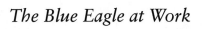

The Blue Eagle at Work

The Blue Eagle at Work

Reclaiming Democratic Rights
in the American Workplace

CHARLES J. MORRIS
With a Foreword by
Theodore J. St. Antoine

ILR Press, an imprint of
Cornell University Press
ITHACA AND LONDON

First published 2005 by Cornell University Press

Printed in the United States of America

Library of Congress Cataloging-in-Publication Data

Morris, Charles J., 1923–
  The blue eagle at work : reclaiming democratic rights in the American workplace / Charles J. Morris.
      p. cm.
  Includes bibliographical references and index.
  ISBN 0-8014-4317-2 (cloth : alk. paper)
  1. Labor unions—Law and legislation—United States.
2. Freedom of association—United States.   3. Collective bargaining—United States.   4. Minority labor union members—United States.   I. Title.
  KF3389.M67 2004
  344.7301'89—dc22

                                            2004012145

Cornell University Press strives to use environmentally responsible suppliers and materials to the fullest extent possible in the publishing of its books. Such materials include vegetable-based, low-VOC inks and acid-free papers that are recycled, totally chlorine-free, or partly composed of nonwood fibers. For further information, visit our website at www.cornellpress.cornell.edu.

Cloth printing   10 9 8 7 6 5 4 3 2 1

This book is dedicated to Minnette

The [prefered] method of coordinating industry is the democratic method. . . . It places the primary responsibility where it belongs and asks industry and labor to solve their mutual problems through self-government. That is industrial democracy, and upon its success depends the preservation of the American way of life.

The development of a partnership between industry and labor in the solution of national problems is the indispensable complement to political democracy. And that leads us to this all important truth: there can no more be democratic self-government in industry without workers participating therein, than there could be democratic government in politics without workers having the right to vote. . . . That is why the right to bargain collectively is at the bottom of social justice for the worker, as well as the sensible conduct of business affairs.

—Senator Robert F. Wagner, Address at
National Democratic Club Forum, May 8, 1937

Contents

Foreword

Specialists in any field have a vested interest in their mastery of the subject. Expertise, after all, is their stock in trade. Assaults on the conventional wisdom can be unnerving if not discrediting. In the pages that follow, such an experience awaits all conscientious readers with a labor background who dare to expose themselves to Professor Charles Morris's provocative, iconoclastic, and ultimately persuasive arguments. He insists that a half-century of American labor law thinking has gone astray in failing to recognize the duty of an employer to bargain with a labor union representing less than a majority of the firm's employees.[1] While the experts will have a field day with the pros and cons, the general reader will have no trouble following Morris's well-honed prose. Anyone can gain much insight into this important if neglected legal issue.

Every labor specialist knows that the American law of collective bargaining is unique. One feature of this uniqueness is the concept of exclusive representation. Once a union has the support of a majority of the employees in an appropriate unit, it is the sole bargaining agent for all the employees in the unit. The National Labor Relations Act (NLRA) requires employers to bargain with a majority union concerning the terms of employment of all the unit's workers. That even includes employees who may vigorously oppose the majority union. This system of exclusive representation is justified on such grounds as industrial stability and predictability, worker solidarity, and employer convenience.

In the absence of a majority union exercising exclusive authority, the law allows an employer to bargain with a union that represents only a minority of the employees. Such negotiations can cover the union's own members and can lead to what is commonly called a members-only contract. But some time in the first decades after the passage of the Wagner Act, the original NLRA, in 1935, it became generally accepted by labor practitioners and scholars that employers had no statutory *duty* to bargain with a minority union. "Majority rule" did not allude merely to exclusive representation; it referred to the only kind of status that conveyed legal obligations.

In 1990, into this seemingly settled scene, stepped that imaginative legal thinker and doughty champion of workers' rights, Professor Clyde Summers.[2] Summers contended that in the analysis of workers' bargaining rights, too much emphasis had been placed on Section 9(a) of the NLRA, which makes a majority union the "exclusive representative" of all the employees in a bargaining unit. In Summers's view this obscured the even more fundamental provision of Section 7, entitling employees to "bargain collectively through representatives of their own choosing."

Section 7 draws no distinctions between majority unions and minority unions. For Summers this meant that when no exclusive representative is present, an employer should be obligated to bargain with a union representing less than a majority of a unit's employees. Yet even Summers conceded: "We have probably proceeded too long on the questionable assumption that the employer has no affirmative duty to bargain with a nonmajority union to now recognize that duty short of a statutory amendment."[3]

Professor Morris will have none of this temporizing. His is no quixotic quest for some shimmering, unattainable ideal. A former labor practitioner himself, Morris is a hard-headed realist who aims for a practical, viable theory that can be sold to the National Labor Relations Board (NLRB) and the courts. So he has dug deep into the legislative history of the NLRA and its predecessor, the National Industrial Recover Act (NIRA). He has also scoured the early Labor Board and judicial decisions that touch on the issue of minority-union bargaining, as well as the major Supreme Court pronouncements that might have some bearing on the question. His exhaustive research efforts have borne rich fruit.

Morris meets head-on the notion that a minority union has no legal bargaining rights and can negotiate on behalf of its members only at the sufferance of the employer. He says he "can report with assurance" that there is not a single NLRB or court decision holding any such thing. The case law reveals the issue has never been squarely faced and resolved. Turning to the positive side, Morris demonstrates convincingly that minority-union bargaining and members-only contracts were common sights in the labor relations landscape at the time the NIRA and the NLRA were adopted. There is not the slightest indication that Congress intended to change that situation.

Perhaps Morris's most personal contribution is his lovingly detailed reconstruction of the world of the NIRA and its Blue Eagle, and the subsequent developments leading to the enactment of the NLRA. Context can be crucial in the interpretation of a statute. What Morris shows is that minority-union bargaining was taken for granted during the critical period of the 1930s. Indeed, members-only contracts were as common as majority-exclusivity contracts, and more so in such major industries as steel and auto. Wouldn't Congress have addressed the issue if it felt that employers were not required to engage in this frequent and sometimes favored form of negotiation? Yet the legislative history contains not a hint of disapproval of minority-union bargaining. And the plain language of Section 7 of the NLRA, unchanged from Section 7(a) of the NIRA and unchanged to this very day, says without qualification or limitation that "[e]mployees" have the "right" to "bargain collectively through representatives of their own choosing."[4] There is no suggestion whatsoever that employees lose this right if they cannot get a majority of their fellows to go along.

Why, then, did the conventional view take hold that employers have a duty to bargain only with majority unions? Morris is convincing on this as well. He points out that in the first decade after the passage of the Wagner Act in 1935, unions won over 85 percent of the representation elections and card-checks conducted by the NLRB. This quick and easy route to recognition meant a majority union was now entitled to exclusive bargaining authority under Section 9(a). Members-only recognition fell into disuse and memories of its prior prominence soon faded. By 1945 a labor leader quoted by Morris even voiced the opinion that employers could only recognize majority unions.

The Morris thesis confronts two big hurdles. The first, cited by Professor Summers, is that for more than half a century the contrary proposition has been accepted. Inertia can be a force in the law. Morris responds, correctly, that civil rights rulings both older and clearer than minority-bargaining principles have been reversed when their errors became manifest. These days, however, labor claims may not be accorded the same high priority as civil rights. The second objection is a practical one. It is entirely possible that two or more hostile minority unions might assert competing bargaining rights in the same unit. That could cause factional divisions among the workforce and serious operational difficulties for an employer. Morris believes, and I agree, that those problems could be worked out. But the NLRB and the courts can be expected to scrutinize such functional factors with a wary eye.

Finally, what might have been an intriguing but redundant modus operandi in the 1940s and 1950s could assume great practical significance in the current industrial relations climate. With union density in the private sector now dipping below 10 percent, the unique American institution of collective bargaining, with all its capacity for economic and humane contributions to our society, stands in need of major rehabilitation. The requirement of minority-union recognition might be the very ingredient to jump-start the process. If the sequence follows that of the 1930s—minority-union bargaining leading to full-scale majority-exclusivity contracts—that will be all to the good. In today's increasingly polarized world, we tend to forget the benefits that a mature, cooperative union-management relationship can bring to the workplace. Management is invariably best qualified to direct the overall enterprise. The workers in the shop, however, are often better able to determine just how a particular operation should be performed.

When Professor Morris first broached his theory about minority-union bargaining, I was close to total skepticism. Most of us are unreceptive to what appears completely at odds with widespread basic understandings. Some will say we have enough difficult questions in the labor field, legal and otherwise, to deal with as it is. But Morris is like an irresistible force—and, more important, he is a thorough researcher, a keen analyst, and a persuasive writer. His remarkable, salutary message deserves our fullest attention.

THEODORE J. ST. ANTOINE

Preface

Law—more than any other factor—controls American labor relations. That being so, why is it that for most private-sector employees the federal law that was expressly designed to bring democratic values to the American workplace in the form of labor unions and collective bargaining is no longer a viable source of those rights? Why is it that although a majority of American workers favor union representation, so few of them are able to obtain it in their own places of employment? And why does the archaic master-servant relationship still prevail in most American workplaces, where antidemocratic and authoritarian procedures continue to govern decision making that affects the employment relationship? And why is it that these conditions flourish without public outcry even though a federal statute expressly declares collective bargaining between employees and employers to be the official policy of the United States?

This book is the product of my quest for answers to these questions. And because these questions and their answers directly affect the public at large—not just legal scholars and labor-law professionals, particularly the concerned community of labor-union and human-resource specialists—I have chosen to write this book in a manner accessible to the general reader. Everyone involved in the employment process—including ordinary workers and managers—should have easy entrée to the fundamental features of the law that governs the right of association in the American workplace. But notwithstanding my calculated intent to avoid legal and academic jargon, I have made every effort to base the book's content on the highest standards of legal scholarship, and I expect the work to be judged according to those standards.

Truth in law is critical to the American legal system. What we are now observing in American labor relations, in my view, is the absence of truth, for there is a missing link in the enforcement of the country's basic labor law—the National Labor Relations Act. This truth is not hidden, however. It is easily visible in that statute, which declares in plain English that collective bargaining shall be available to every employee who wishes to join a union—not just employees who manage to achieve a numerical majority in the employer's bargaining unit. This basic right—which is now internationally recognized as a human right—was the reenactment of protective legislation that was originally passed during the New Deal period under the ubiquitous icon of the Blue Eagle. Although this right, as applied to minority-union bargaining, was widely recognized during the early years following the Wagner Act's passage in 1935, in later years it was conveniently forgotten—that is, until its rediscovery in 1990 by Clyde W. Summers, a professor of labor law at the University of Pennsylvania. However, because the concept of minority-union bargaining flies in the face of conventional wisdom, more than mere recognition is required to restore to the prevailing view the state of the law that Congress intended. Accordingly, my first purpose in the research that led to the preparation of this book was to determine the accuracy of Professor Summers's thesis. That research and subsequent analysis, detailed in this volume, convinced me that the National Labor Relations Act indelibly guarantees the right of minority-union employees to engage in members-only collective bargaining where a majority of the employees have not yet designated an exclusive union representative. It is my contention that when this legal truth is finally recognized and accepted—for which no congressional action will be required—American workers will be able to join unions and achieve the benefits of collective bargaining more easily and more successfully, and from this a strong labor movement may eventually materialize in an economy sorely in need of its countervailing power.

I am indebted to many individuals for their help in making this book possible.

To my academic colleagues in labor law who patiently served as invaluable sounding boards to test what may have first appeared to be a quixotic endeavor, I am especially grateful. They encouraged my efforts, raised many critical questions, offered insightful commentary and suggestions, and ultimately provided me with the comfort of their recognition of the plausibility of my thesis. I therefore extend sincere appreciation to the following professors: Benjamin Aaron, emeritus, University of California at Los Angeles; Charles B. Craver, George Washington University; Cynthia L. Estlund, Columbia University; Joan Flynn, Cleveland-Marshall College of Law; Alan Hyde, Rutgers University, Newark; Joel E. Rogers, University of Wisconsin; Theodore J. St. Antoine, emeritus, University of Michigan; and Clyde W. Summers, emeritus, University of Pennsylvania. And the same special thanks go to Fred Feinstein, former General Counsel of the NLRB, now a visiting scholar at the University of Maryland School of Public Affairs, and to Lance

Compa, senior lecturer at the Cornell School of Labor and Industrial Relations.

I am also deeply indebted to the following industrial relations professors and specialists who read some of my early drafts and provided effective comments and welcome encouragement: Roy J. Adams, emeritus, McMaster University; Richard N. Block, Michigan State University; John F. Burton, Jr., Rutgers University, New Brunswick; Sheldon Friedman, AFL-CIO; James A. Gross, Cornell University; Thomas A. Kochan, Massachusetts Institute of Technology; Andrew Levin, AFL-CIO; Robert B. McKersie, Massachusetts Institute of Technology; Charles M. Rehmus, emeritus, Cornell University; and Hoyt N. Wheeler, University of South Carolina.

And I shall be ever grateful to Peter Zschiesche of the San Diego Employee Rights Center who led me to the case of the seventeen immigrant workers who had been fired for concertedly trying to improve their working conditions, for that case brought me to this book. And I am most grateful to two special law librarians and their colleagues at the two libraries on which I depended so heavily: Frank Weston, now retired, at the University of San Diego School of Law, and Gregory Ivy at Southern Methodist University Dedman School of Law. And to Fran Benson, Editorial Director of Cornell ILR Press; thank you for your long-lasting patience and heartening support.

Yet the first and last person on my list of acknowledgments—the person without whose support this book could never have been undertaken or completed—is my dear wife, Minnette. She helped with editorial assistance, but, more important, she was both patient and encouraging during the book's long years of gestation. To her I am most appreciative.

Introduction
The Blue Eagle Is Not Extinct

Its Labor Law Is Alive and Ready to Fly

Almost all ancient peoples believed the Earth to be flat. And almost all Americans involved in employment relations believe that a minority union has no right to engage in collective bargaining, even where no majority union has yet been designated. But come with me on a journey of legal discovery—or rather rediscovery—and we shall learn that this conventional wisdom is an illusion without foundation and that what will appear to be a new world of labor relations lies beyond. Historically, however, this new legal landscape will be no more new than the new world that Columbus found, but the prospect for change in American labor relations, as with the rediscovery of America, will indeed be new.

My personal journey of rediscovery began in the year 2000 when a friend, Peter Zschiesche, director of the San Diego Employee Rights Center,[1] called my attention to the plight of seventeen immigrant workers for whom he had filed an unfair labor practice charge. These were young men who had been employed at Hi Tech Honeycomb, Inc.,[2] a southern California aerospace subcontracting company. Reacting to their low wages and abysmal working conditions, on the morning of February 10, 1999—without labor-union assistance—they organized themselves into an informal peer group and staged a brief walkout to protest those conditions. The company owner refused to meet with them as a group to discuss their grievances and swiftly retaliated by firing all of them. In response to Zschiesche's request, I provided those workers with pro bono legal representation before the Regional Director and the General Counsel of the National Labor Relations Board (NLRB, or Board). While engaged in such representation, I began to analyze the multiple legal issues posed by their situation and to delve into the labor and legislative history that affected those issues. After lengthy study that continued far beyond the final action in the NLRB case, I was able to confidently reconfirm—contrary to conventional wisdom—that in workplaces where there is not yet a majority/exclusive representative, collective bargaining on behalf of the members of a minority labor union is a protected right fully guaranteed by the National Labor Relations Act (NLRA, Wagner Act, or Act).[3]

The yield from that and further research and analysis forms the core of this book, which also explores the nature of the end product of such members-only union organizing and bargaining and the impact that this rediscovered process will likely have on future labor-management relations in this country. This book is therefore a hybrid of the interrelated disciplines of labor law and industrial relations, with a generous dollop of labor history. Although my primary aim is to provide rigorous and objective legal analyses of the propositions posed herein, the importance of those issues compels me to direct my text to both legal and lay audiences. It is thus my hope that this presentation—in which I have tried to avoid legal and academic jargon—will be of interest and use to a wide range of readers, including lawyers, judges, and administrative personnel who regularly handle labor-law problems, as well as others who deal directly with employee relations on a daily basis (i.e., human resource professionals, union officials and organizers, and individual employees and employers who might desire more knowledge about the legal nature of their own employment relationship) and of course academics and students in all of these fields.

My attention to the iconoclastic thesis that I am here presenting was prompted earlier—in 1990—when I read Professor Clyde Summers's article, *Unions without Majority—A Black Hole*,[4] in which he made an observation that had not appeared in the legal literature since 1936,[5] to wit, that the plain words of the Act "would seem to require an employer, in the absence of a majority union, to bargain collectively with a non-majority union for its own members";[6] and he noted various historical features to support that observation. He suggested, however, that "it may be too late to open this question."[7] Writing separately in 1993, Professors Alan Hyde and Matthew Finkin, although not disagreeing with Summers's premise,[8] contended that because of the passage of time legislative action would be required to reaffirm this true meaning of the law. Rejecting that pessimistic appraisal, I wrote in 1994 that although "the role of the minority union should be reaffirmed and reinvigorated . . . amending the Act is not essential to the confirmation of the existence of the rights of minority unions";[9] nevertheless, I then conceded that amendments, or perhaps the issuance of administrative rules, would be desirable to emphasize and clarify those rights.[10] And so the matter rested—at least for me—until my interest was aroused again by the peremptory firing of those seventeen immigrant workers. Subsequent research that I initiated on their behalf produced considerable new evidence and substantiated that the present law is clear and sufficient, that amendments to the Act—which in any event would be unobtainable in the foreseeable future—are unnecessary and would serve no useful purpose.

What happened to those seventeen workers was a disgrace to American democracy. Those young men, who were of Vietnamese, Cambodian, and Philippine origin[11] and new to America, apparently trusted that this was a land of opportunity where they could improve their lot through hard work and cooperation with others. Lacking the usual fear that traditional American employees typically display toward organizational activity in the workplace, they boldly decided to join together to confront their employer about their grievances. The company, which employed about fifty production workers, manufactured honeycombs (filters made of welded metal that resemble beehive honeycombs) for jet engines. Despite the low wages, which were only slightly above minimum wage for most of the group, the employees' job tasks required considerable skill and attention. The group's chief complaints were that they had been promised wage increases that were either long delayed or never delivered; they had been denied such basic safety protections as gloves (for handling hazardous fluid) and safety goggles and face masks when needed; some of them had been promised promotions which never materialized; some had often been denied rest breaks; and some had suffered verbal abuse from the owner himself.

Operating on the premise that "enough is enough," these aggrieved workers organized and signed a petition for presentation to their employer through a spokesperson whom they had democratically selected. He then asked management for a meeting on behalf of the group, but when that was not promptly forthcoming the aggrieved employees shut down their machines and quietly walked out. Soon after, they gathered at a meeting in a public park near where they lived, and later that day they returned to the factory to renew their request for a group meeting with management to discuss their complaints. The owner denied their request, insisting that the company would not meet with them as a group and would only see them individually. Preferring to maintain their group solidarity, the employees refused to meet alone, whereupon management immediately advised them that they had all forfeited their jobs. They were thus terminated for having engaged in concerted activity that was intended to improve their wages and working conditions through a civilized process of jointly discussing their grievances with management—that is, through a rudimentary form of collective bargaining. Federal law unequivocally states that they "have the right . . . to bargain collectively through representatives of their own choosing . . . ."[12] The Hi Tech owner admitted to one of his supervisors that the reason "he did not want them together as a group [was] because he felt that they would back each other up if he offered something to one employee." This seemed to fly in the face of the congressional intent behind the Act that was meant to create "some equality of bargaining power."[13]

Out of desperation—for they had families to feed—several of the men broke ranks. Later that afternoon, assuming they had no alternative, a few met individually with management, and some were rehired shortly thereafter. A few others were selectively rehired during the next several months. The remainder sought other employment or left the area. Hi Tech Honeycomb had thus effectively squelched this fledgling effort by a group of its employees to achieve self-organization in their new American workplace.

Previous to my being made aware of the happenings at Hi Tech, the NLRB Regional Director had issued a complaint against the company and the case was set for hearing, for the discharges were clearly in violation of well-settled law[14] (although the employer could have obtained the same result legally by replacing—instead of discharging—the striking employees[15]). However, it had not occurred to the Regional Director to seek an order requiring the employer to meet and bargain with the employee group, which was really the key issue. I tried, unsuccessfully, to achieve that objective with an amendment to the complaint, citing as a separate unfair labor practice the company's refusal to meet with the employees as a *group*. The General Counsel declined to consider such an amendment because the case had already been set for hearing and apparently a settlement was deemed likely. In fact, over my objection, the employer eagerly settled the case for 80 percent of lost back wages, a belated offer of reinstatement (a year and a half had elapsed since the discharges), and the posting of an effectively meaningless notice. Thus, for a total payment of only $26,000 for all lost wages, the company was able to relish its success in crushing the organizational efforts of seventeen courageous but naïve employees.

The National Labor Relations Act, or at least its administration, had totally failed these new American workers at the most critical point on the scale of rights protected by the Act—the point of initial organizing and rudimentary collective bargaining. Yet this inaction of Board officials was fully consistent with conventional wisdom, according to which Hi Tech had no duty to bargain with the representative of that employee group, notwithstanding that the group was clearly, in the words of the statute, an "organization[,] committee or plan" formed for the purpose of bargaining collectively with the employer "concerning grievances."[16] When I noted this, together with other legal arguments, to Leonard Page, the NLRB General Counsel at the time, he did not disagree with my construction of the law (indeed four earlier General Counsels had indicated their agreement in similar cases[17]), but he declined to amend the complaint for the reasons already noted, indicating, however, that he would reconsider "this type allegation in a more appropriate case." Unfortunately, however, Page's tenure as General Counsel expired a few months later. The conventional wisdom on this issue thus remains ripe for reconsideration, which is the justification for this book.

About that conventional wisdom—actually *latter-day* conventional wisdom—as Sportin' Life in *Porgy and Bess* reminds us, "it ain't necessarily so."[18] In fact, minority-union recognition by employers, accompanied by bilateral collective bargaining for union members only, was the *original* conventional wisdom on this subject, for such bargaining was commonly practiced following passage of the Wagner Act in 1935. Although the ultimate goal of the statute was the institution of exclusive collective bargaining with majority unions, in workplaces where majority bargaining was not yet established Congress did not intend to bar minority-union members-only bargaining, which was deemed a preliminary stage in the development of mature collective bargaining.[19]

It may come as a surprise to most readers to learn that members-only bargaining was widely practiced by employers and unions during the early years following passage of the Wagner Act. In fact, one of the most influential corporate executives in the nation, Myron C. Taylor, U.S. Steel's chairman of the board and chief policy maker, issued a written formula for union recognition in 1937 that declared that

> The Company recognizes the right of its employees to bargain collectively through representatives freely chosen by them [and] will negotiate and contract with the representatives of any group of its employees so chosen and with any organization *as the representative of its members* . . . .[20]

That is exactly what U.S. Steel did several months later when it signed a *members-only* agreement with the CIO Steelworkers Union,[21] which at the time represented less than a majority of the company's eligible employees. That same pattern was widely followed in most of the steel industry and elsewhere. Eighty-five percent of the original Steelworkers agreements were for "members only," as were 64 percent of the UAW[22] contracts in the auto industry. Indeed, in the late 1930s members-only contracts, which were popular with both the CIO and AFL[23] unions, were just as common as majority-exclusivity contracts.[24] When a union finally achieved majority status under such contracts, which almost always occurred, these preliminary agreements were typically followed by conventional exclusive-recognition agreements. The postenactment industrial relations community was thus putting into effect what scholarly comment on the new law had already observed, for in 1936 E. G. Latham, a fellow of the Social Science Research Council, had written that "it appears to be a reasonable construction [of the Act that] the employer may be bound to bargain with minority groups until . . . 'proper majorities' have been selected."[25] He concluded that "*[I]t is reasonable to suppose that where there is no majority organization at all . . . minority rights are . . . reserved.*"[26]

Notwithstanding that early history, today almost everyone in the field of labor and employment relations takes for granted that American employers have no duty to bargain with any union until its majority status has been certified or recognized, usually as a result of an NLRB election. That assumption has long prevailed despite the fact that the Act clearly indicates that in workplaces where no exclusive bargaining agent has yet been "designated or selected . . . by the majority of the employees" in an appropriate bargaining unit pursuant to Section 9(a),[27] all employees, regardless of majority status, are entitled "to bargain collectively through representatives of their own choosing."[28] At first blush, this literal reading of the law may sound like a radical proposition, but it is not. As the reader will discover, not only is this meaning conveyed by the ordinary language contained in the statutory text, it is also fully supported by unequivocal legislative history. But if that is so, why is it that latter-day conventional wisdom assumes the contrary? In an ironic twist of history, a misunderstanding of the law's protection—or at least an unawareness of that protection—evolved despite the absence of any decisional authority to support the conventional view. As the record will show, neither the NLRB nor the courts have ever held that an employer has no duty to bargain with a minority union for its members only, although in a few cases there are vague dicta—but no decisional holdings—that pay lip service to latter-day conventional wisdom.[29] Notwithstanding the absence of any adverse rulings—in fact all of the related cases are supportive[30]—the early practice of members-only bargaining was abandoned and eventually forgotten. Why?

The reason is simple. After the labor movement had made use of members-only bargaining for only a few years, it quickly became apparent that a faster and less expensive way to obtain exclusive recognition was available through direct NLRB representational processes, usually by means of an election. In the Board's first decade, the unions' success rate through this route was truly phenomenal—in over 85 percent of all NLRB representation cases the unions won recognition.[31] Consequently, out of sheer convenience for most unions, NLRB elections became the favored organizational device. And in a relatively short period of time—which included the period during World War II and the postwar boom that followed—this deceptively easy expedient became habit-forming. From then on, the labor movement made no visible effort to resume organizing through members-only bargaining. And after 1947 unions were busily distracted by massive amounts of litigation engendered by the Taft-Hartley Act,[32] whereupon members-only bargaining was effectively forgotten. Although such institutional forgetfulness may be understandable, it is nonetheless to be regretted, for the premature abandonment of minority-union organizing and bargaining undoubtedly contributed to the steady decline in the density of union membership and coverage.

Employers, however, had no reason to question the dependence on the election process, for elections provided them with an ideal forum in which to mount offensive campaigns against union representation. Thus, in a short time NLRB elections became the centerpiece of the statute and the established norm for union organizing. Accordingly, the interplay of employer self-interest and union acquiescence eventually repressed all institutional memory of the duty to bargain with minority unions, and the lack of wisdom about that duty metamorphosed into the latter-day conventional wisdom. Although labor's retreat from members-only organizing and bargaining was not the product of deliberate decision—it just happened, without any of the principals being aware that it was happening—the impact of that retreat meant that Senator Robert F. Wagner's vision of industrial democracy would be put on hold.

That vision about the role of democracy in the workplace, for which Senator Wagner provided the legislative imprimatur, was neither novel nor revolutionary. The concept of industrial democracy had a long history in American political and economic thought. In the early days of the republic, Albert Gallatin, Treasury Secretary under Thomas Jefferson and James Madison, advocated that the democratic principle of "the political process" be applied as well to "the industrial operation,"[33] and expressions of that goal were reiterated countlessly. For example, the United States Industrial Relations Commission of 1902 declared that only by the introduction of an "element of democracy into the governance of industry [can] workers . . . effectively take part in determining the conditions under which they work."[34] And Louis D. Brandeis renewed that thesis in 1915 when he reminded the country that attainment of "rule by the people . . . involves industrial democracy as well as political democracy."[35]

It was Senator Wagner's view that a partnership between employers and labor unions was an "indispensable complement to political democracy."[36] When he submitted his bill to the Senate in 1935, he therefore envisioned a "new industrial democracy that is bound to come, that is growing, here at our feet, inexorably . . . ."[37] And two years after passage of the Act he reemphasized that

> The struggle for a voice in industry through the process of collective bargaining is at the heart of the struggle for the preservation of political as well as economic democracy in America.[38]

In passing the Wagner Act, Congress clearly intended that employees would participate in the democratic process of determining their working conditions through collective bargaining. In addition to the Act's substantive provisions to that effect, its opening section specifically declared this to be the official policy of the United States,[39] and, despite some wishful thinking to the contrary by the employer community, Congress has never amended that policy.[40]

The collective bargaining process that Wagner envisioned was to begin with the democratic expression of the right of association that would be achieved through the exercise and enforcement of certain basic employee rights, including the right to join labor unions and engage in collective bargaining. These are essentially the same rights that the civilized world later recognized to be fundamental human rights[41] and which the United States reaffirmed by international agreements in 1992 and 1998.[42]

Where are those rights today? As we know too well, they are effectively unavailable to most American workers. Over 90 percent of the employees in the private sector are not working under collective bargaining conditions,[43] and formidable obstacles stand in the way of their obtaining union representation.[44] According to recent polling reports, 50 percent of nonunion workers in America would vote for a union if they were given the opportunity,[45] but under present conditions very few employees will have that opportunity. The international civil rights organization, Human Rights Watch, recently conducted an investigation of the status of workers' freedom of association in the United States and concluded, based on intensively documented evidence, that

> millions of workers are excluded from coverage by laws to protect rights of organizing, bargaining and striking. For workers who are covered by such laws, recourse for labor rights violations is often delayed to a point where it ceases to provide redress. When they are applied, remedies are weak and often ineffective. In a system replete with all the appearance of legality and due process, workers' exercise of rights to organize, to bargain, and to strike in the United States have been frustrated by many employers who realize they have little to fear from labor law enforcement through a ponderous, delay-ridden legal system with meager remedial powers.[46]

Those conclusions have long been recognized, but legislative correction has been unobtainable because of the sixty-member requirement to break a filibuster in the U.S. Senate.[47] But is legislative action the only means to restore the original democratic potential of the Wagner Act? It is my contention that it is not. That Act—despite several amendments and judicially imposed restrictions—still contains the basic elements that are sufficient to achieve meaningful realization of democracy in the workplace.

For that reason, it is my purpose and concern in this book (1) to set forth and explain the original and accurate reading of the NLRA concerning the critical issue of less-than-majority collective bargaining in workplaces where there is no exclusive/majority bargaining agent; (2) to describe how that process can be utilized and developed through traditional unions, and to a limited extent through alternative forms of employee representation; and (3) to provide a reasoned forecast of the resulting impact of these changes on the labor relations landscape.

Before the advent of statutory-based collective bargaining, which began on the railroads with enactment of the Railway Labor Act (RLA)[48] in 1926 and for other employee relations in 1933 with passage of Section 7(a) of the Depression-era National Industrial Recovery Act (NIRA),[49] it had been traditional for unions to achieve bargaining rights based entirely on the extent of their membership—often expressed by a strike for recognition. Elections were not part of the organizational process. Elections for determining union recognition developed relatively late in the history of American industrial relations. And when they finally appeared, they were used primarily to determine which union would be recognized when multiple unions were claiming representation; that was their justification in the railroad industry where such elections were first held.[50] It was not until much later—but rarely prior to passage of the Wagner Act—that another reason for elections developed: to provide an employer with a reliable means to verify whether a union that sought, or claimed, to represent all the employees in an appropriate bargaining unit did in fact represent a majority.

Prior to the time when union recognition was conventionally based on majority selection within a bargaining unit, it was commonly accepted—although usually resisted by employers—that an employer had a duty to bargain with any union that sought to represent its employee-members, whether a minority or a majority union. And this was indeed the prevailing practice under the Blue Eagle "Codes of Fair Competition" promulgated under NIRA Section 7(a), which guaranteed the right of employees "to bargain collectively through representatives of their own choosing"—language that had been derived from the Norris-LaGuardia Act of 1932.[51] Such legislative protection of the right of nonrailroad employees to organize into labor unions and engage in collective bargaining had been preceded by judicial recognition in 1930 of those general rights in the unanimous decision of the Supreme Court in *Texas & New Orleans Railway Co. v. Brotherhood of Railway Clerks*,[52] in which Chief Justice Charles Evans Hughes wrote:

> The legality of collective action on the part of employees in order to safeguard their proper interests is not to be disputed. It has long been recognized that employees are entitled to organize for the purpose of securing the redress of grievances and to promote agreements with employers relating to rates of pay and conditions of work.[53]

The Norris-Laguardia Act and Section 7(a) gave legislative expression to those rights. And the same statutory text that defined those rights in the Blue Eagle codes of the NIRA, which was enacted as a temporary measure, was soon incorporated into permanent law in Section 7 of the 1935 Wagner Act. That statute, which was passed by overwhelming majority vote,[54] explicitly—then and now—guarantees that employees have the right "to bargain collectively through representatives of their own choosing" and provides that it is an unfair labor practice for an employer "to interfere with, restrain, or coerce employees in the exercise of" that right.[55] From the beginning, Senator Wagner emphasized that his bill "creates no new substantive rights"[56] and "does not present a single novel principle for the consideration of Congress."[57] Leon Keyserling, his legislative assistant who drafted the bill, later commented that the "background of the Wagner Act of 1935 is contained in the history of the National Industrial Recovery Act." Blue Eagle labor law thus continued to prevail as the law of the land.

Although minority-union bargaining received brief textual attention in the drafting of Wagner's unsuccessful 1934 bill, such bargaining was never perceived to be an issue in his 1935 bill. In the congressional debate on the latter—the bill that eventually became law—the matter of preliminary minority-union bargaining was but a blip on the legislative screen. It was not a contested issue, for such bargaining was widely recognized and accepted at the time and was taken for granted even by employers; it was thus not deemed controversial. The primary focus of the public debate that preceded passage of the 1935 Act, both in and out of Congress—as legislative history distinctly records—concerned other, more controversial questions: mainly issues of company unions, the closed shop, majority-rule exclusivity, and whether the Act was constitutional. The majority-rule exclusivity concept represented the chosen legislative response to the prevailing problem of dual unionism, where one of the contending unions was almost always a company union. Although the matter of members-only bargaining prior to the establishment of majority representation received no direct attention in the congressional debates, Wagner and Keyserling had carefully and knowingly made certain in the drafting process and in the final text that such bargaining would be protected. At the time, minority-union bargaining was fairly common and was not viewed as a problem requiring special attention, provided no competing union was seeking or claiming recognition. While it is true that employers were generally opposed to outside unions and they vehemently objected to closed-shop unionism, where a minority union was strong enough to obtain bargaining recognition for its own members and was not insisting on exclusive representation, nonmajority status was a nonissue. The legislative history of the enactment of the 1935 Wagner Act shows positively that its authors fully and intentionally protected, in the broad text of the statute, all minority-union bargaining that would occur prior to mature majority-based exclusivity bargaining.

As the reader will learn, numerous aspects of this history support that conclusion. However, one particular feature not previously noted in the literature provides a historical "smoking gun" that unequivocally validates this deduction.[58] Legislative history therefore confirms the plain reading of the textual provisions that recognize the statutory protection afforded members-only bargaining prior to the employees' selection of a majority union. Such a reading—rather than the latter-day conventional wisdom—is the true state of the law. The analyses presented here also establish that this statutory right is part of a fundamental right of association that is consistent with and ultimately protected by the First Amendment of the U.S. Constitution and by international law to which the United States is a confirming party.[59]

It is sad, nevertheless, that after two-thirds of a century, this basic law relating to minority-union bargaining has yet to be judicially articulated in the manner originally intended by Congress. But long delay sometimes happens to the best of statutes. To mention but one, it took more than a century for

Section 1982 of the Civil Rights Act of 1866[60] to begin to be applied in the manner intended by Congress. As the Supreme Court reminded us in *Jones v. Alfred H. Mayer Co.*,[61] the fact that this civil rights "statute lay partially dormant for many years does not diminish its force today."[62] Belated application of that statute to private acts of discrimination regarding disposition of property—like the anticipated belated application of Sections 8(a)(1) and 8(a)(5) of the NLRA to minority-union members-only bargaining—occurred under uniquely similar circumstances: long-held custom and practice to the contrary, conventional wisdom that assumed the statute did not really mean what its words clearly said, and adverse judicial dicta. Better late than never.

It is my hope that this book will help restore an important missing link in the American labor-relations system. That link—by now obvious—is the reinvocation of the methodology of minority-union collective bargaining by labor unions for their members only, for this is the natural preliminary stage in the organizational development of mature, majority-based exclusivity bargaining. When traditional unions reclaim the process of organizing by representing and bargaining on behalf of their members from the very beginning—or at least attempting to do so—they will be returning to their roots. They will be organizing by recruiting dues-paying members—not card-signers or potential voters, which is the common practice today. And even if employers refuse to deal with these minority unions—which is not unlikely for most employers, at least until the NLRB requires it or the judiciary confirms it—membership-based organizing will make infinitely more sense than the current alternative.

An actively organizing members-only union, even without the advantage of formal collective bargaining, can make its mark in the workplace simply by acting like a union. It can assist employees in many different ways, especially regarding concerted action for "mutual aid or protection" (another aspect of Section 7 rights). For example, it can offer a union steward to assist any employee (whether or not a union member) who is called in for a disciplinary interview—a right that is otherwise not available to nonunion employees.[63] And it can provide employees with a variety of social and economic services that are not dependent upon a collective bargaining relationship.[64] Such a fledgling union can thus become a clearinghouse for information and action and an organizational link to an assortment of community activities,[65] all of which are consistent with the role of a new union seeking to prove its worth and expand its membership.[66]

More important, however, the new union will begin to represent its members by engaging in its primary function, which is to negotiate on their behalf about a variety of statutory bargaining subjects affecting their employment,[67] albeit such bargaining will probably be conducted initially on an ad hoc basis. The resulting premajority agreements, which will be legally enforceable, will apply to union members only, although employers will probably extend the same economic benefits to nonunion employees. But noneconomic benefits, such as grievance and arbitration procedures, will apply only to union members.[68] When the minority union finally develops into a majority union—which will likely occur in most instances—it will then become the exclusive bargaining agent for all employees in the unit, whereupon it will be legally entitled to function like any traditional majority union, with collective bargaining applicable to all employees in the unit. The labor-relations system resulting from this rediscovered concept should be infinitely more user friendly than the prevailing system. Employee morale ought to improve significantly, and high-performance workplaces will probably become more prevalent. It is also likely that the advent of members-only bargaining will encourage the creation of a variety of alternative forms of employee representation. Indeed, the process may spawn many nontraditional employee groupings.[69]

My goal in this book is therefore to call attention to a means that already exists in present law to rationalize the respective but interdependent roles of workers and employers. As Professors Paul Osterman and Thomas A. Kochan and their colleagues aptly remind us, "work is a social as well as an economic process [that] involves important moral values and power relationships that are not always reflected in the unregulated workings of market forces."[70] The government is therefore expected to provide a legal environment that reflects the moral values of our society, "leaving the greatest possible amount of control in the hands of those closest to the problems."[71] That is the role of democracy in the workplace, and collective bargaining is its repository.

Simplifying the process of labor organizing—a process that can again be made available to all employees covered by the Act—will open the way to wider and more meaningful employee participation in the collective bargaining process. Under the broad umbrella of the NLRA, the nature of that process can be tailor-made to fit the particular needs of almost any workplace environment. Because the substantive provisions of that Act are brief and simple,[72] collective bargaining can take almost any form the parties voluntarily decide to give it. Properly understood and enforced, the NLRA can thus offer the basis for a vibrant and flexible system of employee relations in which the voices of organized workers can provide a healthy dose of countervailing economic and political power,[73] which is now sorely deficient in the American economy. I shall leave to the economists the task of defining with some degree of precision how such a redistribution of power might address the widening gap between the lowest and highest income earners in the nation. It seems obvious, however, that the renewed presence of a strong labor movement would once again represent a positive force for higher earnings at the bottom- and middle-income levels of the economy and a restraining factor on some of the out-of-control earnings prevailing at the upper levels. If so, this could be a viable means to help replenish the ranks of the vanishing middle class. Such a prospective change is long overdue.

I conclude this introduction by offering the reader some assistance in picking and choosing among the legal, historical, and industrial-relations portions of this book, for I recognize that certain readers may wish to concentrate only on specific parts. For example, most attorneys may be interested mainly in the foundational legal materials, most union and human resources readers may be especially concerned with the "how-to" and policy-oriented sections, and some labor history buffs may prefer to focus on the historical materials. I wish to emphasize, however, that all the materials are integrated and interrelated—and, I hope, they will prove to be clear and understandable to the interested reader.

Here then is a brief outline of the book's organizational format. Chapter 1 begins the account of the pertinent historical factors that preceded passage of the Act. Chapters 2 and 3 continue that story, recounting the relevant parts of legislative history that contribute to the thesis, and Chapter 4 covers postenactment industrial-relations history. Chapter 5 provides legal analyses of the statutory text; and Chapters 6, 7, and 8 examine the thesis from the perspectives of constitutional law, administrative law, and the dimensions of international and human-rights law, respectively. Chapter 9 reviews the current state of decisional law, and Chapter 10 provides a road map for the legal implementation of the thesis. Chapter 11 provides "how-to" guidelines and forecasts for membership-based union organizing. And Chapter 12 closes with an overview of the likely outcome of the prospective changes and their policy implications.

The reader should now be ready for this journey of legal rediscovery, a journey that will reveal that the labor law of the Blue Eagle codes under Section 7(a) of the 1933 NIRA is alive and well in the NLRA of today. The Blue Eagle is at work and ready to fly again.

PART I
The Past as Prologue

I   *Membership-Based Collective Bargaining, the Norris-LaGuardia Act, and Section 7(a) of the National Industrial Recovery Act*

The Origin of the Statutory Specie

Although the underlying concern of this book is the elucidation of statutory law, our interpretative journey begins with an examination of the historical origins of the statutory text here in issue. Because this language has a long-established historical meaning, our narrative begins with a recitation of that text—a critical fourteen-word phrase now contained in Section 7 of the NLRA, the core provision that governs the right of minority unions to engage in collective bargaining on behalf of their employee-members. The phrase simply declares that

> Employees shall have the right to . . . bargain collectively through representatives of their own choosing . . . .[1]

Although that same language is contained in Section 2 (preamble) of the Norris-LaGuardia Act,[2] from which the identical text in Section 7(a) of the Depression-era NIRA[3]–the "Blue Eagle" law–was consciously derived,[4] the administrative—although not the legislative—antecedent of this language dates to yet an earlier instrument, to President Woodrow Wilson's proclamation that created the War Labor Board during World War I.[5] To appreciate the evolutionary origin of this statutory specie, the reader's attention is directed to the documentary excerpts that follow chronologically. These quotations—identified by **boldface** and *italic* emphases (for **substantive** and *prohibitory* language, respectively)—trace the passage of the critical statutory language in a direct line of succession from the World War I proclamation to comparable wording in Sections 7 and 8(1)[6] of the NLRA. This unbroken line of text continues to this very day to establish the right of employees to engage in collective bargaining, including their right to do so through minority unions in workplaces where no majority representative has yet been designated.

From the 1918 National War Labor Board proclamation:

The right of workers to organize in trade unions and to **bargain collectively through chosen representatives is recognized and affirmed.** *This right shall not be denied, abridged, or interfered with by employers in any manner whatsoever.*[7]

From Section 2 of the 1932 Norris-LaGuardia Act:

Whereas under prevailing economic conditions, developed with the aid of governmental authority for owners of property to organize in the corporate and other forms of ownership association, **the individual unorganized worker** is commonly helpless to exercise actual liberty of contract and to protect his freedom of labor, and thereby to obtain acceptable terms and conditions of employment, wherefore, though he should be free to decline to associate with his fellows, **it is necessary that he have full freedom of as**sociation, self-organization, and **designation of representatives of his own choosing, to negotiate the terms and conditions of his employment,** and that *he shall be free from the interference, restraint, or coercion of employers of labor,* or their agents, in the designation of such representatives or in self-organization **or** in other concerted activities for the purpose of collective bargaining or other mutual aid or protection . . . .[8]

From Section 7(a) of the 1933 NIRA:

. . . **employees shall have the right to** organize and **bargain collectively through representatives of their own choosing,** and *shall be free from the interference, restraint, or coercion of employers of labor,* or their agents, *in the designation of such representatives* or in self organization or in other concerted activities *for the purpose of collective bargaining* or other mutual aid or protection.[9]

From Section 7 of the 1935 NLRA (Wagner Act):

Employees shall have the right to self-organization, to form, join, or assist labor organizations, to **bargain collectively through representatives of their own choosing,** and to engage in other concerted activities, for the purpose of collective bargaining or other mutual aid or protection . . . .[10]

And from Section (8)(1) of that Act:

It shall be an unfair labor practice for an employer . . . to interfere with, restrain, or coerce employees in the exercise of the rights guaranteed in section 7 . . . ,[11]

It is self-evident from these passages that the basic fourteen-word bold-face phrase in Section 7 of the Wagner Act, that "**employees shall have the right to . . . bargain collectively through representatives of their own choosing,**" which is the key language here in issue, is identical to the corresponding phrase in Section 7(a) of the NIRA. It is to be further noted that the related prohibitory language (italicized) in Section 8(1) of the Wagner Act, except for immaterial changes in syntax, is likewise identical to the corresponding prohibitory language in NIRA Section 7(a), which also matches similar italicized prohibitory language in Section 2 of the Norris-LaGuardia Act and in the War Labor Board proclamation.

This juxtaposition of text in its various legislative incarnations demonstrates that the substantive law here in issue—albeit not its enforcement procedure—has been continuously in effect in one or more manifestations since 1932: first as congressional policy under the Norris-LaGuardia Act (which is still in effect); thereafter from June 16, 1933,[12] until May 27, 1935,[13] as a statutory requirement for all Blue Eagle codes of fair competition under the National Recovery Administration (NRA); and thereafter since July 5, 1935 (when it became the law in its present form upon the signing of the NLRA by President Franklin Delano Roosevelt), as current law.

Thus when the Wagner Act was first enacted, the critical language in Sections 7 and 8(1)—particularly the basic fourteen-word provision—had already acquired a recognized meaning. Despite some controversy regarding other aspects of Section 7(a) of the NIRA, which will be noted in due course, the language here in issue had never been deemed to require designation of a majority representative as a precondition to collective bargaining, and this is the only language in that statute that mandated such bargaining. By borrowing in 1935 this exact language from preexisting legislation, Congress was identifying and incorporating prevailing legislative meaning.

Although this book focuses primarily on the bargaining requirements applicable to employers vis-à-vis minority unions composed of member employees, part of this examination necessarily sweeps more broadly to include the full scope of congressional intent that motivated passage of the NLRA. Because Congress did not seek to introduce major changes in preexisting substantive law—it sought only to reenact with clarity that same law and make it realistically enforceable—the Wagner Act represented no significant divergence from the way in which the core substantive provisions of the prior law had been viewed and interpreted by the earlier boards that functioned under the NIRA. Such recognition that the Wagner Act's major innovations concerned only *procedures* and *remedies* puts in perspective what Congress intended to achieve in 1935 when it again provided for statutory facilitation of collective bargaining.

From Membership-Based Collective Bargaining to the Enactment of a New Deal for American Labor

Historically, including the years immediately preceding passage of the Wagner Act, collective bargaining as an institution was intertwined with the concept of union membership.[14] As one academic observer wrote in 1927, "[u]nless the employers recognize the union officials as spokesmen for members of the union, there is, of course, no collective bargaining."[15] In 1933, another wrote that

> Recognition is the admission on the part of an employer that his employees have a right to and may negotiate an agreement as a body rather than as individuals and that he recognizes the union as the authorized agent of those of his employees who are its members . . . .[16]

Unions thus normally bargained only on behalf of their members.[17] Union recognition by an employer usually occurred when the union's membership was strong enough to demand and receive recognition—which more often than not resulted from a strike or threat of a strike. Union membership was the sine qua non of collective bargaining.

Majority selection by employees was not a requisite for union representation and collective bargaining. As Milton Derber, in his carefully researched volume on industrial democracy, reported concerning trade unionism in the nineteenth century,[18]

> The majority-rule principle . . . was not an established principle in determining union representation in the workplace. . . . Normally the union established its status by persuading the employer of its desirability or by a showing of strength through a strike. Majority rule played little or no role on the management side.[19]

That description continued to be accurate well into the twentieth century. For example, in its report on collective bargaining in the glass industry prior to 1935, the Twentieth Century Fund concluded that "[s]igning an agreement or obtaining recognition before a substantial union membership had been gained were not uncommon in the industry."[20]

Even the unions' penchant for closed-shop agreements fitted the nexus between membership and collective bargaining. When a union's membership was large enough to represent an effective voice for most if not all of the involved employees, union leaders would usually perceive a need to ensure job security for their members and guaranteed protection for the bargaining process, which only closed-shop agreements could provide efficiently. Moreover, such agreements brought union coverage over otherwise free-riders and also financial contributions from them. On the other hand, when a union was not strong enough to obtain a closed shop or even full recognition, it often settled for a members-only collective agreement,[21] for this was considered a logical step in the organizational process that would eventually lead to total employee recognition. In these scenarios, it was the membership factor that provided the union with agency authority to engage in collective bargaining.

During the pre–Wagner Act years of American labor history, strikes and boycotts, or threats of such activity, were usually a union's only means of securing recognition, for employers vigorously opposed dealing with any outside unions. The list of tactics typically used by employers to avoid unionization is lengthy: companies inundated their employees with anti-union propaganda and threats, frequently enforced yellow-dog contracts,[22] employed labor spies, organized company unions, discharged union adherents, exchanged blacklists of union militants, obtained labor injunctions to suppress union activity, and on a number of occasions resorted to the use of goon squads and armed force.[23] Here is a typical observation from recorded American labor history—this from Foster Rhea Dulles:

> Nor was propaganda the only weapon employed in fighting unionism and promoting the open shop. Many employers continued to force yellow-dog contracts upon employees, to plant labor spies in their plants, to exchange black lists of undesirable union members, and openly follow the most discriminatory practices in hiring workers. It was the old story of intimidation and coercion, and when trouble developed in spite of all such precautions, strong-arm guards were often employed to beat up the trouble-makers while incipient strikes were crushed by bringing in strikebreakers under protection of local authorities.[24]

Elections for recognition were not part of that picture. In most industries, elections and the concept of majority-union exclusivity did not evolve until relatively late,[25] although they appeared earlier in the railroad industry. Acceptance of the majoritarian concept occurred first on the railroads primarily because "railroads were the first major industry where both labor and management advocated the tenets of collective bargaining and sought to develop procedures to make it work."[26] The original Railway Labor Act (RLA) of 1926[27] did not provide for elections, although nonstatutory elections were occasionally utilized on some of the railroads.[28] As a result of the RLA amendments of 1934,[29] however, the National Mediation Board (NMB) was authorized to hold secret-ballot elections, within its discretion, to determine "*who* are the representatives" of a "craft or class"[30] of employees. Those amendments also conferred exclusivity on majority unions by mandating that "[t]he majority of any craft or class of employees shall have the right to determine who shall be the representative of the craft or class for the purposes of this Act."[31] As our historical review will demonstrate, representation elections outside the railroad industry were not resorted to until late in 1933, following enactment of Section 7(a) of the NIRA.[32]

In 1932, the year Norris-LaGuardia was passed, a union's majority was not relevant to an employee's right to designate "representatives of his own choosing to negotiate the terms and conditions of his employment . . . ."[33] That key phrase in the Norris-LaGuardia preamble and its accompanying language was, in the words of Felix Frankfurter and Nathan Green, "intended as an explicit avowal of the considerations moving Congressional action and, therefore, controlling any loyal application of national policy by the courts,"[34] for it was their view that "it is the primary function of the legislature to define public policy."[35] Collective bargaining was thus declared to be the national policy applicable to every employee in America. When the Norris-LaGuardia Act was passed in early March, 1932—well in advance of the national elections—it "was overwhelmingly supported in both the House and Senate and received widespread popular approval."[36] Indeed, that Act set the tone for the New Deal legislation of the following year. The collective bargaining and right-of-association policy described in its preamble became the model for the labor provisions of the new legislation. Its statement of policy, which stressed the importance of the individual employee's right to choose his *own* representative, implicitly affirmed that collective bargaining was not dependent on majority designation.[37] As a Brookings Institution report observed just prior to passage of the Wagner Act,

> The language of this declaration [in the Norris-LaGuardia Act] was truly extraordinary. It expressed a thoroughgoing change of previous legislative policy with regard to labor organization. The act was premised on the idea that there could ordinarily be no equality of liberty of contract between employer and employee except on the basis of organized and collective bargaining. That *the Act contemplated collective bargaining in according with trade union practices* is clear from the fact that it was sponsored by the A. F. of L. and that specific provisions were directed against many of the practices whereby the courts in the past had made it difficult for trade unions to organize and to carry on their activities.[38]

Following the 1932 elections, the new president, Franklin Roosevelt, quickly proceeded to implement his New Deal program to fight the Depression and revitalize the American economy. The Administration's immediate objective was to stimulate business and thereby reduce unemployment. Central among its early legislative programs to achieve those goals was the National Industrial Recovery bill,[39] the principal feature of which was suspension of the antitrust laws to permit companies to join with others in their industry through "codes of fair competition" that would cooperatively regulate prices, production, and labor standards. Pragmatically realizing that full labor support would be essential to the success of that program, the new Administration recognized early in the planning stages that it would need to balance those novel economic freedoms for business with a grant of rights for employees and unions that would promote labor organizing and collective bargaining.[40] To develop and guide this labor portion of the legislative package—which became Section 7(a) of the NIRA—the President turned mainly to Senator Robert F. Wagner of his own state of New York. Wagner, "recognized as the member of Congress most active in the labor field,"[41] seized the opportunity to fashion legislation that would foster his long-cherished objective of linking collective bargaining with the democratic process.

It was Wagner's view that a partnership between industry and labor was an "indispensable complement to political democracy"[42] and that such democratic self-government in industry would require the active participation of workers. He therefore insisted that "the right to bargain collectively is at the bottom of social justice for the worker, as well as the sensible conduct of business affairs[, for] the denial of observance of this right means the difference between despotism and democracy."[43] Wagner's vision of industrial democracy was a manifestation of a venerable and highly respected concept in American political and economic thought. Milton Derber, who traced that idea in his insightful study, *The American Idea of Industrial Democracy, 1865–1965*,[44] reported an early reference attributed to Albert Gallatin, Secretary of the Treasury under both Thomas Jefferson and James Madison, regarding a profit-sharing plan in his Pennsylvania glass works, which was that "[t]he democratic principle on which this nation was founded should not be restricted to the political process but should be applied to the industrial operation as well."[45] And the 1902 *Final Report of the United States Industrial Commission*[46] recommended that democracy be instituted in industry as follows:

> By the organization of labor, and by no other means, it is possible to introduce an element of democracy into the government of industry. By this means only the workers can effectively take part in determining the conditions under which they work. This becomes true in the fullest and best sense only when employers frankly meet the representatives of the workmen, and deal with them as parties equally interested in the conduct of affairs. It is only under such conditions that a real partnership of labor and capital exists.[47]

Senator Wagner was indeed pursuing a long-recognized social objective, a goal that Louis D. Brandeis had described in his 1915 testimony before another industrial relations commission. Viewing the American commitment to social justice as an incident of democracy, Brandeis stressed that

> the end for which we must strive is the attainment of rule by the people, and that involves industrial democracy as well as political democracy. That means that the problem of trade should be no longer the problem of the employer alone. The problems of his business, and it is not the employer's business alone, are the problems of all in it.[48]

Although several draftsmen were ultimately involved in the crafting of Section 7(a), the principal writer was Donald R. Richberg, who had been one of the authors of the Norris-LaGuardia Act.[49] One contemporaneous report on the resulting provision observed that it was obviously patterned after Section 2 of the latter statute, "even to employing much of its phraseology."[50] Richberg's subsequent interpretation of key phrases of Section 7(a), to be noted later, contributes to our understanding of what that language was recognized to mean when the NIRA was in effect.

Section 7(a), in its final version as passed, read as follows:

> Every code of fair competition, agreement, and license approved, prescribed, or issued under this title shall contain the following conditions: (1) That *employees shall have the right to* organize and *bargain collectively through representatives of their own choosing, and shall be free from the interference, restraint, or coercion of employers of labor, or their agents, in the designation of such representatives or in self-organization or in other concerted activities for the purposes of collective bargaining or other mutual aid or protection;* (2) that no employee and no one seeking employment shall be required as a condition of employment to join any company union or to refrain from joining, organizing, or assisting a labor organization of his own choosing; and (3) that employees shall comply with the maximum hours of labor, minimum rates of pay, and other conditions of employment, approved or prescribed by the President.[51]

The President selected Wagner to introduce the NIRA bill in the Senate.[52] It quickly sailed through Congress, and Roosevelt signed it on June 16, 1933.[53] The Blue Eagle, displayed by companies participating in the *codes of fair competition,* now became the symbolic icon of the federal government's new role in labor relations.

Wagner was pleased with the final product. A year later he recalled that in passing Section 7(a), "Congress [had] projected into economic affairs the essence of true democracy, by outlining a system of checks and balances between industry and labor, crowned by governmental supervision and advice."[54]

The Short Life of "Self-Policing" and Mediation

Inasmuch as Section 7(a) contained no explicit means of enforcement, its effectiveness depended on factors that were uncertain or unknown when the statute was passed. On its face, the collective bargaining obligation in Section 7(a) does not appear to have required any precondition other than the presence of an identifiable group of employees who are members of a labor organization that seeks to represent them in bargaining collectively with their employer. The basic fourteen-word provision required no more and no less. This process could embrace either minority- or majority-union bargaining—even proportional bargaining with two or more labor organizations. As labor historian James Gross perceptively recognized, "its wording was susceptible to interpretations that would sanction . . . *proportional* rather than exclusive representation."[55] The provision contained no reference to majority representation.

Shortly after passage of the NIRA, General Hugh S. Johnson, who had been appointed head of the National Recovery Administration (NRA), the agency charged with administering the Act, announced with reference to Section 7(a) that he looked "to this new industrial self-government to be self-policing," although he acknowledged that if there were violations the government "could step in."[56] That concept of "self-policing" remained the policy of the Administration for only a short time, however. Encouraged by the enactment of Section 7(a), the trade union movement undertook a massive organizational campaign that exceeded any such activity since World War I,[57] and in July, immediately after passage of the Act, a wave of strikes swept over the country. In that month, 1,375,000 worker-days were lost due to strikes, and in August the number rose to 2,378,000, which was three times the average for the first half of 1933.[58] The magnitude of these strikes prompted the Administration to immediately create some form of governmental machinery to address the settlement of labor-management disputes;[59] whereupon, on August 5, 1933, President Roosevelt announced the establishment of a National Labor Board (NLB)[60] to assist in the implementation of Section 7(a). This represented the first institutional attempt to shape 7(a) "in the NRA mold of voluntary self-government."[61] However, Roosevelt issued no executive order defining the Board's authority at that time. His announcement simply stated that the Board would "consider, adjust, and settle differences and controversies"[62] among disputing parties. It was not until December 16, 1933, that the President issued his first executive order acknowledging the Board's existence and defining its authority, but that order still left the matter of its jurisdiction in a state of uncertainty.[63] In fact, throughout its tenure, the "Board was never quite sure of its own authority."[64]

In accordance with the Administration's voluntary self-policing approach, the NLB initially concentrated its efforts on conciliation or mediation.[65] Such a program did not seem illogical at the time because the collective bargaining process mandated by Section 7(a) appeared to require only three factors: a union that represented a group of employees, a demand for recognition and bargaining, and an employer who was expected to respond by engaging in good faith negotiations. It soon became apparent, however, that the last part of that scenario rarely occurred, for almost all employers vigorously resisted union recognition unless it was forced upon them by strikes or boycotts. Not surprisingly, most of the strikes then occurring were for recognition.[66] Nevertheless, in the early months of the NLB's existence the Board's leadership made an effort to mold the agency primarily into a provider of mediation.[67] And during that early period no one among that leadership, including Senator Wagner, whom the President had appointed chairman of the NLB,[68] even intimated that Section 7(a) required a union majority as a precondition for recognition and bargaining. Majority status was not yet an issue because labor-management practices prevailing at the time included an eclectic assortment of collective bargaining arrangements, and minority-union and members-only bargaining were almost as common as exclusivity bargaining.[69] In fact, according to one contemporary observer, Minier Sargent, a law professor at Northwestern University writing in the *Illinois Law Review*,

> The concept of a representative selected merely by a majority of the employees in a plant being representative of all, with power to make a contract for all covering terms and conditions of employment for a specified period of time was foreign to the labor relations field in general industry prior to the N.I.R.A. The only principle of majority rule known prior to the statute was the principle of rule by a majority within an organization voluntarily chosen by the employee. . . .[70]

The Collective Bargaining Scene at the Beginning of the National Recovery Administration: The Conference Board Survey

Fortunately, an empirically reliable description of the essential characteristics of labor relations practiced at this important stage in American labor history is available. In November, 1933, the National Industrial Conference Board (Conference Board)[71] conducted "A Statistical Study of Present Practice"[72] in order to determine the nature of collective bargaining as it was being conducted immediately following enactment of the NIRA. The resulting monograph provides nationwide data—not heretofore highlighted—that reveal the make-up of the collective bargaining process during this critical period prior to passage of the Wagner Act.

Conducted only five months after Section 7(a) became effective and shortly after the mid-summer wave of strikes, the Conference Board's survey provides a remarkable portrait of the labor-relations scene in 1933. Because of its early timing, the study records practices that were for the most part already in place prior to passage of the NIRA, although the new legislation and the strikes that promptly followed were bound to have had some impact, albeit minor, which would be reflected in certain parts of the data. Nevertheless, whatever collective bargaining practices might have been added shortly before November, 1933, they would not have been affected by any elections conducted by the NLB mandating exclusivity for majority unions, for such election procedures were not instituted until several months later.[73]

The Conference Board's study was directed to the fields of manufacturing and mining, which were appropriate industries to investigate, for these were the industries most affected by Section 7(a) and the ones that would ultimately be the industries most affected by the Wagner Act.[74] The survey addressed inquiries to a carefully selected representative sample of 10,335 companies.[75] "Companies were asked, in addition to the number of wage-earners employed, whether they dealt with employees individually, through a plan of employee representation [i.e., a company union[76]] or through an organized labor union. [And if] more than one method was used, the number or proportion of workers affected by each policy was asked."[77] The response rate was high and clearly representative of the universe being studied, for

Replies were received from 3,314 companies, which reported an aggregate employment of 2,585,740 wage-earners. This represents approximately 27% of the estimated total number of workers employed in the fields of manufacturing and mining.[78]

The compiled replies are contained in Tables 1 and 2, reproduced here from the monograph.[79]

Table 1
Number and Proportion of Wage-Earners Covered in Survey that Deal with Employer by Methods Indicated

Method of Dealing with Employer	Number of Employees	Percentage of Total
Individually	1,180,580	45.7
Through employee representation	1,164,294	45.0
Through organized labor unions	240,866	9.3
Total	2,585,740	100.0

Table 2

Number and Proportion of Companies and Wage-Earners Affected by Various Policies of Conducting Employer-Employee Relations

Method of Conducting Employer-Employee Relations	Companies	Wage-Earners under			
		Individual Bargaining	Employee Representation	Union	Total
		Number			
Individual bargaining exclusively	2,284	1,013,016	—	—	1,013,016
Employee representation exclusively	556	—	894,327	—	894,327
Union agreement exclusively	230	—	—	189,756	189,756
Combination, individual bargaining and union	147	81,180	—	39,240	120,420
Combination, individual bargaining and employee representation	58	70,248	243,182	—	313,430
Combination, employee representation and union	21	—	15,916	8,140	24,056
Combination, individual bargaining, employee representation, and union	18	16,136	10,869	3,730	30,735
Total	3,314	1,180,580	1,164,294	240,866	2,585,740
		Percentage			
Individual bargaining exclusively	68.9	39.2	—	—	39.2
Employee representation exclusively	16.8	—	34.6	—	34.6
Union agreement exclusively	6.9	—	—	7.3	7.3
Combination, individual bargaining and union	4.4	3.1	—	1.5	4.7
Combination, individual bargaining and employee representation	1.8	2.7	9.4	—	12.1
Combination, employee representation and union	0.6	—	0.6	0.3	0.9
Combination, individual bargaining, employee representation, and union	0.6	0.6	0.4	0.1	1.2
Total	100.0	45.7	45.0	9.3	100.0

The data contained in these tables offer a wealth of information about the nature of labor relations during this seminal period in American industrial-relations history. Although the Conference Board survey provides statistical information concerning employers' relations with both independent unions and company unions—i.e., "employee representation plans"[80]—our present focus is only on the nature of the collective bargaining processes that involved conventional independent unions (i.e., trade unions). Later, however, I shall return to this survey to report what it reveals about the strong presence of company unions during the period immediately before passage of the Wagner Act[81] and to evaluate the ultimate effect their presence had on the legislative process that produced that Act.

The Conference Board data show that a variety of bargaining arrangements prevailed at the time of the study. Table 1 reveals that 45.7 percent of the employees dealt with their employers on an individual basis, 45 percent dealt through employee representation plans (i.e., company unions), and 9.3 percent dealt through independent unions. Table 2 reveals that 68.9 percent of the reporting companies engaged in no bargaining at all with any organizational entity—that is, neither with an independent union nor a company union. The remaining 31.1 percent engaged in bargaining with either an independent union or a company union or both, including arrangements whereby employees in many of the companies also engaged in individual bargaining. This group of 31.1 percent of the companies, representing 1,030 companies in the sample, is the main focus of our attention, for they represented the universe of employers in the survey who bargained collectively with organizational entities, whether independent unions or company unions. Of the percentages and numerical figures applicable to this group of employers, we observe that 230 bargained with independent unions representing 189,756 employees on an exclusive basis,[82] and 186[83] bargained with independent unions representing 51,100 employees[84] on a nonexclusive basis.

The following statistical summaries from the upper half of Table 2 provide the principal bases for the conclusions here presented:

1. Of the 147 companies with a combination of individual and union bargaining, 81,180 of the employees were non-union and bargained individually and 39,240—approximately one-third of the total employees—were members of independent unions who bargained through those unions.

2. Of the 21 companies with a combination of employee representation (i.e., company-union representation) and union bargaining, 15,916 employees bargained through their company unions and 8,140—approximately one-third of the total number of those employees—were members of independent unions who bargained through those unions.

3. Of the 18 companies with a combination of all three types of bargaining, 16,136 employees bargained individually, 10,869 bargained through their company unions, and 3,730—approximately one-eighth of the total

number of those employees—were members of independent unions who bargained through those unions.

These figures indicate, or strongly imply, that where bargaining occurred on a members-only basis, most—if not all or nearly all—such bargaining was with unions that represented less than a majority of the employees in the employing units to which the responding companies referred. In the event, however, that any of these companies also included units in which union employees constituted a majority—which is theoretically possible to a very limited extent, although not likely in significant numbers—collective bargaining at those workplaces would nevertheless have been conducted on a members-only basis, for those companies also engaged in individual bargaining and/or bargaining with company unions. However, because of the relative sizes of the three component groups,[85] as well as the logic of their bargaining situations, I shall assume for present purposes that all such members-only bargaining was conducted with unions that represented less than a majority of the employees in the respective workplace units.

Of the total of 416 companies in the sample that bargained with independent unions, 55 percent did so on an exclusive basis and 45 percent bargained on a members-only basis. The 51,110 union employees who were not involved in exclusive representation (i.e., union employees in the companies that engaged in members-only bargaining) were thus working in varying combinations and job categories in those companies alongside 124,101 other employees who were either wholly nonunion or were represented by company unions. Together, these workers totaled 175,211 employees, a number that may be compared to the only slightly higher number of 189,756 employees covered by exclusive union representation.[86] And extrapolating from the survey group to the nationwide employee populations of companies in mining and manufacturing, we arrive at totals of approximately 189,260 union employees covered by *members-only* collective bargaining, as compared with approximately 702,800 union employees covered by *exclusive* collective bargaining. In other words, of all the union members employed in mining and manufacturing in 1933, approximately 21 percent were represented by minority unions that engaged in members-only bargaining. And, as noted, the percentage of companies that bargained with those minority unions was considerably higher, representing 45 percent of all the companies that engaged in some form of collective bargaining.

The foregoing statistics—with their references to exclusive union bargaining, nonexclusive union bargaining, company union bargaining, and individual bargaining, plus various combinations of the latter three types of bargaining—dramatically portray the eclectic nature of trade-union representation in the manufacturing and mining industries in America at the time Section 7(a) was enacted. These data confirm that members-only collective bargaining through minority unions was a common phenomenon in those industries, and there is no reason to believe that manufacturing and mining were unique in this regard.

Although the findings by the Conference Board may surprise many readers today, that same general information was well known at the time.[87] Contrasting the rock-solid state of union representation in the railroad industry with the fragmented condition of representation then prevailing in other industries, Professor Sargent wrote in 1934:

> Labor has been well organized in the railroad industry for many years. The possibility of independent unions opposed to the unions to which a majority of the employees in a particular craft or class belonged was very remote. On the other hand, the N.I.R.A. applies to all industries generally throughout the country, in many parts of which the employees are either entirely unorganized or are organized into several different unions, with *many employees belonging to unions which cannot claim that their memberships comprise a majority of the employees in the plant or company involved.*[88]

Collective bargaining was indeed closely tied to union membership during the years preceding the Wagner Act. Majority-rule exclusivity bargaining was but one of several patterns of representation and bargaining that existed at that time. Minority-union bargaining was another commonly practiced pattern. It is thus not surprising, as we shall see in subsequent chapters, that in both 1934 and 1935 the drafters of the Wagner Act took special pains to protect premajority collective bargaining, for it was looked upon as an important preliminary stage in the development of mature union bargaining.

Interpretation, Application, and Administration of Section 7(a)

Now that we have a reliable picture of what the labor-relations landscape looked like in the early days of the NIRA when the NLB was established, we can better understand that Board's initial responses to the disputes it encountered. At the beginning, the NLB took the position that only workers had the right to determine how their collective bargaining representatives would be selected,[89] and, as noted, it viewed its role chiefly as a provider of mediation to assist unions and employers in the settlement of their disputes.[90] Eventually, however, events dictated an expansion of that role, for employer opposition to Section 7(a) and the NLB's policies prompted the Board to develop its own procedures for the designation of employee representatives.[91] Lacking any other effective method to require employers to comply with the bargaining requirements of the law, the NLB seized on the strategy of proffering elections as a means to jump-start the bargaining process. Where employers were willing to cooperate, it began holding governmentally supervised elections in "cases in which a conflict existed over the question of who were the bona fide representatives of the employees, and in which the conflict did not appear subject to solution in any other way."[92]

Representation elections were thus initiated as a pragmatic enforcement mechanism by an otherwise powerless NLB, for they were found to be a plausible means of settling disputes in workplaces where the principal issue was union recognition.

Notwithstanding this ad hoc adoption of the election device—which was not even mentioned in Section 7(a)—the Board demonstrated a keen awareness of the broad implications of the basic collective bargaining text contained in that section, for when employers' insisted on dealing only with representatives drawn from their own work force, the NLB wrote and ruled as follows:

> We fail to see how it is possible to put any interpretation on the phrase "representatives of their own choosing" which would make it necessary for employees to choose these representatives from a particular class or a particular group. . . . To give the code the interpretation sought by the company would nullify the employees' right to organize as they choose. . . . The National Labor Board rules, therefore, that employees have the right to choose anyone they may wish as their representative and are not limited in their choice to fellow employees.[93]

The representation election had its inception in the Board's effort to mediate a lengthy strike in the full-fashion hosiery industry. This was one of the prominent strikes in mid-summer of 1933 for which mediation was successful. It produced the notable "Reading formula" that consisted of the following key elements:

> (1) The union called off the strike. (2) Employees were rehired without discrimination. (3) *The Board would hold elections in which the workers would vote by secret ballot for representatives and those so chosen would negotiate with the employers to the end of executing collective bargaining agreements covering wages, hours, and working conditions.* (4) Failing agreement on any of the matters, the parties would submit unresolved issues to the Board for final decision.[94]

This formula set a pattern that was applied—or at least attempted—in many other disputes. Secret-ballot representation elections now became the NLB's chief means of implementing Section 7(a),[95] for when a union won the support of a majority of the employees in a governmentally conducted election it achieved a degree of legitimacy usually not otherwise attainable without a strike. But success under the Reading formula soon proved illusory, for by the end of 1933 most employers had turned against the NLB and were flatly refusing to cooperate with the election process.[96] Accordingly, lacking meaningful enforcement authority, the NLB became increasingly irrelevant,[97] and its decisions—as illustrated by the cases that follow—reflected its institutional frustration.

Those decisions, nevertheless, recognized that the collective bargaining obligation mandated by Section 7(a) was keyed to the employees' exercise of their choice of bargaining representative, and majority status was not a requirement of that obligation. And although a governmentally supervised election could confirm a union's majority status, it was only a proffered enforcement device, not a requisite for bargaining. Illustrative of such decisions was *Edward G. Budd Mfg. Co.*,[98] decided in mid-December, 1933. The Budd company employed from 3,500 to 5,000 workers. Following management's organization of a company union, many employees joined an outside union affiliated with the American Federation of Labor (AFL), which then demanded recognition. When the company refused, stating that it could not recognize the AFL because it already "had employee representation that was operating satisfactorily,"[99] between 1,200 and 1,500 of the employees went on strike to protest that refusal. In its opinion, the Board stated that

> Both the selection of a form of organization and the designation of representatives, as well a the method of designation, are placed by Section 7(a) within the exclusive control of the workers. The law does not tolerate any impairment of this freedom of self-organization.[100]

However, it is unclear from the decision whether the AFL union was seeking to represent all of the company's workers or only its members, for it obviously represented less than a majority. Notwithstanding, the Board affirmed the propriety of bargaining with such a minority union, for it noted that the union committee had been "authorized to speak for a substantial number of the workers," but it criticized the union for its "hasty resort to a strike *before* the process of collective bargaining had been exploited."[101] Implying, however, that the committee may have been claiming to represent *all* of the employees, not just union members, it also stated that if "the committee represented a majority of the employees, the company's refusal to recognize them as representatives for the purpose of collective bargaining was wrongful."[102] In the face of the employer's strong opposition to recognizing any outside union under any circumstances, the Board was obviously powerless to fashion an appropriate remedy. Nevertheless, it ordered a government-supervised election, but it was never conducted because the company refused to comply.[103] The *Budd* case was further evidence that the NLB had indeed become irrelevant, at least to the major part of American industry.[104]

Despite its enforcement problems, the NLB continued its efforts to articulate a viable labor policy under Section 7(a), directing its attention to various aspects of the collective bargaining obligation. On January 31, 1934, in *S. Dresner & Son*,[105] it issued an opinion that reaffirmed that neither a verifiable majority nor an election was a necessary prerequisite to an employer's duty to bargain. The union's majority status was not even an issue for inquiry in that case, where the union had simply "purported to represent the employees"[106] and tendered a contract for bargaining. When the employer refused to deal with the union, a strike occurred. Finding the employer's refusal a violation of the Blue Eagle code under Section 7(a), the Board wrote:

> The record reveals a deplorable misconception by the company of the nature and meaning of collective bargaining. . . . The preemptory rejection of the employees' proposal and the refusal to enter into negotiations with the representatives of the employees are repugnant to the very concept of collective bargaining. . . . The refusal to enter into negotiations left the employees no alternative but to strike.[107]

Although the statute mandated that companies recognize and bargain collectively with representatives of their employees' union regardless of majority status—which General Johnson and NRA General Counsel Richberg fully acknowledged and were publicly asserting[108]—Senator Wagner and most of his colleagues on the NLB preferred to modify that requirement whenever an election was held to determine majority representation so that the victor in that election would be deemed the *exclusive* representative. They considered this approach to be the most effective means to settle contested claims of representation, almost all of which involved competing claims between independent unions and company unions, for these were the most common cases that raised questions concerning representation. In fact, the NLB during its short tenure[109] conducted 546 elections, of which 449 (83 percent) involved "a choice between trade-union representation and some form of nonunion employee representation [i.e., company union]."[110]

In mid-December of 1933 the President finally issued an executive order confirming the NLB's original authority.[111] That order ratified the Board's prior activity—which had included the conduct of many elections—and formally authorized it to "settle by mediation, conciliation or arbitration all controversies between employers and employees which tend to impede the purpose of the National Industrial Recovery Act."[112] It said nothing explicitly, however, about elections. It was not until Executive Order 6580,[113] issued on February 1, 1934, that the Board was given official approval—albeit executive rather than legislative—to hold elections. Thereafter, upon a request by a "substantial number" of a company's employees, the Board was now authorized, pursuant to that executive order, to conduct elections in which "representatives who are selected by the vote of at least a *majority* of the employees voting . . . have been thereby designated to represent *all of the employees eligible to participate . . . for the purpose of collective bargaining.* . . . "[114] Although this authorization appeared to indicate presidential approval of the concepts of majority rule and representational exclusivity, it was not so interpreted by everyone concerned, including the President himself.

Indeed, Executive Order 6580 only exacerbated the festering dispute between the respective administrators of the NRA and the NLB concerning the interpretation of Section 7(a), a dispute about which President Roosevelt's own views often flip-flopped.[115] A showdown—but not the final showdown—was now inevitable. Although the language of Section 7(a) provided no basis for excluding minority-representation collective bargaining—a reality that was recognized by a strong and vocal part of the employer community[116]—such an exclusionary concept was nevertheless the interpretation the majority of the NLB intended to apply wherever a union had been selected by a majority of the employees in an election. The Board majority viewed this approach as a pragmatic means to avoid allowing a continuing role for a company union once it had been defeated by an independent union in a Board-ordered election. Employers, however, disagreed with that approach, favoring instead a concept of "collective bargaining pluralism,"[117] for they preferred dealing with company unions, even when they represented only a minority of the employees. "The statute, in their interpretation, was not meant to establish exclusive agencies of collective bargaining in all units, but to assure the co-existence of as many collective bargaining groups as could find adherents among the workers."[118] Their major concern, however, according to a 1935 Brookings Institution report, was their fear "(1) that the Board's electoral procedure would throw elections to trade unions, and (2) that the winning of an election by a union was but a first step towards the demand for 'union recognition' and the 'closed shop.'"[119] The first fear may have been justified; as the Brookings report noted: "The election returns of the National Labor Board show that where the choice was offered them, the workers favored trade unions rather than company unions in a ratio of about two to one."[120]

The employers had General Johnson and Donald Richberg[121] on their side of the legal argument. Johnson and Richberg reacted to Executive Order 6580 by promptly issuing a joint interpretive statement advising that "Section 7(a) affirms the *right of employees to organize and bargain collectively through representatives of their own choosing;* and such concerted activities can be lawfully carried on by either *majority or minority* groups, organizing and selecting such representatives in such manner as they see fit."[122] They thus reiterated and relied on the basic fourteen-word statutory phrase, giving it its natural meaning.

Although the NLB refused to accept the Johnson-Richberg concept of collective bargaining pluralism when applied to representation elections, it never abandoned its position that a union's majority status was a non-issue when a union was seeking to bargain in places where the employees had not yet selected a majority representative in an election. That position was clearly apparent in its *National Lock Company* decision,[123] which was issued only a week prior to the NLB's embrace of the majoritarian-exclusivity model in *Denver Tramway Corporation.*[124] And following the latter decision, the pre-election minority-union bargaining model was reinforced in the *Bee Bus Line*[125] and *Eagle Rubber*[126] cases, which will be discussed shortly.

On March 1, 1934, bolstered by Executive Order No. 6580, the Board erected a major landmark in American labor history with its issuance of the decision in *Denver Tramway,* which held that where a union had obtained a majority of the votes cast in a government-sponsored election—even though not a majority of the eligible voters—any collective agreement reached between that union and the employer "must apply alike to all employees."[127] The NLB thus inaugurated the *rule of exclusivity* for majority-union representation. Although this is the rule for which *Denver Tramway* is famous, a closer look at that decision reveals a little-noticed feature that sheds much light on the object of our concern, the principle of members-only collective bargaining. That feature is that the Board's policy of representational exclusivity—inaugurated in that opinion—was not only at odds with the Johnson-Richberg approach, it was also at odds with organized labor's reliance on union membership as the customary basis for collective bargaining, for that position was openly espoused in the *Denver Tramway* opinion by both the successful union and the prominent union members of the NLB.

The Board's decision recognized the Amalgamated,[128] an independent trade union, as the employees' new bargaining agent based on the 353 votes that it had received in the election as compared with the 325 votes cast for the Employees Representation Committee,[129] a company union that had previously represented the employees. A total of 714 employees were qualified to vote and 36 failed to vote. Following the election, the Amalgamated submitted a proposed collective bargaining agreement to the company that provided that it was to govern "the relations to exist during the term of this agreement between the company and the *members of said Association.*'"[130] According to this proposal, "in its capacity as exclusive agent, the Amalgamated would bargain collectively for its members alone."[131] The Board majority rejected that members-only approach, insisting that

> Any agreement reached in conformity with this decision must apply alike to all employees of the company. The limitation to its membership in the form of contract submitted by the Amalgamated does not meet this requirement and must be modified accordingly.[132]

Although this holding in *Denver Tramway* established "the cornerstone principles of majority rule and exclusive representation"[133] that would henceforth characterize American labor relations through successive labor boards to the present, in 1934 those principles were not widely accepted. This was certainly evident from the members-only contract that the Amalgamated had proposed to the company, and it was also evident from the positions taken in the case by the two labor members of the Board, William Green, president of the AFL, and John L. Lewis, president of the United Mine Workers (UMW), probably the most influential labor leaders in the country. Although Green and Lewis agreed with the basic ruling that recognized the Amalgamated as bargaining agent, they refused to concur with the requirement by the Board's majority that the union must represent *all employees* under its proposed contract, not just its own members.[134] And almost to the same effect, Pierre duPont, the leading employer member of the Board, submitted a dissenting opinion holding that as to the employees who voted in favor of the Amalgamated, that union should be their representative, but as to the minority who voted in favor of the Employees' Representation Committee, that committee should be their representative.[135] This idea of collective bargaining pluralism, expressed by duPont, was to remain the position of most employers for the duration of Section 7(a)[136] and would be their position during deliberations on the Wagner bill in 1935.[137]

Another case that illustrated organized labor's attachment to the notion of members-only bargaining during the NIRA period is to be found in a 1934 NRA press release. The case involved the American Federation of Full-Fashioned Hosiery Workers and the *Real Silk Company,* where the NLB had supervised a representation election in October 1933. The press release, issued on April 27, 1934, reported that

> The election was won by the Employees' Mutual Benefit Association. Subsequently the Hosiery Workers' Union [which lost the election] demanded that the company bargain with it as well as with the company union on the ground that *as a group, though a minority group, the hosiery workers had a right to bargain with the management.*[138]

The Board rejected the request.[139] The case is significant here because the Hosiery Workers' Union was seeking the same arrangement, i.e., membership-based bargaining, that the Amalgamated had proposed in *Denver Tramway* and that the employer representatives a few months later would advance with reference to the *Houde* case.[140]

Although *Denver Tramway* has come to be viewed as a crucial turning point in American labor history,[141] it should be remembered that in that decision labor leaders Green and Lewis refused to concur with the Board's rejection of members-only representation. It is true that organized labor would later embrace the idea that exclusivity should apply *after* a majority of the employees have selected a bargaining agent, but labor's position in *Denver Tramway* and *Real Silk* emphasized two important contemporaneous factors: *First,* that collective bargaining representation was deemed to be tied to union membership, and *second,* that the NLB's rejection of members-only bargaining was to be applicable only *after* the employees had selected a majority—hence *exclusive*—representative. *Denver Tramway* had no effect on an employer's duty to bargain with a minority union in workplaces where a majority union had not yet been designated; indeed, such minority-union bargaining was commonly practiced at the time.

The majority-rule model of *Denver Tramway* may have expressed the view of the NLB, but it no longer represented the view of the President. Only a few weeks after that decision, Roosevelt abandoned the majority-union position he had espoused so recently in Executive Order 6580. The occasion was his personal intervention in a major dispute in the automobile industry. The United Automobile Workers, affiliated with the AFL, despite fierce resistance from the employers, had organized more than 50,000 workers in that industry. The companies' response was total rejection of any recognition of an outside trade union, a refusal to allow any NLB elections, and rapid organization of numerous company unions. Although the NLB tried to mediate this volatile dispute, it failed. Faced with the threat of a crippling strike, President Roosevelt and General Johnson decided to intercede directly, and they were successful in mediating a settlement that avoided the strike, which the President proudly announced to the American people on March 25, 1934.[142] That settlement agreement, however, rejected the majority-rule model and provided instead for collective bargaining based on plurality or proportional representation. It also established the Automobile Labor Board, which effectively divested the NLB of jurisdiction over that industry. Furthermore, the agreement contained no provision for elections.[143] The automobile settlement thus struck a blow that proved fatal to the NLB's prestige.[144]

Meanwhile, however, the *Denver Tramway* rule of exclusivity, attached to union representation following an election, did not affect the NLB's position that where there was no question concerning representation that called for an election, the employer had a duty to bargain with minority unions without reference to the extent of union membership. The *National Lock*,[145] *Bee Bus Line*,[146] and *Eagle Rubber*[147] cases, previously mentioned, are illustrative of that proposition.

In *National Lock*, which was decided a week before *Denver Tramway*, the NLB reported that during August of 1933 "*many* of the employees formed a federal union,"[148] but it was unable to determine "how many of the employees had joined"[149] by the time of the strike that occurred on August 31. Union employees asserted that on the morning of September 1 they had presented written demands to the company, which the company denied receiving. Without resolving that issue of fact, the Board declared that "[i]f the document was received, the summary rejection by the employer could only be construed as a denial of the rights conferred upon the workers by the statute."[150] The union's majority—or lack thereof—was obviously not an issue. The NLB not only found an interference with the employees' right to bargain collectively, it used the occasion to define the bargaining duty required by Section 7(a):

The collective bargaining envisaged by the statute involves a quality of obligation—an obligation on the part of employees to present grievances and demands to the employer before striking, and an obligation on the part of the employer to discuss differences with the representatives of the employees and to exert every reasonable effort to reach an agreement on all matters in dispute. Negotiations should precede rather than follow the calling of a strike.[151]

It then ruled that the "Board finds as a fact that the National Lock Company interfered with the right of its employees to organize and bargain collectively through representatives of their own choosing."[152]

In *Bee Line Bus Company*, decided May 10, 1934, the NLB again stressed the need to bargain collectively prior to a strike, even though the striking bus drivers were only 77 of the company's 200 drivers.

A week later, in *Eagle Rubber Company*, the Board again found an employer in violation of the statute when it "would not recognize the union or recognize [its] committee as the representative of the employees,"[153] thereby precipitating a strike. As the opinion noted, the "union local involved in the dispute . . . had enrolled practically all the men and a few women, *comprising slightly less than half of the* force of 120 then at work."[154] At a hearing before the Regional Labor Board, the employer pledged "to meet with the chosen representatives of the employees"[155] and take certain other action relating to the reinstatement of striking employees. Notwithstanding that less than a majority of the employees had joined the union, the NLB found that it was

> clear from the evidence . . . that the company has complied neither with the recommendation of the Regional Board . . . nor with its own promises . . . to bargain collectively with their chosen representatives. . . . The statute requires the employer to meet with the duly chosen representative of the employees . . . and to negotiate actively in good faith to reach an agreement. . . . The employees, on their part did not strike without having previously taken reasonable measures to avoid drastic action. [The company's action] was compatible neither with its repeated pledges nor its statutory duty.[156]

These three decisions demonstrate that the NLB did not require an election unless it was requested by a union or a substantial number of employees,[157] although if more than one union were seeking representation it would also conduct an election and the *Denver Tramway* rule of majority-union exclusivity would thereafter apply. Absent any of those circumstances, the unvarnished duty-to-bargain mandate contained in Section 7(a) prevailed regardless of the size of the union's membership. Majority representation was not essential for the NLB to find that an employer's refusal to bargain interfered with employees' rights under Section 7(a).

It had now become apparent, however, that the NLB could no longer cope with the intransigence that typically characterized employer responses to its efforts to implement the requirements of the Act. Judicial enforcement through the Justice Department was difficult to obtain, and the Board was inadequately staffed to handle litigation. When litigation did occur, which was infrequent, it usually proved to be only another means for the employer to delay an election or avoid bargaining.[158] In most employer-violation cases, recommending removal of the symbolic Blue Eagle was the only enforcement medium reasonably available to the Board.[159] Senator Wagner and his associates had been aware of these problems for many months. It was therefore no surprise that on March 1, 1934—the same day the *Denver Tramway* decision was issued—he introduced S. 2926, his "Labor Disputes" bill, the first of his two legislative efforts to correct the enforcement deficiencies of Section 7(a). The stage was now set for final action under the Blue Eagle code and for new legislative activity that would eventually lead to passage of the Wagner Act.

2   *Prelude to the Wagner Act*

The 1934 Labor Disputes Bill and the State of Labor Relations under the Blue Eagle

Wagner's Nine Legislative Drafts

As we have seen in the previous chapter, Senator Wagner, who had been the driving force behind both the drafting and the passage of the NIRA's Section 7(a) and was Chairman of the National Labor Board, was fully aware of the shortcomings of that fledgling body and the weaknesses in the law under which it was attempting to operate. Although the NLB had made some modest progress in mediation and had succeeded in settling many labor disputes through representation elections,[1] its lack of enforcement power rendered it wholly ineffectual in contested cases.[2] Industry generally refused to comply with the Board's orders, and efforts at judicial enforcement created only more delays without resolving the issues at stake.[3] Furthermore, the White House was ambivalent about the Board's mission.[4] Thus, by fall 1933, in the wake of the numerous strikes that had swept over the country, Wagner's frustration with the inadequacy of Section 7(a) brought him to an idea that was to mark the legislative beginning of the Act that was to bear his name. That idea, as told to his legislative aide, Leon Keyserling, was that what the country needed was a labor court to enforce Section 7(a).[5] Recalling that conversation many years later, Keyserling opined that Wagner "didn't have any very definite ideas in his mind as to what he meant by a 'labor court,' I think he thought more of a regulatory court to hear labor matters."[6] That, of course, is what was ultimately achieved in the National Labor Relations Board that was created by the 1935 Wagner Act.

When the President expressed no interest in this new legislative objective, Wagner decided to proceed without White House support.[7] He instructed Keyserling to begin working on a bill, and in January 1934 he hosted an introductory conference on the subject. Present were William Green, John L.

Lewis, Henry Warrum (counsel for the Mine Workers), Charles E. Wyzanski, Jr., (solicitor of the Department of Labor), and of course Keyserling.[8] This group favorably discussed the general outline of a bill that would cover the right to organize and bargain, bargaining units, outside representation elections, majority rule, the duty to bargain, the closed shop, company unions, and the right to strike.[9] Wagner placed Keyserling in charge of drafting the bill—a role that he would hold throughout the life of this first bill and also through final passage of the second bill that became law in 1935.[10]

Wagner relied heavily on Keyserling, who was given "final authority" as to the contents of the proposed bill, subject only to the Senator's approval.[11] A close working relationship developed between the two, and they were apparently in total agreement on all major issues relative to this legislation. Here is Keyserling's description of the remarkable rapport that existed between him and Wagner:

> It was very hard for me to delineate between what the Senator felt and what I felt. I can only say that in a general way, the reason we got along, and the reason I could be effective, was that broadly speaking, we were in agreement. Second, on the more detailed aspects, he relied greatly on my judgment. It was very hard for me to say just where I ended and he began.[12]

Although Keyserling was the primary draftsman of all of Wagner's public statements and materials—including his speeches, legislative bills, and key committee reports—the Senator was kept fully advised at all stages of the work and totally approved of the final product.[13] Keyserling reported that Wagner "didn't go over the details of the legislative drafting [for he] knew that our thinking was generally the same and he had confidence in the people that I was working with. [H]e was a very good reader of language."[14]

Keyserling's immediate task was to draft a bill, titled the Labor Disputes Act, that would create an "industrial court" bearing the currently familiar name of "National Labor Board"; this body would have enforcement authority over the rights contained in Section 7(a) of the NIRA as interpreted by the existing nonstatutory National Labor Board (NLB). Technical assistance was obtained from the NLB's staff.[15] Keyserling drafted the bill in February and Wagner introduced it in the Senate on March 1.[16]

Nine drafts were involved in the process. Eight preliminary drafts, numbered 1 through 8, including drafts 2(a) and 2(b), were published by Professor Kenneth Casebeer in 1989.[17] The ninth and final draft was the bill introduced in the Senate as S. 2926.[18] The reader will find all relevant parts of these drafts and the Walsh substitute bill—the National Industrial Adjustment bill[19] that ultimately replaced Wagner's bill—reproduced in the Appendix to Chapter 2.[20] These drafts tell a remarkable story about the issue of minority-union representation and bargaining at the premajority stage of union organizing and bargaining. They unequivocally show that Wagner and

Keyserling considered, weighed, and specifically covered this minority-bargaining issue; and as we shall see in Chapter 3, that same awareness and consideration continued the following year in the drafting of the bill that was finally enacted as the National Labor Relations Act.

As we examine these early drafts we shall be aware that Wagner and Keyserling preferred the majority-rule concept over its alternative, plurality representation among competing unions, which had been the plan favored by General Johnson and Donald Richberg and the plan adopted in the automobile settlement.[21] However, although Wagner considered majority exclusivity to be the ideal bargaining format for mature collective bargaining, the various changes that occurred in the enabling language in the several drafts indicate that his primary concern was to establish an effective means to settle representation disputes so that collective bargaining—whatever its format—could proceed expeditiously and successfully. These drafts demonstrate that he and Keyserling were conscious of the role played by minority-union bargaining in the organizational process, for it was common knowledge that such bargaining often preceded the establishment of a union's majority.[22] Thus, for workplaces where a majority representative had not yet been chosen, they were careful to avoid any statutory interference with nonexclusive, members-only bargaining. The analyses of the drafts that follow are confined to those provisions relating to such minority-union bargaining.

The most important feature in the drafts is the unchangeable protective language that appears in relevant portions of each,[23] to wit, the key substantive phrase derived from Section 7(a) of the NIRA that guarantees employees the right "*to bargain* (or *of bargaining*) *collectively through representatives of their own choosing.*"[24] I shall refer to this phrase as the *basic collective bargaining provision*. And, as we shall observe in Chapter 3, that same provision—in its original fourteen-word version—was carried over to Section 7 of the 1935 bill as introduced and finally enacted. Standing alone, this basic provision on its face guarantees employees the right to bargain collectively through any union they choose, regardless of how many employees select that union. The provision, however, does not stand alone in any of the drafts, and the manner in which Keyserling and Wagner changed the qualifying text from time to time shows their awareness of the importance of protecting the right of minority employees to bargain prior to establishment of majority representation.

They began the drafting process with reference to the duty to bargain in *Draft 2(a)* by relying on the expansive language of the basic collective bargaining provision,[25] which they qualified only for situations in which a majority of the eligible employees had already selected their majority representatives, in which event those representatives would be "the *sole* representatives of all the employees eligible to participate in such choice."[26]

In the next draft (*Draft 3*) they continued with virtually the same approach, except they added another provision, Section 12(a), that spelled out that employers have a duty "to recognize and bargain collectively [with employee representatives] whether these representatives are or are not employees."[27] This passage thus emphasized that the duty to bargain was not restricted to representatives who were employees of the same company, as many employers had insisted.[28] That this clause was later deleted suggests that the authors were satisfied—in fact preferred, at least in this legislative effort—to rely on the broad coverage and unambiguous simplicity of the basic collective bargaining provision to cover all duty-to-bargain situations except those specifically limited elsewhere in the bill. This is the approach they would eventually take regarding both the identification of bargaining representatives and the practice of minority-union bargaining in the absence of a majority representative.

In the meantime, however, just as they had recently spelled out the duty to bargain with nonemployee representatives, Keyserling and Wagner now experimented with similar specificity concerning the basic provision's requirement for bargaining with minority unions. They introduced text that would confirm and emphasize that where there was no majority representative, the employees still had a right to engage in negotiations (i.e., "dealing") through a nonmajority union or other "group." They inserted language to that effect in *Draft 4* as follows:

> Section 12. (c) Where no representatives have been selected by the majority as provided in the above paragraph, the representatives chosen by any *group of two or more employees* shall represent such *group* for the purpose of dealing with employers.[29]

This draft provision tells us much. In the first place, it shows that Wagner and Keyserling were fully cognizant of the minority-bargaining issue and intended to protect workers in their right to engage in such bargaining. In the second place, it shows that they affirmatively wanted to be certain that the reference to "sole representatives" chosen by a majority, who were granted exclusive bargaining status in Section 12(b), would not be interpreted to mean that such majority representatives were the *only* representatives with whom employers must bargain. In workplaces where there was no majority representative, the employer still had a duty to "deal with"—using the language of Section 12(c)—minority unions for their members only. However, that clause as written had severe defects, which the authors must have seen. As worded, it could have required "dealing"—which was broader than bargaining collectively[30]—with a "group" that was not even a trade union, thereby creating unwanted confusion as to the meaning and reach of the requirement, especially as to rights it could confer on loosely organized groups whose conduct might be viewed as unduly disruptive to an employer's busi-

ness operations. More important, however, such an effort at legislative specificity, with its confusing language, apparently served to reinforce the conclusion that the plain meaning of the basic collective bargaining provision
needed no elaboration—an approach that the draftsmen would apply in the
next draft to the problem of nonemployee representation that Section 12(a)
had been designed to solve. And, as we shall see in Chapter 3, it was also the
approach adopted the following year in the final drafting of the Wagner Act.

Accordingly, in *Draft 5* Keyserling and Wagner abandoned both Sections
12(a) and 12(c). Section 12(a) was changed to a general recognition clause—
with no specific reference to the permissibility of nonemployee representatives—and Section 12(c) was deleted entirely. Shortly afterward, in *Draft 6,*
the revised Section 12(a) was likewise deleted entirely.

Draft 6 also tells us that although the collective bargaining process was
well known at the time and had been clearly defined in several NLB decisions,[31] Wagner and Keyserling nevertheless seemed uncertain about relying
solely on the basic collective bargaining provision to define an employer's
duty to bargain. Therefore, to further delineate that duty, they inserted a new
Section 11(b) with language derived from the Railway Labor Act that made
it an unfair labor practice for

> An employer to refuse to recognize and/or deal with the representatives of
> (his) employees or to fail *to exert every reasonable effort to make and main-
> tain agreements* with such representatives concerning wages, hours, rules
> and other conditions of employment.[32]

Draft 7 included only one new provision, and that was unrelated to the
area of our concern. *Draft 8,* the penultimate draft, contained several textual changes that were minor and mostly cosmetic. The latter draft is significant, however, because it was the one originally sent to the Senate committee,
containing both the basic collective bargaining provision, Section 4, and the
provision for majority representation and exclusivity, Section 7 (derived
from Section 12(b) of *Draft 5*). But before the bill was introduced, Wagner
and Keyserling deleted Section 7 entirely,[33] thereby eliminating the majority-exclusivity bargaining concept.[34]

The *Ninth and Final Draft* is the Labor Disputes bill that Senator Wagner
introduced on March 1, 1934, as S. 2926. It presents enlightening insights
concerning the minority-bargaining issue, for the deletion of the former Section 7 removed entirely the requirement of majority-rule collective bargaining. The bill, in Section 207(a), simply granted the Board discretionary
power to certify representatives "that have been designated and authorized
to represent employees" and authorized the use of secret-ballot elections or
other appropriate methods to assist in making those determinations. It was
totally silent regarding the subject of majority representation, thereby con-

firming that an employer would have a duty to bargain with any union that represented its employees—whether a majority or minority union—for this was required by Section 5(b).[35]

The drafting of the 1934 Labor Disputes bill thus patently indicates that Wagner was seeking to protect the collective bargaining process in all of its stages. And majority exclusivity was not to be a statutory mandate. In fact, only when a dispute arose would the Board intervene to settle a question of representation.

Congressional Action, the Walsh Bill Substitute, and Public Resolution 44

Reviewing in detail the reception Wagner's Labor Disputes bill received in Congress will serve no useful purpose here.[36] It suffices to note that it did not fare well. Employer opposition, which was intense and vocal, concentrated primarily on the provisions that outlawed company unions and allowed independent unions to obtain closed-shop agreements. The National Association of Manufacturers (NAM) mobilized industry to fight the bill and appealed for the President's assistance in that endeavor.[37] The press was overwhelmingly opposed to the measure,[38] and the "Administration spokespersons were either ambivalent (Secretary Frances Perkins) or conspicuously absent (General Johnson)."[39] It was inevitable that the bill would also suffer from the concessions the President had made to the automobile industry while it was pending, for employers pointed to the inconsistency between that settlement and Wagner's bill.[40] Employers also raised constitutional and numerous other objections.[41] The major obstacle, however, was that it was feared "that so controversial a measure would drag a weary Congress through the Washington summer [and] the President and the Democratic leadership were anxious to call a halt to [Congress's] extraordinary output before the fall elections. . . ."[42]

Nonetheless, Congress was under considerable pressure to pass some kind of labor legislation, for the Administration was impatient with industry's refusal to comply with Section 7(a) and it felt a need to respond to the heavy load of strikes that had occurred that spring and summer, a significant number of which concerned disputes over recognition.[43] Senator David I. Walsh of Massachusetts, chairman of the Senate Committee on Education and Labor—and fully in control of the committee at that time—was determined to respond to those pressures. With the assistance of Charles Wyzanski, solicitor of the Labor Department, he drastically revised, renamed, and presented as a new bill, S. 2926, which the committee reported on May 26. That bill, now retitled the "National Industrial Adjustment Bill"—better-known as the Walsh bill—presented a watered-down version of most of the strong passages in Wagner's bill[44] and added a provision that prohibited coercion of employees from any source, whether employers or unions.[45] Features of the Walsh bill pertinent to our interest here are reproduced in the Appendix to Chapter 2.[46] The most notable of those features was contained in Section 10(a), which left to the Board's discretion whether "the representatives agreed upon by the majority of employees in an appropriate unit shall represent the entire unit. . . ."[47] The Board might thereafter apply either majority, proportional, or plurality representation in structuring its elections. Here was further evidence that Senator Wagner, who joined in supporting the Walsh bill, was mainly interested in favoring collective bargaining as a *process*, regardless of its eclectic manifestations.

"The Walsh bill momentarily obtained the support of virtually all the key government figures: the President, the Department of Labor, the NRA, the Senate Committee, and Wagner."[48] Such virtually unanimous support within the New Deal Administration was indeed a one-of-a-kind phenomenon. That so many diverse views were briefly reconciled suggests that the bill conveyed different meanings to different interests.[49] The press, however, was not enthusiastic. Of the seventeen newspapers that commented on the issue, thirteen were unfavorable,[50] and both industry and organized labor were "less than friendly."[51] The NAM harshly denounced the measure, the U.S. Chamber of Commerce strongly opposed it,[52] and automobile industry executives called upon the White House to administer the *"coup de grâce."*[53]

Although it was soon apparent that the Walsh bill could not be passed, the Administration still needed some kind of legislative victory in the labor area prior to the upcoming fall elections, preferably a statute with bipartisan support. The unions were restless, and an impending labor crisis in the steel industry was threatening the economy. The President reacted by requesting and obtaining separate legislative proposals from Wysanski and Richberg.[54] He then called a White House conference on June 12. Present were Senators Walsh and Wagner, majority leaders Senator Joseph T. Robinson and Representative Joseph W. Byrns, Labor Secretary Perkins, and also Wysanski and Richberg. With both memoranda in front of him, Roosevelt dictated Public Resolution No. 44 in essentially the form in which it was submitted to Congress on the following day.[55] That sparsely worded resolution empowered the President to create a new labor board (or boards) that would be authorized to conduct investigations, with subpoena power, in controversies arising under Section 7(a) and to hold elections and issue enforceable orders. Congress promptly abandoned the Walsh bill and enacted the resolution with only a minor change.[56] The President affixed his signature on June 19,[57] and Congress promptly adjourned.

Organized labor did not openly oppose Resolution No. 44, but the AFL resented the Administration's role in killing Wagner's Labor Disputes bill and was disappointed in the resulting compromise. Industry "maintained a discreet public silence,"[58] but industrial leadership privately indicated that the resolution was not expected to pose any great problem.[59] Although this stopgap measure failed to resolve the major issues under Section 7(a), and Senator Wagner was determined to go forward with permanent remedial legislation after the elections, Public Resolution No. 44 nevertheless had a significant impact on the ultimate direction of American labor law and policy. Its National Labor Relations Board, established by presidential executive order,[60] would provide the organizational format for the statutory NLRB that would be created by Wagner's successful legislative effort the following year.

The President appointed three able and talented members to this new Labor Board: Lloyd K. Garrison, dean of the University of Wisconsin Law School, as chairman; Harry A. Millis, professor of economics at the University of Chicago; and Edwin A. Smith, Commissioner of Labor and Industry for the Commonwealth of Massachusetts.[61] This Board, like its predecessor National Labor Board, would favor elections as the most satisfactory means of ascertaining employee preference when there was a question concerning representation. One of its earliest decisions, *Houde Engineering Corp.*,[62] established the basic pattern for representation elections and defined the duty to bargain required by Section 7(a).

The *Houde* Case and Its Significance

"Of all the [old] NLRB's opinions, none was more controversial or more opposed by employers than the board's August 30, 1934 judgment concerning good faith bargaining and majority rule in the *Houde Engineering Company* case."[63] The case was a carry-over from the prior NLB, which had conducted an earlier election at this automotive-parts manufacturing company. The United Automobile Workers (UAW), a federal labor union affiliated with the AFL, had received 1,105 votes, and a company union, the Houde Welfare and Athletic Association, had received 647; about 400 employees did not vote. Having achieved a clear majority, the UAW requested recognition and bargaining on behalf of all the employees. The company refused to grant such exclusive recognition. It proceeded instead to meet every week or two, first with the Association's committee and then with the UAW's committee, or vice versa. The subjects discussed at these meetings generally concerned only "matters of secondary importance [such as] toilet facilities, safety measures, lighting and ventilation, coat-racks, [and] slippery stairs;"[64] regarding one item of general importance, group insurance, it met only with the Association and reached a decision without consulting the UAW. Admitting frankly that it had no intention of entering into any collective bargaining agreement, the company contended that it had satisfied the bargaining requirements of the statute by meeting and holding discussions with both unions. It claimed that the statute required it to meet with both the majority and the minority representatives. In this seminal decision rejecting that pluralistic concept of collective bargaining, the NLRB disagreed. It declared that the company's policy of dealing first with one group and then the other defeated the objects of the statute and inevitably produced rivalry, suspicion, and friction between the leaders of the two committees. Accordingly, the Board observed that

> the company's policy, by enabling it to favor one organization at the expense of the other, and thus to check at will the growth of either organization, was calculated to confuse the employees, to make them uncertain which organization they should . . . adhere to, and to maintain a permanent and artificial division in the ranks.[65]

The Board also rejected the company's proposal to deal with a composite committee made up of representatives of both unions in proportion to the votes each had received in the election, which would have been a plan similar to the automobile settlement.[66] Noting that the majority union was opposed to this proposal, it concluded that such process "would have hindered true collective bargaining."[67] The Board ruled that the proper interpretation of Section 7(a) required "that the representatives of the majority should constitute the exclusive agency for collective bargaining with the employer."[68] This was the majority-rule concept that was later to be incorporated into Section 9(a) of the 1935 Wagner Act.

Most of the historical attention on the *Houde* case has focused on the manner in which the Board resolved conflicting claims of union representation by applying the rule of exclusivity for a union that demonstrates majority support in a governmentally sponsored election.[69] After first noting that it was not laying down a rule as to what should constitute an appropriate bargaining unit, the Board expressed the following regarding the scope and limits of that majority-exclusivity ruling:

> *Nor does this opinion lay down any rule* as to what the employer's duty is where the majority group imposes rules of participation in its membership and government which exclude certain employees whom it purports to represent in collective bargaining, or where, in an election, representative have been chosen by a mere plurality of the votes cast, or by a majority of the votes cast but by less than a majority of all employees entitled to vote; or *where the majority group has taken no steps toward collective bargaining or has so abused its privileges that* **some minority group might justly ask this Board for appropriate relief.**
>
> *Subject to these qualifications, the Board confines itself to holding that* **when** *a person, committee or organization has been designated by the majority of employees in a plant or other appropriate unit for collective bargaining, it is the right of the representative so designated to be treated by the employer as the exclusive collective bargaining agency of all employees*

in the unit, and the employer's duty to make every reasonable effort, when requested, to arrive with this representative at a collective agreement covering terms of employment of all such employees.[70]

In view of the importance of *Houde* to our understanding of its later codification in Section 9(a) of the Wagner Act,[71] it behooves us to examine carefully what the opinion said and did not say. That is not difficult, for it is evident from the foregoing statement that the Board went to great pains to emphasize the express limitations on its ruling. First, it indicated that the decision did not "lay down any rule" beyond its holding applicable to majority unions in appropriate bargaining units. It left open—with an implication of ready availability of enforceable Board orders—the question of relief for minority-union bargaining where there was no proper majority representative. Note the specific reference to "minority group . . . justly" asking the Board for "appropriate relief." I join with Professor Clyde Summers in his conclusion that regarding the boldface and italicized part of the statement, "[t]he inference is that in the absence of bargaining by a majority union, there is an obligation to bargain with a non-majority union."[72] Second, the Board made absolutely certain that its rule of majority exclusivity would apply only "*when*" majority status was designated by the employees. The Board thus left no doubt that majority status was not a prerequisite for bargaining under the basic collective bargaining language of Section 7(a).

The *Houde* case had an immediately impact on the industrial relations community. Although the AFL lauded the Board for its decision,[73] employers were quick to condemn it. The NAM encouraged employers to ignore the decision until competent judicial authority had reviewed it, and this may have contributed to a boycott of the Board's processes by many employers.[74] The *New York Times* reported that the decision had led "to an almost complete strangulation of the labor boards in their efforts to obtain elections."[75] The decision was also sharply criticized in three contemporary law review articles that provide both useful analyses and revealing insights concerning the ultimate significance of the case.

In the first article, Professor Minier Sargent, Assistant Professor of Law at Northwestern University, construed the text of Section 7(a) that "*employees shall have the right to* organize and *bargain collectively through representatives of their own choosing*"[76]—the italicized portion being the exact fourteen-word phrase that was later reenacted in Section 7 of the NLRA—and observed that this language "may well be merely a statutory recognition of . . . previously existing rights"[77] because for "many years it has been customary for each employee to select his own union or organization to act for him in collective bargaining."[78] Noting that "[p]rior to the N.I.R.A., however, employees had no legal protection, in the exercise of these rights, against interference on the part of the employer,"[79] he concluded that

The construction of Section 7(a) adopted in the *Houde* case narrows the previously existing rights of the individual employee in that it takes from him the right to bargain with his employer through a representative of his own choice unless his choice coincides with that of the majority of his fellow employees. The statute on its face purports to recognize and protect the existing rights of employees, not to narrow them.[80]

Sargent reminded us that his position was consistent with the prior interpretation expressed by Hugh Johnson and Donald Richberg, that collective bargaining under Section 7(a) "could be carried on by either majority or minority groups"[81] and also with the position President Roosevelt had expressed in the automobile settlement.[82] Although the *Houde* Board purported to base its decision both on what it perceived to be the implied meaning of Section 7(a) and on the election authorization contained in Public Resolution No. 44, Sargent argued that the language of the latter and its legislative history would not support the concept of majority exclusivity. Whether or not he was correct in that assessment is no longer relevant, for Congress by its enactment of Section 9(a) of the Wagner Act the following year gave statutory status to the *Houde* ruling on postelection representational exclusivity. The Sargent article, however, is highly relevant for the light it sheds on contemporary interpretation of the statutory language of Section 7(a), for that language is the language of Section 7 in the current Act.[83]

The other two articles were by Raymond S. Smethurst[84] of the legal staff of the National Association of Manufacturers and Cornelius W. Wickersham[85] of the New York Bar. Both presented the prevailing management interpretations of Section 7(a) and the *Houde* case. Although Smethurst's disclaimer indicated that he was reflecting his own views, those views were fully consistent with his NAM credentials and the NAM's well-documented position on the issues.[86] And Wickersham left no doubt that his views were the views of the management community, for he titled his article *The NIRA from the Employers' Viewpoint*. As to the ruling of the Board in *Houde*, Smethurst criticized the "policy-making activities of this administrative agency,"[87] concluding that "there is considerable doubt whether Congress intended such a result from Section 7(a) or Public Resolution 44."[88] His view as to the meaning of Section 7(a) was thus similar to Professor Sargent's. Wickersham viewed Section 7(a) in the same manner, specifically endorsing a statement by Richberg that "[t]he right of self-organization certainly includes the right of each man to decide for himself with what men he desires to be associated."[89] Criticizing the *Houde* Board for having exercised a "judicial function,"[90] he concluded: "It is difficult to see how it can be seriously contended that [employees] must bargain, not through representatives of their own choosing, but through representatives chosen by someone else."[91]

The messages conveyed by the foregoing articles and their contemporary timing yield two important lessons that will be valuable in ascertaining congressional intent in the later codification of the *Houde* rule in the NLRA. First, their analyses of Section 7(a) substantiate the conclusion that the basic fourteen-word phrase asserting the right to collective bargaining, standing alone, does not support the rule of majority exclusivity. The *Houde* Board's application of that rule was simply an administrative device to favor the majority-exclusivity concept, which many deemed to be the most effective form of collective bargaining; but it was also a means to prevent an employer from further dealing with a company union that had lost an election to an independent union. This approach was therefore essentially the same as that of the prior NLB in *Denver Tramway*[92] and motivated by the same reasons. Second, these law review articles—especially the two avowedly employer-oriented pieces—firmly and consistently construed the basic fourteen-word phrase as a guarantee of the right of each worker to engage in collective bargaining through a representatives of his own choosing, unrestricted by the choice of others. This was management's position throughout the duration of Section 7(a), as illustrated by the organized employer support of the Johnson-Richberg position,[93] by the DuPont dissent in *Denver Tramway*,[94] and by the settlement agreement in the automobile industry.

Who was right in the construction of Section 7(a) regarding majority exclusivity bargaining, the *Houde* Board or the employers? I can only answer that question in the manner of the rabbi in the classic Jewish joke reiterated in *Fiddler on the Roof*:

> *Board:* We are right for the reasons stated in our *Houde* opinion.
> *Rabbi:* Yes, you are right.
> *Employers:* That can't be. We are right because of the clear language of the statute and the many reasons we have described.
> *Rabbi:* You know . . . you are right too.
> *Bystander:* But Rabbi, they can't both be right.
> *Rabbi:* You know, you are right too.

The rabbi was also right because the Board was right to the extent that it had administrative authority to provide a pragmatic mechanism that would achieve more effective collective bargaining when two or more unions were claiming representation, the employers were right because they were correctly reading the literal language of the statute, and the bystander was right because ultimately Congress resolved the issue by giving statutory status to the *Houde* rule and its limitations.

The *Houde* case certainly left its mark. As Professor James A. Gross observes: "The conflict and confusion surrounding the *Houde* decision demonstrated the growing need for a clear statement of a national labor policy 'one way or the other,' either by executive action, court decision, or legislation."[95] The time was ripe for another legislative attempt by Senator Wagner.

The Labor Relations Scene in Late 1934 and Early 1935

What features characterized American labor relations when the *Houde* case was dominating the legal scene? This was the period immediately before and during congressional consideration of Wagner's second and successful legislative attempt. The most visible features on the industrial landscape at that time were widespread strikes, for the year 1934 "yielded the highest strike-load in over a decade."[96] Strikes, however, were but the tip of the iceberg. Unions and workers had been responding rapidly to the receptive climate for labor organizing under the Blue Eagle. Nevertheless, although trade-union membership was growing rapidly, company-union membership was growing even more rapidly because employers were likewise active and "Section 7(a) actually stimulated more than it checked the introduction of company unions."[97] Accordingly, "[c]oncurrent with [the] growth in trade-unionism was an even greater increase in company unions."[98] Although trade-union membership increased from 3,144,300 in 1932 to 4,200,000 in 1935,[99] company unions, which had covered 1,263,194 employees in 1932, increased to 2,500,000 employees in 1935.[100] As Professors Harry A. Millis and Royal E. Montgomery noted,

> The gains by company unions and trade unions in number of adherents had been approximately equal, but the coverage of the former had about doubled, while the membership in trade unions had increased about one-third. . . . During those three years company-union coverage increased from approximately 40 per cent to almost 60 per cent of the estimated trade-union membership.[101]

Aware of this rapid growth of employer-created company unions, Senator Wagner and his supporters viewed such entities as a major impediment to the organization of legitimate unions and the functioning of genuine collective bargaining.[102] That awareness accounts for the prominence the company-union issue received in the drafting of both the 1934 and 1935 Wagner bills and in subsequent legislative debates. As we observe in the next chapter, a major focus of congressional consideration regarding the 1935 bill (S. 1958) was centered heavily on this issue. In contrast, there was no explicit congressional debate about the issue of our present and primary concern— the matter of minority-union or members-only bargaining—for that was not deemed controversial. The following glimpse at the condition of labor relations prevailing at that time is accordingly confined to those two issues: the first hotly contested and the second not contested at all.

My principal sources of data for this historical snapshot are three contemporary studies. The earliest is an analysis of the results of all representation elections conducted by the NLB under Section 7(a),[103] which Emily Clark Brown of Vassar College published in January 1935, just weeks before

Senator Wagner introduced S. 1958.[104] The second source is a volume entitled *Labor and the Government*[105] published by the Twentieth Century Fund while that bill was still pending in Congress. And the third is a study by the U.S. Bureau of Labor Statistics (BLS) comprising a comprehensive description of the history and nature of existing company unions, based on a nationwide survey conducted in April 1935.[106] Although these three studies provide detailed information about company unions during the New Deal period, our present concern is neither with the manner in which such entities functioned nor with their characteristics—our only concern is with the role those organizations played in shaping the legislative process relative to the subject of minority-union representation.

It was widely recognized at the time that company unions were almost always the creation of employers, not employees. And according to the BLS study, in 89 percent of the cases a desire to improve personnel relations was not the dominant factor motivating employers to establish company unions; rather, the major factors were (1) defensive responses to trade-union headway in the plant or locality, (2) the influence of the NIRA, and (3) strikes, either current or recent.[107] According to that study, "[a]bout 80 percent of the company unions were originated solely by management."[108] The Twentieth Century Fund's study also concluded that "[t]he initial move for introducing a plan in practically all cases comes from management."[109] Senator Wagner recognized the source of such plans, for on March 12, 1934, he told the Senate that "[t]he company union is generally initiated by the employer;"[110] and by the following year when he introduced S. 1958, the bill that was to become the Wagner Act, he had available convincing evidence, revealed by Clark's study, that when employees were given a choice they strongly preferred representation by independent outside unions rather than by company unions.[111]

The foregoing and similar data sent a strong message that a company union was probably the most potent weapon an employer could use to ward off successful organizing by an independent union. It was thus to be expected that the most hotly contested labor-related debates in the next session of Congress would be about company unions and the efforts of Wagner and his supporters to eliminate them by means of his forthcoming bill.

Regarding the least-contested issue, we recall from Chapter 1—particularly from data contained in the Conference Board's study[112]—that at the beginning of the New Deal, membership-based union representation was almost as common as exclusive union representation. But was that also true in early 1935? Although there are no quantitative studies showing the full extent of minority-union bargaining in that year, the BLS survey does provide limited but supportive evidence that such representation and bargaining continued to be quite common. Unlike the 1933 Conference Board study, however, the BLS survey centered only on company unions and their various manifestations—thus, it did not yield any direct information about employee relations generally. It made no inquiry regarding practices by companies that had no company unions who dealt with some employees individually and with others through independent unions. Nevertheless, in the process of distinguishing and enumerating the universe of employers and workers who were involved in company unions, that study revealed some data—albeit incomplete—relevant to the subject of minority-union relationships. Consistent with the Conference Board's report, the BLS study indicated that a large number of employers dealt with both trade unions and company unions and reconfirmed that "[d]uring the N.R.A. period there was a tendency for trade-unions and company unions to exist in the same establishment."[113] Furthermore, its report on the relative proportions of those arrangements was similar to that found by the Conference Board. The BLS report concluded that "[a]bout 30 percent of the companies at the time of the 1935 study dealt with one or more trade-unions as well as with company unions"[114]—an implicit acknowledgement of members-only union representation with accompanying collective bargaining. Although that study focused on company unions and not on independent unions, there is no reason to believe that in workplaces where there were no company unions, minority-union dealings would be any different from that described in the 1933 Conference Board report.[115] Moreover, the fact that minority-union members-only bargaining accelerated immediately following passage of the Wagner Act[116] tends to support that conclusion.

We have thus learned that on the eve of congressional consideration of the 1935 Wagner bill, minority-union bargaining was a highly visible part of the industrial-relations landscape. It was, however, but one of several types of employee relations then prevailing in the nation's workplaces. Those practices included (1) employers dealing directly with individual employees; (2) employers dealings with various forms of company unions; (3) employers dealing on an exclusive basis with independent unions (often with closed-shop agreements); and (4) employers dealing with independent unions on a members-only basis, but with other employees on an individual basis, or through company unions, or both.

3   *The NLRA Bill in Congress*

What Happened on the Way to Passage

The First Three Drafts of the Wagner Act

The 1934 fall elections for Congress gave Senator Wagner a relatively free hand to achieve passage of his ideal version of a labor bill, for the Democrats now commanded a lead of 45 in the Senate and 219 in the House.[1] As the *New York Times* observed, "[t]he President and his New Deal won the most overwhelming victory in the history of American politics,"[2] and Wagner took full advantage of the favorable political climate. He promptly directed his aide, Leon Keyserling, to prepare a new and stronger bill, using the 1934 Labor Disputes bill as a basic framework.[3] The final draft was to be ready for early introduction in the new Congress. Although Wagner proceeded in this new undertaking without Roosevelt's support, at least not until near final passage, the President refrained from interfering directly with the overall legislative objective or with the process that produced the end result.[4]

Five published drafts were involved in the effort; the first two resulted in a carefully honed bill that was introduced in the Senate on February 21, 1935.[5] We shall examine the pertinent features of all five drafts,[6] the first three of which are treated in this section. The relevant texts of all the drafts are reproduced in the Appendix to Chapter 3.[7] An analysis of these texts will reveal—as did our examination of the drafts of the 1934 bill—a conscious intent by Senator Wagner and his colleagues to protect the right of workers to bargain collectively through minority unions prior to their obtaining full majority representation. Not surprisingly, however, the focus of public and political attention on the substantive features of the 1935 bill, which bore the designation S. 1958, was concentrated elsewhere, on the two controversial issues that had dominated the 1934 congressional debates—the matter of company unions and the majority-exclusivity rule, the latter being the ultimate goal of Wagner' concept of collective bargaining. The closed shop was also an issue, although to a lesser yet significant extent. Details of the legislative debates on those controversial issues are well documented elsewhere[8] and will not occupy our attention here. Our principal attention will be directed—as it was on the 1934 bill—toward those provisions of the drafts and their legislative history that relate to pre-majority-union bargaining. As the record indicates, such bargaining was deemed important but not controversial; hence, it was never the subject of direct public or legislative debate.

We begin our examination with the *First NLRA Draft,* which bears Professor Kenneth Casebeer's designation: "November, 1934, modified from last Wagner version of Labor Disputes Act, May 5, 1934."[9] This draft adopts the section numbering that was retained in the final bill when it was passed, with Sections 1, 7, 8, and 9(a) providing a policy declaration, a statement of general rights, a listing of unfair labor practices to enforce those rights, and a majority-rule designation of representatives applicable to appropriate bargaining units, respectively. This first draft contained four features of significance to our inquiry:

First, following the example of the Walsh substitute version of S. 2926, the declaration of policy was strengthened. It stated that the "policy of the United States" is to protect

> the exercise by the worker of full freedom of association, self-organization, and designation of representatives of this own choosing, for the purpose of negotiating the terms and conditions of his employment or other mutual aid or protection.

This is basically language from the Walsh Bill,[10] which is infinitely stronger than the declaration in the original S. 2926 as introduced by Wagner in 1934.[11] This new text conveys an unambiguous intent to guarantee workers "full freedom of association" and to make collective bargaining the norm for labor relations in the American workplace. This policy declaration remained unchanged in the various drafts until the last draft reported out of Conference Committee, when it was strengthened even further;[12] the "full freedom of association" language is contained in the Act as it stands today.

Second, the text of the all-important Section 7 was left blank, but with a note by Keyserling: "to be dictated." This clean-slate approach to the most important section in the bill points to a rethinking by Wagner and Keyserling as to how the basic rights from Section 7(a) of the NIRA would be repackaged. The language they ultimately settled on did not appear until the draft introduced in the Senate three months later. That language, as we shall see, remained faithful to Section 7(a) of the NIRA—a simple but flexible text that would characterize the nature of the final legislative product.

Third, this draft contained, as Section 8(5), an unfair labor practice applicable to employers as follows:

> To refuse to bargain collectively with the representatives of his employees.[13]

This clause was shown to have been "added by Francis Biddle, chairman of the old National Labor Relations Board,"[14] one of the key figures with whom Keyserling worked during the drafting process.[15] He was also the acknowledged source of the two alternative versions of this provision contained in the *Third NLRA Draft*[16] and the version that appeared in the amended bill that ultimately passed.[17] Significantly, the bill that was later introduced in the Senate did not contain this or any other separate duty-to-bargain unfair-labor-practice provision. Such inclusion here, followed by exclusion later—plus the fact that several of the earlier drafts of the 1934 Labor Disputes bill contained various versions of a specific duty-to-bargain provision[18]—attest to the ambivalence that Wagner and Keyserling evidenced regarding the inclusion of any specific bargaining provision in the 1935 bill.[19] It is noteworthy, however, that this Section 8(5) provision contained neither a suggestion nor a requirement that the duty to bargain was limited only to unions with Section 9(a) majority status.

Fourth, this draft, in Section 9(a), restored the mandatory principle of majority exclusivity to the bargaining process. That concept had not been mandatory in either version of the 1934 Labor Disputes bill.[20] This new section also contained a *first proviso* that expressly recognized the right of minority groups to bargain collectively when no representative has been designated by a majority of the employees in the bargaining unit, which further demonstrated the authors' continuing concern about guaranteeing the duty to bargain with a minority union prior to the selection of an exclusive majority representative. This text reads in its entirety as follows:

> Sec. 9(a) Representatives designated or selected for the purposes of collective bargaining by the majority of the employees in the unit appropriate for such purposes, shall be the exclusive representatives of the entire unit for the purposes of collective bargaining in respect to rates of pay, hours of employment, and other *basic* conditions of employment: *Provided,* however, *that any minority group of employees in an appropriate unit shall have the right to bargain collectively through representatives of their own choosing when no representatives have been designated or selected by a majority in such unit:* and Provided further, that nothing in this section shall prevent any individual or minority group of employees at any time from having representatives of their own choosing to present grievances to their employer, or from engaging in self-organization for their mutual protection or benefit.[21]

The first proviso implies that Keyserling, presumably in consultation with Wagner, was still seeking suitable language to protect members-only collective bargaining rights for workers prior to their achieving mature bargaining that would include all the employees in a bargaining unit. The genesis of this proviso is found in Section 12(c) of Draft 3 of the 1934 Labor Disputes bill.[22] This new version corrected the earlier ambiguity problem of "*dealing*" with employers[23] by substituting "the right to *bargain collectively,*"[24] but the impracticality inherent in bargaining collectively with "any minority group"—as distinguished from bargaining with a conventional labor organization—remained. To require employers to bargain with *groups* of non-union employees (including amorphous or ad hoc groups) would have posed a multitude of difficulties and would have been perceived as confusing and unworkable—a prospect that was evidently soon realized by the drafters, for this scattershot legislative approach was abandoned in favor of the simple and direct language that would ultimately be contained in the yet-to-be-drafted Section 7. Despite the textual shortcomings of this early version of Section 9(a), however, its tentative reinsertion of specific minority bargaining rights provides further proof of Keyserling's and Wagner's continued concern about the need to protect workers in their entitlement to collective bargaining at the pre-majority stage of union representation, which, as we have seen in earlier chapters, was a prevailing and noncontroversial practice under Section 7(a) of the NIRA.

Another aspect of this preliminary version of Section 9(a) contributes to our understanding of the intent behind that same section as it was finally worded in S. 1958 as introduced. The text in this *First Draft* contains a reference to "*basic* conditions of employment,"[25] which generally means essential and common working conditions applicable to all employees similarly situated within a bargaining unit, such as general categories of wage rates and job classifications, as distinguished from other more individualized conditions of employment that might apply only to designated workers such as union members where no union yet represents a majority of the employees. This distinction regarding "basic" conditions reappears in subsequent legislative debates and committee reports and is commented on later.

The next draft—the *Second NLRA Draft*—is Wagner's original bill that was introduced as S. 1958 on February 21, 1935, and referred to the Senate Committee on Labor and Education. The striking feature of this draft is its simple elegance. This is the draft which, except for minor revisions and the deletion of its injunction and arbitration provisions, became the National Labor Relations Act. In this bill, Wagner and Keyserling successfully, as intended, "recast the measure in a simple conceptual pattern."[26] As Irving Bernstein, a labor historian, has described their newly compressed format, their "emphasis was on the *enforcement of rights* rather than the adjustment of differences [and] they broadened administrative discretion by employing *general enabling language.* This flexibility applied to such areas as the *unfair labor practices,* determination of appropriate unit, and restitution of the worker for losses suffered."[27]

Most important of all, this draft contained the long-awaited Section 7, which encapsulated the basic guarantees of employee rights—the essence of the entire statute—into one sentence of forty-one common words of plain meaning. Predictably, that sentence included, without embellishment, the familiar basic fourteen-word phrase that had been contained in Section 7(a) of the NIRA, which in turn had been derived from the Norris-LaGuardia Act and earlier sources.[28] Here is that Section 7, the relevant text of which is still in the law today:

> Sec. 7. *Employees shall have the right* to self-organization, to form, join, or assist labor organizations, *to bargain collectively through representatives of their own choosing,* and to engage in concerted activities, for the purpose of collective bargaining or other mutual aid or protection.[29]

On March 11, 1935, the Senate committee submitted a memorandum comparing S. 1958 with the last version of S. 2926, in which it reported that this Section 7 "is drawn from section 3(1) of last year's bill, although the form has been somewhat changed."[30] In that same memorandum, William M. Leiserson[31] explained that "[t]his section, while newly added in S. 1958, is nothing more than a *verbatim recital* of the various rights granted employees under Section 7(a)."[32] Here then was familiar text deliberately chosen for the reenactment of the same fundamental and substantive labor law that had existed under the Blue Eagle.

S. 1958 contained only four unfair labor practices. The first, Section 8(1), made all of the foregoing rights fully enforceable by declaring it an unfair labor practice for an employer

> to interfere with, restrain, or coerce employees in the exercise of the rights guaranteed in section 7.

The other three unfair-labor-practice provisions related to problem areas where specific prohibitory language was deemed appropriate.[33] Although none of these provisions is central to our immediate concern, one passage does contain text strongly supportive of the minority-union bargaining position advanced herein; and, as we shall later observe, a minor modification made in that text corroborates the intended meaning of Section 8(5). I refer to Section 8(3)—or more specifically to the closed-shop proviso to that section—which implicitly acknowledged the prevalence of contemporary minority-union bargaining. The significance of this feature is discussed following our examination of Section 8(5) in the *Third NLRA Draft.*[34]

Conspicuous by its absence from the draft of the bill as introduced was Section 8(5)—the duty-to-bargain clause for which Francis Biddle had lobbied. Wagner and Keyserling decided that such a specific provision was unnecessary, preferring to rely on Section 8(1) to enforce the broad collective bargaining requirement contained in Section 7 under which a refusal to bargain represented an *interference* with workers' right to bargain collectively. Although Wagner's and Keyserling's reasons will be elaborated on later in this chapter, it is here noted that their exclusion of a specific duty-to-bargain unfair labor practice was consistent with their intent to present a broadly worded bill with a simple conceptual pattern. That same bare-bones approach was apparent in the new—and final—version of Section 9(a). Consistent with their deletion of Section 8(5), they also deleted the *first proviso* in Section 9(a)—which contained the confusing reference to "any minority group"—for it was no longer required or appropriate.

Section 9(a) was the sole provision in the bill designed to shape the nature of mature collective bargaining, which was the bill's ultimate objective for it established the concept of exclusive bargaining for unions that represented a majority of the employees in an appropriate bargaining unit. Here is the opening and relevant portion of this provision.

> Sec. 9. (a) Representatives designated or selected for the purposes of collective bargaining by the majority of the employees in a unit appropriate for such purposes, shall be the exclusive representatives of all the employees in such unit for the purposes of collective bargaining. . . .

That clause, in juxtaposition with the other two pertinent provisions of the bill as introduced, describes the essential characteristics of the collective bargaining requirements in the Wagner Act and reveals the unvarnished intent of the drafters. The full bargaining duty was contained in just two provisions: in the basic fourteen-word phrase in Section 7 and in its unfair-labor-practice enforcement provision in Section 8(1), for an employer's refusal to bargain would constitute an *interference* with the employees' right to engage in collective bargaining just as the old NLRB had construed Section 7(a) of the NIRA in *Houde Engineering Corp.*[35] The only qualification to that Section 7 right was the single clear and simple statement in Section 9(a) indicating that when and if a majority of the employees in an appropriate unit designate or select a bargaining representative, that representative will be their sole representative. Accordingly, where employees have not selected a majority representative, the full bargaining duty contained in Section 7 remains intact, fully applicable to all employees who desire to exercise their right to engage in collective bargaining through a representative of their own choosing.

I have focused attention on these three simple clauses in order to highlight the pivotal importance of the basic collective bargaining phrase in Section 7, for Section 9(a) says nothing about the duty to bargain, leaving that mandate entirely to Sections 7 and 8(1). As we shall see, that mandate was never altered, and the subsequent addition of Section 8(5) was meant to enhance the duty to bargain, not to diminish it.

We shall now examine what I have designated the *Third NLRA Draft*, which contained various proposed amendments initiated by Keyserling and others. The physical condition of this draft is relevant. The proposed changes were inserted directly onto an official Senate print of S. 1958 bearing the printed date February 15, 1935, and also the printed calendar (i.e., introduction) date of February 21, 1935.[36] Some of the changes are typewritten inserts and others are handwritten; the draft also contains handwritten annotations by Keyserling indicating the source or sponsor of the various proposals.[37] These proposals were evidently inserted between February 21, when the printed version of the bill appeared, and March 11, when the Senate committee submitted its memorandum to the Senate comparing S. 1958 with the S. 2926 substitute of the previous year. This is evident from the fact that this memorandum contained most—but not all—of these proposals accompanied by statements from their sponsors,[38] and some—but again not all—of these proposals were ultimately adopted by the committee and thus appear in the final bill that the committee recommended for passage on May 2, 1935.[39]

This draft, which Professor Kenneth Casebeer labels "New Preamble, Amendments in Committee/ Annotated by L. Keyserling in margin,"[40] consists of various additions, deletions, and changes in wording to S. 1958. Some of these changes were submitted by other participants with whom Keyserling was consulting, and some originated directly from Keyserling and/or Wagner. The other sponsors were identified as Labor Secretary Perkins,[41] AFL Counsel Charlton Ogburn, Senator William E. Borah, and Compliance Chief William H. Davis and Chairman Biddle of the old NLRB.[42]

Although a number of the proposed changes in this draft had major impact on the final legislative product,[43] one in particular had a direct bearing on the nature of the duty to bargain under Section 8(5) and therefore deserves our close attention. Those proposals—for there were actually two versions submitted—were alternative texts of what was intended to be a new separate unfair labor practice, Section 8(5). These two versions show conclusively that Section 8(5), which was belatedly added to S. 1958 when it was reported by the Senate committee on May 2, was never intended to confine an employer's bargaining duty to majority unions only. Although this meaning is clear from the literal language of Section 8(5) in the final bill,[44] the following inside look at its drafting process indisputably confirms that reading. An insert flap, appended at the point of a handwritten insertion of the numeral "(5)" following Section 8(4), contains the handwritten identification "Biddle" and the following typewritten text:

(5) To refuse to bargain collectively with the representatives of his employees, subject to the provisions of Section 9(a).

or, (5) *To refuse to bargain collectively with employees through their representatives, chosen as provided in Section 9(a).*[45]

These alternative presentations once again demonstrated Wagner's and Keyserling's keen awareness of the minority-bargaining issue. More important, however, they specifically show the joint consideration that Wagner, Keyserling, and Biddle gave to the matter, for Biddle actually drafted alternative language (the second version) that would have excluded any minority-bargaining obligation from Section 8(5). That version, however, was specifically rejected by Biddle and Keyserling (obviously with Wagner's approval)—and also by the Senate committee, as demonstrated by the fact that many of the other proposals in this draft, including the first version of Section 8(5), were later adopted by the committee as amendments in the final bill recommended to the Senate. When Biddle made his first public plea in Congress for inclusion of Section 8(5) on March 11[46] it was with reference to the first version only, which was the version the committee reported on May 2 after Wagner had withdrawn his objection to its inclusion.[47]

The second and rejected version is important to our investigation, for it tells us how Section 8(5) would have read if Biddle—or the Congress—had intended that an employer be required to bargain *only after* a majority of its employees had "designated or selected" a majority representative, with no obligation to bargain with a minority union prior to establishment of such exclusive-majority representation. This carefully worded alternative version of Section 8(5), had it been adopted, would have required an employer to bargain *only* with representatives "chosen as provided in Section 9(a)," hence only with a union *after* it had been selected by a majority of the employees in an appropriate bargaining unit. The word "chosen" was obviously derived from the common root of "choosing" contained in the basic collective bargaining provision incorporated in Section 7: "representatives of their own *choosing.*" The fact that this second version was rejected clearly indicates that the authors of the Wagner Act never intended the bargaining duty under Section 8(5) to apply only if and when a majority representative was selected.[48]

We now examine the confirming role of Section 8(3) in our analysis, for the closed-shop proviso to that section contains two features supportive of minority-union collective bargaining.[49] First, the thrust of the clause recognizes the existence of such bargaining, for the proponents' public-policy justification for compelling union membership was found in the requirement that only unions that represent a *majority* of the employees could qualify for closed-shop agreements. As legislative history expressly confirms,[50] employers and minority unions could enter into collective bargaining contracts, but only majority unions would be permitted to enter into closed-shop contracts. Second, regarding the changes made in the *Third NLRA Draft,* it is apparent that Keyserling, with the approval of the Senate committee, deliberately and knowingly decided not to use the second version of Section 8(5) that contained the phrase "chosen *as provided in Section 9(a),*"[51] for the same phrase, "*as provided in Section 9(a),*" was inserted into Section 8(3)—presumably at or about the same time—in handwriting on the same page just two inches above the second 8(5) insert-proposal in this draft,[52] a phrase that was in fact later added by committee amendment to Section 8(3) and is still a part of the Act.

As we have seen from our review of the foregoing three drafts of S. 1958, Wagner and Keyserling fully protected the right of employees to engage in collective bargaining with their employer on a members-only basis *prior* to establishing mature majority-based bargaining. The survey of legislative history that follows shows that protection of this right also prevailed in the final legislative action on the bill.

Congressional Consideration

What the Hearings, Debates, and Committee Reports Reveal

Unlike most major congressional legislation, the content of the Wagner Act was truly the product of a single legislator, Senator Wagner. Such were the times and such was the man. From introduction to final passage he was in full control.[53] The Wagner Act was most assuredly *his* Act, although he received assistance from many sources.[54] Accordingly, his unilateral development and composition of the bill provide us with a high level of certainty regarding legislative intent, for which we are fortunate to have available the remarkably full history of the drafting process that I have outlined in this and the preceding chapter.

It was the goal of Wagner and his supporters to create a permanent statute that would replace Section 7(a) of the NIRA, which was soon to expire.[55] Having recognized that Section 7(a) was devoid of meaningful enforcement procedures—indeed it had proved to be virtually unenforceable[56]—they considered it a fatally flawed statute. Drawing on his knowledge and experience under Section 7(a), Lloyd K. Garrison, the first chairman of the old NLRB, described the enforcement problems under that statute:

> There were only two means of enforcement, and neither was satisfactory. The first was, upon noncompliance by an employer, to refer the case to the NRA for removal of his Blue Eagle. . . . But in most cases it meant nothing, and then the only recourse was to refer the matter to the Department of Justice for prosecution in the courts, which would have been too slow and cumbersome to accomplish anything, and it was not attempted by the Department except in a few ill-starred cases.[57]

The Wagner bill was therefore intentionally designed to be substitute legislation that would correct the shortcomings of Section 7(a). S. 1958

achieved this by codifying, clarifying, and slightly strengthening the substantive rights contained in the earlier law and by incorporating and giving
statutory status to the majority-rule concept that the old NLRB had adopted
by decision and practice. To administer and enforce those rights and corresponding duties, the bill created a new labor board that "was styled National
Labor Relations Board to provide continuity with the existing agency."[58]
Thus, the new bill was not intended to create new law but rather to reestab-
lish old law, adding clarity and teeth.[59] The recognition of that purpose is of
prime importance to the construction of the Wagner Act, for, as Professor
William Eskridge points out, "when Congress borrows a statute, it adopts
by implication interpretation placed on that statute, absent express statement to the contrary."[60]

The purpose of the Wagner bill was made well known to Congress. Although Senator Wagner presented the most comprehensive of the arguments
favoring the bill, a parade of other distinguished witnesses also explained the
need for this legislation and its intended meaning. From the beginning, it was
emphasized that "the purpose of the bill is to encourage collective bargaining, just as the purpose of section 7(a) is to encourage it."[61] The witness who
presented what was perhaps the most articulate exposition of the reasons for
the bill and a concise description of its contents was Harry A. Millis, Chairman of the Department of Economics at the University of Chicago. The following highlights from his testimony will provide the reader with the gist of
the items in issue and the rationale that motivated passage of the Act. Although most of these excerpts have no direct bearing on the history of the
narrow issue of minority-union bargaining, I include them here so that this
issue, which was noncontroversial and not the focus of debate, may be
viewed in the broader context of the subjects that were central to the debate.
Citing his long experience as "an economist and practical student of industrial relations,"[62] Professor Millis submitted the following in support of Senator Wagner's bill.[63]

> **First.** *That the great majority of wage-earners are employed under such
> conditions that they must act in concert with reference to wage scales,
> hours, and working conditions if they are to have a reasonably effective
> voice as to the terms on which they shall work.* Without organization there
> is in most modern industry unequal bargaining power, for the individual
> worker, as compared to the employer, is ignorant of the market situation
> and of employment opportunities; he has little or no reserve power in funds
> in hand; he fears to push a claim vigorously lest he be discriminated against
> or lose his job; he is likely to reason that it is better to accept or to retain
> employment on adverse terms than to lose working time while waiting for
> another job; he finds himself, unless peculiarly fortunate, pitted against
> other seekers of work and the cheaper man is likely to be the successful bid-
> der; if he has employment, the terms of his contract, like the railway time-
> table, is "subject to change without notice."

Second. *That in pre-code days and only to a lesser extent since the codes were adopted, the average employer, however appreciative he may have been of the value of good employment conditions and the needs of his workers, has been under the necessity of reducing costs because of the . . . practices of his less socially minded competitors. . . .* Informed labor leaders and observers recognize that most employers really wish to do what is fair but that competition frequently prevents them from doing what they would like to do in labor matters. . . . The truth, as I see it, is, however, that the competitive demand for labor, while important, does not go far in protecting the workers against long hours, excessive overtime, fines, discharge without sufficient cause, and objectionable working conditions. . . . One is thus driven to the conclusion that hours of work and conditions of work—things which intimately concern workmen, are best decided collectively—through legislation or through collective bargaining, and some of them are not easily subject to legislative control. This is particularly true of a reasonable degree of security of tenure.

The case for collective bargain is only less strong with respect to wages. In a boom period, when prices are rising and profits are good, it is true that business is very active and bidding for labor generally becomes keen. . . . But in more normal times, though progress is made and most workers are finding employment, wage advances are hesitantly offered, and there is more or less room for under payment, even for a considerable degree of exploitation. For there are groups with very limited mobility, and new accessions to the labor supply and displaced workers are more or less eagerly seeking employment on such terms as their limited individual bargaining ability will secure for them. . . . Within the given industry or locality there are the lower obstructive wages paid by hard-boiled managers. . . . The fact is that wages depend to a considerable extent upon the policies of the employers, as so many investigations have disclosed.

Third. *That a measure of control of wages is necessary if the needed relationship between consuming power and production is to be maintained and general instability checked.* I have spoken of the need for organization of labor and collective bargaining if workers and the typical employer are to have substantially equal bargaining power and if conditions are to be standardized and a plane of fair competition is to be established in industry. More recently a new doctrine has been invoked, not only in support of collective bargaining in defending labor's wage interest but also in furthering and obtaining a higher standard of living for the wage earners. I refer of course to the doctrine of high wages and mass purchasing power which has played an important role in this country in recent years and which underlies so much of the "new deal." The doctrine is that wages must be made high and kept high to provide the mass purchasing power required to maintain a market-outlet for goods produced.

Fourth. *That if and when collective bargaining is definitely freed from*

undue militancy, as it can be when wise management and good labor lead-
ership are brought into cooperation, special problems connected with col-
lective bargaining clear up and there are opportunities for gain to all
parties. Reference may be made to union-management cooperation. . . .
There has been much of it in organized industry and it can be greatly and
profitably extended with the exercise of patience and brains. Many employers have found that they can conduct their business more satisfactorily
on a union than on a nonunion basis.

Such is the positive case for organization of labor and collective bargaining. . . . I, therefore, maintain that organization and intelligent and
honest collective bargaining has a sound basis in economics.

In this rather long statement I have explained my general approval of the
declaration of policy of the Wagner bill. Permit me now to make some observations on the several sections of the measure. This proposed measure,
it should be noted, would replace existing legislation expiring June 16,
next, and would be effective indefinitely.

. . . The proposed National Labor Relations Board would have functions similar to those of the Federal Trade Commission and certain other
independent agencies of the Government. As a quasi-judicial agency, it
should be, and should be known to be, independent of influence by any executive officer or department. . . . In my opinion an independent but coop-
erating board, such as described, would render the Government the best
and a valuable service.

I wish to comment next on *sections 7 and 8. These are designed to de-*
fine more accurately and to clarify section 7(a) of the National Industrial
Recovery Act.

. . . *Section 7(a) of the National Industrial Recovery Act and sections 7*
and 8 of the Wagner bill have a common object, namely, to give the work-
ers the same freedom to organize as they choose, as employers have to or-
ganize employers' associations and trade associations. Nothing more is
involved than equalization of the law as between workers on the one hand
and employers on the other.

. . . Paragraph 2 of section 8 [regarding company unions] is necessary if
the right to organize as the workers wish is to be reasonably well safeguarded. . . . It is a matter of common knowledge . . . that employee-representation plans have frequently been virtually forced upon employees; the
employees had no real voice in the matter. . . . Furthermore, many of the
plans have been dominated by the employers and their agents. . . . This sort
of thing must be placed under effective ban of the law if the right to organize and to bargain collectively, possessed by employers, is to be possessed
by labor.

. . . The fact is that there is little difference in the general social philosophy of American workers and American employers. The fact is that, with
rare exceptions, when collective bargaining is engaged in for a time, ad-

justments are easily made and a cooperative relationship, with rough ideas of fairness, is developed.

. . . Coercion of labor by labor alone needs discussion [especially] unionization through pressure of the closed shop. . . . Frequently the closed union shop, especially if it would involve discharge of employees for nonmembership in a union is under the ban of State law. It is evidence that it is the thought of the drafters of this bill not to interfere with State law upon the subject. This, I think, is desirable. The closed union shop is likely to cease to be an issue and practically to disappear when active employer opposition to organization and collective bargaining and discrimination against union men cease. . . . I approve of the proviso contained in (3) [of Section 8.] The object of the proviso is merely to permit, so far as Federal law is concerned, employers and unions by mutual agreement to provide for the employment of union men *only where a majority of the employees in a collective bargaining unit are already union members.*

Perhaps the most contentious provision of the bill is found in section 9. I refer to majority rule. The section would give legislative confirmation to the rulings of the National Labor Board in the Denver Tramway and to the rulings of he National Labor Relations Board in the Houde and other cases. . . . *All it means is that the representatives of an established majority in an appropriate unit shall be the exclusive representatives of all employees in that unit* for the purpose of collective bargaining in respect of rates of pay, wages, hours of employment, and the like—where there must be standards or the common rule, which should be settled for a period of time . . . standards sound management must apply to all. . . . *Nothing can be said for dealing with first one group and then with another, except that it makes it possible for the employer to play off one group against another and thus defeat real collective bargaining.*

. . . *Proportional representation of all groups is plausible and democratic and finds an analogy in the Government arrangements of some of the more liberal countries. . . . Such an arrangement [however] in a plant or industry tends to keep the organizational situation open and plastic, while majority rule tends to maintain and to increase the strength of the representation plan or union which has succeeded in obtaining a recognized majority. . . . So long as there are two or more rival organizations functioning through a composite committee or council, difference will be exhibited in conference. . . . In other words, friction and jealousy between organizations will almost certainly be exhibited by their representatives on the committee or council. . . . Not only is labor likely to be weak in bargaining under a scheme based upon proportional representation; there will not be the same centralized responsibility for finding solutions for production or cost problems* as has been experienced in the cases of such union organizations as the Amalgamated Clothing Workers and which has proved to be of much value to the manufacturers.

[Regarding enforcement:] The really weak and not infrequently unfair part of the present emergency legislation is found in the provisions for the enforcement of the law. In an effort to remove this weakness and to do more even justice, this bill would change radically the enforcement proceedings.

The foregoing catalog by Professor Millis of the contents of S. 1958 and the proponents' reasons for its passage were directed to the areas in legislative contention. Debate over substantive provisions[64] focused on the issues of majority rule versus pluralism, company unions, and to a lesser extent the closed shop and absence of regulation of coercive union conduct. Hundreds of pages of statements and testimony in the legislative history are devoted to these subjects.

On the other hand, the subject of minority-union bargaining prior to the designation of majority representation was not an issue in the debates. Discussion and committee consideration concerning the majority-rule concept centered only on the requirements for mature—i.e., fully established—collective bargaining. Although the prevalence of minority-union members-only bargaining was common knowledge[65] and the history of the legislative drafts demonstrated that the draftsmen were well aware of the need to protect such bargaining, this practice was not viewed as controversial. Accordingly, minority-union bargaining prior to the establishment of an employee majority was not a challenged concept, and employers in particular supported the right of employers to bargain with all employee representatives, whether minority or majority.[66]

The proponents of the bill were strongly of the opinion that majority-rule collective bargaining—the bill's solution to the problem of dual unionism—would mean more effective bargaining. On the other hand, the employer lobby advocated the alternative of fragmented pluralistic representation. As might have been expected, this issue was a major subject of discussion in the legislative record. Senator Wagner intensively promoted the majority-rule concept for established collective bargaining, for it was his view that "collective bargaining can be really effective only when workers are sufficiently solidified in their interests to make one agreement covering all."[67] On the other side of the debate, the employer lobby advocated plurality bargaining, opposed the majority rule as a denial of the rights of minorities, and asserted that the Board's authority to determine the bargaining unit would lead to a closed shop.[68] In that context, employers vigorously defended the right of minority unions to engage in collective bargaining. Attention during the congressional debates, however, was concentrated on the anticipated presence of multiple unions and on whether a minority union should have bargaining rights *after* a majority union had been chosen. There was no discussion about minority-union bargaining *prior* to the establishment of majority representation. That was a non-issue in the debates, for, as we have observed, throughout the New Deal period the business lobby was on record favoring all minority-union bargaining and Wagner and Keyserling had already taken pains in the text of the bill to protect pre-majority-union bargaining.

Numerous statements by the proponents of the bill indicated full recognition that the majority rule would apply to bargaining only *after* the employees had exercised their selection of a majority representative under Section 9(a). There was never a question about the nonapplicability of that restriction *prior* to majority selection. For example, following the addition of Section 8(5) to the bill, Senator Wagner, referring to Section 9(a), cautioned that

> Majority rule makes it clear that the guaranty of the right of employees to bargain collectively through representatives of their own choosing must not be misapplied so as to permit employers to interfere with the practical effectuation of that right by bargaining with individuals or minority groups in their own behalf *after* representatives have been picked by the majority to represent all.[69]

And the Senate committee's report on the amended bill, referring to the operation of Section 9(a), likewise stated that

> Majority rule carries the clear implication that employers shall not interfere with the practical application of the right of employees to bargain collectively through chosen representatives by bargaining with individuals or minority groups in their own behalf, *after* representatives have been picked by the majority to represent all.[70]

This was consistent with the old NLRB's opinion in *Houde Engineering Corp.*,[71] discussed in Chapter 2, which had noted the role of that Board regarding an employer's duty to bargain with a minority union when there was no properly designated majority union. Wagner and Keyserling, and hence also the congressional committees, crafted Section 9(a) to be the statutory codification of the rule in *Houde*. It will be recalled that *Houde* established the concept of exclusivity for designated majority unions but left untouched, and implicitly recognized, the employer's duty to bargain with minority unions prior to the employees' selection of a majority representative. That was the congressional understanding of *Houde* and also the common perception, as illustrated by an exchange between a witness at the Senate committee hearing and Senator Wagner in which Walter Lippmann, the popular newspaper columnist, was quoted with reference to the *Houde* case: "that this very decision upholding the majority principle clearly recognizes that it applies *only* when there is in fact a majority."[72] The Wagner bill thus contemplated that minority-union bargaining could and would occur *prior* to invocation of Section 9(a) procedures and that such bargaining would be fully protected by the broad fourteen-word provision in Section 7 guaranteeing employees the right to bargain collectively through representatives of their own choosing. That was the clear message of the text, and such meaning was supported by the administrative law decision that it was codifying.

There was indeed extensive debate about majority rule, and elections were looked upon as one of the best means to settle disputes over union representation; but the disputes that were anticipated concerned the determination of the *choice* of which union would represent the employees, not *whether* employees would have representation.[73] Accordingly, in commenting on the need to enforce the duty to bargain, the Senate committee report focused on choice, stating that "the procedure of holding governmentally supervised elections to determine the *choice* of representatives of employees becomes of little worth if after the election its results are for all practical purposes ignored."[74] And the report of the House Committee on Labor, in commenting on Section 9 elections, declared that "[t]he question will ordinarily arise as between *two or more* bona fide organizations competing to represent the employees."[75] It also noted, however, that the election authority was broad enough to cover cases in which only one group was pressing for recognition and its claim was being challenged, although it acknowledged that such utilization would apply only when the union was claiming to represent *all* the employees in the unit. As to such claims, William Green, President of the American Federation of Labor, testified that an election was a "satisfactory way to determine by whom employees want to be represented *when an employer challenges the right of a union to bargain for all the employees....*"[76]

The arguments for majority rule contained in the committee reports and legislative debates were made in the context of competing unions and the necessity that the majority union have exclusive authority to negotiate for all the employees. The primary purpose of an NLRB election was to determine which, if any, union was to be given exclusive representation rights, thereby empowering it to represent nonconsenting employees. A secondary purpose was to confirm the existence of majority representation when a union was claiming exclusive bargaining rights and the employer was challenging that claim. An election would serve no purpose, however, when the union was claiming only representation of union members, not exclusive representation. And there was never any suggestion in the legislative debates that a majority of employees, by preferring individual bargaining, could thereby deprive a minority of their right to bargain for themselves thorough their own union.[77]

As we have learned in the preceding chapters, elections under Section 7(a) were required only in those cases—such as in the *Houde* case—where a union was seeking to represent *all* the employees and its claim was being challenged either by the employer or by another union, which was almost always a company union. And it will be recalled that in January 1935, just prior to consideration of S. 1958 by the Congress, the U.S. Bureau of Labor Statistics published a study reporting on all representation elections that had been conducted by the National Labor Board, a total of 183 elections in 546 bargaining units. Almost all—89 percent—involved multiple unions, and 83 percent of all elections were held between an independent union and a company union. Only 11 percent involved a single union.[78] Those elections combined, however, represented but a small and partial showing of the worker population covered by the NLB cases. As the author of the study observed,

> The final statistical report of the Board reported that more than 4,000 cases involving over 2,000,000 workers had been handled by the boards.[79] Against these figures are the 183 elections, in 546 industrial units, with somewhat more than 100,000 votes in the election cases of the boards. *The elections therefore do not necessarily represent the relative strength of various types of representation among all cases which reached these boards. They cover only those cases in which a conflict existed over the question of who were bona fide representatives of the employees,* and in which the conflict did not appear subject to solution in any other way.[80]

As I have noted, Section 8(5) was not added until the Senate committee amended S. 1958 in May of 1935. Details concerning the how and why of that afterthought amendment have a direct bearing on the issue of minority bargaining. As our review of the *First NLRA Draft* earlier in this chapter revealed, Senator Wagner saw no need to include a separate unfair-labor-practice provision to spell out the employer's duty to bargain. It had been his and Keyserling's view that the employer's duty to bargain was adequately covered by Sections 7 and 8(1), which implicitly but plainly established that a failure to meet and bargain constituted an *interference* with the employees' right to bargain collectively through their chosen representatives.[81] Wagner's testimony to that effect was unequivocal. On the opening day of the Senate committee hearing on S. 1958 he testified:

> [W]hile the bill does not state specifically the duty of an employer to recognize and bargain collectively with the representatives of his employees . . . such a duty is clearly implicit in the bill. *To attempt to deal with his men otherwise than through representatives they have named for such purposes would be the clearest interference with the right to bargain collectively.*[82]

In support of that conclusion, Wagner quoted the following excerpt from the now-familiar *Houde*[83] decision construing the fourteen-word passage in Section 7(a) that was identical to the text in Section 7 of his bill:

The right of employees to bargain collectively implies a duty on the part of the employer to bargain with their representatives. [T]he incontestably sound principle is that the employer is obligated by the statute to negotiate in good faith with his employees' representatives; to match their proposals, if unacceptable with counter proposals; and to make every reasonable effort to reach an agreement.[84]

By 1935 the nature of the collective bargaining obligation under Section 7(a) was well established.[85] The *Houde* Board, citing several prior decisions,[86] had written regarding that obligation:

These phrases are full of meaning. The right of employees to bargain collectively implies a duty on the part of the employer to bargain with their representatives. Without this duty to bargain the right to bargain would be sterile; and Congress did not intend the right to be sterile.[87]

The foregoing confirmations of the duty-to-bargain requirement in the original Wagner bill clearly indicate that Section 8(5), which was later added, would provide nothing more than emphasis to the duty already contained in Sections 7 and 8(1).

Why were Wagner and Keyserling so reluctant to include a separate duty-to-bargain provision? As reported by Professor Gross, "Wagner was particularly concerned that an explicit good faith bargaining requirement in S. 1958 would intensify and strengthen attacks on the bill by making it more vulnerable to charges that the law would require an employer to reach an agreement with a union and that the agreement be written—that is, a kind of compulsory arbitration."[88] Notwithstanding that objection, Francis Biddle lobbied early and hard for the inclusion of a specific bargaining provision—as was evident from our review of the preliminary drafts of the bill[89]—and he continued that lobbying with his testimony at the Senate and House committee hearings.[90] Finally, the old NLRB establishment, "through the persuasiveness of Biddle, Garrison and others . . . prevailed upon Senator Wagner to include a duty to bargain section in the bill."[91] Consequently, ten weeks after Wagner had introduced his original bill, the Senate committee—with virtually no discussion of the amendment within the committee—reported its revised bill, the *Fourth NLRA Draft,* containing the Section 8(5) amendment, to wit, the first version that Biddle had presented in the *Third NLRA Draft.*[92] The Senate passed the amendment pro forma without debate.[93]

Biddle and the Senate committee had been careful, however, to protect the full scope of the original bargaining duty contained in the basic fourteen-word provision in Section 7, for that duty was limited only by the unchanged requirement in Section 9(a) that when and if employees designate a *majority* representative in an appropriate unit, such representative would become the employees' *exclusive* representative. Biddle made that limitation clear when he rejected the alternative version of Section 8(5) prepared for consideration in the *Third NLRA Draft*.[94] His stated reason for the selected amendment was to strengthen the bargaining requirement, not to diminish it. At the Senate committee hearing, he said that in order to avoid disagreement and confusion "this [bargaining] duty should be expressed in the act;"[95] and at the House committee hearing he stated, "I don't like legislation by implication."[96] Indeed, the Senate and House committee reports both reconfirmed the supremacy of Section 8(1) in the strongest of terms, for they added the following admonishments concerning each of the four specific unfair labor practices that followed Section 8(1), including Section 8(5).

Senate Report:

The four succeeding unfair-labor practices are *designed not to impose limitations or restrictions upon the general guaranties of the first,* but rather to spell out with particularity some of the practices that have been most prevalent and most troublesome.[97]

House Report:

The succeeding unfair labor practices are intended to amplify and state more specifically certain types of interference and restraint that experience has proved require such amplification and specification. *These specific practices, as enumerated in subsections (2), (3), (4), and (5), are not intended to limit in any way the interpretation of the general provisions of subsection (1).*[98]

The committee reports thus reaffirmed the full scope of the duty to bargain protected by Section 8(1), expressly rejecting any concept of 8(5) as a limitation on the preexisting Sections 7 and 8(1), thereby confirming that Congress did not intend for Section 8(5) to be a basis for confining an employer to a duty to bargain only with Section 9(a) majority representatives.

That same message was contained in an address to the Senate on May 15 when Senator Wagner personally reconfirmed the supremacy of Section 8(1) by explaining that

the succeeding four unfair-labor-practice provisions, *without narrowing in any way the widest possible application of the first,* enunciate with particularity the concrete acts which have been the most fertile source of trouble in the past.[99]

Accordingly, as the record demonstrates, there is not the slightest suggestion that when Senator Wagner agreed to accept Francis Biddle's proposed addition of Section 8(5) that he was also agreeing to the elimination of the guaranteed right of collective bargaining that precedes the establishment of majority and exclusive union representation; nor is there any indication to that effect in the Senate and House committee reports. In fact, the House report's explication of the majority rule did not even mention Section 8(5); it focused only on Sections 8(1) and 9(a). Furthermore, it indicated that the Section 9(a) exclusivity limitation had no application *prior* to selection of a majority representative in an appropriate bargaining unit, for it stated:

> As a necessary corollary it is an act of interference (under Section 8(1)) for an employer, *after* representatives have been so designated by the majority, to negotiate with individuals or minority groups in their own behalf on the basic subjects of collective bargaining.[100]

The distinct implication of this statement, like that of the caveats recognized by the old NLRB in the *Houde* case,[101] is that *prior* to such designation it would be an act of interference for an employer to refuse to bargain with any organizational representative of the employees' own choosing, regardless of the percentage of employee membership in that organization.

It is significant that prior to the addition of Section 8(5) the pertinent text of Section 9(a), with its provision for majority designation and corresponding mandatory exclusivity, was already contained in Senator Wagner's proposed bill in its present and unaltered form. That timing reconfirms that the collective bargaining rights provided by Sections 7—already enforceable through unfair-labor-practice proceedings under Section 8(1)—were not dependent on Section 8(5) and that all that was intended by the belated addition of Section 8(5) was the provision of specific reinforcement of the employer's obligation in the collective bargaining process. Francis Biddle so indicated when he recommended the provision, urging simply that the duty be "expressed"[102] rather than "implied."[103] Plainly, with or without Section 8(5), Section 9(a) could have no effect on minority-union bargaining prior to the establishment of exclusive majority representation.

The bill as passed (*Fifth and Final NLRA Draft*) contained only a minor change pertinent to our area of concern, which was to emphasize the *concerted* nature of the rights guaranteed by the Act, for in the declaration of policy in Section 1 "worker" was changed to "workers" and the phrase "representatives of his own choosing" was changed to "representatives of *their* own choosing."[104] Unquestionably, Congress was thereby emphasizing that the workers' rights being guaranteed were meant to be exercised in concert.

Postscript: From Hyperbole and Ambiguity to Clarification and Reaffirmation

Now a digression, followed by a welcome clarification and reaffirmation. In an effort to learn whether there was any evidence—however minuscule—of any lawmaker's impression that the Wagner bill was intended to deny employees the right to engage in collective bargaining through a minority union of their own choosing prior to the selection of a majority union, I diligently searched the congressional record. I found no such evidence. I did find, however, some hyperbole and ambiguity in a snippet of one early statement in the record that was later repeated twice in slightly edited but similar versions, and then used again in a completely revised and corrected version. Although an analysis of that brief passage supports my thesis—in fact the corrected version strongly reconfirms it—by way of anticipatory discouragement of anyone who might erroneously cite that snippet to bolster latter-day conventional wisdom, I shall here spell out its history and real meaning. Accordingly, as part of the leave-no-stone-unturned approach that I have attempted to employ in my research, I present the following with reference to the passage in question.

The passage was the product of Leon Keyserling's busy pen. Recall that Keyserling was the primary draftsman of all of Wagner's public statements relating to the bill[105] and also the author of both the Senate and House reports on the bill.[106] The passage—for it was a single passage, although it was used three times before being corrected—first appeared in an early prepared statement that Senator Wagner presented at a hearing before the Senate committee.[107] Citing the example of the *Houde* case, which involved both an independent union and a company union, Wagner, as previously noted, argued in favor of the majority rule expressed in that case, which was now codified in Section 9(a) of his bill. He hypothesized a situation in which most of the employees favored union representation but their allegiance was divided among competing unions, which would usually be an independent union and a company union. As we have observed, Wagner and Keyserling considered the bill's *exclusivity* concept to be superior to the opposing concept of *plurality* representation. To make that point, Wagner's presentation to the committee contained the following statement, which is the focus of our immediate attention:

> Students of industrial relations are in most unanimous accord that it is practically impossible to apply two or more sets of agreements to one unit of workers at the same time, *or to apply the terms of one agreement to only a portion of the workers in a single unit.* For these reasons, collective bargaining can be really effective only when workers are sufficiently solidified in their interests to make one agreement covering all. This is possible only by means of majority rule.[108]

The analysis of this passage, which I have divided into six parts, reveals both its hyperbole and its ambiguity. We begin with the hyperbole parts. First, "practically impossible" does not mean "impossible," and the reference to "really effective" collective bargaining is not inaccurate when confined to mature, majority-based exclusive bargaining. The phrase says nothing, however, about early-organizational collective bargaining, which was not an issue regarding Section 9(a), for that section applies only *after* a majority representative has been selected. Second, the industrial relations community was certainly not "in most unanimous accord" in favor of majority rule. The vocal management community was strongly united in its opposition, preferring the plurality rule that President Roosevelt and General Johnson had negotiated for the automobile industry and their unions;[109] plurality representation also existed elsewhere in American industry.[110] Third, Wagner's hyperbole was intended to apply only to postmajority determinations of representation, for he was speaking about his bill as it existed at the time, *when it did not contain Section 8(5);* hence, the statement could not have been construed, even by implication, as a denial of bargaining rights to minority-union employees *prior* to invocation of the majority-designation requirement of Section 9(a). Furthermore, as we shall see, even in its later incarnations the statement never made reference to or purported to rely upon the Section 8(5) amendment.

Now for the ambiguity parts. Fourth, the described scenario was not intended to apply *prior* to the selection of union representation by a majority of the employees in a bargaining unit; this is apparent both from the statement's context because Wagner quoted from *Section 9(a)* to explain "[m]ajority rule as set forth in the present bill,"[111] and also from his response to a follow-up question from Senator Walsh[112] in which he expressly clarified that he was referring to the time "*after* representatives have been picked by the majority to represent all."[113] Fifth, the reference to the difficulty in applying the terms of an agreement to only a portion of the workers in a single unit implies the existence of a *unit,* a concept that becomes applicable only *after* the provisions of Section 9(a) and (b)[114] are invoked. Members-only agreements, not being applicable to employees who are not union members, do not depend on bargaining-unit determinations and the unit concept is irrelevant to such bargaining. Wagner's quoting of text from Section 9(a) confirmed that meaning. Sixth, the reference to the "terms of one agreement" and the application of "two or more sets of agreements" implies only *basic* terms covering *basic* conditions of employment, not to terms applicable to individual employees covered by a members-only agreement. Although this is logical, it is also what was clearly intended, for, as we shall soon see, Keyserling later edited this passage by repeatedly adding the word "basic" to clarify the statement's intent.

The significant aspect of Senator Wagner's relatively innocuous statement is that Keyserling later recycled virtually the same statement when he composed the Senate committee report on S. 1958, and he used it again in Wagner's lengthy speech to the Senate following issuance of that report. Such recyclings thus could not have had any reference to Section 8(5) in view of the preamendment timing of the original version. That time factor is especially noteworthy regarding the recycled statement in the Senate report issued on May 2, for that statement, which follows, is identical to Wagner's preamendment hearing statement except for minor editing:

> Since it is wellnigh [*sic*] universally recognized that it is practically impossible to apply two or more sets of agreements to one unit of workers at the same time, *or to apply the terms of one agreement to only a portion of the workers in a single unit,* the making of agreements is impracticable in the absence of majority rule.[115]

There is a similar excerpt in Wagner's later speech to the Senate.[116]

As I have noted regarding the original version, it is apparent from the context of these statements that they referred only to an advanced stage of union development, when two unions, one of which was expected to be a company union, are both claiming representation. The passage is a defense of the single majority-based collective agreement *versus* multiple agreements in a pluralistic collective bargaining environment. The Senate committee report and the speech both made clear—in fact, with identical language in the paragraph that followed—that this scenario applies only "*after* representatives have been picked by the majority to represent all,"[117] not before they were picked.

That these statements were originally written and used prior to the Senate committee's addition of Section 8(5) to the bill confirms that they were not based on that newly added unfair-labor-practice provision. Indeed, as I have noted earlier, the Senate report and Wagner's speech both explained that the four specific unfair labor practices, including Section 8(5), were "not designed to impose limitations or restrictions on the general guarantees" contained in Sections 7 and 8(1). Needless to say, the previous six-part analysis of hyperbole and ambiguity in the original passage in Wagner's earlier presentation also applies to these recycled versions.

The final note about the next recycling of this passage is a welcome one. When Keyserling drafted the report for the House Labor Committee he obviously recognized the ambiguity in his earlier versions, for he now clarified the language (1) by omitting entirely the key erroneous phrase, "*or to apply the terms of one agreement to only a portion of the workers in a single unit,*" (2) by making multiple insertions of the word "basic," using it in the same manner as he had previously used that word in the first draft of Section 9(a),[118] and (3) by softening the hyperbole. Accordingly, when the passage reappeared on May 17 in the report of the House committee, it now read, together with related phrases, as simply a rational presentation of the case for majority-union exclusivity *after* a majority of the employees in an appropriate unit have chosen a union of their choice. Once again, the statement wholly ignores Section 8(5), relying instead on Section 8(1), and in the *opening paragraph* it is clearly keyed to the pertinent time factor, signifying that this description applies "*after* representatives have been so designated by the majority."[119] Here is the final version of the statement in full—not just the recycled parts—including one part previously quoted:

> *Majority rule.*—Section 9(a) incorporates the majority rule principle, that representatives designated for the purposes of collective bargaining by the majority of employees in the appropriate unit shall be the exclusive representatives of all the employees in that unit "for the purposes of collective bargaining in respect to rates of pay, wages, hours of employment, or other conditions of employment." As a necessary corollary it is an act of interference (under sec. 8(1)) for an employer, *after* representatives have been so designated by the majority, to negotiate with individuals or minority groups in their own behalf on the *basic* subjects of collective bargaining.
>
> The misleading propaganda directed against this principle has been incredible. The underlying purposes of the majority rule principle are simple and just. As has frequently been stated, collective bargaining is not an end in itself; it is a means to an end, and that end is the making of collective agreements stabilizing employment relations for a period of time, with results advantageous both to the worker and the employer. There cannot be two or more *basic* agreements applicable to workers in a given unit; this is virtually conceded on all sides. If the employer should fail to give equally advantageous terms to nonmembers of the labor organization negotiating the agreement, there would immediately result a marked increase in the membership of that organization. On the other hand, if better terms were given to nonmembers, this would give rise to bitterness and strife, and a wholly unworkable arrangement whereby men performing comparable duties were paid according to different scales of wages and hours. Clearly then, there must be one *basic* scale, and it must apply to all.
>
> It would be undesirable if this *basic* scale should result from negotiation between the employer and unorganized individuals or a minority group, for the agreement probably would not command the assent of the majority and hence would not have the stability which is one of the chief advantages of collective bargaining. If, however, the company should undertake to deal with each group separately, there would result the conditions pointed out by the present National Labor Relations Board in its decision in the . . . *Houde* Engineering [case].[120]

The House report thus removed both the ambiguity and the hyperbole from this justification for majority rule. In so doing, it reiterated—in accordance with the plain language of Section 9(a)—that this provision applies only *after* majority selection, and this was reconfirmed by reference to the *Houde* case, which had been expressly limited to the postelection scene.[121] It also clarified that the perceived disadvantage of applying terms of one agreement to only a portion of the workers in a single unit referred only to *basic* conditions of employment, not to the individualized or minority-group conditions that would probably be the subjects of bargaining with a premajority union for its employee-members only.[122]

In the final analysis, the recycled passage viewed in context, especially after its metamorphosis into the form it later took in the House report, fully supports the thesis of this book regarding congressional intent concerning membership based minority-union bargaining prior to the employees' selection of a majority representative.

Legislative History in Conclusion

The historical record shows conclusively that Senator Wagner and his principal draftsman, Leon Keyserling, were fully aware of the need to protect minority-union bargaining, which was fairly common at the time and continued to be widely used following passage of the Act.[123] The textual history of the preliminary and final drafts documents their efforts; and when Section 8(5) was added as an afterthought that resulted from Francis Biddle's persistent urging, care was taken by Biddle and the Senate committee to reject a text that would have confined the duty-to-bargain obligation to Section 9(a) majority representatives only.[124] The only serious area of legislative contention relating to collective bargaining concerned the establishment of the exclusivity rule for majority-union bargaining. Proponents of the Wagner bill deemed that rule the best way to achieve effective bargaining, whereas the alternative of pluralistic representation, which employers favored, would have fragmented the bargaining process among competing unions. Minority-union bargaining that precedes the selection of a majority representative was thus a non-issue in the legislative debates. Although the fanfare that surrounded the collective bargaining process during those debates focused on majority rule and governmentally conducted representation elections, members-only minority-union bargaining also emerged from the same legislative process, although quietly and without fanfare.

4 *How Lack of Wisdom Became Conventional Wisdom*

Union Elections Are Habit-Forming

For several years following the passage of the Wagner Act in 1935, there was never any legal question raised as to the scope of its bargaining requirements, either as to minority-union members-only bargaining or majority-union exclusivity bargaining. Both types of bargaining had prevailed earlier under the Blue Eagle administration of Section 7(a) of the NIRA and both were now widely accepted under the new NLRA. Unions and employers continued to agree to members-only contracts. During those early years, such contracts proved pragmatically useful to both unions and employers. At places where unions had organized a substantial number—but less than a majority—of a company's bargaining-unit employees and majority support did not seem likely or easily attainable, these membership-based contracts were welcomed and many such agreements were signed. Unions viewed these agreements as a preliminary stage in the organizational and collective bargaining process. When majority-union membership was finally achieved, such contracts were almost always followed by conventional exclusivity agreements. During those years employers did not contend that they had no legal duty to bargain with minority unions for members-only contracts; on the contrary, numerous companies engaged in such bargaining and signed many such agreements—often readily—for they considered this limited type of recognition a lesser evil than exclusive recognition, which was usually accompanied by a demand for a closed shop. The only legal question of serious consequence raised by employers during the first two years following enactment of the new statute concerned its constitutionality, which the management community vigorously and incessantly challenged[1] until the Supreme Court put that issue to rest in *NLRB v. Jones & Laughlin Steel Corp.*[2] In my research, I found no evidence or suggestion that premajority members-only bargaining during that period was ever considered a challengeable legal issue.

Despite the constitutional cloud that hovered over the NLRB for the first 21 months of its existence, labor unions at that time took full advantage of the Act's pro-union impetus—which was psychological as well as legal—and they proceeded to organize vigorously and with remarkable success. Union membership grew phenomenally—jumping from 3,317,000 in 1935 to 8,200,000 in 1938[3]—notwithstanding that the labor movement was simultaneously splitting itself into two rival camps, the old American Federation of Labor (AFL) and the new Congress of Industrial Organizations (CIO).[4]

Of the newly signed collective bargaining contracts, members-only agreements were as common as exclusivity agreements, and their coverage was perhaps even more extensive. In 1938, the Bureau of National Affairs issued a report entitled *Union Recognition as Shown in Contracts*[5] in which it published "typical recognition provisions" derived from twenty-three recently concluded collective bargaining contracts. That report noted that these contracts generally fell into two different patterns: "In some . . . the union is recognized as the exclusive bargaining agent for all employees. In others the union is recognized as bargaining agent for those employees only who are or may become members of the union."[6] Of the twenty-three provisions examined, thirteen (or 57 percent) were of the members-only type, eight (or 35 percent) provided for exclusive representation, and two were ambiguous as to coverage. A variety of industries were covered by these members-only contracts. The CIO agreements included two steel companies, two automobile manufacturers, a rayon manufacturer, a silk manufacturer, an electric equipment manufacturer, and a rubber manufacturer. The AFL agreements included two public utilities, a steel-products manufacturer, a cement manufacturer, and a publishing company.[7]

Use of the Act's broad bargaining coverage was especially common in the steel industry. In 1940, Professor Robert Brooks, who had been given wide access to the archives of the United Steelworkers of America, described the organizational pattern employed by the CIO's Steel Workers Organizing Committee (SWOC) as follows:

> During the first wave of organizing activity in 1936–37, the S.W.O.C. contented itself very largely with securing contracts which provided for recognition of the union as the bargaining agent only for members of the union. Of the 486 contracts signed before January, 1938, 60 per cent were for "members only." This 60 per cent included all the U.S. Steel contracts and most of the larger companies. Consequently, the relative importance of members only was far greater than indicated by the percentage figure.[8]

In fact, the most important breakthrough occurred at U.S. Steel.[9] In summer 1936, Myron C. Taylor, its board chairman and chief policy maker, privately arrived at a written formula for union recognition that later became known as "the Myron Taylor formula for industrial peace."[10] It read as follows:

> The Company recognizes the right of its employees to bargain collectively through representatives freely chosen by them without dictation, coercion or intimidation in any form or from any source. It will negotiate and contract with the representatives of any group of its employees so chosen and *with any organization as the representative of its members,* subject to the recognition of the principle that the right to work is not dependent on membership or non-membership in any organization and subject to the right of every employee freely to bargain in such manner and through such representative, if any, as he chooses.[11]

A year after passage of the Act, here was—in essence—recognition and acceptance by the country's largest employer of the broad scope of the duty-to-bargain requirements contained in the new law.

Meanwhile, SWOC organizers in the field were busy persuading steelworkers to sign *membership* cards[12]—not merely authorization cards, such as are commonly used by unions today to secure an election.[13] By January 1937, SWOC had enrolled 125,000 steelworker members.[14] However, because it lacked a majority at U.S. Steel,[15] the union's leadership—John L. Lewis and Philip Murray—resolved to accept Taylor's formula for less-than-majority recognition. And Taylor, rather than engage in a bitter fight against unionization—which was the union-avoidance approach currently practiced by management in most industries, especially in the automobile industry—decided that it was in the best interests of U.S. Steel and its subsidiaries to comply with the new law and bargain with this outside union that had been chosen by substantial numbers of the companies' employees.[16] Accordingly, on March 2, 1937, U.S. Steel signed an agreement recognizing the SWOC as collective bargaining agent for those employees who were its members.[17]

The U.S. Steel members-only agreement became a model that was soon followed at many other steel companies.[18] By December 15, 1937, of the 445 contracts entered into by the SWOC, 85 percent provided for members-only recognition.[19] "On the basis of number of employees embraced, the model agreement had a coverage of 98 percent of all those working under contracts with the union."[20] Of the 403 steel industry contracts signed in 1938—including renewals of expiring agreements—155 (38 percent) limited recognition to union members only. In 1939, fifty-six (14 percent) stipulated recognition for members only.[21] That decline in members-only agreements represented the natural progression in the organizational process, for when steelworker union membership reached majority status—whether demonstrated by an NLRB election or otherwise—the members-only agreement was replaced by an exclusivity agreement.

What happened in steel was also happening in many other workplaces in

American industry. Here is a snapshot view of union organizational status recorded by the Twentieth Century Fund in 1942:

The status of the union varies considerably from industry to industry (and within industries), depending, in the main, upon the age of the organization and the length of time collective bargaining has been in effect. Most unions seek a closed, union or preferential shop, but newly organized ones usually have difficulty in winning any one of these from employers traditionally opposed to unionism. Ten years ago most agreements provided for the closed shop. In recent years there have been more exceptions than at any time since the 1880's; unions were willing to take what they could get in order to secure a foothold in areas previously closed to them. For example, *many agreements in the 1930's with new industrial unions in the mass production industries stated that the union was to bargain for members only. However, as collective bargaining gained more general acceptance and as unions won National Labor Relations Board elections, these "membership" agreements were generally replaced by contracts designating the union as exclusive representative of all employees,* except certain groups such as supervisors and salaried employees. Agreements of this type are prevalent in the rubber and auto industries.[22]

General Motors (GM), the giant of the auto industry, was a part of this pattern, but reluctantly. Although GM had "set out systematically to destroy the union in its plants,"[23] after a series of sit-down strikes and pressure from the White House, and following dogged mediation by Michigan's governor Frank Murphy, GM's management—perhaps with knowledge of the ongoing negotiations between Lewis and Taylor regarding the impending settlement at U.S. Steel[24]—agreed on February 11, 1937, to recognize the United Automobile Workers (UAW) as the representative of its members only; on April 6 Chrysler followed suit with similar recognition.[25] And like the CIO steelworkers, the UAW could not at that time have won an election on the basis of its own membership.[26] The members-only agreement thus emerged as a critical organizational tool. By 1938, of the 537 auto industry contracts signed by the UAW, 343 (i.e., 64 percent) were members-only agreements.[27]

As previously noted,[28] members-only agreements were also widespread in industries other than steel and auto. In fact, it was such an agreement with an electrical public utility company that was in issue in *Consolidated Edison Co. v. NLRB*,[29] where the Supreme Court expressly affirmed the legality of members-only minority-union agreements.[30] However, neither the Court nor the NLRB had occasion to rule directly on the issue of compulsory bargaining with member-only minority unions. As a strict legal proposition, this issue remained unsettled. Nevertheless, extensive contemporary acceptance of the process suggested *de facto* recognition of this bargaining requirement. And certainly from the standpoint of feasibility and future acceptance, the fact that such minority bargaining was commonly and successfully practiced is of major importance to our inquiry and to the ultimate administrative and judicial disposition of this issue.

At the time, unions looked upon these membership-based agreements as merely a temporary means to an end, for they were convinced—as had been Senator Wagner and the Congress—that for collective bargaining to achieve maximum effectiveness, exclusive representation, hence majority status, was necessary. Accordingly, during the early Wagner Act years unions sought exclusive recognition by a variety of means, depending on the circumstances prevailing at the time in the targeted company or industry. Members-only agreements were one of those means, for they were viewed as useful stepping-stones on the path to majority membership and mature collective bargaining. What occurred at GM and Chrysler—as in the steel industry—was exemplary of that pattern. These temporary agreements provided the UAW with a bully platform inside the workplace from which to demonstrate the advantages of union representation and thereby increase employee support to the point where majority status could be easily and conclusively achieved. Accordingly, following NLRB election victories in 1940, the UAW was officially certified as the exclusive bargaining agent for 130,000 workers at GM and for 50,000 workers at Chrysler.[31] By 1942, nearly all the plants where the UAW had first achieved recognition on a members-only basis were now locked in for "sole bargaining rights."[32] An example of that transitional process was confirmed by the Seventh Circuit U.S. Court of Appeals when it upheld a Board order that required a recalcitrant employer to confer exclusive recognition on a formerly members-only UAW union after it had attained majority status.[33]

Not surprisingly, however, members-only agreements became increasingly rare after 1940. And soon they were but a memory, for unions were more often bypassing that early bargaining stage, seeking instead—and in most cases obtaining—majority bargaining rights directly through NLRB representation ("R" case) procedures. Consequently, in only a few years members-only bargaining all but vanished from the industrial-relations scene. What caused such a major shift in the unions' organizational strategy?

The answer to that question is to be found primarily in the Labor Board's representation statistics. From the beginning of the new Board's existence, union organizers had made prompt and effective use of Section 9 procedures, and such use increased rapidly because during those early years the Board generally provided the easiest and most expeditious route to organizational success. Filing representation petitions often produced recognition agreements even without formal NLRB intervention, and Board agents usually processed elections and payroll checks fairly quickly in those days, at least in places where the employer was not engaging in serious unfair labor practices. Unions indeed discovered that the fastest and least expensive way to achieve majority recognition from most employers was through NLRB procedures. Although in most cases this process required an election, certification was frequently granted on the basis of a payroll check, i.e., a comparison of the union's membership cards with the employer's payroll records.[34] Consequently, during the Board's first decade, unions were successful in winning recognition in almost nine out of every ten representation cases. As a result, this path of least resistance led to a relatively quick abandonment of members-only bargaining and ultimately to a widespread unawareness of the legal basis for such bargaining.

The following statistics explain why it was so easy for unions to stray from the practice of relying on members-only agreements as a preliminary step to exclusive majority representation. In 1937, the Board's first full fiscal year, unions obtained recognition or certification in 421 of the 465 active representation cases—a win rate of 90.1 percent.[35] By fiscal year 1938, the Board's processes had become more familiar and more popular and unions achieved recognition or certification in 1,789 of 1,996 active cases—89.6 percent.[36] In 1939, of 1,356 active cases, unions were recognized or certified in 1,184 cases—87.3 percent.[37] In 1940 unions successfully obtained recognition or certification in approximately[38] 1,714 of 1,985 active cases—86.3 percent.[39] In 1941, the last fiscal year prior to World War II, of 2,568 elections and payroll checks, unions won 2,127—82.8 percent.[40] In 1942, the first of the World War II years, the Board conducted 4,212 elections and payroll checks, almost twice the number of the previous year, of which unions won 3,635—86.3 percent.[41] In 1943, the Board conducted 4,153 elections and payroll checks, of which unions won 3,580—86.2 percent. That was the year in which the number of employees in units in which unions obtained recognition exceeded 1 million for the first time.[42] In 1944, unions won 3,983 elections and payroll checks out of a total of 4,712 conducted—84.5 percent.[43] In 1945, the Board conducted 4,919 elections, of which unions won 4,078—82.9 percent. And, in 1946, the Board conducted 5,589 elections and payroll checks, of which unions won 4,446—79.5 percent.[44] Thus, during the first ten full fiscal years of the Board's existence, the average win rate for unions in representation cases was 85.5 percent. NLRB elections had indeed become habit-forming in a relatively short period of time.

Organized labor recognized and appreciated the critical role that the Labor Board was performing, for it had greatly facilitated the expansion of union membership. For example, the president of the AFL Office Employees International Union called the Act "a powerful stimulant to the growth of trade union organization [which] is graphically illustrated by the fact that approximately 15,000,000 men and women in the United States are members of trade unions in 1945, as compared with 3,000,000 ten years ago."[45] However, it was this rapid and phenomenal growth in union membership, attributed to the Act and the Labor Board's presence, that proved to be the chief factor contributing to the loss of institutional memory, or unawareness, of the earlier role that members-only bargaining had played in the organizational process.

As the previously noted "R" case statistics attest, the unions' concentration on the election process had accelerated during the war years. Such reliance was undoubtedly aided by the Board's own emphasis on "R" case procedures, for they provided a relatively simple pattern for bargaining-unit determinations, conduct of elections, and certification of majorities for exclusive union representation.[46] That quick and easy process coexisted in sharp contrast with the Board's more tedious unfair-labor-practice complaint ("C" case) procedures,[47] which required long and drawn-out contested hearings and time-consuming determinations through administrative reviews, usually followed by reliance on the courts. Although final results in the "C" cases were usually successful, many of their outcomes were unsatisfactory or uncertain, especially regarding compliance.[48] It was thus entirely logical that the Board as an institution would be focused, as it was indeed, on "R" cases and the concept of majority representation, for the scheme of the Act contemplated mature—hence majority/exclusive and appropriate-unit—collective bargaining. Although protected by the Act, minority-union bargaining, even as a prelude to majority representation, was never the Board's center of attention. Nor was it the common view of the Act. Just as minority-union members-only bargaining had not been a controversial issue during the congressional debates,[49] it was likewise not a controversial issue during the early years after passage of the Act, even though it was widely practiced. It is therefore not surprising that members-only bargaining was not a subject of major interest at the Labor Board, and it was also soon forgotten by the industrial-relations public at large.[50]

That first decade was also the time when the American labor movement was engaged in fierce organizational rivalry between the AFL and the CIO. And the last half of that decade included the prewar build-up of defense industries, especially during the period of the Battle of Britain, which was followed by massive and rapidly expanding industrial activity that accompanied World War II. These momentous historical factors had a powerful and lasting impact on the growth and shape of organized labor in America. Although unions gained in strength during the war, they did so without special emphasis on organizing.[51]

When the war was over, the industrial-relations scene was immediately transformed by a record number of strikes. At the beginning of 1946, a "staggering total of 2,000,000 industrial workers were simultaneously on strike,"[52] and during the twelve-month period following the end of the war 5,000,000 workers engaged in strikes for a total of 120,000,000 days of idleness.[53] The largest of these strikes occurred in the critical industries of coal, steel, auto, railroad, and meat packing.[54]

There were also several major strikes in 1947;[55] however, the most significant labor-relations event of that year was passage of the Taft-Hartley

Act,[56] which initiated a whole new environment for American labor relations. Among the immediate changes introduced by that legislation was the phenomenon of unions becoming busily engaged in a multitude of legal defensive actions generated by the numerous union restrictions that the new law had created.[57] Such extensive litigation represented distractions of major proportions that contributed to a decline in union organizational activity, which was already significantly impaired by procedural and substantive changes engendered by the Taft-Hartley amendments.[58] At that stage in history, union organizational activity and the employers' responses were now focused almost exclusively on NLRB election procedures. For all practical purposes, members-only recognition was now entirely forgotten—a tribute to the short life span of institutional memory.

As a consequence, only a few years after Taft-Hartley, the NLRB and its union and employer constituents were routinely viewing majority-union bargaining—which was certainly the ultimate goal intended by the Act—as the *only* bargaining contemplated by the Act. Although unions had originally favored NLRB elections out of sheer convenience, their reliance on the election process had now become routine, with attendant misunderstanding of the true scope of bargaining offered by the statute. Employers, of course, had no reason to question such dependence on the election process because an election campaign gave management the ideal forum in which to mount offensive activities against union representation. Professor Summers accordingly observes that "unions seem to have been captured and imprisoned by the misconception of the function of majority rule."[59] That misconception, however, was but the outgrowth of custom. As we have noted, that custom, or habit, evolved after members-only bargaining had ceased to flourish, having been replaced by the "R" case process of establishing union majorities through formal NLRB representation procedures. This became the standard operating practice for most unions. Thus was born the latter-day conventional wisdom that assumes that majority-union representation is the sine qua non of collective bargaining. Not surprisingly, by 1976 even the Labor Board, in an occasional indirect reference,[60] and at least one labor-law publishing service, in a careless headnote,[61] gave brief voice to that conventional assumption. Lack of wisdom had finally become conventional wisdom. Section 7, however, with its guarantee of the employees' right to "bargain collectively through representatives of their own choosing," remains on the statute books ready to be employed once again by minority employees and their unions in workplaces where there is not yet a majority representative. Although organized labor may have forgotten this key feature in the Act, that bargaining mandate remains fully intact—a sleeping giant waiting to be reawakened.

PART II
The Legal Parameters

The Search for the Phantom Provision

The Statutory Text Means Exactly What It Says

An Introduction to Statutory Interpretation: The Primacy of Plain Meaning

As we have learned in the preceding chapter, latter-day conventional wisdom would have us believe that employers are only required to recognize and bargain with majority unions, which in most instances means only unions that have been so selected through an NLRB election. If that were a correct reading of the statute, an employer would have no duty to bargain with a minority union for its members only even in workplaces where no Section 9(a) majority union is currently designated. As our review of legislative history has demonstrated, however, that legal conclusion was not intended by Senator Wagner or the Congress, and the practices of the parties immediately following passage of the Act likewise rejected such a narrow reading. In order to determine whether the statutory text contains any provision that might support the current conventional wisdom, this chapter focuses primarily on language in the text, for that is ordinarily the main source for ascertaining statutory meaning. And because this chapter is intended to be a free-standing exposition of exactly what Congress mandated in that text, I apologize to the reader in advance for the unavoidable repetition of some of the basic elements noted in previous chapters.

According to the statute's wording, what exactly did Congress enact in 1935 concerning minority-union collective bargaining? Does the Act retain the right that prevailed under the Blue Eagle—under Section 7(a) of the National Industrial Recovery Act (NIRA)—whereby all employees were entitled to bargain collectively through a union of their own choice without regard to majority or unit requirements except in workplaces where a majority representative has already been selected? That was certainly the congressional intent.[1] Although Section 9(a) clearly requires exclusive representation in workplaces where a majority of the bargaining-unit employees have designated a representative pursuant to that provision, does that requirement also mean that where a majority representative has not been so designated there can be no enforceable collective bargaining with a nonmajority union? In other words, is the bargaining requirement under the current Act more restrictive than it was under the NIRA? We know from Chapter 3 that Congress intended to continue its protected coverage of minority-union bargaining to the same extent that such coverage prevailed under the NIRA. Did it succeed? And is the meaning of the applicable text understandable and without ambiguity? A judicial construction of that text, which will occur eventually, will look first to the wording of the provisions in issue—hence this chapter, in which text is emphasized and only passing reference is made to supportive legislative history.

When courts resort to legislative history it is usually because the statutory language is unclear or ambiguous. In this instance, as our examination will confirm, the text of the statute is clear on its face. Nevertheless, legislative history—which we have already reviewed—has an important role to play, for when the linguistic meaning of ordinary words and phrases in statutory provisions match the meaning revealed by legislative history, such meaning is confirmed and reinforced. And, needless to say, if any unanticipated ambiguity were to be found regarding the meaning of statutory text, legislative history will be important in clarifying the intent of that text.

This chapter accordingly examines closely the relevant statutory provisions. And, as we shall observe, the common words and phrases contained in those pertinent passages do not support latter-day conventional wisdom that assumes an employer never has a duty to bargain with a minority union. On the contrary, the text positively conveys the meaning that where no exclusive representative has been designated by a majority of the employees in an appropriate unit, Sections 8(a)(1) and/or 8(a)(5)[2] guarantee the right of nonmajority employees to engage in collective bargaining with their employer through a union of their own choosing. I carefully searched the entire statute for any provision that might conceivably indicate the contrary, but that search proved unproductive. In the end, I could only conclude that the latter-day conventional wisdom is supported by only a phantom provision— verily, a provision that does not exist.

The analysis that follows demonstrates that the meaning I attribute to the statute is fully supported by the Supreme Court's arsenal of "traditional tools of statutory construction" referred to in its seminal *Chevron*[3] decision, including legislative history noted in earlier chapters. This construction satisfies both the traditional *plain meaning rule* of statutory construction and the *new textualist* approach to such construction.[4] If we employ even the strictest process advocated by the latter approach—that "[c]ourts should interpret statutes based on the ordinary meaning of the words used in the statute and various rules of grammar and syntax, such as the interpretative canon that a court must interpret a statute so as to give every word some effect,"[5]—the resulting interpretation is the same. Professor William Eskridge has noted that "textualism appeals to the rule of law value that citizens ought to be able to read the statute books and know their rights and duties."[6] Such a reading is especially important regarding the NLRA, for ordinary workers ought to be able to rely on the plain language of that statute, which tells them quite simply that they have a right "to bargain collectively through representatives of their own choosing." In this instance, it should and does mean exactly what it says.

The Supportive Case Law

Notwithstanding popular belief supporting the conventional wisdom's view of the issue in question, there have been no cases decided by either the NLRB or the courts sustaining that view, a condition that I explore in depth in Chapter 9. There are several cases, however—six from the Supreme Court and four from the Board—that are consistent with the proposition that the Act guarantees the right of employees to engage in members-only minority-union bargaining where a majority representative has not yet been designated or selected. None, however, had occasion to reach that final conclusion. But because these cases verify the legality of minority-union bargaining and their products—members-only bargaining contracts—and because they support the rationale for the type of bargaining advanced herein, these ten decisions provide the ideal backdrop for our examination of what the statutory text literally says about this subject.

The first Supreme Court case was *NLRB v. Jones & Laughlin Steel Corp.*,[7] the critical decision in which the Court affirmed the constitutionality of the Wagner Act. The Court there expounded on the basic purpose and thrust of the rights protected by the Act, stating that

> the right of employees to self-organization and to select representatives of their own choosing for collective bargaining . . . is a *fundamental right.* Employees have as clear a right to organize and select their representatives for lawful purposes as the respondent has to organize its business and select its own officers and agents. . . . Long ago we stated the reasons for labor organizations. [The] union was essential to give laborers opportunity to deal on an equality [basis] with their employer.[8] We reiterated these views when we had under consideration the Railway Labor Act of 1926.[9]

The Court having thus characterized the collective bargaining right of association as a "fundamental right," it should be treated accordingly.[10] As a fundamental right, it logically must be available to all covered employees, not just to majority employees, for in the normal progression of societal conduct majority groups begin as minority groups. If minority-union employees are barred from engaging in collective bargaining, not only are they denied the immediate benefits of their association, they are also likely to be denied any future benefits, for their ability to achieve majority-status association will have been severely impaired, as history has amply demonstrated.[11] Such an extreme limitation is inconsistent with the characteristics of a fundamental right.

The next relevant Supreme Court case was a 1938 decision that directly examined the legality of a members-only collective bargaining agreement. As Chapter 4 has demonstrated, such agreements were quite common at that time. The case was *Consolidated Edison Co. v. NLRB.*[12] The several companies involved had entered into collective agreements with the International Brotherhood of Electrical Workers (the Brotherhood), an AFL affiliate, and its local unions. Under those agreements, the Brotherhood was recognized as the collective bargaining agency "for those employees who are members of the Brotherhood."[13] In response to a charge filed by the United Electrical and Radio Workers of America, a CIO affiliate, the NLRB held those agreements invalid under Sections 8(1) and 8(3), the latter provision being the prohibition against discrimination to encourage or discourage union membership. Significantly, however, the Board dismissed the charge that had alleged a violation of Section 8(2), the provision that proscribes employer domination or interference with the formation or administration of a labor organization. The Board thereby confirmed that members-only union recognition and bargaining are not unlawful under that section of the Act.[14] As to the Board's holding that the agreements violated Section 8(1) and 8(3), the Court reversed the agency. Writing for the Court, Chief Justice Hughes declared that

> The Act contemplates the making of contracts with labor organizations. That is the manifest objective in providing for collective bargaining. Under §7 the employees of the companies are entitled to self-organization, to join labor organizations and to bargain collectively through representatives of their own choosing. [The contracts] simply constitute the Brotherhood the *collective bargaining agency for the employees who are its members.* [T]here is nothing to show that the employees' selection as indicated by the Brotherhood contracts has been superseded by any other selection by a majority of employees of the companies so as to create an exclusive agency for bargaining under the statute, and in *the absence of such an exclusive agency the employees represented by the brotherhood, even if they were a minority, clearly had the right to make their own choice.*[15]

The Court's determination regarding the legality of such contracts, even if made by a minority union, was unequivocal. Having thus established that these agreements are appropriate and legal under the NLRA, it should logically follow that "in the absence of [a majority] exclusive agency"[16] there is also a duty to bargain with such a minority union for a members-only contract, although that issue was not before the Court in *Consolidated Edison*.

In the 1961 *Bernhard-Altmann*[17] case, which we examine for another but related reason in Chapter 9,[18] Justice William O. Douglas, in his partial dissent, elaborated on the role of members-only bargaining, declaring that

> We have indicated over and again that, absent an exclusive agency for bargaining created by a majority of workers, a minority union has standing to bargain for its members.[19] . . . Honoring a minority union—where no majority union exists or even where the activities of the minority union do not collide with a bargaining agreement—is being respectful of history. Long before the Wagner Act, employers and employees had the right to discuss their problems. In the early days the unions were representatives of a minority of workers. The aim—at least the hope—of the legislation was that majority unions would emerge and provide stabilizing influences.[20]

Justice Douglas thus recognized the preliminary—but highly important—organizational nature of minority-union bargaining. He also reminded us that "[t]he Board has frequently recognized that recognition of a minority union as representative of its members only was not an unfair labor practice."[21] And although it was his partial dissent that stressed the role of minority-union bargaining, the Court's majority opinion acknowledged the accuracy of his observation (disagreeing only as to the appropriate remedy in the case), for Justice Tom C. Clark, writing for the majority, qualified the Court's holding by noting that

> the violation which the Board found was the grant by the employer of exclusive representation status to a minority union, *as distinguished from an employer's bargaining with a minority union for its members only.*[22]

A year after *Bernhard-Altmann,* the Court decided *Retail Clerks v. Lion Dry Goods, Inc.,*[23] where the issue was the enforceability, under Section 301(a) of the Taft-Hartley Act,[24] of a union-management contract that was not a collective bargaining agreement with an exclusive majority union. In the course of holding that contract (a strike-settlement agreement) enforceable, the Court reiterated that "'members only' contracts have long been recognized."[25]

Later that same year the Court decided *Washington Aluminum,*[26] holding that a strike by a minority group of employees over a work-related grievance was protected concerted activity under Section 7. Although that strike represented concerted activity for "mutual aid or protection"—conduct discussed and defined later in Chapter 9[27]—it provides a model for the legality of strikes that may be conducted by minority unions as part of their collective bargaining process.[28]

Last in this review of related Supreme Court authority, it is useful to pon-
der what Justice William J. Brennan wrote for the Court in 1984 when he
construed the intent of Congress in enacting Section 7. In *NLRB v. City Disposal Systems, Inc.*,[29] he said:

> Congress sought generally to equalize the bargaining power of the em-
> ployee with that of his employer by allowing employees to band together
> in confronting an employer regarding the terms and conditions of their
> employment. There is no indication that Congress intended to limit this
> protection to situations in which an employee's activity and that of his fel-
> low employees combine with one another in any particular way. [W]hat
> emerges from the general background of §7—and what is consistent with
> the Act's statement of purpose—is a congressional intent to create an equal-
> ity in bargaining power between the employee and the employer through-
> out the entire process of labor organizing, collective bargaining, and
> enforcement of collective bargaining agreements.[30]

That assessment of what Congress intended provides a fitting guideline for
implementing the meaning of Section 7 regarding minority-union bargaining. Just as most businesses start out as small enterprises, most employee organizations begin as small groups of workers. The normal growing process
for union organizations and collective bargaining—especially when that
process is compared to and treated equally, as was intended, with the normal growing process for typical businesses—should invariably include the
early stages of collective bargaining. Before the Wagner Act was passed,
members-only bargaining provided this maturation function, and it continued to serve that same purpose during the early years following passage of
the Act. As Justice Brennan's reading of the intended coverage of Section 7
connoted, such bargaining is entitled to the protection of that section. That
is essentially what the literal language of the statute requires, as this chapter
demonstrates.

The Labor Board has also acknowledged that members-only or nonexclusive collective bargaining, as well as its resulting agreements, are contemplated by the Act and lawful under both Sections 8(a)(1) and 8(a)(2).
Three cases directly recognize and confirm those concepts: in 1938 *The
Solvay Process Company*,[31] in 1950 *The Hoover Company*,[32] and in 1952
Consolidated Builders, Inc.[33] And a fourth case, *Lundy Mfg. Corp.*, decided
in 1962,[34] is consistent with this same minority-union recognition thesis.

In *Solvay Process*, the Board specifically held—as it had previously ruled
in *Consolidated Edison*[35] prior to the Supreme Court's review of that case—
that an employer's execution of a members-only collective agreement does
not constitute an act of *domination* or *interference* with the formation or administration of a labor organization in violation of Section 8(2).

In the *Hoover* case, the Board declared that an employer, faced with the
rival demands of two unions, "may, without violating the *Midwest Piping*[36]

doctrine grant recognition to each of the claimants on a members-only basis."[37]

In *Consolidated Builders,* the Board subsequently cited the declaration in *Hoover* to support its holding that inasmuch as "an employer may grant recognition to each of two rival unions on a members-only basis[,] *a fortiori,* [it] may grant recognition on a nonexclusive basis to a minority union, as here, there was no rival union claim."[38]

And in *Lundy,* which is discussed in Chapter 9,[39] the Board recognized that, where there was no exclusive bargaining agent, an ad hoc group of employees had the right to deal with their employer on a group basis regarding grievances.

As the foregoing cases indicate, it has long been recognized that where there is no exclusive majority-union representative, members-only collective bargaining and resulting agreements are proper and lawful under the Act. The time is now ripe for a decision (or decisions) also holding that an employer has an enforceable duty to recognize and bargain with a minority union for such members-only agreements.

Where Is the Phantom Provision? A Statutory Analysis

The Act's General Purpose

Although my immediate objective here is to probe all the passages in the Act that bear on the question of minority representation, the general purpose behind the entire Act must first be taken into account in order to view the target provisions in proper perspective. The congressional purpose thereby revealed is a major aid to statutory interpretation.[40] To that end, the authors of the statute accommodated by writing a preamble that fully explained the Congress's intent, for they were anticipating intensive judicial scrutiny, although at the time their primary concern was the issue of constitutionality.[41] Their general, but nevertheless targeted, intent was spelled out in Section 1[42] as a statement of the "policy of the United States," a policy that was to be achieved

> by encouraging the practice and procedure of collective bargaining and by protecting the exercise by workers of full freedom of association, self-organization, and designation of representatives of their own choosing, for the purpose of negotiating the terms and conditions of their employment or other mutual aid or protection.[43]

The similarity between that language and comparable language in the preamble to the Norris-LaGuardia Act and Section 7(a) of the National Industrial Recovery Act is readily apparent and not coincidental, as the historical data reviewed in Chapter 1 indicate.[44]

The reference to "collective bargaining" for workers in the Act's preamble is exceedingly broad, employing the all-inclusive phrases of "*full* freedom of association"[45] and "representatives of *their own choosing.*"[46] The provision makes no reference to excluding any workers covered by the Act[47] from access to collective bargaining. And there is certainly no suggestion that collective bargaining rights would be unavailable prior to establishment of majority representation; in fact, the concept of majority and exclusive representation does not even appear in the preamble. That section simply emphasizes that collective bargaining is to be the norm for all workers who choose to be represented for such a purpose. As will be apparent from our examination of the pertinent statutory provisions, the preamble's "public justification approach"[48] is consistent with the Act's substantive contents.

Collective bargaining was and continues to be the national labor policy. That it is still the policy was strongly reconfirmed in 1949 when Congress amended the Wagner Act by passage of the Taft-Hartley Act;[49] and subsequent amendments made no changes in that policy.[50] The Taft-Hartley reconfirmation is especially meaningful because the original House version would have completely eliminated the Wagner Act's declaration of policy; instead, the conference committee retained the critical Wagner Act language, and the only changes made to the preamble in the final bill are irrelevant to our concerns.[51] Furthermore, in recommending the Taft-Hartley bill for final passage, Senator Robert A. Taft, the bill's chief sponsor, pointed out that

> the committee feels, almost unanimously, that the solution of our labor problems must rest on a free economy and on *free collective bargaining.* The bill is certainly based on that proposition.[52]

And during the Senate debate preceding the vote to override President Harry S. Truman's veto, Senator Taft again emphasized that the bill "is based on the theory of the Wagner Act. . . . It is based on the theory that the solution of the labor problem in the United States is *free, collective bargaining. . . .*"[53]

Accordingly, the statement of policy regarding collective bargaining contained in the Section 1 preamble provides a major directional guideline for interpreting the provisions in the statute that guarantee collective bargaining. Those provisions, which are relatively short and straightforward, consist of *three* basic statutory clauses, *Sections 7, 8(a)(1),* and *9(a),* which contain the essence of the rights and obligations that relate to the collective bargaining process. These basic clauses are supplemented by four unfair-labor-practice clauses, *Sections 8(a)(2),*[54] *8(a)(3),*[55] *8(a)(4),*[56] and *8(a)(5),*[57] which supply enforcement emphasis and specific detail concerning employer violations that Congress deemed most common and especially egregious. Of these supplementary clauses, only Section 8(a)(5) relates directly to the matter of collective bargaining.[58] The remaining provisions of the original Wagner Act pertained to jurisdiction, definitions, administration, and remedies. None of the substantive provisions with which we are here concerned were affected by either the Taft-Hartley or the Landrum-Griffin amendments.

Section 7: The Labor Bill of Rights

The first and foremost of the basic clauses is *Section 7*. Its full text is a virtual *bill of rights* applicable to all workers covered by the Act. [59] Although several provisions of the Act are involved in the determination of collective bargaining rights, the critical language here in issue is to be found in the familiar fourteen-word clause in Section 7 that states that

> *Employees shall have the right to* self-organization, to form, join, or assist labor organizations, [and] to *bargain collectively through representatives of their own choosing. . . .*[60]

This short but comprehensive clause—the italicized words that are derived from prior congressional legislation[61]—says simply and without ambiguity that all employees covered by the Act have a right to engage in collective bargaining.

Absent limiting language elsewhere in the statute, Section 7 thus makes it clear that every worker is so entitled and that no distinction is made between minority and majority representation. The *"shall"* in the provision is unequivocally mandatory.[62] And because *"to bargain collectively"* involves a process that was well understood in common usage at the time of enactment,[63] such accepted meaning was patently the meaning intended by Congress.[64] At the time of the Act's passage, collective bargaining was a process so well-known that it did not require explanation in the "definitions" section of the Act.[65] As the legislative history indicates, it was a familiar process that had been described frequently by the two prior labor boards under Section 7(a) of the NIRA, the most notable of which was the depiction in the *Houde Engineering*[66] decision that Senator Wagner quoted and relied on in support of the duty to bargain required by Section 7.[67] In that description, the old NLRB had recognized that the phrase in question was "full of meaning,"[68] that collective bargaining requires the employer to "negotiate in good faith with his employees' representatives; to match their proposals, and to make every reasonable effort to reach an agreement."[69] The concept of collective bargaining was thus well established and fully recognized when the Act was passed. In fact, its basic definition was contained in a contemporaneous report by the Twentieth Century Fund, which recorded that

> Collective bargaining is the act of carrying on negotiations over the terms of employment between the representatives of *organized* employees and their employers which if successfully consummated, results in a trade agreement (often referred to as a "collective agreement"), either written or unwritten. A trade agreement . . . is an agreement or contract between an *employee organization* and an employer, or a group of employers, which stipulates for a fixed period of time the wages, hours and working conditions in accordance with which the contracting parties offer and accept employment.[70]

This understanding of collective bargaining was so common and widely accepted that it was essentially the meaning contained in the authoritative *Webster's New International* (second edition) unabridged dictionary, published one year prior to passage of the Act (a dictionary definition contemporary with enactment of statutory language is a proper factor for judicial consideration).[71] *Collective bargaining* was there briefly defined as: "Negotiation for the settlement of the terms (for example, as to wages) of a labor contract between an employer, or group of employers, on one side, and an *organized* body of workers on the other."[72] Consistent with that standard definition and the Twentieth Century Fund's longer description, it is evident that the statutory words "self-organization" and "labor organizations" in Section 7 are plainly phrases that were intended to be complimentary to the "bargain collectively" language in that same provision. Collective bargaining contemplated by the statute thus requires the *presence of* and *representation by* an *organized* group of employees, hence a *labor organization*.[73]

When the Supreme Court recognized that "the right of employees to self-organization and to select representatives of their own choosing for collective bargaining . . . is a *fundamental right*,"[74] it was correctly characterizing congressional intent, for (in addition to other supportive features in the statute) Congress had inserted the qualifying word "own" to emphasize this right of selection; it was therefore employing straightforward language that requires no amplification for interpretation.[75] Its all-inclusiveness clearly means that this right applies to all covered employees unless limited by a specific statutory exception found elsewhere in the Act. Congress included only one such exception:[76] the single limitation in Sections 9(a) that imposes a bargaining representative not of the employees' own choosing *when and if* a majority of them in an appropriate unit designate an exclusive representative.

It may also be noted that the use of the *plural* "representatives" in Section 7, later repeated in Section 8(a)(5), suggests the possibility of more than one bargaining representative among the employees.[77]

The foregoing review patently demonstrates that Section 7 standing alone does not require that collective bargaining be confined to any special group of employees. As Professor Clyde Summers perceptively observes, "Section 7, by its terms, makes no distinction between a union with a majority and a union without a majority."[78] Indeed, it would be difficult to conceive of stronger or more precise language than that which Congress selected to convey the meaning that every worker covered by the Act has a fundamental right to engage in collective bargaining through a union of his or her own choosing; and the only limitation on that right is the unambiguous provision contained in Section 9(a) that yields the individual right to yet another democratic concept, that of *majority rule* when and if a majority of the employees in a bargaining unit decide to exercise that prerogative. Prior to that occurring, however, all employees who so choose—albeit a minority—retain the right to engage in collective bargaining for themselves through their own union, that is, through members-only collective bargaining.

Section 8(a)(1): The Universal Enforcer

The second relevant basic clause in the Act is *Section 8(a)(1)*. It is the instrument that provides the enforcement mechanism for the totality of employee rights contained in Section 7, for it broadly declares that it is an unfair labor practice for an employer

> to interfere with, restrain, or coerce employees in the exercise of the rights guaranteed in section 7. . . .

The Labor Board has traditionally and consistently recognized the all-inclusive scope of this clause by automatically including a Section 8(a)(1) allegation whenever a violation of any other Section 8(a) unfair labor practice is found or alleged.[79] Section 8(a)(1), however, independently provides express protection against an employer's interference with or restraint of the employees' "right . . . to bargain collectively through representatives of their own choosing," thus including for enforcement purposes the bargaining rights of minority unions, subject only to the limitation applicable when and if a majority union is selected pursuant to Section 9(a).

As we noted in Chapter 3, the Senate and House committees reporting on the final version of the Wagner bill expressly emphasized that the four unfair-labor-practice provisions following Section 8(1)—including Section 8(5), the duty-to-bargain provision—imposed no limitations or restrictions on the guarantees contained in Section 8(1).[80] Section 8(a)(1)—with or without Section 8(a)(5)[81]—therefore provides full authority for enforcement of an employer's duty to bargain with a minority union for a members-only collective agreement whenever and wherever there is no exclusive majority representative. The implications of this concept are treated more extensively later in this chapter.

Section 9(a): Majoritarian Exclusivity for Mature Collective Bargaining

The third basic clause relating to collective bargaining is *Section 9(a)*. This is the provision in the *representation procedures* (i.e., "R" case) portion of the statute—as distinguished from the *rights and unfair labor practices* (i.e., "C" case) portion contained in Sections 7 and 8—that defines the majoritarian and exclusivity standard applicable to fully established collective bargaining. It provides, in pertinent part, that

> Representatives designated or selected for the purposes of collective bargaining by the majority of the employees in a unit appropriate for such pur-

poses, shall be the exclusive representatives of all the employees in such unit for the purposes of collective bargaining in respect to rates of pay, wages, hours of employment, or other conditions of employment. . . .

As the historical materials in Chapter 3 demonstrate, this clause is the single and key provision of the Wagner Act that was expressly designed to establish what Congress deemed to be the ideal form of mature collective bargaining, to wit: majority and exclusive representation and bargaining covering all employees in an appropriate bargaining unit. However, as we have often noted, this clearly stated limitation on the Section 7 right of all employees "to bargain collectively through representatives of their own choosing" applies only where and after a majority of the employees in an appropriate bargaining unit have chosen an exclusive representative. Professor Summers accurately explains the interaction of Sections 7, 8(a)(1), and 9(a) as follows:

> Section 7 states as one of employees' basic rights, the right "to bargain through representatives of their own choosing." It is not stated as a qualified right to bargain through a representative of the majority's choosing but of "their own" choosing. This is, of course, qualified by section 9(a), but that qualification, by its terms, applies only when there is a "representative selected by a majority." The employer's refusal to meet and deal with a non-majority union would "interfere" with its members' exercise of this section 7 right "to bargain through representatives of their own choosing," contrary to Section 8(a)(1).[82]

Accordingly, unless and until majority representation is established, collective bargaining rights contained in Sections 7 and 8(a)(1), and logically also in Section 8(a)(5),[83] remain applicable. On the other hand, such rights would not exist if there were any provision in the Act that limited collective bargaining to Section 9(a) majority unions only.[84] Conventional wisdom assumes that such a provision exists, but it is the phantom provision that we have yet to find.

Although the foregoing brief examination of the text of Section 9(a) would seem to establish sufficiently that it is not the phantom provision, additional analysis of that clause is nevertheless appropriate to dispel any doubt as to its meaning. First, it should be noted that the text of Section 9(a) does not address in any manner the subject of bargaining *prior* to designation of a majority representative. It addresses only the question of majority rule once it has been established. Furthermore, as we have observed in Chapter 3 and as Professor Summers accurately concludes, the "history of the majority rule principle shows that its purpose was not to limit the ability of a non-majority union to represent its own members, but to protect a majority union's ability to bargain collectively."[85] Section 9(a) is simply the provision that establishes the principle of exclusive majority rule, and during congressional debates it was the only provision in the bill cited with reference to that principle.[86] As our review of legislative history has revealed, the essence of that debate concerned only majority versus plurality representation. The proponents of the Wagner bill were concerned about the problem posed by competing unions, especially when one of those unions was a company union. The record of union elections under Section 7(a) of the NIRA had exposed the serious problem of multiple unionism that frequently followed the election of a majority representative, which is what Wagner was seeking to avoid.[87] As we have learned, the congressional debate was not about representation by a minority union *prior* to the selection of a majority representative; it was about representation *after* an election—about whether the losing minority union could continue to bargain on behalf of its own members.[88] It was Wagner's view and that of others who supported his 1935 bill, S. 1958, that if plural representation were allowed following the selection of a majority union an employer could play off one group against the other, thereby reducing substantially the bargaining power of the majority union. Requiring the majority union to represent all employees in a bargaining unit, including nonconsenting employees, was therefore deemed the most appropriate means to produce more effective bargaining. But there was nothing in the legislative history to suggest that majority employees who prefer not to be represented by a union could deprive a minority who desire such representation of their right to bargain "through representatives of their own choosing." And there was certainly nothing to suggest that when a minority group of employees choose to join a union prior to an election and seek to bargain for their union members only, that they can be deprived of their Section 7 right to engage in such bargaining. It might seem that with such repetition I am beating a dead horse with an overemphasis on the obviously limited scope of Section 9(a). This is true, but I do so in order to impress on the reader the critical factor that it was Section 9(a)—not Section 8(5)—that provided the totality of congressional consideration of the majoritarianism issue prior to passage of the Act.

Section 8(a)(5): The Afterthought Enforcer

In our search for the phantom provision, Section 8(a)(5)—the last unfair-labor-practice subsection following Section 8(a)(1)—looms as the most logical candidate for examination because at first glance this clause might appear to concern only a duty to bargain with a majority representative selected in accordance with Section 9(a). Furthermore, Section 8(a)(5) is the weak straw that proponents of current conventional wisdom are most likely to grasp in their effort to defend the status quo. On careful reading, however, it is soon evident that this provision does not prohibit minority-union bargaining where there is no currently designated majority union, and this reading coincides with the intent shown by its legislative history. As we have seen in Chapter 3, the authors of the Act made a positive and successful effort to carefully craft language that would avoid prohibiting the duty to bargain with a minority union prior to establishment of Section 9(a) representation.[89]

Section 8(a)(5) is simply the supplemental provision that establishes that it is an unfair labor practice for an employer, in the language of the provision,

> to refuse to bargain collectively with the representatives of his employees, subject to the provisions of section 9(a).

On its face, that text merely reinforces the duty to bargain contained in Sections 7 and 8(a)(1). Thus it is only an enforcer of Section 7 rights, not a limiter of those rights. Although this should be apparent from the plain language of the text, we also know from both the Senate and House committee reports on the final Wagner bill and the absence of any debate when the provision was added, that this nonlimiting feature was specifically what Congress intended.[90] That nonlimiting qualification is particularly significant for this subsection, for Senator Wagner had intentionally omitted Section 8(5) when he introduced S. 1958 in 1935.[91] As we have observed in Chapter 3, it was Wagner's view that the employer's duty to bargain collectively was adequately covered by Sections 7 and 8(1), which implicitly—yet indisputably—established that an employer's failure to meet and bargain would constitute a Section 8(1) *interference* with the employees' right to bargain collectively through their chosen representatives. Wagner's testimony to that effect was unequivocal.[92] We have also learned that the late addition of Section 8(5) was only an afterthought by Wagner. Francis Biddle had lobbied persistently for its inclusion, and more than two months after the original bill was introduced it was finally added in committee with Senator Wagner's acquiescence.[93] This fifth subsection, however, was only intended to enhance the bargaining obligation, not to limit it. But even if Section 8(5) had been included in the original bill, there is nothing in its language that absolves an employer from its duty to bargain with a minority union prior to the designation of a majority union.

Because the exclusivity clause in Section 9(a) was intended to avoid fragmentation of collective bargaining where two or more unions were seeking or claiming representation, that subsection was properly referenced in Section 8(5). The phrase "subject to the provisions of section 9(a)"—with its plural designation of "provisions"—was therefore inserted to indicate the statutory provisions, i.e., *conditions,* that would apply if and when bargaining was conducted by a majority union as the employees' exclusive representative. Section 9(a) contains several such conditions. The *first* and most relevant is that once a majority of the employees in an appropriate unit select or designate their representative—whether by election or other satisfactory means—the employer thereafter has no duty to bargain with any other employee representative; indeed the employer is prohibited from such bargaining. This was the Act's codification of the rule of the *Houde*[94] case under Section 7(a) of the NIRA, which, as we know, did not affect the duty to bargain in workplaces where there was no majority representative. The inclusion of the "subject to" phrase was thus necessary to avoid the appearance of a conflict with that section if a minority union should seek to bargain after a majority union had already been selected. The *second* bargaining condition in Section 9(a) is applicable to a representative claiming majority status, to wit, the requirement of a "unit appropriate" for bargaining. The *third* condition (or group of conditions) is the delineation of mandatory subjects of collective bargaining. And the *fourth* is a *proviso* relating to the adjustment of certain types of grievances.[95]

The foregoing rationale plainly expresses the intent of the phrase in question, and it is consistent with the meaning derived from ordinary English usage of the word combination "subject to." Indeed, the comma reinforces that meaning. To equate this combination, following a comma, with the phrase "in accordance with" without a comma—as some status-quo adherents might wish to do—would be a patently erroneous reading. Even if there were no comma, attributing a narrower meaning (i.e., requiring bargaining *only* with a majority representative) would be awkward and implausible (and certainly contrary to legislative history); with the comma, such a meaning is impossible. As Professor William Eskridge notes regarding a familiar canon of statutory construction, "Congress is presumed to follow accepted punctuation standards, so the placement of commas and other punctuation is assumed to be meaningful."[96] Thus, according to its ordinary meaning, the phrase "subject to the provisions of section 9(a)" simply means that the *conditions* of Section 9(a) were intended to be applicable—no more and no less. Accordingly, in workplaces where there is no "designated or selected" majority representative, Section 9(a) is not applicable. Had Congress intended to exclude minority unions entirely from the protection of Section 8(5), thereby confining the bargaining duty to majority unions only, it could have—and most likely would have—easily done so by saying so. The Senate committee, hence the Congress, had that opportunity but deliberately rejected it.

As we have learned in our review of the early drafts of the NLRA bill in Chapter 3, the authors of the Wagner Act were keenly aware of the minority-union bargaining issue. Experimenting with several drafts, they consciously chose language that would assure that the duty to bargain with a majority union would not exclude the duty to bargain with a minority union prior to the establishment of majority representation. Recall that Francis Biddle had drafted a rejected version of Section 8(5) that would have excluded minority unions entirely from the protection of that provision.[97] I remind the reader of that rejected language, for it would have made it an unfair labor practice for an employer

> to refuse to bargain collectively with employees through their representatives, *chosen as provided in Section 9(a).*[98]

Here then is proof positive—indeed a "smoking gun"—revealing that if the authors, including the Senate committee that reported the bill, had desired to limit the bargaining duty under Section 8(5) to majority unions only, they were fully aware of the precise language to use and how to use it.[99] Legislative history thus confirms that the draftsmen of the Act knowingly decided not to do so, preferring instead to leave untouched the unequivocal bargaining duty contained in Section 7—collective bargaining "through representatives of their own choosing"—which could not be interfered with or restrained by an employer without violating Section 8(1) and which with the addition of Section 8(5) was now reinforced by a separate duty-to-bargain unfair-labor-practice subsection. This bargaining duty remains fully applicable to any legitimate minority union until such time as the employees in an appropriate bargaining unit select a majority representative pursuant to Section 9(a).

Although that conclusion has been long forgotten, immediately after passage of the Act an observation to that effect was made by an astute observer writing in the *George Washington Law Review.*[100] In 1936, E. G. Latham recognized that a "reasonable construction" of Sections 8(5) and 9(a) means that

> where representatives have been designated by *"proper majorities"* the employer is under a duty to bargain collectively with such representatives and with no others in the unit. [However] the employer may be bound to bargain with minority groups until such *"proper majorities"* have been selected. In such a case, since Section 9(a) will have no application, the bargaining authority of representatives designated by minority groups will be limited to those employees who *voted for them.*[101]

Obviously that conclusion applies equally to employees who are *members* of "minority groups," for membership affiliation rather than voting is more likely to be the basis of selection in workplaces where the NLRB is not conducting an election—a phenomenon that is more apparent in hindsight today than in Latham's time. Citing the Senate committee report, Latham concluded that "*[i]t is reasonable to suppose that where there is no majority organization at all . . . minority rights are . . . reserved.*[102]

Patently, Section 8(5) is not the phantom provision. It was simply intended to reinforce the duty to bargain with representatives of the employees' "own *choosing*"; it was not intended to limit that duty beyond the limits contained in Section 9(a).

The Duty to Bargain under Section 8(a)(1) — An Ace in the Hole

In the unlikely event (unlikely in my view because of the plain meaning of the text and strong legislative history) that Section 8(a)(5) were to be judicially interpreted as a bargaining requirement applicable *only* to representatives that achieve majority status under Section 9(a), such a construction would nevertheless have no effect on an employer's duty to bargain with a minority union where there is no designated majority representative. That is so because even if the unfair labor practice defined in Section 8(a)(5) were to be thus narrowly construed to compel an employer to *bargain only with a majority union under Section 9(a) conditions,* the statute nowhere prohibits other collective bargaining required by Section 8(a)(1). By its own terms, Section 9(a) cannot be activated until a majority representative is "designated or selected," and there is nothing in 8(a)(5)—or any other provision—that confines bargaining solely to the requirements of 9(a). The thrust of 9(a) is on the "exclusive" nature of representation *when and if* majority status is established. Until that condition occurs, however, this exclusivity feature is inactive. Section 8(a)(1), on the other hand, remains fully active, thus requiring—wholly apart from Section 8(a)(5)—an employer to bargain with a minority union where one exists for employees who are its members, although not for other employees.

As was intended, Section 8(a)(1) has always played an important role during preliminary stages of union organizing that typically precede mature majority-based collective bargaining. Accordingly—not being otherwise limited by any statutory provision—in workplaces where there is no Section 9(a) majority representative, employees are entitled to bargain collectively through representatives of their own choosing, for that is what Section 7 guarantees and what Section 8(a)(1) enforces. Therefore, in the unforeseen event of a restrictive judicial reading of Section 8(a)(5) supporting the conventional-wisdom construction of the Act, an independent right to engage in minority-union bargaining for members only would still be enforceable as *residual coverage* under Sections 7 and 8(a)(1)—a type of coverage that is commonplace for other aspects of Section 7 law.

The best-known examples of such residual coverage concern employee discharges and suspensions that violate Section 8(a)(1) but not Section 8(a)(3). Although Section 8(a)(3)[103] is the primary unfair-labor-practice provision designed and applied to protect workers from unlawful discharges and other denials of "terms and conditions of employment," it is not the only unfair-labor-practice provision employed for that purpose. Section 8(a)(1) *independently* protects employees from such conduct, particularly including discharges and suspensions that do not violate Section 8(a)(3) but nevertheless violate Section 7. The Labor Board, from its earliest days, and with full support from the Supreme Court,[104] has relied on the broader language of Section 7 to protect employees from denial of "term or tenure" of employment in violation of that section, even though the employer's action may not have involved "discrimination . . . to encourage or discourage membership in any labor organization" in violation of Section 8(a)(3). For example, that residual aspect of Section 8(a)(1) has often been used to obtain reinstatement and back pay for employees who were terminated or suspended for engaging in protected concerted activity preliminary to formal union organizing even where there is no discriminatory motive.[105] Examples of such cases are legion.[106] No one would argue that because Section 8(a)(3) covers most of the discharges and suspensions directly relating to union activity that Congress thereby intended to confine application of the Act only to such conduct specifically covered by that subsection. Such confinement to the limits of the textual definition of an 8(a)(3) unfair labor practice—as would also be true regarding the limits of a Section 8(a)(5) violation—would be unthinkable, for it would eviscerate the intended broad coverage of Section 7.

As was demonstrated in Chapter 3, the congressional committee reports on the final drafts of the Wagner bill made clear why certain conduct was redundantly covered by separate inclusion in the four unfair-labor-practice subsections following Section 8(1). In the words of the Senate report, it was "to spell out with particularity some of the practices that have been most prevalent and most troublesome,"[107] and in the House report it was "to amplify and state more specifically certain types of interference and restraint that experience has proved require such amplification and specification."[108] Both reports, however, emphasized the primacy of Section 8(1), with the House report stating that the other four subsection "are not intended to limit in any way the interpretation of the general provisions of subsection (1)"[109] and the Senate report stating that the last four subsections "are designed not to impose limitations or restrictions upon the general guarantees of the first. . . ."[110] I cannot imagine any stronger or more explicit indication of legislative intent concerning the nonlimiting relationship of the four subsidiary subsections to the general provisions of the first subsection, Section 8(a)(1).[111] Consequently, regardless of how Section 8(a)(5) might be interpreted, the independent and residual duty to bargain under Section 7, fully enforceable under Section 8(a)(1), remains intact. Accordingly, however Sections 8(a)(1), 8(a)(5), and 9(a) are construed, an employer is under a statutory obligation to bargain with a minority union for members-only representation in any workplace where there is no designated majority representative in an appropriate bargaining unit.

Wrapping Up: The Natural Meaning Is the Meaning

Based on language of the Act standing alone, it should now be apparent that in workplaces where employees have not yet selected a majority representative, the statutory text does not support an exclusion of an employer's duty to engage in good-faith collective bargaining with a minority union that seeks to bargain only on behalf of its employee members. Such a duty exists and is enforceable. Both legislative history and text leave no doubt as to this conclusion, and—as we observe in later chapters—constitutional and international-law considerations also mandate this reading. Related case law already points in that direction and, as we shall see in Chapter 9, there is no case law to the contrary. Although conventional wisdom may suggest that the only bargaining duty countenanced by the Act is bargaining with a majority union in an appropriate unit, such conventional wisdom, like the emperor, has no clothes, and the provision in the Act on which it is supposedly based does not exist—it is indeed a phantom.

I therefore conclude—notwithstanding the passage of time and widespread habituation to conventional wisdom—that the National Labor Relations Act is now ripe for enforcement that will protect the rights of minority-union employees to engage in effective collective bargaining. There is no credible basis for the Board or the courts to hold otherwise. Latter-day custom and practice, unsupported by decisional authority, do not outweigh plain statutory meaning that is substantiated by legislative history and the more relevant custom and practice that prevailed immediately following enactment. As then Justice William H. Rehnquist wrote in *Griffin v. Oceanic Contractors*,[112] "[t]he words chosen by Congress, given their plain meaning, leave no room for the exercise of discretion. . . . Our task is to give effect to the will of Congress, and where its will has been expressed in reasonably plain terms, 'that language must ordinarily be regarded as conclusive.'"[113] Furthermore, it cannot be argued that the prevailing practice under latter-day conventional wisdom is working, for the congressional declaration asserting that "collective bargaining" is the "policy of the United States" is obviously not being achieved.[114] The law is indeed ready for long-overdue administrative and/or judicial clarification.

6 *The Constitutional Dimension*

With Deference to *Catholic Bishop, DeBartolo,* and *Beck*

As I have demonstrated in the earlier chapters, the National Labor Relations Act guarantees minority labor unions the right to engage in collective bargaining in all workplaces under NLRB jurisdiction where the employees are not currently represented by a majority union pursuant to Section 9(a). And as I demonstrate later in Chapter 8, that interpretation is consistent with United States obligations under international law, to wit, the Covenant on Civil and Political Rights, which this country ratified in 1992, and the *ILO Declaration on Workers Rights,*[1] to which the U.S. became a party in 1998.[2] This chapter presents yet another consideration: the impact of the U.S. Constitution on the interpretation of the NLRA with regard to minority union bargaining. Although legal analysis based on the statute alone is strong and persuasive, I would be remiss if I were to ignore the additional authority that the Constitution brings to this issue. I am well aware, however, that during the early Wagner Act years such an approach would have been neither apparent not appropriate, for the Supreme Court had not yet articulated a broadly-based right of expressive association under the First Amendment. But today, in view of the Court's subsequent development of a substantial body of applicable freedom-of-association jurisprudence, it is entirely proper to examine this question in light of the late twentieth-century cases that bear directly on this issue.

Before analyzing those cases, however, I hasten to announce that I do not contend that the Constitution guarantees collective bargaining as such. But the right of association as defined by the Court in a series of landmark decisions does have a perceptible impact on the construction of the NLRA, especially concerning the right of workers to join labor-union associations of their choice and the reciprocal role of the federal government regarding the activities of such associations, including collective bargaining and other forms of concerted activity. That impact is essentially indirect, however, because of the long-established doctrine expressed in *Crowell v. Benson*,[3] where the Court asserted that

> When the validity of an act of Congress is drawn into question, and even if a serious doubt of constitutionality is raised, it is a cardinal principle that this Court will first ascertain whether a construction of the statute is fairly possible by which the question may be avoided.[4]

The application of that doctrine would certainly not be new to the NLRA, for the Supreme Court employed it in three landmark cases, *Catholic Bishop*,[5] *DeBartolo*,[6] and *Beck*.[7]

What follows in this chapter is an explication of the proposition that if the Act were construed to deny employees the right to engage in collective bargaining because their union represented less than a majority of the bargaining-unit employees where there is no majority/exclusive union to represent them, such denial would raise—at the very least—a serious question of constitutionality. Although the analyses that follow demonstrate, in my opinion, that such a construction would be unconstitutional, under *Crowell v. Benson* and its progeny a finding of unconstitutionality would not necessarily follow. As the Court expressed that doctrine in *DeBartolo*, "where an otherwise acceptable construction of a statute would raise serious constitutional problems, the Court will construe the statute to avoid such problems unless such construction is plainly contrary to the intent of Congress."[8] As both the statutory and legislative records have revealed, the minority-union rights asserted herein are plainly in accordance with the intent of Congress, certainly not contrary to that intent. Accordingly, the courts could easily declare such rights to be protected by the statute and thereby avoid making a constitutional determination. It is my view, however, that if the Act were to be interpreted today as not requiring an employer to bargain with a minority union regarding its employee members where no majority representative has been selected in accordance with Section 9(a), such a construction would violate the freedom of association guaranteed by the First Amendment. The bases for my conclusion are contained in the following discussion.

First Amendment Freedom of Association: An Introduction

First Amendment freedom of association, which is an amalgam of several First Amendment freedoms, particularly speech, assembly, and petition, is especially important to the democratic process. As Alexis de Tocqueville wisely observed,

> The most natural privilege of man, next to the right of acting for himself, is that of combining his exertions with those of his fellow creatures and of acting in common with them. The right of association therefore appears to

me almost as inalienable in its nature as the right of personal liberty. No legislator can attack it without impairing the foundations of society.[9]

Citing that observation, Justice John Paul Stevens, writing in *NAACP v. Claiborne Hardware*[10] in which the Court found a consumers' boycott to be protected freedom of association, emphasized that "one of the foundations of our society is the right of individuals to combine with other persons in pursuit of a common goal by lawful means."[11] This is what workers do when they organize and join a labor union. The unfettered right to so organize—which, as we shall see, is protected by the First Amendment—was a democratic goal expressly intended to be protected also by the NLRA. Not only does Section 7 spell out "the right to self-organization," the Act's statement of policy couples "protecting the exercise by workers of full freedom of association [and] self-organization" with the process of "collective bargaining."[12]

Accordingly, this book is about the right of association, an essential freedom in a democratic environment. It specifically concerns the right of *workers* to associate, which is a right about which American jurisprudence has long conferred special status. The rationality in that status, however, did not come easily. It was achieved only after more than a century of harsh judicial repression of the labor movement, repression that used (aside from the legal recognition of slavery[13]) the law of criminal conspiracy, the concept of restraint of trade, and the heavy hand of the labor injunction.[14] Early in the twentieth century, however, a perceptible change in the public's attitude toward organized labor occurred—a change that was first reflected in congressional legislation, beginning most conspicuously with the Clayton Act of 1914. That statute declared that "the labor of a human being is not a commodity or article of commerce" and that labor organizations "instituted for the purpose of mutual help" shall not be "construed to be illegal combinations or conspiracies in restraint of trade."[16]

The judiciary eventually followed suit in its labor-related cases, although with significant wavering over a period of many years.[17] But In four notable cases the Supreme Court supplied strong judicial recognition of the workers' right of association. In the first case, *American Steel Foundries v. Tri-City Central Trades Council,*[18] Chief Justice William Howard Taft emphasized that a labor union "was essential to give laborers an opportunity to deal on equality with their employer."[19] And he spelled out the *raison d'être* for employees associating in unions: "They united to exert influence upon [the employer and] to induce him to make better terms with them."[20] Although the Court had not yet articulated that this right of association was protected by the First Amendment, Taft's opinion appeared to be an expression of such a fundamental right. The Court's next declaration of the workers' right of association came again from the Chief Justice, this time from Chief Justice Hughes, who wrote in the *T. & N. O.* case[21] that "[i]t has long been recognized that employees are entitled to organize for the purpose of securing the redress of grievances and to promote agreements with employers relating to rates of pay and conditions of work."[22] Two years later, Congress again contributed with passage of the Norris-LaGuardia Act,[23] which stressed the necessity of a worker having "full freedom of association, self-organization, and designation of representatives of his own choosing, to negotiate the terms and conditions of his employment."[24] That statute effectively outlawed the use of labor injunctions and supplied the impetus for the Court's subsequent reaffirmation and clarification of the Clayton Act in the *Hutcheson* case,[25] the third of these bellwether decisions, which I expand upon later.[26] And, as we have observed and studied in earlier chapters, Congress in 1935 replicated those same organizational rights in the Wagner Act; and in 1937, in *Jones & Laughlin*,[27] the fourth case here noted, the Court characterized "the right of employees to self-organization and to select representatives of their own choosing [as] a *fundamental* right."[28]

It is obvious today that what Congress and the Supreme Court were conveying in those early statements about workers' organizational rights was but a manifestation of the freedom of expressive association that the Court later, in another series of cases beginning in 1958, confirmed to be protected by the First Amendment.[29] By 1984, this "communal dimension"[30] of individual human rights was already well established when Justice Brennan in *Roberts v. United States Jaycees*[31] provided the following summary description of this nonspecifically worded[32] First Amendment freedom, which became known as freedom of *expressive* association:

> the Court has recognized a right to associate for the purpose of engaging in those activities protected by the First-Amendment—speech, assembly, petition for the redress of grievances, and the exercise of religion. The Constitution guarantees *freedom of association* of this kind as an indispensable means of preserving other individual liberties.[33]

It is my position that First Amendment freedom of association would be violated if the Act were construed to permit employers legally to refuse to bargain with unions for their employee-members when such membership does not constitute a majority in an NLRB-designated appropriate bargaining unit. This is so because such an interpretation and its consequences would entail *state action*[34] that seriously impairs the employees' freedom of association without furthering any compelling governmental interest. Such state action would be substantial, for it would be based on each of three recognized Supreme Court tests, to wit, *indirect state action*, the *Lugar*[35] two-part test of state action, and *direct state action*. Applications of these tests are discussed in the next three sections of this chapter. The absence of any compelling governmental interest is treated in the section that follows, and the final section concludes with the resulting avoidance of the constitutional issue.

Indirect State Action

The Supreme Court's first overt formulation of the First Amendment right of freedom of association was contained in *NAACP v. Alabama,*[36] which together with another National Association for the Advancement of Colored People (NAACP) case, *Bates v. City of Little Rock,*[37] exemplifies *indirect* state action that is remarkably parallel to the indirect state action that would be involved if the NLRA were misconstrued to exempt employers from a duty to bargain with a minority union where there is currently no majority union.

Both the *Alabama* and *Little Rock* cases concerned governmental requirements of public identification of NAACP members during the early years of the civil rights movement. In the *Alabama* case it was claimed that the membership lists were required for disclosure in litigation instituted by the state's attorney general regarding the association's alleged status as an out-of-state corporation, and in the *Little Rock* case the membership information was sought pursuant to ordinances of two cities concerning identical license-tax requirements. In the former case, the Court began its consideration of the issue by observing that "[i]t is beyond debate that the freedom to engage in association for the advancement of beliefs and ideas is an inseparable aspect of the 'liberty' assured by the Due Process Clause of the Fourteenth Amendment, which embraces First-Amendment freedom of speech."[38] In the *Little Rock* case, the Court added that the framers of the Constitution considered peaceable assembly to lie at the foundation of government and that it was beyond dispute that the First Amendment protected freedom of association for the purpose of advancing ideas and airing grievances. In both cases the Court held that requiring disclosure of members' identification was violative of the members' freedom of association because, as it pointed out in the *Alabama* case, "it may induce members to withdraw from the Association and dissuade others from joining it."[39] And in the *Little Rock* case it specifically noted that, in addition to evidence that public identification of members had been followed by fear of harassment and threats of bodily harm,

> [t]here was also evidence that fear of community hostility and economic reprisals that would follow public disclosure of membership lists had discouraged new members from joining the organization and induced former members to withdraw. This repressive effect, while in part the result of private attitudes and pressures, was brought to bear only after the exercise of governmental power had threatened to force disclosure of the members' names.[40]

Indeed, the governmental bodies in both cases had argued that the deterrent effects had resulted from private community pressures rather than from state action. The Court rejected that argument, explaining that "[t]he crucial factor is the interplay of governmental and private action, for it is only after the initial exertion of state power represented by the production order that private action takes hold."[41] That appraisal of *indirect state action* closely resembles the indirect state action that would be involved if employers were exempted by the NLRA from the bargaining obligation at issue herein. The deterrent effect of the forced disclosure of NAACP membership thus sets the stage for our examination of the indirect state action that would occur if an employer, pursuant to governmental authority, refused to bargain with a less-than-majority union. If the Act granted such an exemption, the resulting *chilling effect*[42] on the employees' desire to join a union, although immediately attributable to the employer's private conduct, would have been engendered by governmental action. Such action would deny employees their freedom of association protected by the First Amendment.

As the foregoing NAACP cases illustrate, First Amendment restraint fully applies to indirect state action. In fact, the Supreme Court has long recognized the role of such indirect action in the context of labor legislation. With reference to the potentially restraining effect that union-shop agreements have on the exercise of free speech by dissident employees, the Court asserted in *Abood v. Detroit Board of Education*[43] that the constitutional scrutiny of potential deprivation of First Amendment freedom, notwithstanding that it is accomplished by the private action of a union, "was not watered down because the union shop agreement operated less directly than" express governmental action. It therefore quoted with approval from Justice Douglas's concurrence in *Machinists v. Street*[44] that "since neither Congress nor the state legislatures can abridge [First Amendment] rights, they cannot grant the power to private groups to abridge them. As I read the First Amendment, it forbids any abridgement by government whether directly or indirectly."[45]

In like manner, if the NLRA confined the statutory bargaining obligation to majority unions only, such a limitation would have an appreciable chilling effect on union organizing. Just as the Supreme Court found that disclosing the identity of NAACP members would dissuade potential members from joining that association and induce existing members to withdraw, the same effect would be achieved when employers condition their bargaining with a union on the prior establishment of majority status. Nor is this deterrent effect based on speculation, for it is the prevailing de facto situation throughout the country, for almost all the parties involved in employee relations already believe that such limitation is required by law. This condition demonstrably results in nonunion employees refraining from joining any union that cannot yet engage in collective bargaining, for to do so would expose them to economic retaliation by their employer. This is like the "fear of community hostility and economic reprisals" that the Court described in *Bates v. Little Rock.*

Fear of economic reprisals in the typical American workplace is immediate and serious, with the reprisals ranging from the withholding of wage increases or promotions to the finality of discharge. The public record establishes that in companies where the employer's obligation to bargain does not occur until the union wins an election, there is a high probability that many employees whose union sympathies become known to the employer will be discharged or be subjected to other employment discrimination in order to discourage union representation.[46] As a result, employees are denied a critical element in the associational process—the right to join and form their labor organization at a time of their own choosing. As the law presently functions de facto (although not de jure), employees are effectively prevented from becoming members of a labor organization until after that organization proves that it represents more than 50 percent of the employees, at which time—in most cases—none of the employees will yet be members of the organization. This is truly a Catch-22 situation for employees trying to organize a union association. Freedom of association is thus stood on its head, for a labor association's effective right to exist must first be established before workers can even join that association.

If Congress permitted private employers to refuse to meet and deal with less-than-majority associations of employees that seek to represent only their members, the federal government would be indirectly—but effectively—inhibiting the initial establishment and natural growth of such associations. The government would thus be dictating the selection of the individuals who are allowed to associate as members of the group. As the Supreme Court stated in *Boy Scouts of America v. Dale,*[47] "actions that may unconstitutionally burden this freedom [of association] may take many forms, one of which is 'intrusion into the internal structure or affairs of an association' like a regulation that forces the group to accept members it does not desire."[48] The same would be true if the government, either directly or indirectly, forced the group to exclude members that it does desire.

Clearly, under the test of *indirect state action,* minority-union bargaining is entitled to constitutional protection under the First Amendment.

The *Lugar* Two-Part Test

Assessing the denial of collective bargaining rights to minority-union employees pursuant to the Supreme Court's *two-part* approach in *Lugar v. Edmonton Oil Co., Inc.,*[49] also yields a finding of state action that deprives employees of their First Amendment freedom of association. Here is the clearly worded two-part standard the Court formulated in *Lugar* to identify the critical elements that substantiate a deprivation of federal or constitutional rights:

> Our cases have . . . insisted that the conduct allegedly causing the deprivation of a federal right be fairly attributable to the State. These cases reflect *a two-part approach* to this question of "fair attribution." *First, the deprivation must be caused by the exercise of some right or privilege created by the state* or by a rule or conduct imposed by the State or a person for whom the state is responsible. . . . *Second, the party charged with the deprivation must be a person who may fairly be said to be a state actor. This may be because he* is a state official, because he has acted together with or *has obtained significant aid from state officials,* or because his conduct is otherwise chargeable to the State.[50]

Lugar involved a simple fact situation. Creditors, pursuant to a state statute, had attached a debtor's property without notice or hearing, and a writ of attachment was written by the county clerk and executed by the sheriff. Justice Byron R. White, writing for the Court's majority, posed the question of "whether [the creditors], who are private parties, may be appropriately characterized as 'state actors,'"[51] to which his opinion responded: "While private misuse of a state statute does not describe conduct that can be attributed to the State, *the procedural scheme created by the statute obviously is the product of state action.*"[52] Accordingly, the Court ruled that the "Court of Appeals erred in holding that in this context 'joint participation' required something more than invoking the aid of state officials to take advantage of state-created attachment procedures."[53] It held that such statutory procedures were "sufficient when the state has created a system whereby state officials will attach property on the ex parte application of one party to a private dispute."[54]

Applying the *Lugar* two-part test to the minority-bargaining issue herein produces the following typical scenario. An employer, pursuant to the latter-day conventional-wisdom reading of the statute, is granted the *privilege* of refusing to bargain with employees who are members of a minority union. Needless to say, with such ostensible encouragement from the governmentally created statute, the employer takes full advantage of that privilege. In accordance with that reading and also the *Linden Lumber* case,[55] it makes known that it will not recognize or bargain with any union unless it first proves its majority status through a governmentally conducted election. Operating on that same premise, plus fear of discharge or other retaliation should their pro-union sympathies become known to the employer, employees who would otherwise have joined this fledgling union, with expectations that it would soon bargain collectively, now refrain from doing so. They have thus been deprived of their right of association by their employer, who has now become a *state actor*, for it *"has obtained significant aid from state officials,"* to wit, from the statute and from the NLRB and its agents. Furthermore, if these pro-union employees—despite conventional wisdom—were to join the minority union and engage in a strike and a proscribed secondary boycott[56] to support their demand, the employer would probably lose no time in (1) permanently replacing them, (2) filing a Section 8(b)(4)[57] secondary-boycott charge with the NLRB, and (3) seeking injunctive relief under Section 10(l).[58] If the conventional reading of the statute were the correct reading, governmental agents would grant the requested relief and, when the replaced employees filed their Section 8(a)(3) charges to regain their jobs, the agency would summarily dismiss those charges.[59] As we know very well, the first part of this scenario actually happens today, for it is based on the *presumed* state of the law. Clearly, under the *Lugar* test, the workers' First Amendment freedom of association would be denied if the presumed state of the law were in fact the law. This minority-union scenario is infinitely stronger than were the facts in *Lugar,* where the creditors could have given notice to the debtor without prejudice to themselves, for a hearing actually did occur later; whereas in the minority-union scenario, the state-actor employer sees no reason to make a choice—the employer simply does what the law is deemed to permit and that inaction (i.e., not bargaining) has an undeniable chilling effect on the employees' freedom to join the association "of their own choosing."[60]

That depicted scenario is not materially different from the actual scenarios in *International Association of Machinists v. Street*[61] and *Communication Workers v. Beck,*[62] which construed the union-shop provisions of the RLA and the NLRA respectively. In both cases, the Supreme Court avoided finding violations of First Amendment freedom of speech and association by following the familiar axiom that "[f]ederal statutes are to be so construed as to avoid serious doubt of their constitutionality."[63] Employing the *Lugar* analysis, *Street* and *Beck* each involved unions—i.e., private parties—that exercised a *privilege* granted them by a federal statute to enter into union-shop contracts with agreeable employers. Had those statutes been construed to allow unions to exact funds from dissident employees to support political causes or for other non–collective bargaining purposes with which they disagreed, those unions would certainly have been *state actors* responsible for depriving the dissident employees of their First Amendment freedoms. *State-actor unions* under union-shop provisions are thus the equivalent, for First Amendment purposes, to *state-actor employers* under the NLRA's duty-to-bargain provisions. What is sauce for the goose is sauce for the gander.

Accordingly, under the *Lugar* two-part test, employers who refuse to bargain with a qualified minority union are state actors depriving employees of their freedom of association—unless such conduct is also barred by the NLRA, as it surely is.

Direct State Action

Direct state action[64] is state action—a truism indeed, but that is what Congress ordained with the passage of the NLRA. Prior to the existence of the Act and its predecessor statute, Section 7(a) of the NIRA,[65] the configuration of labor unions and collective bargaining in the United States was based on voluntarism and the exercise of economic power, although with an emerging yet largely undefined common law[66] that was coupled with hortatory but passive congressional declarations.[67] Since 1935, however, the bulk of the American labor-relations system (i.e., that which is subject to the jurisdiction of the NLRA) has been defined by that statute and compelled by its law. Although it might be argued that such *generalized* federal control is sufficient to implicate the presence of state action shaping the parameters and functions of labor unions vis-à-vis First Amendment freedom of association, I do not so contend here. Rather, I rely on *specific statutory provisions* which, as I shall explain, directly control the organization and operation of labor unions. I also show that if the bargaining provisions of the Act do not in fact require an employer to bargain in good faith with a less-than-majority union where no exclusive majority representative has been designated, it follows that these specific provisions will have directly deprived employees of their First Amendment right of association without a compelling governmental interest to justify such deprivation.[68]

Before examining these critical provisions, however, I call attention to three cases in which the Supreme Court has already enforced the First Amendment protection of some of the secondary, although nevertheless important, functions of labor unions when those functions were being infringed upon by direct state action. These functions were ruled on in *Trainmen v. Virginia,*[69] *Mineworkers v. Illinois State Bar Association,*[70] and *United Transportation Union v. State Bar of Michigan.*[71]

In *Trainmen,* the Court struck down an injunction restraining a union from recommending attorneys whom it considered honest and competent to represent its members and their families in claims arising from on-the-job injuries or deaths. Notwithstanding the state's allegation that such recommendations and related assistance constituted the unlawful practice of law and solicitation of legal business, the Court held that such actions were protected under the First Amendment's guarantee of freedom of association. It noted that the union's program was designed to shelter its members from hazards related to their securing proper legal representation under federal statutes that affected safety conditions and appropriate compensation for work-related injuries and deaths. Inasmuch as these were appropriate union functions, the Court concluded that

> It cannot be seriously doubted that the First-Amendment's guarantees of free speech, petition, and assembly give railroad workers the right to gather

together for the lawful purpose of helping and advising one another in asserting the rights Congress gave them in the Safety Appliance Act and the Federal Employers' Liability Act, statutory rights which would be vain and futile if the workers could not talk together freely as to the best course to follow.[72]

In the *Mineworkers* case, the Court struck down an injunction against the union's practice of employing a salaried attorney to represent members in workers' compensation claims. Here again, the Court found that First Amendment "rights to assemble peaceably and to petition for a redress of grievances"[73] applied, which it characterized as being "among the most precious of the liberties safeguarded by the Bill of Rights."[74]

In *United Transportation Union,* which concerned an injunction obtained by a state bar association to restrain a union from recommending selected attorneys to represent members and their families in Federal Employers' Liability Act cases, Justice Hugo L. Black recalled that in *Mine Workers* the Court had upheld "the First-Amendment principle that groups can unite to assert their legal rights as effectively and economically as practicable";[75] therefore, the Court once again "upheld the right of workers to act *collectively* to obtain affordable and effective legal representation."[76]

So much for direct state action that seeks to regulate a union's secondary functions. As the Supreme Court indicated long ago in the *Tri-City*[77] and *T. & N. O.*[78] cases, the essential purpose of a union is to deal on an equal basis with an employer in order to redress grievances and promote collective agreements relating to rates of pay and conditions of work[79]—in other words, to engage in collective bargaining. That is the union's primary function. Having received the foregoing First Amendment protections for some of its secondary functions, a union is entitled, a fortiori, to like protection for its primary function.

Recall from Chapter 4 that in the early years following passage of the Wagner Act minority-union members-only contracts were common. It was with reference to that environment that Chief Justice Hughes wrote in 1938, in *Consolidated Edison,*[80] that when the "Brotherhood"[81] negotiated collective bargaining contracts with Consolidated's companies it was doing what the "Act contemplates,"[82] and "in the absence of . . . an exclusive agency the employees represented by the Brotherhood, *even if they were a minority,* had the right to make their own choice."[83] The Court stated that "[t]he Brotherhood and its locals were entitled to solicit members and the employees were entitled to join. These rights . . . are of the very essence of the rights which the Labor Relations Act was passed to protect."[84] And noting the nature and role of such contracts, the Court explained that

The contracts do not claim for the Brotherhood exclusive representation of the companies' employees but only representatives of those who are its

members, and the continued operation of the contracts is necessarily subject to the provision of the law by which representatives of the employees
for the purpose of collective bargaining can be ascertained in case any question of "representation" should arise. §9.[85]

Thus, early in the Act's history, the Court showed its awareness of the role
of minority-union members-only bargaining. It commended the process and
declared it lawful. Such bargaining was widely viewed as an interim—although perfectly natural—stage in the development of mature collective bargaining. It was expected, however, that members-only bargaining would be
replaced eventually by exclusivity bargaining. Therefore, whenever a question concerning representation arose under Section 9, an NLRB election
would be available to determine the majority/exclusive bargaining agent.
The Court in *Consolidated Edison* thus correctly described the process of establishing a labor union's *primary* activity. Accordingly, if congressional action deprives workers of their right to engage in this early phase of the
associational process, their freedom of association will have been substantially impaired. And because there is no compelling state interest to justify
such impairment, the First Amendment will have been violated.

This brings us to an examination of *specific provisions* of the amended
Act that severely limit the right of labor-union associations to organize and
function naturally, especially during the initial and growth stages of their
development. Can Congress constitutionally mandate these associational
limitations without also providing the affected minority unions with a com-
pensatory statutory right, such as the right to engage in minority bargaining? That is the critical question before us. The provisions are the following:

1. The *secondary-boycott* provisions in Section 8(b)(4) and paragraphs
(A) and (B) of (ii),[86] with the exception of the phrases "threaten, coerce,
or restrain" in (ii) and "forcing and requiring" in said paragraphs (A) and
(B) to the extent that such phrases refer to elements of physical or violent
conduct (but not excluding references to voluntary withholding of work,
picketing, and other nonviolent activities that might produce economic
consequences).

2. Section 8(b)(7),[87] which limits and/or prohibits most *organizational*
and *recognitional picketing*, but only to the extent that such provision might
be deemed a limitation or prohibition on striking and/or picketing for members-only recognition and bargaining, as distinguished from exclusive recognition and bargaining.[88]

3. Section 10(l),[89] the *mandatory injunction* provision applicable to union
conduct where there is "reasonable cause to believe" that a union has violated a portion of Sections 8(b)(4) or 8(b)(7).

4. Section 303,[90] the *damage-suit* provision applicable to secondary-boycott violations under Section 8(b)(4).

As we have seen, the first section of this chapter concerns the presence of *indirect state action* and the second concerns the role of the employer as *state actor;* both state-action concepts are based on the *chilling effect* that an employer's absolute refusal to bargain has on a union's organizational progress. The four statutory provisions just cited, however, restrain freedom of association in a less subtle way—they *directly* and *deliberately* prohibit a union from engaging in natural and otherwise legal organizational activity, which raises another basic question. If the Act does not require an employer to bargain with a minority union, does that union retain its prestatutory right to compel bargaining through self-help? In other words, if a union cannot use the statute to enforce bargaining, is it otherwise exempt from restrictions imposed by that statute, i.e., by the four provisions? And can it attempt to force an employer to bargain as it commonly did prior to passage of the Act? According to the plain language of each of these four restrictions, the answer is *no* to both forms of the question. These statutory limitations are total and severe. Accordingly, this is not a condition in which an association on its own might function without dependence on the legal enforceability of the Act, for employers as a rule will not voluntarily bargain with a union unless forced to do so, either by law or by economic persuasion, as the history recounted in Chapters 1 and 2 confirms. The congressional sanctions contained in the aforesaid provisions, however, absolutely prevent a premajority union from pressuring an employer to engage in collective bargaining. Compare this state of affairs with what a minority union could legally do before the enactment of the restrictive provisions.

As we have learned in earlier chapters, prior to passage of the Wagner Act—in fact, also prior to Section 7(a) of the NIRA—majority status was irrelevant to a union's collective bargaining activity.[91] Preceding the enactment of Section 7(a)—and frequently after its passage—workers and their newly organized unions generally relied on their ability to strike as a means to achieve recognition and bargaining, and those strikes often included secondary activity. Section 7(a) provided a modicum of relief, however, for although unions were still forced to depend on strikes—actual or threatened—to achieve recognition, they at least now had the Blue Eagle imprimatur of federal law on their side, and an employer's refusal to bargain was deemed an unlawful interference with their right to "bargain collectively through representatives of their own choosing."[92] Majority status was not a requirement. That point is well illustrated by several cases discussed in Chapter 1.[93] To appreciate what a nonmajority union is required to give up under the foregoing restrictive amendments to the NLRA, we need only examine one of those cases, *Eagle Rubber Company,* and relate it to the Supreme Court's decision in *United States v. Hutcheson.*[94]

In *Eagle Rubber,* a minority union "comprising slightly less than half"[95] of the workforce requested recognition and a discussion about working conditions. The employer at first refused to grant recognition, but later, at the urging of the U.S. Conciliation Service, agreed to "confer" but not to recognize. Thereafter, several union adherents were laid off amid evidence of discrimination against union activity, but the company repeatedly refused to meet with the union representatives, all of which precipitated a strike. The National Labor Board held, as previously noted,[96] that the company's refusal to recognize the union constituted a violation of the NIRA. Clearly, in 1934 employees had a right to engage in collective bargaining through a minority union and to strike for recognition,[97] and they did so both before and after passage of the Wagner Act. Even after passage of that Act, however, unions in the real world knew that for such rights to be meaningful they had to be supported with the right to strike and picket.

In those early days, what would a strike for recognition entail? It might entail what the law allowed. The state of the law concerning strikes and picketing prior to the Taft-Hartley Act was best described by Justice Felix Frankfurter's opinion in *United States v. Hutcheson*.[98] Here are the essential facts of that case. At issue was the conduct of the Carpenters' union[99] in its picketing in St. Louis of both the Anheuser-Busch plant and the adjacent Gaylord Container Corporation. The Carpenters' primary dispute, which was with the construction companies that were then building additional facilities for Anheuser-Busch and Gaylord, concerned the assignment of work to members of the Machinists' union[100] instead of to members of the Carpenters' union. Although their dispute was with the construction contractors, the Carpenters picketed both Anheuser-Busch and Gaylord.[101] This was a textbook example of secondary picketing.

The case arose from an indictment that had charged a criminal conspiracy in violation of the Sherman Antitrust Act.[102] Relying on what it viewed to be the congressional reassertion and clarification in the Norris-LaGuardia Act[103] of the original intent of the Clayton Act,[104] the Supreme Court held the Carpenters' conduct not to be a violation of the Sherman Act.[105] Justice Frankfurter, the author of the Court's opinion, contributed this now-famous description of what constitutes lawful union conduct under the antitrust statutes:

> So long as a union acts in its self-interest and does not combine with non-labor groups, the licit and illicit under §20 are not to be distinguished by any judgment regarding the wisdom or unwisdom, the rightness or wrongness, the selfishness or unselfishness of the end of which the particular union activities are the means.[106]

Justice Frankfurter's *Hutcheson* decision thus provided judicial reiteration of the public policy about which Professor Frankfurter had written concerning the Norris-LaGuardia Act prior to its passage, in which he had stated that

> The whole bill flows logically from its avowed public policy. By particularization it aims to give that policy content and meaning. Thus, section

3[107] seeks to effectuate the *rights of free association* and to secure genuine representation in *collective bargaining.*[108]

Free association and *collective bargaining* were thus intended to be interwoven rights proclaimed by Congress through the Norris-LaGuardia Act, now reinforced by the Court's correlated reading of that Act together with the Clayton Act. Those rights clearly included secondary activity, for that was the conduct in which the Carpenters' union was engaged in *Hutcheson.*

Did Congress intend to narrow this permissible conduct with passage of the Wagner Act? Certainly not. As the *Hutcheson* case indicated in 1941, a union's right to engage in secondary picketing was alive and well and legally protected. And in 1942 the Second Circuit Court of Appeals, in an opinion by Judge Learned Hand, expressly confirmed that "a 'sympathy strike' or secondary boycott"[109] was conduct protected by the "mutual aid or protection" clause of Section 7 of the NLRA. All of that changed in 1947, however, when Congress enacted the Taft-Hartley Act, which, in three of the provisions previously noted, outlawed most forms of secondary picketing. Those provisions were made broadly applicable to all labor unions, whether they represented a majority, a minority, or no employees at all.[110] This extensive reach of Section 8(b)(4) was illustrated in *Longshoremen (ILA) v. Allied International,*[111] in which the Supreme Court held that a union's boycott of cargoes arriving from or destined for the Soviet Union violated that provision. On the other hand, in *Railroad Trainmen v. Terminal Co.,*[112] a case that concerned the interpretation of the Railway Labor Act, Justice John Marshall Harlan observed that the absence of a provision in the RLA like the NLRA's Section 8(b)(4) indicated that unions under the former statute could lawfully engage in secondary picketing, such as was involved in that case, for "[i]mplicit in the statutory scheme . . . is the ultimate right of [unions] to resort to *self-help.* . . ."[113]

The natural purpose of a labor union is to engage in collective bargaining. Without the ability to exercise this bargaining function, there is no incentive, rhyme, or reason for such an association to be organized or even to exist, for it would be incapable of doing what it was designed to do. Under the conventional-wisdom view of the bargaining obligation contained in the NLRA, not only would an employer have no duty to recognize and bargain with a minority union, such union would have no way to force the employer to bargain. On the other hand, *but for the existence of Section 8(b)(4) and the other limiting provisions previously noted,* a minority union would be free to attempt to persuade an employer to grant recognition and bargaining by engaging in a strike, utilizing both primary and secondary picketing. In the face of such economic pressure, many employers would undoubtedly yield to such demands and would negotiate members-only collective-bargaining agreements regardless of whether such bargaining was required by the Act. Thus, had Congress confined its prohibition of secondary activity to

Section 9(a) majority/exclusivity unions only, many minority unions would be able to achieve collective bargaining regardless of the presence or absence of an enforceable right to bargain. But because such self-help is not available, a labor organization cannot function on its own without dependence on legal enforceability of the bargaining obligation. Consequently, under the restrictive reading of the duty-to-bargain provisions here in issue, vast numbers of workers are prevented—as a result of congressional action—from organizing into labor unions.

I do not here question Congress's constitutional authority to outlaw secondary and other conduct in the previously noted provisions. However, if those provisions apply to minority members-only unions (which the secondary-boycott passages obviously do[114]) and if employers are under no legal obligation to bargain collectively with those minority unions, then Congress has curtailed the legitimate activities of these associations without a compelling governmental purpose to justify such an infringement of a First Amendment freedom. This is state action in its most controlling form. Not only does it not foster collective bargaining—which is the national policy mandated by the statute—it actually diminishes the opportunity for such bargaining, for it makes it impossible for a minority union to function as a union. Permitting *only* majority unions to function thwarts the normal associational growth process and makes it more difficult—indeed well-nigh impossible in most cases—for workers to achieve union representation.

In summation, if the conventional reading of the bargaining provisions of the Act were to be deemed valid, then Congress would be *directly* denying minority unions the right to operate as unions; on the one hand, they would deny them the right to bargain by law and, on the other, they would bar them from using such self-help as Justice Harlan described in the *Terminal Case* (i.e., striking or picketing, including secondary picketing) to persuade the employer to grant recognition and bargaining. Such governmentally imposed organizational impotence would stifle the associational process that the First Amendment is supposed to protect.

Having articulated the case for the existence of direct state action under the NLRA, I now digress briefly to view how our good neighbor to the north treats a related underinclusion problem that arose pursuant to its constitutional requirement of freedom of association. I refer to the 2001 decision of the Supreme Court of Canada in *Dunmore v. Ontario (Attorney General)*,[115] which ruled on an amendment to the Ontario Labour Relations Act (LRA) that removed agricultural workers from LRA coverage. The Canadian Court held that this legislative *exclusion* from the Ontario labor-relations regime violated the "freedom of association" guaranteed by Section 2(d) of the Canadian Charter of Rights and Freedoms, i.e., the Canadian "Bill of Rights."[116] According to Justice Michel Bastarache, who wrote the Court's lead opinion, the central question posed by the amendment was: "can excluding agricultural workers from a statutory labour relations regime,

without expressly or intentionally prohibiting association, constitute a substantial interference with freedom of association?"[117] Responding to that
question, his opinion pointed out that the LRA

> provides the only statutory vehicle by which employees in Ontario can as-
> sociate to defend their interest and, moreover, recognizes that such associ-
> ation is, in many cases, otherwise impossible. This recognition is evident
> not only from the statute's protections against unfair labour practices, but
> from the express "right to organize" it inscribes. . . .[118]

Bastarache observed that "Without the Protection of the LRA, Agricultural
Workers are Substantially Incapable of Exercising their Freedom to Associate."[119] And although the Court found that their freedom to organize was
substantially impeded by exclusion from protective legislation, it recognized
that it was still necessary "to link this impediment to state, not just private,
action.[120] With reasoning similar to that employed by the U.S. Supreme
Court in the NAACP cases previously discussed,[121] the Canadian Supreme
Court found such state action and declared that the exclusion of agricultural
workers by the amending statute in Ontario was unconstitutional. Here is
the heart of the Court's state-action finding:

> The most palpable effect of the [amending legislation is] to place a *chilling
> effect* on non-statutory union activity. By extending statutory protection to
> just about every class of worker in Ontario, the legislature has essentially
> discredited the organizing efforts of agricultural workers.[122] [Furthermore]
> the didactic effects of labour relations legislation on employers must not be
> underestimated. . . . [T]he wholesale exclusion of agricultural workers
> from a labour relations regime can only be viewed as a stimulus to inter-
> fere with organizing activity.[123]

The Canadian experience is thus reminiscent of what we have witnessed in
the United States with de facto exclusion of minority-union bargaining—employers have indeed been stimulated to interfere with organizing activity.

The Absence of a Compelling Governmental Interest

As the preceding analyses has established, if the NLRA were construed to
deny minority-union employees the right to engage in collective bargaining
in workplaces where there is no exclusive majority representative, this would
constitute governmental action that deprives those employees of their right
of association. Such rights can be denied by regulatory action only if there is
"a compelling state interest in the regulation."[124] Addressing the issue of
such permissible regulation, the Supreme Court declared in *Claiborne Hardware* that

Governmental regulation that has an incidental effect on First-Amendment freedoms may be justified in certainly narrowly defined instances. . . . This Court has recognized the strong governmental interest in certain forms of economic regulation, even though such regulation may have an incidental effect on rights of speech and association."[125]

However, such regulation or other governmental action "which may have the effect of curtailing the freedom to associate is subject to the *closest scrutiny.*"[126]

Can that threshold of *close scrutiny* be met if collective bargaining under the Act is narrowly confined to recognized or certified Section 9(a) majority unions only? What salutary purpose, if any, could Congress have to deny a minority association of employees the right to bargain collectively on a members-only basis in workplaces where no exclusive majority representative has been designated? None whatever, for such denial would actually be counterproductive to the establishment of mature, majority-based exclusivity bargaining, which was the ultimate congressional objective. But Congress unquestionably has a right to make the rational decision to limit the proliferation of labor organizations once a majority of the employees in a bargaining unit select a single organization as their representative, and it thus has the correlative right to provide that such organization will be the *exclusive* representative of all the employees. That regulation of associational rights has been approved by the Supreme Court in several cases, including *Abood v. Detroit Board of Education*[127] in which the Court reiterated the standard explication of the congressional rationale for majority-union exclusivity as follows:

The principle of exclusive union representation which underlies the National Labor Relations Act . . . is a central element in the congressional structuring of industrial relations. . . . The designation of a single representative avoids the confusion that would result from attempting to enforce two or more agreements specifying different terms and conditions of employment. It prevents inter-union rivalries from creating dissension within the work-force and eliminating the advantages to the employee of collectivization. It also frees the employer from the possibility of facing conflicting demands from different unions, and permits the employer and a single union to reach agreements and settlements that are not subject to attack from rival labor organizations.[128]

This is the same rationale that proponents of the Wagner bill expressed prior to passage of the Act in their support of exclusive representation.[129] And like the justification they advanced, the Court's reference in *Abood* to multiple-union problems is directed entirely to the stage of mature or established collective bargaining, not to bargaining that precedes the selection of a majority representative. Indeed, as legislative history has demonstrated, the drafters of the Act took great pains to protect the right of minority unions to bargain prior to the designation of a Section 9(a) representative.[130]

It is true that granting exclusive bargaining rights to a union *after* it achieves majority status represents a palpable infringement on the freedom of association of employees who do not wish to be represented by the majority union. But, as we noted in *Claiborne Hardware*, an "incidental effect on First-Amendment freedoms may be justified in certain narrowly defined instances," such as this, where the substitution of a democratically selected majority representative supplies substantial public benefits, as is described in the passage from *Abood*. Depriving employees of their right of association *prior* to the selection of an exclusive representative, however, is unrelated to those benefits and would represent a classic example of overbroad legislation for which there is no constitutional justification.[131]

Clearly, it was not the intent of Congress to prohibit minority unions from bargaining prior to the consummation of a Section 9(a) selection, nor would it serve the Act's purpose to discourage such preliminary-stage bargaining. On the contrary, as we have observed, the Supreme Court itself has affirmatively encouraged such bargaining, for, as the Court stated in *Consolidated Edison*, that is what the "Act contemplates."[132] And the Court also expressed its approval in three other prominent cases.[133] The NLRB has likewise indicated similar express approval in three of its cases, and it rendered another decision consistent with that proposition.[134] In addition, four NLRB General Counsels—two appointed by Republican presidents and two by Democratic presidents—indicated, by their advocacy, that negotiations over grievances could be required between minority groups of employees and their employers in workplaces where there was no majority representative.[135] With this wealth of favorable prior judicial and administrative reaction, there should be no reason for the Board or the courts to question the propriety of minority-union bargaining here under consideration.

Perhaps most telling of all, however, is the historical fact that such minority bargaining prevailed extensively during the first few years following passage of the Act,[136] and the multitude of members-only contracts that were consequently executed attest to the success of the process that Congress intended and Justice Douglas articulated in the *Bernhard-Altmann* case.[137] With reference to the role of minority unions, he wrote that "[t]the aim—at least the hope—of the legislation was that majority unions would emerge and provide stabilizing influences."[138] That is exactly what happened in the late 1930s.

Inasmuch as I am dedicated to conscientious scholarship, my original preference at this point was to play devil's advocate and propose a rationale for congressional exclusion of members-only premajority collective bargaining that could be objectively tested. I abandoned that approach, however, when I was unable to conceive of any rationale for such an exclusion that might be deemed even remotely reasonable and consistent with the Act's express objective. It appears to be self-evident that denying minority employees the right to engage in such bargaining bears no "reasonable relationship to the achievement of the governmental purpose asserted as its justification,"[139] for the governmental justification here is the encouragement and establishment of collective bargaining. Accordingly, we must conclude that if minority-union members are denied this right to bargain in order to support the abstract concept of majority-union bargaining, we will have a case of legislative overbreadth best described as throwing out the baby with the bath.

Avoidance of the Constitutional Issue

The foregoing discussion establishes that constitutional implications flowing from the issue of First Amendment protection of freedom of association in the workplace is a substantial factor to be reckoned with in the evaluation of relevant statutory meaning. As we have seen, the presence of this constitutional factor is based on the verifiable existence of state action by any or all of three different means: by indirect state action, by the employer as state actor, and by direct state action. These are serious considerations that would require careful weighing if the statute were interpreted—notwithstanding the overwhelming authority to the contrary—to deny minority-union employees their qualified right to bargain collectively as described herein. However, such constitutional issues can—and certainly should—be avoided entirely.

As noted at the beginning of this chapter, the Supreme Court's familiar approach to the construction of any congressional legislation that poses a serious question of constitutionality is to avoid the question by choosing a construction that does not raise such an issue unless such a construction "is plainly contrary to the intent of Congress."[140] (And as will be observed in Chapter 8, this is essentially the same approach the Court applies to statutory construction involving an obligation under an international treaty, to wit, "an act of Congress ought never to be construed to violate the law of nations, if any other possible construction remains. . . ."[141])

The *DeBartolo*[142] case provides the ideal model for disposition of the First Amendment question posed here. That case concerned a First Amendment issue of free speech in which the Labor Board had construed the phrase "threaten, coerce, or restrain" contained in a secondary-boycott subsection of the Act[143] to prohibit the peaceful distribution of union handbills at a shopping mall. The union contended that the handbills were a truthful expression of the existence of a labor dispute that urged potential customers to refrain from shopping at a mall where substandard wages were being paid to construction workers. The Court rejected the Board's construction of the statute, declaring that it "must independently inquire whether there is another interpretation, not raising these serious [constitutional] concerns."[144] It thus concluded, adopting the union's construction, "that the section is open to a construction that obviates deciding whether a congressional prohibition of handbilling on the facts of this case would violate the First Amendment."[145]

Following that model, if the Act were construed to exempt an employer from its duty to bargain with employees represented by a minority union where there is no Section 9(a) majority union, such a construction would raise the issue of a denial of the First Amendment's freedom of association without any redeeming feature. Clearly, however, such a result is avoided entirely by construing the Act to recognize that these minority-union employees have an enforceable statutory right to bargain collectively—a construction not "plainly contrary to the intent of Congress." Indeed, it is wholly in accord with such intent.

With such a construction, the Act's guarantee in Section 7 that "[e]mployees shall have the right to self-organization, to form, join, or assist labor organizations, [and] to bargain collectively through organizations of their own choosing" will have been accorded the First Amendment status that has always been implicit in this statutory language. This was recognized by the Supreme Court in *NLRB v. Gissel Packing Co., Inc.*,[146] where Chief Justice Earl Warren noted that an employer's free-speech right to communicate its views to its employees under Section 8(c)[147] "merely implements the First-Amendment. . . . Thus an employer's rights cannot outweigh the *equal* rights of the employees to associate freely, as those rights are embraced in 7 and protected by 8(a)(1)."[148] The First Amendment right of association is indeed a *fundamental right* for employees. That same right is embedded in Section 7 of the statute[149] and is entitled to constitutional consideration.[150]

7 *The* Chevron *Two-Step Process as an Alternative Approach*

National Labor Relations Board Approval Would Represent a Rational Construction Consistent with the Act

As the preceding chapters have demonstrated, the National Labor Relations Act definitely requires that where a majority of the employees in an appropriate bargaining unit have not designated an exclusive representative, an employer has a duty to bargain collectively with a minority union that seeks to bargain on behalf of its member-employees. It is the basic premise of this book that such a duty is *mandatory* under the statute. The purpose of this chapter, however, is to consider an alternative proposition: that if the meaning of the statute were considered to be unclear (i.e., deemed to be silent or ambiguous on the subject) the NLRB, in accordance with step two of the Supreme Court's *Chevron*[1] doctrine, should exercise its *discretionary* authority to adopt the proposed reading of the statute and require bargaining where the aforesaid minority-union conditions prevail. In fact, as I explain later, that course would even be suitable if the Board were satisfied that such a reading is mandated by the Act.

As followers of administrative law are well aware, the *Chevron* doctrine is the Supreme Court's articulation of its prevailing rule defining judicial deference to an administrative agency's determination of statutory meaning. In *Chevron*, the Court outlined a two-step process for such review. As to step one, it said that

> When a court reviews an agency's construction of the statute which it administers, it is confronted with two questions. First, always, is the question whether Congress has directly spoken to the precise question at issue. If the intent of Congress is clear, that is the end of the matter; for the court, as well as the agency, must give effect to the unambiguously expressed intent of Congress.[2]

In a footnote accompanying step one, the Court reiterated that the "judiciary is the final authority on issues of statutory construction";[3] therefore, if "a court, employing *traditional tools of statutory construction,* ascertains that Congress had an intention on the precise question at issue, that intention is the law and must be given effect."[4] It is my position that the conclusions revealed in the previous chapters, using "traditional tools of statutory construction," leave no doubt about congressional intent on the issue in question. If there were a doubt, however, then step two of the *Chevron* doctrine would apply. The Court defined that second step as follows:

> If, however, the court determines Congress has not directly addressed the precise question at issue, the court does not simply impose its own construction on the statute, as would be necessary in the absence of an administrative interpretation. Rather, if the statute is silent or ambiguous with respect to the specific issue, the question for the court is whether the agency's answer is based on a permissible construction of the statute.[5]

In a footnote to step two, the Court stressed that a "court need not conclude that the agency construction was the only one it permissibly could have adopted to uphold the construction, or even the reading the court would have reached if the question initially had arisen in a judicial proceeding."[6] Accordingly, if the statutory provisions here in issue were to be deemed unclear, the Labor Board would theoretically be free to declare that an employer has a duty to bargain with a premajority union for its members only because such a determination would be a *permissible* construction of the Act even if the reviewing court disagreed with the wisdom of that policy.

I am well aware that although the Supreme Court continues to espouse its adherence to *Chevron,* the evolution of its reviews of administrative-agency statutory construction since the promulgation of the doctrine in 1984 has been inconsistent. Indeed, the Court's majority has increasingly found reasons not to invoke the second step, thus avoiding deference to administrative statutory interpretation. As Professor Richard J. Pierce, Jr., concluded in the mid-1990s, the Court's

> post-*Chevron* jurisprudence is so confused that it is difficult to determine what remains of the original, highly deferential test. This inconsistency in applying the test is largely attributable to post-*Chevron* changes in the choice of "traditional tools of statutory construction." . . . As the Court has changed the mix of "tools" it uses and the ways in which it uses those tools, it has gradually ceased to apply step two . . . to uphold an agency construction of ambiguous statutory language, because it rarely acknowledges the existence of ambiguity.[7]

That tendency has continued, culminating most notably in the *Brown & Williamson*[8] decision, in which the issue was the Food and Drug Administration's conclusion that nicotine is a "drug" within the meaning of the enabling statute, thereby subjecting tobacco products to the agency's jurisdiction. The Court paid dutiful lip service to the *Chevron* formula, but avoided finding any ambiguity in statutory language by declaring that "[t]he meaning—or ambiguity—of certain words or phrases may only become evident when placed in context."[9] Thus, regarding the regulation of tobacco, the Court said that "the meaning of one statute may be affected by other Acts, particularly where Congress has spoken subsequently and more specifically to the topic at hand."[10]

Not surprisingly, *Chevron* and the Court's ambivalent treatment of its applications have spawned a plethora of scholarly comment and debate,[11] particularly regarding the new ways to use traditional tools of statutory construction, noted by Professor Pierce, whereby the Court arrives at an unambiguous statutory meaning under step one, thus avoiding a step-two determination of whether the agency's "interpretation is rational and consistent with the statute,"[12] which is the standard test of permissibility. The principal debate, both on and off the Court, has concerned the role of legislative history in the determination of statutory meaning; and several new labels— plus old labels revived—have surfaced to describe various theories of interpretation, including "new textualism,"[13] "hypertextualism,"[14] "public choice theory,"[15] "public justification,"[16] "interpretativism,"[17] "intentionalism,"[18] and "statutory default rules."[19] For our purposes, however, it suffices to examine the NLRA simply with reference to its plain language and its legislative history, without reference to trendy labels.

Inasmuch as plain language supports this book's minority-bargaining thesis, Justice Antonin Scalia's admonition in his concurring opinion in *Cardoza-Fonseca*[20] serves to underscore that conclusion.[21] Eschewing a resort to legislative history, Justice Scalia insists that "Judges interpret laws rather than reconstruct legislators' intentions," contending that "[w]here the language of those laws is clear, we are not free to replace it with an unenacted legislative intent."[22] As to the current issue, an objective observer ignoring legislative history would have to conclude that the critical duty to bargain contained in the language of Section 7 would still be enforceable under Section 8(a)(1) even if Section 8(a)(5) were disregarded,[23] although it need not be disregarded; the totality of the statutory language standing alone indicates that the exclusivity requirement in Section 9(a) is wholly conditional and inoperable until a majority representative is selected. On the other hand, if the observer recognizes the importance of legislative history—as do most members of the Court—the same conclusion follows.[24] As Justice Stephen G. Breyer wrote prior to his appointment to the Supreme Court, and as he has often viewed the process in his opinions on the Court, "[l]egislative history helps a court understand the context and purpose of a statute."[25] In this instance, the context and purpose of the NLRA revealed by its legislative history strongly confirms that Congress intended to retain the then-existing right of minority unions to engage in collective bargaining prior to the selection of an exclusive majority representative.[26]

Despite its checkered history, *Chevron* remains a viable framework for judicial review of administrative statutory action. Its two-step procedure is especially useful when applied to broadly worded legislative provisions in which Congress has demonstrably intended to grant an agency authority to engage in decision making consistent with manifest statutory policy. The National Labor Relations Act fits that category. However, no guarantee comes with this package, for the Supreme Court's record of judicial construction of the NLRA is spotty at best.[27] Nevertheless, the prospect for the current issue under *Chevron* is extremely favorable.

In the past, in cases in which the Labor Board had construed the NLRA, the Court often articulated the components of a "permissible construction of the statute" and usually—but by no means always—found them satisfied by the Board's interpretation. As early as 1944, in *NLRB v. Hearst Publications, Inc.*,[28] the Court declared that "where the question is one of specific application of a broad statutory term in a proceeding in which the agency administering the statute must determine it initially, the reviewing court's function is limited."[29] And more recently, in *NLRB v. United Food and Commercial Workers*,[30] the Court expressly applied *Chevron's* second step and declared that "we have traditionally accorded the Board deference with regard to its interpretation of the NLRA as long as its interpretation is *rational and consistent with the statute.*"[31] The Court repeated that standard when it approved the Board's no-presumption rule that rejected the employer's presumption of union opposition by striker replacements in *NLRB v. Curtin Matheson Scientific, Inc.*,[32] where it added that "a Board rule is entitled to deference even if it represents a departure from the Board's prior policy."[33] And in *Holly Farms*[34] it again relied upon step two of *Chevron* when it approved the Board's interpretation of the statutory terms "employee" and "agricultural laborer." It also there cautioned that "administrators and reviewing courts must take care to assure that exemptions from NLRA coverage are not *so expansively* interpreted as to deny protection to workers the Act was designed to reach."[35] That statement of policy should be equally applicable to the avoidance of *narrowly* interpreting NLRA coverage so as to exclude substantial numbers of workers whom its collective bargaining provisions were "designed to reach."

The Court in *Chevron* emphasized that

> If Congress has explicitly left a gap for the agency to fill, there is an express delegation of authority to the agency to elucidate a specific provision of the statute by regulation. Such legislative regulations are given controlling weight unless they are *arbitrary, capricious, or manifestly contrary to the statute.*[36]

Accordingly, if the Labor Board were to deem the statutory provisions in issue ambiguous, it would have *discretionary* authority to fill the gap and achieve the same end as that produced by the mandatory construction described in the previous chapters, for the resulting regulation would not be "arbitrary, capricious, or manifestly contrary to the statute."

In view of the strong legislative policy that permeates both the existing statutory language[37] and applicable legislative history,[38] there should be no doubt that if and when the NLRB determines that premajority members-only bargaining is a protected right enforceable under the Act, such determination will be held to be "rational and consistent with the statute." How could a court conclude otherwise in view of the fact that the Supreme Court has already on several occasions approved such members-only bargaining and contracts generated by such bargaining?[39] And this is likewise applicable to the Labor Board, for it too has approved such recognition.[40]

Although such endorsements by the Supreme Court and the Board indicate that members-only collective bargaining is already implicitly regarded as "rational and consistent with the statute," it is nevertheless appropriate to examine this bargaining process on the merits. Inasmuch as such bargaining was commonplace when the Act was passed, had Congress disapproved, it would surely have outlawed the practice entirely, just as it did for employer-controlled company unions.[41] Instead, it only prohibited the practice in bargaining units where it would interfere with exclusivity bargaining *after* a representative had been designated by a majority of the employees. As bargaining history and statutory text both confirm, Congress was careful not to impair the right of employees to bargain prior to that designation. As we have seen, such preliminary bargaining by minority unions was commonly accepted as a natural stage in the development of the collective bargaining process. And as the early history of the Act demonstrated, such premajority bargaining almost always led to exclusive-majority bargaining;[42] hence, it is consistent with the Act's policy favoring collective bargaining. But even aside from such organizational justification, minority bargaining can serve other important functions in workplaces where there is no exclusive representative. Although many of those functions are discussed in Chapters 11 and 12, the following description, which offers a brief introductory rationale for the practice, is also appropriate to the thrust of this chapter.

If employees with common interests can join together and organize themselves informally—thus satisfying the broad definition of a "labor organization" under Section 2(5)[43]—they can more effectively meet and confer with management to resolve their common problems. In all but the tiniest of workplaces, meaningful dialogue about working conditions requires *group* presence; and to achieve maximum benefit, that dialogue ought to be a two-way discussion, not merely a unilateral chain-of-command message from management. A labor organization, however small or informal, will almost always be better suited for this process than no organization at all, particularly in establishments where employees are alleged to have a significant voice regarding their conditions of employment. At the early stages, however, minority bargaining may be more likely to resemble "meet and confer" sessions than negotiations under traditional collective bargaining, but the group format will at least give interested employees an audible voice to which management will be required to listen. Grievances will thus be more likely to be settled amicably and satisfactorily, and employees will not need to resort to more confrontational forms of concerted activity in order to attract management's attention.[44] In time, as the fledgling union grows in membership, its effectiveness will probably increase, and in due course it should become a fully operational majority union. It is this organizational function that provides the major—but not the only—role and justification for minority-union bargaining.[45]

Notwithstanding the logic of the propositions presented in previous chapters, it is not essential that the Labor Board be convinced that the Act mandates qualified minority-union bargaining. Under *Chevron,* it will suffice if the Board simply requires such bargaining as a *permissive* construction of the Act, just as it has exercised that discretionary authority, with judicial approval, in many earlier decisions, for example, (1) when it recognized in *Republic Aviation*[46] that Section 7 protects employees engaged in union solicitation on company premises during nonworking time, (2) when it recognized in *Weingarten*[47] that an employee called in for an anticipated disciplinary interview in a unionized establishment has the right to be accompanied by a union representative, and (3) when it provided in *Epilepsy Foundation*[48] for the right of a nonunion employee to have the presence of a coworker in that same type of interview in a nonunion establishment. Similarly, recognition of qualified minority-union bargaining would be the right thing to do even if it were not the required thing to do.

The D.C. Court of Appeals easily found the Board's ruling in *Epilepsy Foundation* to be a permissive gap-filling interpretation of the Act under *Chevron* step two.[49] The current Board, however, although it recognized the validity of the extension of *Weingarten* rights to nonunion employees in *Epilepsy Foundation,* chose to overrule that decision in its recent *IBM Corporation*[50] case. Thus, henceforth, nonunion employees will no longer have the benefit of *Weingarten* rights, a factor about which I comment in Chapter 11. But notwithstanding this latest retraction of workers' rights, *Epilepsy Foundation* still provides an instructive example of an appropriate application of *Chevron* step-two decision making, and it also points up the difference between an empty Section 7 right and a meaningful one, for the majority opinion stated:

> We disagree with our dissenting colleagues' assertions that Sec. 7 of the Act gives nonunionized employees only the right to seek the assistance of a coworker at an investigatory interview, not the right to the actual assistance. It is the actual presence of the coworker, not the request for one, that

affords employees the ability to act in concert for mutual and or protection. In our view, *the right to make such a request is devoid of any substance without a corresponding right to have the request granted.*[51]

By the same token, it is the actual required meeting with the employer, not the request for a meeting, that affords employees the ability to engage in meaningful bargaining for settlement of their grievances through representatives of their own choosing. Unquestionably, employees presently have the right to organize themselves into a minority union and *request* that their employer meet and deal with them as a group for the adjustment of their grievances. But that is obviously an empty and meaningless privilege as long as the employer is free to refuse such a request with impunity, insisting instead on either no meetings at all or divide-and-conquer private meetings with individual employees. The reader will recall from the Introduction[52] the Hi Tech employer's reply when seventeen of his employees sought to meet with him as a group. His action and the NLRB General Counsel's timid reaction made a mockery of the right of workers to engage in rational collective activity that Section 7 was designed to encourage and protect.[53] The only recourse available to that group was to engage in the futile act of walking off the job, which they felt compelled to do without ever having had an opportunity to meet with their employer in an attempt to resolve their differences amicably. If an employer is not required to meet and bargain with such a group—which fulfills the statutory definition of "labor organization"[54]—then Section 7 will have been stood on its head, for the absence of such a requirement *discourages* rather than encourages collective bargaining, forcing the employees to deal only individually with their employer, notwithstanding the clear language of Section 7 to the contrary.[55]

Epilepsy Foundation offered an insightful guideline for correcting that imbalance, for the Board's majority opinion states that

> The likelihood that any particular concerted activity will ultimately achieve its intended result is not the controlling consideration in determining whether that activity is protected by Sec. 7 of the Act. What is important is that employees are afforded the *opportunity* to "engage in concerted activities for mutual aid or protection."[56]

The same is true of employees seeking to bargain as a group to settle grievances and improve working conditions. This cannot occur unless they are afforded the *opportunity* to meet with the employer on a group-representation basis. It takes two to tango.

Epilepsy Foundation, despite its untimely demise, thus represented a cautious step forward toward correcting the imbalance that has long existed because of the erroneous belief that an employer has no duty to deal with any group of employees prior to the establishment of exclusive majority-union representation by certification or recognition. The Board majority in that case also called attention to a dissenting Board member's query as to "why nonunionized employees should be entitled to the presence of a coworker in an investigatory interview when nonunionized employees are not entitled to the presence of a coworker at meetings to discuss *other issues.*"[57] The majority properly responded that such a question was not encompassed within the *Weingarten* rationale and that speculation about "other circumstances involving nonunionized employees is not before us today."[58] Nevertheless, that dissenting Board member posed a valid question that now awaits an answer. When the Board considers the minority-bargaining question outlined in this volume, it will be presented with the ideal opportunity to address those "other issues" left open in *Epilepsy Foundation.*

When the members-only minority-bargaining issue reaches the Board, it will be appropriate that its determination be made in two parts: first, as a *mandatory* requirement of the statute in accordance with the rationale contained in the earlier chapters and, second, in the alternative, as a *discretionary* determination of statutory meaning in accordance with the rationale contained in this chapter. But if for any reason the Board chooses not to hold that the minority-bargaining proposition is mandatory, it may—and in fact should—make a discretionary *Chevron* step-two ruling, either as a construction of ambiguous language or as the filling of a gap left by Congress for agency resolution. In fact, the Board could issue such a *permissive* ruling even without reaching the *mandatory* construction issue, although such timidity is not recommended.

Regardless of the Board's choice, a court of appeals or the Supreme Court can independently hold that the statute *requires* the recognition of premajority bargaining, reversing if necessary a contrary NLRB interpretation, for it is unquestionably the court's authority to make such a ruling when the "statute's meaning is plain."[59] However, as we have seen, a court would have no authority under *Chevron* to overturn a favorable ruling by the Board that properly falls within the step-two discretionary area of *permissible* construction, even if it disagrees with the wisdom of that construction. Thus, a determination by the Board that adopts the proposed thesis—either as a single *permissive* construction or as a dual *mandatory and alternatively permissive* interpretation—would present a favorable format on appeal. This is so because if an appellate court were inclined to hold that the language and intent of the statute is ambiguous, it would not be free to reverse the Board's discretionary interpretation inasmuch as *Chevron* recognizes that it is the function of the administrative agency, not the court, to construe an ambiguity or omission, provided only that such construction is "rational and consistent with the statute."[60]

Chevron might also bar an adverse judicial determination as to the meaning of the Act regarding the basic matter in issue, for if the Board were to hold—as a permissive construction—that there is no qualified duty to bargain with a minority union, and if the reviewing court were to agree with that holding, the court would only be approving a second-step construction of the statute. This would not prevent the Board at some future time from revisiting the issue and deciding otherwise, just as the current Board revisited the *Weingarten* issue for nonunion employees in *IBM Corporation.* This is what *Chevron* teaches. On the other hand, if the Board were to hold that there is a duty to bargain with a premajority union, it is difficult to envision the Supreme Court overruling that interpretation inasmuch as the Court has already approved such practice,[61] and plain statutory language and strong legislative history support that interpretation.[62]

Chevron clearly has an important role to play in resolving the issue of minority-union bargaining for union-member employees prior to the establishment of exclusive-majority representation.

8   *The International Human-Rights Dimension and U.S. Obligations under International Law*

This chapter adds a fourth tier to the legal premises on which minority-union members-only collective bargaining is based. The previous chapters have demonstrated three distinct grounds for such bargaining: first—and foremost—that statutory construction mandates this right to bargain, for it is derived from specific language in the Act[1] and is strongly supported by legislative history;[2] second, that the right rests on the freedom of association guaranteed by the First Amendment to the U.S. Constitution;[3] and third, that in the event the Act is deemed ambiguous, the NLRB is vested with administrative discretion, pursuant to the *Chevron*[4] doctrine, to declare and enforce such right, for it represents a rational construction consistent with the statute.[5]

The fourth tier of legal support for this right, treated in this chapter, is the international human-rights dimension. This dimension, which is based on strong moral underpinnings, represents an enforceable legal obligation, although it does not constitute an independent cause of action. It provides no means for enforcement other than through existing American legal institutions (i.e., the National Labor Relations Board and the federal courts) functioning pursuant to United States law but in accordance with international standards to which this country is a legally committed party. As further support for the interpretation of the collective bargaining requirements of the NLRA here asserted, this fourth dimension adds the weight of international human rights expressed in legally binding provisions in international compacts that the United States has officially affirmed.

It may come as a surprise to many readers to learn that the right of association in the workplace is considered a fundamental human right required by international law. As this chapter explicates, the United States is legally obligated under these international standards to promote freedom of association for workers and their right to engage in collective bargaining. This obligation stems primarily from two sources. The first is the International Covenant on Civil and Political Rights (ICCPR or Covenant), which the United States ratified in 1992 with certain reservations.[6] The second is the *Declaration on Fundamental Principles and Rights at Work* (1998 ILO Declaration),[7] which the International Labor Organization (ILO) adopted in 1998 with the full support of the U.S. delegation, including its employer representatives.[8] These two compacts recognize that the freedom to join a union and to engage effectively in collective bargaining are basic human rights—indeed, they are rights premised on a substantial moral foundation.

The Human-Rights Background of the Right of Association

That the right of workers to form and join trade unions to deal with employers is a fundamental human right is not a new concept. Its origins are rooted deeply in diverse sources, including not only traditional trade-union movements[9] and familiar socialist doctrine,[10] but also in the American progressive agenda of the early twentieth century[11] and in solid theoretical support provided by the Catholic Church.[12] As to these sources I highlight here only the latter two, for they are probably the least familiar to the general reader.

As Professor Harry W. Arthurs cogently observes, "American progressivism clearly influenced the normative and institutional architecture of important international regimes such as the UN Declarations of Human, Social and Political Rights and the ILO Conventions on Freedom of Association and on Collective Bargaining."[13] And as Professor David L. Gregory emphasizes, "[t]he right to unionize is expressly regarded as a human right in Catholic social teaching."[14] Indeed, as early as 1891, in *Rerum Novarum* (Concerning New Things),[15] Pope Leo XIII recognized the importance of workers' associations and agreements between workers and employers. And to commemorate the ninetieth anniversary of *Rerum Novarum,* in 1981 Pope John Paul II issued *Laborem Exercens* (On the Nature of Work)[16] in which he reiterated the right of workers to unionize. Again, in 1987, in his major social encyclical *Sollicitudo Rei Socialis* (On Social Concern),[17] Pope John Paul "expressly reminded the world that the rights of workers and unions are fundamental human rights."[18]

These familiar human-rights principles, although derived from widely different sources, have coalesced and now find their expression in international law. Professor James A. Gross places the relationship between union organizing and bargaining within this broader framework of human rights and democracy, asserting that

> the right to strike, to organize, and to bargain collectively are species of the independent right of freedom of association. The violation of the freedom

to associate denies individuals what they need to live a fully human life. The freedom of association is also an essential component of democracy.[19]

And Professor Roy J. Adams, a strong and frequent voice in the enlarging chorus of labor-oriented human-rights advocates, adds that "the right to collective bargaining means that working people have a fundamental human right to co-determine their conditions of work and to select representatives of their own choosing in order to negotiate those terms on their behalf."[20]

Although I recognize and support these expressions of moral imperatives, the only imperative that I ask the American judiciary to rely upon is the imperative of this country's international legal obligations, notwithstanding their morally motivated origins. Such obligations, which are based directly on the aforementioned international compacts—the ICCPR and the 1998 ILO Declaration—are entirely consistent with the statutory and constitutional requirements presented in earlier chapters.

These two documents were preceded by many decades of related international developments for which the United States, despite its unquestioned status as a democratic role model, acted mostly as a bystander. The first major event in this developmental history was the creation of the ILO pursuant to the Treaty of Versailles in 1919. Although the ILO was strongly supported by the U.S. delegation—in fact, Samuel Gompers, president of the American Federation of Labor, was elected president of the commission that established the ILO[21]—isolationist sentiment at home prevented U.S. acceptance of the Versailles treaty, membership in the League of Nation, and membership in the ILO. The United States did not join the ILO until 1934.[22]

Before World War II had ended, the ILO held a ground-breaking conference in Philadelphia in 1944 during which it adopted its major statement of policy and purpose, now known as the *Declaration of Philadelphia*. This declaration, which was subsequently incorporated into its constitution,[23] reaffirmed that "labour is not a commodity [and that] freedom of expression and of association are essential to sustained progress. . . . "[24] Among that declaration's several objectives was recognition of "the solemn obligation of the International Labour Organization to further among the nations of the world programs which will achieve . . . *the effective recognition of the right of collective bargaining*."[25] And that document affirmed "that the principles set forth in this Declaration are fully applicable to all peoples everywhere. . . . "[26] Membership in the ILO thus committed the member states to an affirmative obligation to further those objectives, a conclusion that was latter confirmed by the 1998 ILO Declaration.[27]

In 1948 the General Assembly of the United Nations adopted and proclaimed the Universal Declaration of Human Rights (UDHR),[28] which characterizes as "human rights" the "right of peaceful assembly and association" and the "right to form and join trade unions for the protections of [one's] interests."[29] The United States formally agreed to those key provisions when it later ratified the ICCPR.

Two other important international documents that have functioned globally without ratification by the United States are ILO Convention No. 87, *Concerning the Freedom of Association and the Protection of the Right to Organize,* adopted in 1948,[30] and Convention No. 98, *Concerning the Application of the Principles of the Right to Organize and Bargain Collectively,* adopted in 1949.[31] The relevant provision in Convention 87 is reminiscent of the language in Section 7 of the NLRA. It provides that "workers . . . shall have the right to establish and . . . to join organizations of their own choosing . . . "[32] and that the ratifying state shall "take all necessary and appropriate measures to ensure that workers . . . may exercise freely the right to organize."[33] Convention 98 provides that, subject to national conditions, appropriate measures shall be taken "to encourage and promote the full development and utilization of machinery for voluntary negotiation between employers or employers' organisations and workers' organisations, with a view to the regulation of terms and conditions of employment by means of collective agreements."[34] The ostensible reasons for the United States not ratifying those conventions were fear they would override various features of American labor law and a concern that our federal system would raise serious problems regarding the effect of state laws.[35] Organized management and organized labor for several decades have engaged in bitter and protracted debate over this ratification issue. I do not review the history of that debate here because it would serve no relevant purpose.[36] Furthermore, from a pragmatic standpoint, this nonratification issue was rendered relatively moot by the U.S adoption of the 1998 ILO Declaration, which I treat later in this chapter.

The International Covenant on Civil and Political Rights

Now to our examination of the legal implications of the two international compacts to which the United States has agreed. We begin with the *International Covenant on Civil and Political Rights,*[37] which was ratified with five "Reservations," five "Understandings," four "Declarations," and one "Proviso."[38] This compact, the ICCPR, was adopted by the United Nations General Assembly in 1966, signed by President Jimmy Carter in 1978, and ratified by President George H.W. Bush with the concurrence of the Senate in 1992. Accordingly, it is now a treaty that is part of the "supreme Law of the Land."[39] When this Covenant was presented to the Senate for approval, the Senate Foreign Relations Committee provided the following explanation of its function and purpose and what would be required of the United States as a ratifying party:

> The Covenant guarantees a broad spectrum of civil and political rights, rooted in basic democratic values and freedoms [and] obligates each State Party to respect and ensure these rights, to adopt legislative or other nec-

essary measures to give effect to these rights, and to provide an effective remedy to those whose rights are violated.[40]

The Covenant is part of the international community's early efforts to give the full force of international law to the principles of human rights embodied in the Universal Declaration of Human Rights and the United Nations Charter. The Civil and Political Rights Covenant is rooted in western legal and ethical values. The rights guaranteed by the Covenant are similar to those guaranteed by the U.S. Constitution and the Bill of Rights.[41]

The provisions of the ICCPR that have a bearing on the collective bargaining features here in issue include the following:

The *Preamble* (identifying the rights protected in the Covenant as *human rights*) recognizes

> that these rights derive from the inherent dignity of the human person [and] that, in accordance with the Universal Declaration of Human Rights, the ideal of free human beings enjoying civil and political freedom and freedom from fear and want can only be achieved if conditions are created whereby everyone may enjoy his civil and political rights, as well as his economic, social and cultural rights. . . .

Article 2 (concerning implementation) provides that

> 1. Each State Party undertakes to respect and *to ensure to all individuals* within its territory and subject to its jurisdiction the rights recognized in the present Covenant . . . ,
> 3. Each State Party to the present Covenant undertakes:
> (a) *To ensure* that any person whose rights or freedoms are herein recognized are violated shall have *an effective remedy* . . . ;
> (b) *To ensure* that any person claiming such a remedy shall have his right thereto determined by competent *judicial, administrative,* or *legislative* authorities, or by any other competent authority provided for by the legal system of the State, and to develop the possibilities of *judicial* remedy;
> (c) *To ensure* that the *competent authorities shall enforce such remedies when granted.*[42]

Article 22 (concerning right of association and trade unions) provides that

> 1. Everyone shall have the freedom of association with others, including *the right to form and join trade unions for the protection of his interests.*
> 2. *No restrictions may be placed on the exercise of this right other than those which are prescribed by law and which are necessary in a democratic*

society in the interests of national security or public safety, public order
(ordre public), *the protection of public health or morals or the protection
of the rights and freedoms of others. . . .*[43]

None of these provisions was the subject of any reservation by the United
States, which did attach specific reservations to several other provisions of
the Covenant, for example Article 20, relating to war propaganda and in-
citement to discrimination,[44] and Articles 6 and 7, relating to capital punishment and cruel and unusual punishment.[45] Those reservations, which
have been subjects of much scholarly attention[46] and some litigation,[47] are
not relevant here.

Although none of the *reservations* specified by the United States is pertinent to our present interest, one *understanding* and two *declarations* attached by the U.S. are relevant to the provisions that I have quoted.

Understanding No. (5) provides

That the United States understands that this Covenant *shall be implemented by the Federal Government to the extent that it exercises legislative
and judicial jurisdiction over the matters covered therein. . . .*[48]

Declarations (1) and (2) provide

1. That the United States declares that the provisions of *articles 1 through
27* of the Covenant are *not self-executing.*[49]
2. That it is the view of the United States that States Party to the Covenant should wherever possible *refrain from imposing any restrictions
or limitations on the exercise of the rights recognized and protected by
the Covenant. . . .*[50]

I first address the "not self-executing" (NSE) declaration, which has
aroused considerable academic attention and comment.[51] That feature,
however, need not be of concern to the investigators of labor-related human
rights, for it affects only the *procedural* aspects of applying Article 22 and
does not affect its substantive application to the interpretation of the National Labor Relations Act. The binding substantive mandates of the ICCPR
are fully enforceable,[52] including the obligation of the United States to ensure that all workers, including those under the jurisdiction of the NLRA,
have a meaningful right to join trade unions for their "protection," which—
as we have seen and shall see further—necessarily incorporates the right to
engage in collective bargaining.

Although much scholarly writing has addressed the meaning and implication of NSE features in treaties,[53] there can be no question about what the
U.S. Senate intended by the inclusion of the NSE declaration regarding judicial enforcement of the ICCPR provisions relevant to our concern. When it

presented the Covenant for ratification, the Senate Committee was remarkably candid about that intent, stating without qualification that "[t]he intent is to clarify that the Covenant will not create a *private cause of action* in U.S. courts."[54] In other words, no independent cause of action can arise directly under the Covenant. Consequently, although the Covenant's provisions do not furnish any basis for a separate cause of action, they may be raised and fully relied upon in an action arising under existing domestic law,[55] and courts and administrative agencies will enforce the treaty provisions appropriate to the matter in issue. Except for the provisions for which reservations were appended, the substantive mandates of the Covenant are not diminished by the NSE feature.[56] That feature thus poses no problem regarding the enforcement of trade-union-related rights, for they can be raised in unfair-labor-practice charges, complaints, or cases arising under Sections 7 and 8 of the Act. By such means, the United States is bound by the treaty to enforce the provisions to which it attached no reservations, especially the Preamble, Articles 2 and 3, and paragraphs (1) and (2) of Article 22.

Accordingly, the United States is required to exercise its "judicial jurisdiction"[57] "to ensure to all individuals [their] rights recognized in the present Covenant,"[58] "[t]o ensure that [they] have an *effective* remedy,"[59] and "that the competent authorities shall enforce such remedies when granted."[60] This means that the federal courts and the NLRB have an obligation to interpret and enforce the NLRA in conformance with Article 22 of the Covenant. In so doing, they will be complying with what Chief Justice Rehnquist in *Weinberger v. Rossi* reminded us "has been a maxim of statutory construction"[61] since Chief Justice John Marshall's 1804 decision in *The Charming Betsy*, to wit, that "an act of congress ought never to be construed to violate the law of nations, if any other possible construction remains. . . ."[62] This is the criterion the Supreme Court applied in 1962 to its construction of the NLRA when, in order to conform to the standards of international law, it interpreted the Act's coverage—again relying on *The Charming Betsy*—to exclude employees of foreign flag-of-convenience ships from the Act's coverage.[63] As the astute reader will recognize, this approach to the construction of a domestic statute vis-à-vis an issue of international law is essentially the same as that which the Court applies in a case of statutory construction that raises a serious question of constitutionality. As we have observed in Chapter 6, "where an otherwise acceptable construction of a statute would raise serious constitutional problems, the Court will construe the statute to avoid such problems unless such construction is plainly contrary to the intent of Congress."[64] Thus, the courts will be expected to treat statutory issues, whether arising under the Constitution or under international law, according to the same basic standard—that is, to make every reasonable effort to construe the statute consistent with and not in violation of either the Constitution or the treaty. And there is yet another principle of construction germane to this issue that the Supreme Court enunciated in

Asakura v. City of Seattle,[65] to wit, that "treaties are to be construed in a broad and liberal spirit, and, when two constructions are possible, one restrictive of rights that may be claimed under it and the other favorable to them, the latter is to be preferred."[66] This guideline is especially appropriate to the construction and enforcement of a human-rights treaty.

Clearly, Article 22 of the ICCPR commits the United States to ensuring that all workers have an unrestricted right "to form and join trade unions for the protection [of their] interests," for "no restrictions may be placed on the exercise of this right [unless] "necessary . . . in the interests of national security or public safety, public order, . . . protection of public health or morals . . . or rights and freedoms of others. . . ." This commitment is further reinforced by *U.S. Declaration (2),* that a state party to the Covenant "should wherever possible refrain from imposing any restrictions or limitations" on such rights.

Applying the foregoing Supreme Court canons of construction to the reconciliation of the NLRA and the ICCPR, it follows that there is no justification for construing the former in a manner that would severely and effectively restrict the right of employees to join labor unions to protect their interests. But if the conventional-wisdom's view of NLRA bargaining limitations were to prevail, the only unions most American employees could safely join would be the ones that have already been recognized or certified as majority representatives. We know this to be true because, historically, retaliations by private-sector employers against known pro-union employees in nonunion workplaces typically produce a chilling effect that severely restricts the right of their employees to form or join unions.[67] Such a restriction—which is built into the majority-only concept of bargaining—is not remotely related to national security or any other exception named in the Covenant and would, if required by law, violate Article 22. Accordingly, in addition to their domestic statutory responsibilities under the NLRA, the federal courts and the NLRB are mandated by international law to secure to workers their unrestricted right to "form and join trade unions" for the "protection" of their interests, which therefore includes unions having a right to bargain on behalf of their members both *before* and *after* establishment of exclusive majority representation. Giving effect to this plain meaning of the bargaining provisions of the NLRA avoids "violat[ing[the law of nations." Thus, Article 22 does not become a Catch-22, and *The Charming Betsy sails on.*

The foregoing conclusions concerning the relationship between Article 22 of the ICCPR and the reciprocal provisions of the NLRA are consistent with the legislative history that preceded the Senate's approval of ICCPR ratification. In response to certain labor-related questions raised by Senator Daniel P. Moynihan, the Senate Foreign Relations Committee noted the absence of "explicit provisions" in Article 22 and called attention to the NSE feature of the proposed ratification, reminding Senator Moynihan that the treaty, therefore, "would not . . . become *directly* enforceable as United States law in U.S. courts."[68] This was certainly true, for enforcement is left to *indirect*— but no less valid—procedures of the NLRB and the courts. Consequently, the absence of explicit procedures in the treaty does not affect the enforceability of Article 22. The Senate Committee's response also noted the Administration's opinion that the covenant "does not, and will not, require any alteration or amendment to existing Federal and State labor law."[69] Regarding the issue here under consideration (without reference to other unrelated issues), I am fully in agreement that no such statutory amendment is required.

There is also another aspect of the ICCPR that has a direct and positive bearing on the current subject, and that is the relationship between the right of association under this treaty and the right of association under the First Amendment and also the combined effect of those relationships on the construction of the NLRA. The key to these issues is to be found in another response given by the Senate Foreign Relations Committee to a question posed by Senator Moynihan. He asked: "Does Article 22 of the Covenant alter or amend existing legal requirements under the National Labor Relations Act . . . ?" The committee's response was unequivocal:

> *No.* Article 22 only provides for a general right of freedom of association, including the right to form and join trade unions for the protection of his [*sic*] interests. These rights are fully contemplated by the First Amendment to the U.S. Constitution with respect to free speech, petition and assembly.[70]

That answer tied together all three sources of legal rights for American workers. The Senate committee, which was also speaking on behalf of the George H.W. Bush Administration, thus confirmed for the record the applicability of the First Amendment's protection of the right of association to the *private sector* under the NLRA—for which *state action*[71] was not perceived to be a problem. Such protection was conceded to apply to "a general right" to form and join trade unions, which was considered to be "fully contemplated" by both the First Amendment and the Covenant. This was a reiteration of the Bush Administration's position expressed at the beginning of the Senate report: that the "Administration has concluded that the rights of association embodied in Article 22 of the Covenant are general rights of association contained in the First Amendment. . . ."[72] And to underscore that this was not merely an allusion to a non-labor-specific right of association but was intended to be a right applicable *specifically to workers,* the committee repeated three times that mantra tying together Article 22 and federal labor law.

Recall from Chapter 6 that the freedom of association guaranteed by the First Amendment compels a reading of the NLRA that is supportive of the role of less-than-majority unions to engage in collective bargaining in private-sector workplaces where there is no majority union. As explained there, this conclusion is based primarily on the proposition that to limit collective bargaining to established majority unions unduly restricts employees' right to join an association that functions as a trade union and that such a restriction is not supported by any compelling governmental interest. It is thus significant that the Senate Foreign Relations Committee and the Bush Administration recognized that the application of Article 22 of the ICCPR is identical to the application of constitutional requirements under the First Amendment and that this Constitutional provision also pertains to the private-sector workplace.[73] That being so, the same reasons noted in Chapter 6 to avoid an unconstitutional construction of union-bargaining requirements under the NLRA are also applicable to the requirements of international law under the ICCPR.

The 1998 ILO Declaration on Fundamental Principles and Rights at Work

Now to our review of the other international compact that affects this country's labor-law obligations—the *1998 ILO Declaration on Fundamental Principles and Rights at Work*.[74] Although the ICCPR broadly concerns the right of workers to form and join trade unions for *protection* of their interests, the extent of that protection is reinforced and clarified by this 1998 Declaration, which expressly spells out that such protection includes "*the right to collective bargaining.*"

We begin this examination by returning to the Senate Foreign Relations Committee's response to Senator Moynihan as to the meaning of Article 22 of the ICCPR. The Senate Committee there made an effort to distinguish that provision from ILO Convention 87, asserting that the latter sets out "*specific* protections of trade union rights that are not contemplated by Article 22 [which] 'does not make any *explicit* provision for the series of safeguards laid down in' ILO Convention 87."[75] Indeed, Convention 87 does contains a number of explicit safeguards regarding the internal operation of trade unions and their legal personalities. Likewise, ILO Convention 98 contains several reasonably definite provisions concerning organizational and collective bargaining procedures and protections. Although the lack of specificity in Article 22 may have seemed significant to the Bush Administration in 1992—a concern that was not well founded, as we have learned in the preceding section—such concern is now of little importance following the adoption of the 1998 ILO Declaration, for that document expressly incorporates the basic requirements of Conventions 87 and 98.[76]

When the Declaration was adopted at the International Labor Conference in Geneva in 1998, it was "hailed as a landmark achievement by the U.S.

delegates."[77] The instrument "committed the 174 countries belonging to the ILO to respect four principles embodied by seven ILO core conventions [including 87 and 98] and to promote application of the principles by all members. . . ."[78] Here are its relevant provisions.

The Declaration *"Recalls"*

> that in freely joining the ILO, all Members have endorsed the principles and rights set out in its Constitution and in the Declaration of Philadelphia,[79] and have undertaken to work towards attaining the overall objectives of the Organization *to the best of their resources* and fully in line with their specific circumstances . . .[80]

and *"Declares"*

> that all Members, even if they have not ratified the Conventions in question, have an obligation, arising from the very fact of membership in the Organization, *to respect, to promote, and to realize in good faith,* and in accordance with the Constitution, the principles concerning *the fundamental rights which are the subject of those conventions,* namely:
> a. freedom of association and the *effective* recognition of the right to collective bargaining. . . .[81]

Enforcement of the Declaration is the responsibility of each member state.[82] This is a binding obligation that is fully recognized. In fact, Abraham Katz, president of the U.S. Council for International Business (USCIB), which officially represents U.S. business interests at the ILO, confirmed that "[f]or the first time, the ILO has articulated a set of basic principles for workers' rights *to which every member country of the ILO must adhere by virtue of membership.*"[83]

The United States is thus required under the Declaration to comply with the basic rights contained in Conventions 87 and 98, a duty which for our purposes is sufficiently spelled out in the consolidated phrases from the text as an *"obligation . . . to promote . . . the effective recognition of the right of collective bargaining."* Obviously, the U.S. government has not in recent years promoted the *effective* recognition of that right. Indeed, in its official *Follow-Up Report* to the ILO in 1999[84] the Bill Clinton Administration acknowledged that failure, reporting that

> The United States has an elaborate system of substantive labor law and procedures. . . . Nonetheless, the United States acknowledges that there are aspects of this system that *fail to fully protect the rights to organize and bargain collectively* of all employees in all circumstances. The United States is concerned about these limitations. . . .[85]

Aside from that candid acknowledgement, it is widely known and fully documented that the United States does not comply with ILO standards regarding the right of workers to engage in collective bargaining.[86] As the Dunlop Commission concluded in 1994, "[t]he evidence reviewed by the Commission demonstrated conclusively that current labor law is not achieving its stated intent of encouraging collective bargaining and protecting workers' right to choose whether or not to be represented in their workplace."[87] And as Human Rights Watch reported more recently, elements of U.S. labor law and practice "frustrate rather than promote workers' freedom of association."[88] Certainly the current and conventional assumption, that certification or recognition of employee majority status is a precondition for union representation, provides employers with both the incentive and the means to deprive most private-sector employees of their right to engage in collective bargaining. Consequently, under the present assumed interpretation and enforcement of the NLRA, "[m]any workers who try to form and join trade unions to bargain with their employers are spied on, harassed, pressured, threatened, suspended, fired, deported or otherwise victimized in reprisal for their exercise of the right to freedom of association."[89]

The 1998 ILO Declaration thus provides additional international support for judicial and administrative recognition of the right of *all* employees covered by the NLRA—not just majority employees—to gain *effective* access to union representation and collective bargaining.

The Covenant and Declaration Compel a Broad Construction of the Collective Bargaining Obligation under the National Labor Relations Act

The United States has a duty to comply with its international-law commitments. The immediate nature of that duty concerns statutory construction of the NLRA's collective bargaining provisions in conformance with provisions in international agreements that are appreciably more specific than corresponding language in the First Amendment to the U.S. Constitution, for these international compacts expressly refer to "trade unions" and "collective bargaining." As we have seen, the intertwined texts of the ICCPR and the 1998 ILO Declaration mandate a broad construction of NLRA bargaining provisions that will expressly *ensure in good faith that all workers have the right to form and join trade unions for the protection of their interests and to respect and promote the effective recognition of collective bargaining.* These international objectives can be attained for all employees subject to the jurisdiction of the NLRA by interpreting that Act in accordance with the policy already contained in the Act[90]—a policy that is basically the same as the aforesaid international-law requirements. The NLRB and the courts thus have an obligation to enforce the plain meaning of the comparable text in Section 7 of the Act, that "[e]mployees shall have the right to self-organization, to form, join, or assist labor organizations [and] to bargain collectively through representatives of their own choosing . . . ," which in the immediate context simply means recognizing that the statute grants employees the right to engage in collective bargaining in all workplaces, even where there is no exclusive-majority representative.[91] To deny minority-union employees that right by *restricting* collective bargaining solely to majority unions would not only violate the NLRA, it would also—as *The Charming Betsy* reminds us—"violate the law of nations."

When U.S. labor law is finally clarified on this issue, this nation will be making common cause with other democratic industrialized nations. In almost every advanced industrial democracy, trade-union representation and collective bargaining routinely thrive as the accepted norm, and their labor-relations practices tend to conform to high international standards.[92] It is now time for the United States to join with these other countries and guarantee that the democratic values expressed in international law also become readily available in the American workplace.

9   *The Current State of the Law*

The Issue Is Defined and the Slate Is Clean

What Exactly Is the Issue to Be Resolved?

Oddly, this chapter is mostly about nothing—specifically, the two middle sections contain nothing relevant to the issue posed by this book. Those sections, which cover the related case law, literally contain nothing to indicate that either the NLRB or the courts have ever determined the issue in question. This may come as a surprise to many readers, especially to those who might have assumed that latter-day conventional wisdom had some basis in law, that somewhere there was at least one decision holding that under the National Labor Relations Act an employer had a duty to bargain *only* with a union that represents a majority of its employees in an appropriate bargaining unit. I can report with assurance that there are no such decisions. Indeed, even the latest edition of the American Bar Association's highly respected and authoritative treatise on the law of the National Labor Relations Act, THE DEVELOPING LABOR LAW,[1] contains no discussion of the issue, and not a single case is cited therein to support the popular proposition that the duty to bargain requires the existence of a majority representative. The authors and editors of that treatise have simply assumed conventional wisdom to be the law; and inasmuch as I was the editor-in-chief and principal author of the first and second editions of that work, I confess that I too was equally ignorant or naïve at the time about the issue, for I also failed to challenge the conventional wisdom. Such is the power of conventional wisdom and forgotten history.

There has also never been an adjudication of the more specific issue of whether an employer has an obligation to bargain collectively on a members-only basis with a union that represents a minority of its employees where a Section 9(a) majority representative has not been designated. When such a decision is finally issued—which I hope will be soon—the adjudicating Board or court will be writing on a clean slate. As our examination of statutory construction has demonstrated and as our review of legislative history has confirmed, the prospective ruling on this issue should be that an employer is required by Sections 8(a)(1) and/or 8(a)(5) to bargain collectively with its union-member employees through the labor organization they have chosen—albeit a minority union—provided no other union has been designated or selected by a majority of the employees in an appropriate bargaining unit.

The sole purpose of this chapter is to demonstrate the nothingness in the few extant cases that might suggest to the casual observer that a majority union is in fact a legal necessity for bargaining under the Act. A clear understanding of the issue in question, however, is a prerequisite to a meaningful examination of those cases. The nature of the basic issue is revealed in the straightforward proposition that separates this issue from other subjects with which it might be confused. The proposition with which we are concerned is the employer's duty to bargain collectively with a minority union for its employee-members only. We are not here concerned about the duty to bargain—or more accurately the absence of such a duty—with a minority union that *falsely* claims or implies, whether by words or deeds, that it represents all of the bargaining-unit employees, for such a union is simply a minority union trying to act like a majority union. Nor are we concerned here about an employer's duty to deal with a minority *ad hoc group* of unorganized employees that seeks only adjustment of grievances and does not seek collective bargaining. In the two sections that follow, we examine decisions in both of the last two categories, for these are the cases that might have provided the sources of some of the confusion.

The first section concerns the *false-majority* class of cases. A word of caution about these decisions is in order, for the issue in such cases might easily be mistaken for the main issue. These are decisions in which a minority union was claiming or seemed to be claiming—either overtly or implicitly by its demands or actions—exclusive and majority status. In each of these cases, the resulting holding or relevant assertion in the opinion was a predictable and proper denial of such right of representation. These decisions posed or implied this simple question: Does an employer have a duty to bargain with a minority union as the *exclusive* representative of its employees when in fact such union does not represent a majority of the employees in the bargaining unit? The answer to that question is a resounding no. Unfortunately, however, a careless reader might misconstrue one or more of the conclusionary statements contained in these opinions to be a generalized declaration that a minority union never has a right to engage in collective bargaining, whereas such statements only express the uncontested truism that a minority union has no right to bargain as an exclusive-majority union.

As to the second class of cases—those involving the issue of *group griev-*

ances—a preliminary explanation is again in order because the features of that issue highlight the distinctive dual tracks that Congress provided for the protection of concerted activity under Section 7. The *first track* is the category of "*collective bargaining*"; the second is the category of "*mutual aid or protection.*" Although I am unaware of any such prior labeling of these two distinct types of protected activity, I believe the designations I have appended are useful in distinguishing between the salient features that characterize the two types of activities. They may even aid in avoiding some future misunderstanding and confusion, such as was evidenced in certain imprecise language used in some of the opinions in the cases that we shall be examining.

The short text of the original Wagner Act language in Section 7—still the pertinent text in the present amended Act—is here repeated so that the reader may more easily examine the critical difference between these two tracks as they are displayed in the statutory language itself:

> Sec. 7. Employees shall have the right to self-organization, to form, join, or assist labor organizations, to bargain collectively through representatives of their own choosing, and to engage in concerted activities for the purpose of collective bargaining or other mutual aid or protection. . . .

As I have noted frequently throughout the earlier chapters, the fourteen words in this provision that spell out the employees' right to bargain through minority unions is the composite phrase: "Employees shall have the right . . . to bargain collectively through representatives of their own choosing. . . ." For present purposes, the critical and distinguishing phrase in that passage is "to bargain collectively," for the conduct protected by that phrase embraces only *collective bargaining,* not any other form of interaction between employers and employees.

As noted previously,[2] the statutory words "self-organization" and "labor organizations" are complimentary to the phrase "to bargain collectively" in Section 7. It is thus self-evident from the statutory text that the contemplated collective bargaining process requires the existence of an identifiable *organization* that engages in or seeks to engage in *collective bargaining,* not merely an *ad hoc* amorphous group or any other "employee representation committee or plan in which employees participate"[3] that does not seek to engage in collective bargaining. The last quoted language was added to the statutory definition of "labor organization" in Section 2(5) in order to cover all forms of company unions, not just those organized along the lines of traditional unions that routinely engage in collective bargaining. The express purpose of the added text was thus intended to achieve broader unfair-labor-practice coverage under Section 8(a)(2).[4] Although such a "committee or plan" may be a labor organizations for various purposes—although primarily for purposes of Section 8(a)(2)—such an entity is not a labor organization for purposes of bargaining under Section 7 unless the process of *collective bargaining* is a part of its *raison d'être.*[5] In the rare situation in which such a "committee or plan" might properly be classified as a "labor organization"[6] it would ordinarily be one that "exists for the purpose, in whole or in part, of *dealing with* employers concerning grievances, [and so forth],"[7] but not necessarily for the purpose of engaging in collective bargaining. The Supreme Court in the seminal *Cabot Carbon*[8] case, having observed that the Act's definition of "labor organization" was intentionally phrased to include such "employee-representation committees and plans in order that the employers' activities in connection therewith shall be equally subject to the [unfair labor practice] application of section 8,"[9] declared that the broader term *"dealing with"* in Section 2(5) is not synonymous with *collective bargaining*. And as the Board has held in several cases, employees' ad hoc committees or plans are generally not classified as Section 2(5) "labor organizations."[10] This is not to say, however, that such ad hoc groups cannot become labor organizations, indeed even become collective bargaining labor organizations. They would simply need to be *organized,* however loosely, and seek to engage in *collective bargaining*—a metamorphosis that would surely be consistent with the stated policy of the Act. I hasten to add that such a transition to collective bargaining status may be quite informal and still satisfy the bargaining requirements of Section 7.[11]

When we evaluate the central issue herein it is important that we not confuse the two different categories of concerted activity protected by Section 7. Members-only bargaining concerns the right of a minority organization of employees to *"bargain collectively"* with their employer but not the right of an ad hoc group of unorganized employees to *deal* with their employer *"for mutual aid or protection."* These separate functions are closely related and complementary, but their legal underpinnings are vastly different. Section 7 protects not only collective bargaining—the process—but also "other concerted activities *for the purpose of collective bargaining"*—which is the language that I refer to as *first track* protected concerted activity. This is language that protects concerted activity that is *ancillary* to the collective bargaining process, including such activities as union meetings, economic strikes, picketing, grievance participation, arbitrations, and various additional collective bargaining and related activities. The *"other"* (i.e., non–collective bargaining) concerted activities are protected by what I refer to as the *second track* of Section 7. The text is unambiguous as to the distinction between the two types of activities, specifically referring to "concerted activities for . . . *other* mutual aid or protection." Although "collective bargaining" is a form of "mutual aid or protection," the phrasing of second track language is expressly limited to *other* forms of such activity. It is thus a catch-all provision that covers many different types of employee conduct,[12] but not activities involving collective bargaining, for the latter are separately protected under first-track language. NLRB case law is replete with examples of second-track "other" protected concerted activities, particularly the activity of *unorganized* employees involving protests, discussions, and efforts to call attention to or seek correction of work-related complaints that may concern such matters as work schedules,[13] staffing problems,[14] unfair leave practices,[15] wage disparity,[16] unsafe working conditions,[17] employment discrimination,[18] objectionable supervisory behavior,[19] and so forth. The list of concerted non–collective bargaining activities for "mutual aid or protection" is lengthy and growing. Illustrative of the broad scope of this statutory provision is the Supreme Court's decision in *Eastex, Inc. v. NLRB*,[20] which construed second-track protected concerted activity to include concerted action directed to individuals and institutions outside the employing enterprise, specifically to administrative and judicial forums and to legislators. Such appeals by employees were deemed protected because their intent was "to improve terms and conditions of employment or otherwise improve their lot as employees through channels outside the immediate employee-employer relationship."[21] Although second-track protection is applicable both to unionized and nonunionized employees, it is especially important for the latter, as the Sixth Circuit Court of Appeals observed when it characterized the purpose of the "mutual aid or protection" provision as "protecting unorganized employees who need to speak for themselves as best they can."[22]

Later, our attention in the group-dealing cases will be focused on Board opinions that involve protected concerted activity on the part of groups of nonunion employees who complained about compensation or other unsatisfactory working conditions for which they sought, or intended to seek, their employer's response and adjustment. These cases concern employees who joined together informally, often spontaneously, for "*mutual aid or protection*" in an effort to obtain adjustment of their grievances by seeking to deal with their employer as a group, although not through collective bargaining. It is these second-track cases—and especially dicta in some of their opinions—that should not be confused with the primary issue of a minority group of *union* employees seeking to engage in "*collective bargaining*" when their objective is not "*other* mutual aid or protection" but rather, and specifically, "to bargain collectively," which is a first-track objective.

As we shall observe in our review of those decisions, the Labor Board has occasionally touched upon the non–collective bargaining *dealing* process in cases in which informal groups of unorganized employees—usually on an ad hoc basis—have engaged in protected spontaneous strikes to support their grievances. The issue raised[23] by such cases, however, is not whether the employer is obligated to *bargain collectively* with the group, but whether it is obligated to *deal with* the group *qua group* instead of with the employees individually. That is an important question, but it is not a question involving "collective bargaining," which is the principal concern of this book.

As the reader knows well, it is the thesis of this book that in workplaces where there is no majority representative an employer has a duty to bargain with an "organized" group of employees, even if this is a minority union; this is mandated by clear language in the Act and fully supported by legislative history.[24] Accordingly, as we have learned in Chapter 7, such a construction of the statute falls within *step one* of the Supreme Court's *Chevron*[25] doctrine, for the Act is here neither silent nor ambiguous; hence, the intent of Congress can be determined by using "traditional tools of statutory construction."[26] In applying that doctrine to the NLRA, the Court has stressed that "if a statute's meaning is plain, the Board and the reviewing courts 'must give effect to the unambiguously expressed intent of Congress.'"[27] On the other hand, the process of determining whether an employer has a duty to *deal with* a group of nonunion employees regarding their grievances requires the construction of *nonspecific* statutory text, i.e., the second-track "mutual aid or protection" phrase, which falls within *step two* of the *Chevron* doctrine because "the statute is silent or ambiguous with respect to the specific issue."[28] Thus, to determine this *dealing* issue, the Board can properly exercise a high degree of administrative discretion in its interpretation; indeed, the courts "have traditionally accorded the Board deference with regard to its interpretation of the NLRA as long as its interpretation is rational and consistent with the statute."[29] That issue—whether "mutual aid or protection" language ought to include the right of an informal group of employees to present their grievances as a group to their employer for adjustment—is certainly an important question, and I personally believe that it should be answered by the NLRB in the affirmative. That would be a "permissible construction of the statute"[30] because it is an interpretation that is "rational and consistent with the statute;"[31] again, however, that question is not the issue posed by this book.[32]

The reader might then well ask: Why should there be a distinction between *collective bargaining* with an employer by a union and *dealing with* an employer by a group of non-union employees regarding grievances? The short answer is that the former is required by the unambiguous text of the statute, whereas the latter is not. But the reason behind that answer lies in the fact that Congress had a specific intention with regard to conventional unions and the right of employees to engage in collective bargaining through representatives of their own choosing that is reflected in the language of Section 7. That intention goes to the heart of the statute. Other concerted activity may be related to that objective—such as informal group activity that eventually leads to union organizing—and some group activity may be deemed independently worthy of protection because it is supportive of workers in a nonunion environment.[33] But as to all such unorganized group activity, Congress relied on the Board's discretion and expertise to determine, consistent with the objectives of the statute, which of these second-track activities should be protected; and the NLRB and the courts have long recognized that there is a distinction between *protected* and *unprotected* concerted activity under Section 7.[34] As to the right to engage in collective bargaining, however, Congress had a specific objective in mind and it left no room for discretion as to *whether* that primary duty should be exercised. *How* it should be exercised is largely a matter for the Board's discretion, but not *whether* it should be exercised. Thus, notwithstanding the Board's injection of broad and unrelated dicta in a few of its opinions in nonunion group-action grievance cases, which we examine following the false-majority cases, such dicta should not be confused with the issue of minority-union collective bargaining.

The False Majority Cases

The false-majority cases—of which I have found only eight—are all distinguished by a single critical feature that appears in various forms. In each case, the minority union in question did not seek to represent only its members, and/or it failed to disclaim exclusive representational status, and/or it claimed—or conveyed the impression—that it was acting or seeking to act on behalf of all the employees in the bargaining unit when in fact it did not represent the majority. And some of the opinions contain careless and unnecessary commentary about the union's nonmajority status, which, however, does not affect the basic thrust of those cases. The eight cases are *Segall-Maigen, Inc.,*[35] *Mooresville Cotton Mills,*[36] *Wallace Manufacturing Co.,*[37] *Brashear Freight Lines, Inc.,*[38] *National Linen Service Corp.,*[39] *Olin Industries, Inc.,*[40] *Agar Packing & Provision Corp.,*[41] and *International Ladies' Garment Workers. v. NLRB (Bernhard-Altmann Texas Corp.)*[42]

Segall-Maigen, the earliest of these decisions, involved a variety of unfair labor practices, one of which was an allegation in the complaint that the employer had violated Section 8(5) by refusing to bargain with a union designated by "a majority of the employees"[43] in an appropriate bargaining unit. After counting and comparing the union employees with the total number of employees in the bargaining unit, the Board found no majority and therefore concluded that the union "is not by virtue of Section 9(a) of the Act the *exclusive* representative of the employees."[44] Thus, in the first year of the Act's history, the Board showed its full awareness that the *exclusivity* claim was the real issue in such cases, specifically citing Section 9(a) to make the point. Furthermore, the union did not seek to represent union members only; that feature was never the issue in the case.

Mooresville Cotton Mills raised the same issue of claimed majority. The complaint alleged a violation of Section 8(5) by the employer's refusal "to discuss certain grievances with the *duly designated representatives of the employees.*"[45] However, the Board found that at the time of the alleged refusal to bargain the union represented only approximately 424 members among the employer's 1,400 employees;[46] hence, the employer had no duty to bargain about the grievances raised by the union because it was seeking to represent the employees generally, not just its own members. The grievances in question were clearly generic in nature, directed to "practices which were tending to promote discontent among the employees,"[47] including a request for the adoption of a rule applicable to all employees, to wit, "a fair rule for the hiring and discharging of workers."[48] Consequently—obviously referring to the union's effort at general representation—the Board stated that "[i]t is not an unfair labor practice within the meaning of Section 8, subdivisions (1) and (5), of the Act for an employer to refuse to discuss grievances with employee representatives when such representatives do not represent a majority of his employees."[49] The issue of minority-union bargaining for its members only was not before the Board, nor was it addressed in the foregoing statement.

In *Wallace Manufacturing,* the complaint alleged that the employer had refused "to bargain collectively with the *representatives of its employees*"[50]—hence a claim of exclusive representation. The facts, however, established that the union's membership did not constitute a majority of the employees in the unit; accordingly, the Board held that "we cannot find that the respondent refused to bargain collectively. . . ." Here again was a false-majority case, not a case where the minority union was seeking to bargain for its members only.

Brashear was another garden-variety false-majority case. The union sought to discuss the terms of a proposed agreement covering all the employees in a unit of truck drivers, but the employer refused to bargain, questioning the union's majority status. Six of the drivers then engaged in a strike, which the Board found to be less than a majority of the employees at the time, whereupon the refusal-to-bargain charge was dismissed.

National Linen Service Corp[51] was another case in which the union "*claimed* . . . to represent a majority of the employees,"[52] but the Board found no refusal to bargain because it did not appear that the union represented a majority of the employees in the bargaining unit.

Olin Industries was a case involving a union that was refusing to comply with the filing requirements of Section 9(f), (g), and (h)[53] and was accordingly boycotting use of the Board's procedures. The facts, however, indicated that it was attempting to represent the employees generally and attempting to act as their sole representative. To protest the employer's refusal to bargain about the prevailing general grievances of rolling mill employees, including schedule changes relating to weekend work and bonus payments for consecutive work beyond five shifts, the union called a strike. The matters being protested were typical collective bargaining subjects that would affect all employees. The employer argued that it was under no duty to meet with the union committee regarding those grievances because the union was not the exclusive bargaining representative. The Board found that the employer's failure to meet had precipitated the strike, which was concerted activity protected by Sections 7 and 8(a)(1). However, inasmuch as the union was seeking to act on behalf of the employees generally, the Board noted that "[w]hile the Respondent was under no legal obligation to meet with the Union, there is nothing in the Act which removes from its protection concerted activity aimed at securing a meeting between the Employer and the Union to discuss grievances."[54] The duty to bargain with a minority union for members only was never the issue. Indeed, the union's nonexclusive status was wholly unrelated to the Board's decision, which found the employer guilty of numerous and serious unfair labor practices, none of which involved bargaining.

In *Agar Packing* the union had made an effort to discuss a worker's discharge with the employer, but the employer refused to meet with the union concerning the matter and this precipitated a strike. The Board upheld the union's right to protest the discharge and to seek the employee's reinstatement. Regarding the employer's argument that it was under no duty to meet with the union committee because the union was not the employees' exclusive bargaining agent, the Board gratuitously commented: "While the Respondent was under no legal obligation to meet with the Union, there is nothing in the Act which removes from its protection concerted activity aimed at securing a meeting . . . to discuss [the dischargee's] reinstatement."[55] This assertion concerning the absence of legal obligation clearly referred to the union's appearing to act like an *exclusive* bargaining agent, which it was not.[56] In any event, the statement was unnecessary to this feature of the Board's decision, for the strike was held to be a fully protected concerted activity under Sections 7 and 8(a)(1). There was no allegation in the complaint about a refusal to bargain either under Section 8(a)(1) or Section 8(a)(5). Refusal to bargain was not an issue in the case, and there was certainly no reference, directly or indirectly, to members-only bargaining.

In *Bernhard-Altmann*, the Supreme Court affirmed the Board's ruling that it was an unfair labor practice for an employer and a union to enter into an agreement in which the employer recognized the union as the *exclusive* representative of the employees in a bargaining unit when in fact it did not represent a majority of those employees. It was not a sufficient defense that the union and the employer both believed in good faith that the union had the consent of a majority of the employees. The Court's opinion emphasized that the "vice in the agreement" was "the *exclusive* representation provision," which it pointedly "*distinguished from an employer's bargaining with a minority union for its members only.*"[57]

The preceding cases are fully consistent with the plain-language requirement of Section 9(a): that if a union seeks recognition or is recognized as the employees' exclusive bargaining representative, it must in fact have been "designated or selected" by a majority of the bargaining unit employees. Indeed, as the Supreme Court declared in *Bernhard-Altmann*, the vice in such cases is the matter of "exclusive representation." None of these cases support the proposition that an employer's duty to bargain applies only to unions that meet the majority requirement of Section 9(a), and—as the cases that follow illustrate—the Board has never cited or relied on any of these cases for such a proposition. Accordingly, there is nothing in these false majority cases that stands in the way of an employer's duty to bargain with a minority union in workplaces where there is no Section 9(a) representative.

The Group-Dealing Cases

Now for the *group-dealing* cases—of which there are four—all of which involve second-track mutual-aid-or-protection concerted activity. These cases have either posed or alleged the issue of whether an employer has an obligation under Section 8(a)(1) to meet with a group of nonunion employees or their representative in an effort to resolve group grievances when so requested. Does the employer commit an unfair labor practice when it refuses such a meeting, insisting instead on dealing with the employees on an individual basis only? Obviously that issue is not the one posed by this book, but three of these group-dealing cases nevertheless contain statements in their dicta that suggest, in accordance with latter-day conventional wisdom, that the duty to bargain applies *only* to bargaining with majority-exclusive representatives. The opinions in those cases are apparently the only NLRB decisions that have expressed such a position, albeit vague or ambiguous and in dicta. Nevertheless, despite the absence of actual holdings—and none of these cases even mentions members-only collective bargaining—these decisions invite our attention in order to avoid confusing their unrelated dicta with the real issue that is our concern. Furthermore, all four cases reveal—notwithstanding latter-day conventional wisdom—that there has been affirmative support from the Board itself, and also from five authoritative officials within the Board's hierarchy, for the proposition that Sections 7 and 8(a)(1) require an employer to *deal with* a group of employees concerning their grievances despite the absence of an exclusive-majority representative. Although that proposition concerns only *Chevron*[58] step-two discretionary decision making that relates to track-two concerted activity under Section 7 (i.e., "mutual aid or protection"), such affirmative positions are fully consistent with the minority-bargaining premise advanced here; hence, they deserve our attention.

The first of the group-dealing cases was *Lundy Manufacturing*,[59] in which the Board found a violation of Section 8(a)(1) when the employer refused to meet with an employees' grievance committee that it considered to be unduly influenced by a union it had not recognized. The Administrative Law Judge (ALJ), with the Board's approval, found that

> there was no recognized bargaining representative of the employees, nor was [there] any valid collective-bargaining agreement covering the pro-

cessing of grievances in effect at the time.[60] Therefore, *the Company was under statutory obligation to at least accept and meet with and discuss grievances with the committee.*[61]

Although the company seemed to base its refusal to meet on its belief that the nonrecognized union was seeking backdoor recognition through the grievance committee, the ALJ expressly found "that the committee merely requested the company to accept or recognize it for handling grievances and did not, as urged by the company, demand exclusive recognition as the representative of the employees for that purpose or any other purpose."[62] The Board therefore held that the refusal to deal with the committee violated Section 8(a)(1), which according to Professor Alan Hyde "seems to assume that there are circumstances in which an employer might be ordered to 'entertain a grievance' although it could not be ordered to bargain. . . ."[63] He attributes the Board's finding—correctly in my view—to the weight it placed on the proviso to Section 9(a), noting, however, that such "proviso will not bear that weight after [the Supreme Court's] opinion in *Emporium Capwell Co. v. Western Addition Community Organization,*"[64] which held that an employer's obligation to listen to an employee grievance must rest on "the main part of 9(a)," not on the proviso.[65] Although that is certainly true, the Board's finding would today be fully supportable under the *Chevron* step-two premise.[66] Recognizing the importance and the potential of *Lundy,* Professor Hyde opines:

> Most American workers today are in the same situation as the workers in *Lundy Manufacturing.* They have no majority union, no stewards, no grievance system. (They do not even have a defunct "company union!") They are trapped in a "vacuum" in which their section 7 rights rest on hope. *Lundy Manufacturing* offers some hope that employers might become obligated to meet with nonmajority factions, at least in "vacuums."[67]

Lundy thus represents an affirmative ruling by the NLRB that a group of unorganized employees who seek to deal with their employer regarding their grievances *qua group* (i.e., concertedly) have that right under the Act. Unfortunately, the Board has not repeated that holding in subsequent cases, although many responsible individuals within the NLRB establishment, as we shall observe, apparently continued to believe *Lundy* to be the current state of the law.

Unfortunately, the conventional—but contrary—wisdom spilled over into a trilogy of Board decisions during a five-year period from 1976 to 1981. Those cases were *Swearingen Aviation Corp.,*[68] *Pennypower Shopping News, Inc.,*[69] and *Charlston Nursing Center.*[70] As we have learned in Chapter 4, it is a fact of history that after World War II both unions and employers, with few exceptions,[71] became dependent upon—indeed addicted to—the election process. Thus, for many decades almost everyone in the industrial relations community has assumed that a union has no right to bargain unless it represents a majority of the employees in an appropriate unit. It is therefore not surprising to find this conventional view reflected in a few NLRB opinions four decades after passage of the Act, even though such expressions were unnecessary to those decisions. Although we shall carefully examine these cases in the following pages, in the end there will be nothing to show but superfluous references irrelevant to their outcomes and therefore not precedential—in other words, pure *obiter dicta*.[72] And because these cases involve ad hoc groups of unorganized employees who were only seeking resolution of their grievances—not organized unions seeking to bargain collectively for their members only—any dictum in these opinions that implies there is no duty to bargain with a union that does not represent a majority of the employees in an appropriate unit can be labeled "double dictum." Nor should it be overlooked that the complaints issued in those cases represented serious efforts by four General Counsels of the NLRB and one ALJ to obtain rulings from the Board consistent with *Lundy,* to wit, that in the absence of an exclusive-majority representative an employer is obligated to meet and deal with its employees as a *group*—rather than individually—when so requested, regarding their grievances. Various findings of fact and procedural problems in those three cases, however, thwarted full adjudication of that issue; consequently, *Lundy* remains the only true Board holding on this subject.

The first of the trilogy was the *Swearingen Aviation* case. Its primary feature was a protected *Washington Aluminum*[73]–type walkout by a group of twenty-four employees. A digression to explain *Washington Aluminum* is here in order. In that decision, the Supreme Court addressed the issue of protected concerted activity by a group of unorganized employees who had engaged in a walkout to protest unsatisfactory working conditions—specifically a bitterly cold plant—without first having given the employer an opportunity to respond to their complaint. That lack of responsive opportunity was the employer's defense for having discharged the participants in the spontaneous strike. Setting "the tone that made allowances for the employees' lack of sophistication and organizational experience"[74] in exercising their Section 7 rights, the Court declared that

> We cannot agree that employees necessarily lose their right to engage in concerted activities under 7 merely because they do not present a specific demand upon their employer to remedy a condition they find objectionable. The language of 7 is broad enough to protect concerted activities whether they take place before, after, or at the same time such a demand is made. To compel the Board to interpret and apply that language in the re-

stricted fashion suggested by the respondent here would only tend to frustrate the policy of he Act to protect the right of workers to act together to better their working conditions.[75]

In *Swearingen,* the employer, like the employer in *Washington Aluminum,* had also discharged the striking employees, thereby converting their walk-out into an unfair-labor-practice strike.[76] The critical issue in the case was whether the employer had unlawfully refused to reinstate the strikers following their request for reinstatement, for there was a question about the unconditionality of their offer to return to work. However, among the charges raised by the General Counsel in the complaint was an allegation that the employer had violated Section 8(a)(1) by refusing to allow the group's spokesperson to present grievances for adjustment on behalf of both himself and other employees.[77]

The factual details relating to the alleged failure of the employer in *Swearingen* to deal with the group—an issue that ultimately turned out to be irrelevant to the outcome of the case—are not significant here.[78] The bottom line was that the ALJ found that the facts established that the employer had not refused to deal with the group; accordingly that allegation was dismissed from the complaint, and this should have ended the matter. Instead, however, the ALJ gratuitously offered his own view of assumed conventional wisdom by adding the following dictum:

> I am *aware of no authority* for concluding that such conduct would have violated the Act. [In no case that] I know of has it been held violative of Section 8(a)(1) for an employer to refuse to entertain and adjust grievances in circumstances such as those present here where there is no collective bargaining agreement with an exclusive representative of employees in an appropriate unit requiring it to do so.[79]

On review, the Board ignored that superfluous comment, for there was nothing before it on that issue, and this matter therefore never reached the court of appeals that reviewed the case.[80] Accordingly, General Counsel John Irving had no opportunity to present an argument on the merits of his position on that issue, either before the Board or the court.[81] The foregoing dictum in *Swearingen* thus stands only for the vague and uninformed opinion of one ALJ and nothing more. And of course that dictum can also be termed double dictum because the case involved an effort at group dealing, not minority-union collective bargaining. Nevertheless, as we shall note shortly, *Swearingen* was later inflated to unreal proportions.

In the next case, *Pennypower Shopping News, Inc.,* General Counsel Irving made another effort to correct the conventional wisdom, but that effort was again frustrated by unforeseen circumstances at the ALJ level.[82] The factual scenario involved another *Washington Aluminum* walkout. Eleven employees had joined together on a Friday evening to present a petition to management in which they listed certain economic demands and grievances; whereupon, after announcing they would return on Monday, they simultaneously and concertedly quit work. Returning on Monday as promised, they met with the production manager through whom they attempted to arrange a meeting with the general manager. The latter, however, refused to meet with them as a group, stating that he would meet only with each employee individually. The following excerpt from the ALJ's report provides a revealing glimpse at a frustrating—but not unusual—workplace story that vividly describes how these unorganized employees felt, what they believed their rights to be, and their disappointment with the rejection they had received from their employer.

> On Tuesday, employee Debra Leisek called Walton [the general manager] on the phone and started by apologizing. "I started off by saying that I knew that we had done some things wrong. . . . I asked him if I could come in and talk to him. I said, 'I know that you don't want to talk to the whole group, but how about a grievance committee? We've elected a grievance committee, a small one of five. Will you talk to us? And he said 'We don't have a committee at Pennypower, Debbie.' . . . He said, 'if you'd like to make an appointment with me, I'll be happy to talk to you.' Having agreed to meet with Walton alone the next morning, Leisek that same day again met with the rest of the strikers. Their group decision was, still in Leisek's words at the hearing: "maybe it would be just better to just remain as a group, because *we knew we had the right to stay as a group.* We did not have to talk to him individually, and so we decided I wouldn't go, and we decided that Peggy would call and tell him.[83]

The contested fact-issue in the case was whether the production manager had either advised the employees at the Monday meeting that they were discharged—or else had given them reason to believe they were discharged—or whether he had simply told them they would be replaced. The ALJ found that they had not been discharged, concluding that the production manager had only "said they would be replaced";[84] the Board, however, remanded the case for a hearing *de novo* because it determined that this issue could not be resolved without credibility findings. Apparently the case was ultimately settled, for there is no record of any further hearing or supplemental ALJ or Board decision. Our interest in the case stems from the Board's curious reference in its opinion on remand to the employer's refusal to meet with the group *qua group*—which was never a pivotal question in the case. The Board now inserted its own new and confusing dictum—but only in a footnote—in which it said:

We do not, however, disagree with the Administrative Law Judge's conclusion with respect to [the employer's] lawful right, *in these circumstances,* to refuse to deal with the strikers except on an individual basis and we accordingly adopt his dismissal of that allegation of the complaint as a matter of law.[85]

What did the Board mean by "in these circumstances"? Did it mean *for this case only*? No matter, for it was pure dictum that should and could have been avoided. More significantly, it gave no indication that it was overruling its holding in the *Lundy* case.

The aforesaid dictum in *Pennypower* may have been the reason why the drafters of the complaint in the last of the group-dealing trilogy cases, *Charlston Nursing Center,* posed in the alternative the issue of the employer's refusal to meet with employees as a group.[86] Nevertheless, the ALJ treated that allegation as a material issue and it was fully litigated at the hearing.[87] Although the *Pennypower* dictum by footnote was curious, this latest and final episode in our story of "nothingness" was—as Alice would say—even "curiouser and curiouser!"[88] The employees in *Charlston* were an unorganized "group of over 40 nurses aides"[89] who, like the employees in *Pennypower,* were under the impression that their employer had an obligation to meet with them as a group. When he failed to do so, they concertedly walked out—once again a *Washington Aluminum* second-track mutual-aid-or-protection strike. This time the ALJ perceptively found that the employer's "admitted refusal to meet with them as a group . . . was clearly an unfair labor practice."[90] He stated that

It is well settled that an employer may not refuse to discuss wages, hours, or working conditions with a group of its employees in favor of meeting with them individually since *such conduct is antithetical to concerted activity protected by Sec. 7 of the Act.*[91]

It is unknown whether he based that conclusion on the *Lundy* case, but he was certainly in agreement with the positions taken by the four NLRB General Counsels who had posed that issue in the complaints in the three cases here under review. This ALJ found the strike to be an unfair-labor-practice strike that had been caused by the employer's refusal to meet with the employees as a group; he therefore recommended that the striking employees be reinstated regardless of any replacement employees who might have been hired following the strike.

When *Pennypower* reached the Board, the plot thickened—this plot, of course, was only a story line in a work of fiction, not a nefarious scheme. Without intending any disrespect for the Board as an institution—which I hold in high regard—I must nevertheless report that in this instance the

Board, like Alice, soon strayed into the realm of make-believe. Based on its examination of allegedly undisputed facts, it declared that

> Respondent did not absolutely refuse to meet with the employees as a group, but merely refused to meet with the employees as a group at that time because of a prior commitment. . . . Therefore, under all the circumstances of this case, we find that Respondent did not violate Section 8(a)(1) of the Act by refusing to meet with the nurses aides. . . .[92]

That conclusion, based on the Board's assessment of the facts, was not necessarily unreasonable, and it should have fully disposed of the matter, for now there had been no refusal to meet or deal with the group. Instead, however, the Board chose to step into Wonderland and produce a work of pure legal fiction that would further confuse the subject at hand. That fiction was divided into four parts.

In the first part, the Board stated that it did not agree with the ALJ's "finding that [the employer's] refusal to meet with the nurses aides as a group violated Section 8(a)(1) of the Act,"[93] and it volunteered the assertion "that *generally* an employer is under no obligation to meet with employees or entertain their grievances upon request where there is no collective-bargaining agreement with an exclusive bargaining representative requiring it to do so."[94] That assertion of law was unadulterated *obiter dictum,* wholly unnecessary to any issue, for the Board had expressly found that the employer had not refused to meet with the group. The Board was thus acting like the Queen of Hearts: "Sentence first—verdict afterwards."[95] Indeed, that was the order in which the Board issued its assertion of law and its finding of fact: first its aforesaid dictum of law—afterwards its "verdict" of fact, which was that the employer *had not refused* to meet with the group.[96]

In the second part, the Board cited as the *sole* basis for its assertion of law the ALJ's dictum in *Swearingen Aviation* and its own footnote dictum in *Pennypower Shopping News*—portraying those citations, however, not as dicta but as holdings. It thus ignored the text of the statute and its own ruling in *Lundy.*

In the third part, the Board literally misrepresented that the Fifth Circuit Court of Appeals' opinion in *Swearingen Aviation*[97] had affirmed the ALJ's dictum, for it averred that the court had *enforced* the Board's decision "in pertinent part,"[98] whereas the specific matter of the employer's alleged refusal to allow presentation of the group grievance—which the ALJ in *Swearingen* had found not to be a refusal at all—was never even addressed either by the Board or the court. In fact, the court expressly omitted the ALJ's dictum concerning the employer's alleged refusal to meet with the group's representative, stating: "we enforce *only* that part of the Board's order finding Section 8(a)(1) violations for threatening employees with discharge, discharging striking employees, and refusing to reinstate [three named employees] upon their unconditional offers . . . to return to work."[99]

The fourth part concerns the Board's reference in its dictum-assertion to the absence of a "collective bargaining agreement with an exclusive bargaining representative," for the ALJ had made a ruling, which the Board adopted, that the "group of over 40 nurses aides" was not a "labor organization" within the meaning of the Act;[100] hence, it was not a collective bargaining organization. The Board thus determined in *Charlston*, as it had in a previous case[101] on which the ALJ had relied, that an ad hoc group of unorganized employees that seeks to present grievances to their employer is not a *labor organization* within the meaning of the Act. Accordingly, not only was the Board's legal assertion obiter dictum because it was commentary "unnecessary to the decision in the case and therefore not precedential,"[102] it was another example of double obiter dictum because the factual situation did not involve a labor organization—it only involved an *unorganized* group of employees seeking to deal with their employer for mutual aid or protection, in other words, Section 7 second-track activity; it was not an effort by an organized group of employees to engage in "collective bargaining" through a labor union.

A saving grace—or better yet a saving face—may be the Board's use of the qualifier "generally" in its dictum in *Charlston*. Thus, if the Board in a future case were to take the position that this dictum had some precedential value, it would not be bound to follow it or even overrule it, for if an employer might *generally* have no obligation to meet and therefore *deal* with an *unorganized* group of employees "where there is no collective bargaining agreement with an exclusive representative requiring it to do so," there would still be an obligation to meet with the representative of an *organized* group of employees who seek to *bargain collectively* on a members-only basis through their labor-union representative, provided of course there is no exclusive-majority representative at that time in their workplace unit. But regarding the dealing with an unorganized group concerning grievances—the *Chevron* step-two issue—there is still the *Lundy* case, which should prevail unless and until it is overruled.

Charlston Nursing Center might just as well have been a case from Wonderland, for had it been only a dream it would have been easier to explain. But like Alice, the Board will eventually awaken, at which time it should realize that there is undreamed of potential in Section 7 yet to be explored.

A Clean Slate

This concludes our search for and examination of any and all cases that might have adjudicated and ruled on the matter of minority-union bargaining. We found nothing because there was nothing. Using familiar tools of the lawyers' trade to determine whether the Board had ever ruled on the issue in question,[103] I attempted to gather all possible related utterances in every case associated with this subject. What I learned was that none of the decisions had ruled on the issue in question and that none had been cited in subsequent cases concerning this issue.[104] Furthermore, with the exception of the Supreme Court's supportive *Bernhard-Altmann*[105] decision, all the examined opinions were in obscure cases. From an adjudicatory standpoint, the issue is clearly an open question.

It should be noted further, however, that this absence of adjudicatory history also means that restricting an employer's duty to bargain with only Section 9(a) majority unions, even where none exists, cannot be justified simply on the basis of its having been the practice for a long period of time. This is so because the essential conditions for such a holding, such as prevailed in *NLRB v. Bell Aerospace Company,*[106] are entirely missing here. The Supreme Court there held that a long-standing construction of the statute—in that case involving the exclusion of managerial employees from the Act's coverage—could not be changed by the Board many years later where the conditions were the following: (1) the construction was not specified in the statutory text but was consistent with legislative history, (2) the Board had explicitly and consistently ruled directly in accordance with that construction in no less than six cases[107] and indirectly in many more, (3) the appellate courts, without exception, had confirmed such rulings, and (4) it was this reading that was deliberately permitted to stand when Congress later amended the Act. In other words, the Court in *Bell Aerospace* relied on strong and multifaceted legal precedent, not on unsupported conventional wisdom.

Inasmuch as we have found nothing useful in the decisions we examined in this chapter, why have I subjected the reader to such detailed analyses of these cases? I have done so because the conventional wisdom about exclusive majority-union bargaining is so deeply ingrained in the psyche of the American industrial-relations community that I deemed it necessary to conduct this all-inclusive assessment in an effort to enlighten any skeptical reader who might still be clinging to a belief that the conventional wisdom had some support in case law. To the nonskeptical reader, I apologize accordingly. As we have learned, the cases here reviewed have established that when the Board and the courts finally write on this issue, they will be writing on a clean slate. And because I am not displeased that we found nothing in the existing case law, I am happy to close this chapter with Porgy's joyful expression, "I got plenty o nuttin and nuttin's plenty fo me."[108]

PART III
Implementation and Its Aftermath

10 *Obtaining Imprimaturs from the Labor Board and the Courts*

Alternative Routes to Legal Acceptance

Having provided the reader with historical and legal authority for members-only collective bargaining—including converge of the statutory, constitutional, and international-law bases for such authority—I now turn to the tasks of spelling out how NLRB and judicial acceptance of that objective can be accomplished and what might be expected from the outcome of such an achievement. This chapter addresses the essential process of legal implementation. The next chapter, Chapter 11, describes a proposed organizational methodology that might be usefully employed to establish minority labor unions and how such unions can complement the union organizational process. And Chapter 12 provides what I consider to be a plausible forecast of the natural and likely evolution of these new organizational structures, their interaction with employers and other employees, and their possible impact on American society.

Setting the Stage for Legal Implementation

The legal implementation of minority-union bargaining will probably begin with the planning and processing of test cases, and ideally there should be a multitude of such potential cases. Here are three reasons why this effort should be spread among as many different organizational sites as possible.

First, a large number of members-only organizational drives will provide a variety of legal situations. Inasmuch as there are several means by which such tests could or should occur, described later, and law cases are frequently settled and thus yield no legal precedent, it will be useful to have available multiple choices in order to obtain a reasonably prompt and satisfactory resolution of the legal issues that will be advanced. Furthermore, a wide variety of geographical locations can provide an element of choice in the selection of judicial forums for appellate review and possibly direct district-court actions, should such become necessary in the event the NLRB General Counsel refuses to issue the necessary complaint.

Second, the organizational process to be described in Chapter 11 is one that ought to be followed regardless of whether it succeeds in achieving formal decisional authority for members-only bargaining within a reasonable period of time. That process, which calls for organizing employees from the very beginning by means of a viable and functioning labor union—even where the employer is actively engaged in anti-union conduct—will be more likely to achieve majority status than the more traditional method of campaigning for authorization cards and election votes.[1] Thus, if a union were to begin an organizational drive in which one of its objectives, or even possibilities, is to establish a fact situation to test the members-only bargaining thesis, it would be in no worse a position—and probably a better one—if it later chose to switch to a more traditional election-based campaign in the event its legal case were initially unsuccessful or inordinately delayed by the litigation process. Consequently, as many potential test efforts as possible should be undertaken, and they should be accompanied by appropriate educational programs to familiarize the active participants with the new concepts and objectives. These efforts should involve several different unions, and it will be advantageous if the organizational campaigns and legal actions are coordinated.

Third, widespread and highly visible attempts by minority-union employees to achieve collective bargaining with recalcitrant employers could help foster awareness by the public and the media—especially the national media—of the pressing need for this proposed legal reform. Efforts should therefore be made to disseminate information and education about these organizational efforts and the expectation of forthcoming administrative and judicial relief. Creating a critical mass of favorable public opinion will be important to the attainment of the ultimate objective, for widespread discussion and debate can help to create a sympathetic atmosphere conducive to NLRB and judicial articulation of what might otherwise be deemed a startling outcome. Erroneous conventional wisdom can thereby be discredited, and the democratic right of association can be on its way to restoration in the American workplace.

Most employers will undoubtedly resist these efforts to obtain members-only recognition and bargaining; and refusals to bargain, plus other anti-union conduct, will undoubtedly continue to some extent even after a final judicial decision is issued confirming the legitimacy of this rediscovered bargaining duty. Although the newly discovered organizational process may bring into being several different kinds of representational structures,[2] the fledgling organizations that are most likely to produce the necessary test cases will probably be minority-membership unions sponsored by traditional affiliated unions, for they will be the ones financially capable of supporting the necessary litigation.

Implementation through Normal National Labor Relations Board Procedures

Because of the absence of a general right of an aggrieved party to independently file suit for violation of the NLRA, and because the NLRB General Counsel has exclusive jurisdiction to issue complaints and bring cases before the Board for final orders,[3] obtaining an NLRB decision on the central question will be difficult—or at least delayed—if the General Counsel is not supportive of the legal objective. This is so because of the presumptive unreviewability of the General Counsel's refusal to issue a complaint.[4] As the labor-law community is well aware, the normal practice under the Act is for a party to file a charge with an NLRB Regional Director, which brings the alleged commission of an unfair labor practice to the attention of the General Counsel's office. If that office (i.e., the General Counsel) deems the charge meritorious, a complaint will be issued. Thereafter, unless a settlement is reached, the case proceeds to a hearing before an ALJ and then to the Board for its consideration and final order.[5] However, if the General Counsel refuses to issue a complaint, other means will need to be employed to obtain judicial determination of the minority-union bargaining issue.

It will of course be preferable if the General Counsel issues a complaint, whereupon the Board will consider the case and render its decision in due course without judicial intervention prior to the Board's decision, for deciding cases is the Board's primary responsibility. In this instance, as previously noted, the Board's decision might be twofold in nature. Initially, it could and should hold that under the clear requirements of the statute, in a workplace where there is no Section 9(a) exclusive-majority representative, a minority union is entitled to recognition and bargaining on behalf of its employee members and an employer who refuses such recognition or bargaining is committing an unfair labor practice. In addition, however, even if the statutory language were to be deemed ambiguous or silent as to this issue, the Board could and should deliver an alternative ruling declaring the same holding, for such a determination would represent a rational construction of the statute consistent with the congressional purpose embodied in the Act, hence a *permissible* construction under step two of the *Chevron* doctrine.[6] The reader is here reminded of that doctrine and the reasons presented in Chapter 7 for supporting such a dual determination by the Board.[7]

What if, however, the General Counsel refuses to issue a complaint based on the proposed minority-bargaining thesis? Should that happen, four other approaches are available to achieve litigation of the issue. Proponents could pursue judicial intervention either by direct court action or by picketing, or they could proceed through either of two rarely used devices: a piggy-back amendment to a complaint in a hearing being conducted by an ALJ or a petition to the Board for substantive rulemaking.

Implementation through Direct Judicial Intervention

Either or both of the following scenarios describe appropriate direct judicial actions that could produce the desired result. The first involves a suit in federal district court to mandate that the General Counsel issue a complaint. The second involves picketing for members-only recognition. This would probably cause the employer to file an unfair-labor-practice charge alleging violation of Section 8(b)(7),[8] whereupon the Regional Director—assuming she or he determines that there is reasonable cause to believe the charge to be true—would petition a federal district court for a Section 10(l)[9] injunction.

Direct Legal Action against the General Counsel

This first scenario concerns a role that the judiciary must occasionally perform either by direct district-court action or by extraordinary appellate action. Such judicial intervention becomes possible when an administrative agency patently misconstrues key statutory language as to which the statute is silent regarding judicial review and there is no factual issue to be resolved. Such intervention would be appropriate if the NLRB General Counsel refused to issue a complaint to enforce the proposed minority-union bargaining, for such a refusal would deny the Board—the agency charged with initial responsibility for interpreting the statute—an opportunity to exercise its assigned function of interpreting and rendering a final order that would be subject to ordinary judicial review.[10] Notwithstanding popular perception about the unreviewable discretion of the NLRB General Counsel to issue a complaint, there are indeed limits to such discretion. Although the Supreme Court has never ruled directly on the issue of General Counsel unreviewability, it has on several occasions indicated in dicta that a general rule to that effect exists,[11] and I do not contest that proposition. The Court, however, has also recognized several exceptions applicable to this rule. Five cases in particular define the principal areas of exception: *American Federation of Labor v. NLRB*,[12] *Leedom V. Kyne*,[13] *Boire v. Greyhound Corp.*,[14] *Heckler v. Chaney*;[15] and *Citizens to Preserve Overton Park. Inc. v. Volpe.*[16]

In *American Federation of Labor* the Supreme Court posed the basic question of whether a claimant is "precluded . . . from maintaining an independent suit in a district court to set aside the Board's action because contrary to the statute."[17] It later answered that question in *Leedom v. Kyne. Kyne* involved a direct action in federal district court by a union of professional employees seeking to vacate an NLRB certification that violated a statutory provision prohibiting the grouping of professional and nonprofessionals in the same bargaining unit without affording the professionals an election to determine their consent to such inclusion. In allowing the suit, the Court said that

> "absence of jurisdiction of the federal courts" would mean "a sacrifice or obliteration of a right which Congress" has given professional employees, for there is no other means within their control . . . to protect and enforce that right. . . . This Court cannot lightly infer that Congress does not intend judicial protection of rights it confers against agency action taken in excess of delegated powers.[18]

Later, in *Boire v. Greyhound,* the Court stressed that the *Kyne* exception was a narrow one, applicable only where the Board had patently misconstrued the Act, and it would not be applied where there was a question of fact to be reviewed.

Although *Kyne* involved the Board's violation of a negative statutory provision, "its rationale has been held to be equally applicable when . . . the Board or its agents act in disregard of an affirmative or mandatory command,"[19] and its rationale has likewise been applied to actions or inactions of the Board's General Counsel and Regional Director.[20]

Although the Supreme Court has not specifically ruled on the reviewability of the NLRB General Counsel's authority to issue complaints, its decisions involving other administrative agencies subject to the same provisions of the Administrative Procedure Act (APA)[21] are here applicable. Recognized judicial exceptions to the doctrine of unreviewability of discretionary administrative action indicate that such authority is directly reviewable where the issue is one of *pure statutory construction* and the matter has not been committed to the agency's sole discretion or where a right under the Constitution is involved,[22] provided no other adequate remedy is available. In *Heckler v. Chaney* the Court addressed the central issue that defines the limits on the NLRB General Counsel's discretionary authority regarding judicial review of agency action allegedly "committed to agency discretion by law" within the meaning of Section 701(a)(2) of the APA.[23] The Court spelled out specific guidelines for determining when a refusal of an agency to initiate action is subject to judicial review.[24] In an opinion by then Justice Rehnquist, the Court indicated that "an agency's decision not to take enforcement action should be *presumed* immune from judicial review under §701(a)(2),"[25] but in so stating the Court declared that

> we emphasize that the decision is *only presumptively unreviewable;* the presumption may be rebutted where the substantive statute has provided guidelines for the agency to follow in exercising its enforcement powers.

Thus, in establishing this presumption in the APA, *Congress did not set agencies free to disregard legislative direction in the statutory scheme that the agency administers.*[26]

The *Heckler* opinion pointed with approval to *Citizens to Preserve Overton Park. Inc. v. Volpe* regarding the "threshold question"[27] of whether the agency's action was at all reviewable and quoted the following excerpt from the opinion in that case, the essence of which applies to the issue here under consideration:[28]

In this case, there is no indication that Congress sought to prohibit judicial review and there is most certainly no "showing of 'clear and convincing evidence' of a . . . legislative intent" to restrict access to judicial review.[29]

Similarly, the Secretary's decision here does not fall within the exception for action "committed to agency discretion." This is a very narrow exception. . . . The legislative history of the Administrative Procedure Act indicates that *it is applicable in those rare instances where "statutes are drawn in such broad terms that in a given case there is no law to apply.'*"[30]

The NLRA is patently not such a statute.

Regarding the constitutional issue, the Court in *Heckler* did not directly address the matter of unreviewability of discretionary action where "a colorable claim is made . . . that the agency's refusal to institute proceedings violated any constitutional rights;"[31] however, such an exception has long been recognized. Judge Learned Hand, writing for the Second Circuit Court of Appeals in 1949, declared that "if a constitutional question were raised [and] this assertion of constitutional right is not transparently frivolous, it gave the District Court jurisdiction. . . ."[32]

The foregoing judicial precedents establish that if the Labor Board's General Counsel refuses to issue a complaint, and thus prevents the Board from ruling on the critical issue in question, such inaction violates the APA and provides sufficient basis for a district court to issue a mandamus-type order requiring issuance of a complaint. For these purposes, the district court would thus be the reviewing court granting relief under Section 702 of the APA to persons suffering "legal wrong" because of agency action or inaction; and, pursuant to Section 706(1) of that Act,[33] such court could "compel agency action unlawfully withheld" and set aside the General Counsel's refusal to issue a complaint as "arbitrary, capricious, an abuse of discretion, . . . not in accordance with law,[34] [or] contrary to constitutional right. . . ."[35]

Although such a determination would be fully supported by the cases here noted, its logic is independently compelling and elementary. Congress intended for the NLRB to interpret the Act and issue decisions under that Act, and it provided for judicial review of those decisions.[36] It did not confer final interpretative authority on a General Counsel over whom there would be no judicial review. Notwithstanding this logic, if it were concluded that the General Counsel does have unreviewable authority to issue a complaint, regardless of the considerations just discussed, it would follow that such a determination would constitute a *final order* of the Board. Accordingly, because "[a]ny person aggrieved by a final order of the Board granting or denying in whole or in part the relief sought may obtain a review of such order in [an appropriate] United States Court of Appeals,"[37] such direct appellate action would provide another route to judicial relief. Although the appellate court might exercise any of several remedial options under such circumstances, it is most likely that it would remand the case to the Board for initial hearing and consideration.

Whatever the judicial route taken, a remedy is bound to be available to correct a refusal by the General Counsel to issue a complaint on such a critical issue of law. Professor Bernard Schwartz's observation is appropriate here:

> [T]here is no place for unreviewable discretion in a system such as ours. Provided that the case is justiciable, all discretionary power should be reviewable to determine that the discretion conferred has not been abused. What the English courts call the *Wednesbury* principle[38] is just as valid in American administrative law. Under it, the reviewing court should always be able to determine that the discretion has not been exercised in a manner in which no reasonable administrator would act.[39]

Picketing for Members-Only Recognition

The second possible scenario for obtaining direct judicial intervention if the General Counsel refuses to issue a complaint supportive of members-only and minority-union bargaining involves picketing for such recognition and bargaining. Such picketing would be directed at an employer and workplace where there is currently no exclusive majority-union representative. The key to such an action lies in Section 8(b)(7), the Landrum-Griffin amendment that restricts organizational and recognitional picketing, and Section 10(l), the Taft-Hartley mandatory-injunction provision that applies to picketing where there is "reasonable cause to believe" that Section 8(b)(7) has been violated.[40] To activate this approach, a minority union would request recognition and bargaining on behalf of its "members only," being careful not to claim representation of a majority of the employees in any appropriate bargaining unit or to seek bargaining on behalf of all employees in such a unit. The employer, in accordance with latter-day conventional wisdom, will presumably deny that request, whereupon picketing may begin. Such picketing should simply protest the employer's refusal to recognize and bargain with the union for its employee-members only. To assure this critical limitation of intention, I also recommend that the picket signs expressly disclaim any organizational purpose and any intent to represent all of the employees in a likely bargaining unit—or for that matter any employees who are not presently members of the union.

Obviously, the target of such picketing should be an employer and location where picketing can be reasonably effective—perhaps at customer entrances of a retail establishment, at a loading dock of an employer's primary place of business,[41] or at both such locations. After picketing has continued for "a reasonable period of time,"[42] the employer may be expected to file an unfair-labor-practice charge with the Labor Board alleging violation of Section 8(b)(7). (The alternative would be for the employer to recognize and deal with the minority union, which would be a surprise but certainly welcome.) Section 8(b)(7), in pertinent part, basically prohibits picketing

> where an object thereof is forcing or requiring an employer to recognize or bargain with a labor organization *as the representative of his employees* or forcing or requiring the employees of an employer *to accept or select such labor organization as their collective bargaining representative,* unless such labor organization is currently certified as the representative of such employees [and] such picketing has been conducted without a petition being filed within a reasonable period of time not to exceed thirty days. . . ."[43]

After the charge is filed, it will either be dismissed because the necessary elements for a violation of Section 8(b)(7) will be perceived to be lacking or a determination will be made to issue a complaint, in which event the Regional Director, on behalf of the General Counsel, will file a Section 10(l) injunction in federal district court to restrain the picketing pending Board determination, for such filing is mandatory if the NLRB officer "has reasonable cause to believe such a charge is true and that a complaint should issue. . . ."[44] Of course, the proper legal determination should be dismissal of the charge entirely because the picketing would have neither an *organizational purpose* nor a purpose to obtain *exclusive recognition* for all the employees in the bargaining unit—which is what the provision prohibits—in which case the minority union would retain its right to picket.[45] But if a petition for a 10(l) injunction is in fact filed—which would be likely inasmuch as this hypothetical General Counsel has refused to issue a complaint on behalf of a minority union seeking to bargain—the issue in question will then be presented to the court for interim adjudication. The union's defense to the petition and charge will be that its picketing was for members-only recognition and bargaining, not for recognition as the exclusive representative of all the employees in the bargaining unit, which is the only recognition proscribed by Section 8(b)(7).

Not only is the latter reading the natural interpretation of "employees" in the provision, it is also the only meaning intended by Congress—as the legislative history makes unmistakably clear and as settled case law confirms. Section 8(b)(7) was enacted as part of an extensive package of new and amended labor-reform legislation in 1959. The sole public purpose of the provision was to ban "blackmail picketing" and "top-down" organizing.[46] And the Board and the courts have indicated that only picketing to obtain recognition for *all* the employees in the bargaining unit (i.e., exclusive recognition) is proscribed by the *recognition* part of Section 8(b)(7). As the Supreme Court explained in *Iron Workers (Higdon Contracting Co.)*,[47] the interpretation of the provision "is rooted in the generally prevailing statutory policy that a union should not purport to act as the collective-bargaining agent for *all* unit employees, and may not be recognized as such, unless it is the voice of the majority of the employees in the unit."[48] The reader is here reminded that the Wagner Act's goal and ultimate objective was mature bargaining based on majority and exclusive representation, but this is not to be confused with the Act's broad protective umbrella in Section 7 that guarantees a wide range of collective action, including *preliminary* minority-union bargaining that precedes majoritarian-exclusivity bargaining. The *Higdon* Court also noted with approval that Section 8(b)(7) "has not been literally applied"[49] and offered the example of Board rulings holding that a recognized (but not certified) union that pickets an employer to require bargaining to enforce an already executed collective bargaining contract does not violate the Act.[50] Another example of a nonliteral reading of the provision is the confirmed recognition that picketing to protest a non-union employer's failure to pay area-standard wages does not violate the Act.[51]

Clearly, picketing to require an employer to recognize and bargain with a minority union for its members only would not violate Section 8(b)(7), for, as Professor Alan Hyde rightly summarizes the applicable law, "picketing to seek 'members-only' recognition is not organizational, recognitional, or in derogation of an incumbent union."[52] Accordingly, a federal district court faced with that issue in a Section 10(l) injunction proceeding should deny the injunction. But if the court were to hold otherwise, its order would be appealable and the issue would be on its way to final resolution. It is also likely that a determination that such picketing does not violate the Act would be appealed by the employer or submitted to the Board for its full consideration. In either event, judicial review would be available.

Implementation through a Piggy-Back Motion
to Amend a Section 8(a)(3) Complaint

The next approach could be labeled the "accidental traveler" approach. As most readers are aware, in the normal course of a union's organizational campaign employees are often discharged to discourage union membership, which is—needless to say—a violation of Section 8(a)(3).[53] If that should occur to an employee who is a bona-fide member of a minority union,[54] the union should not only file an unfair labor practice charge with the NLRB, it should also request that the employer engage in good-faith bargaining regarding the discharge, for discharges are mandatory subjects of collective bargaining.[55] If the employer refuses, which is likely, the charge should thereafter include not only an allegation of a Section 8(a)(3) violation but also a separate claim of refusal to bargain under Sections 8(a)(1) and 8(a)(5). If the General Counsel declines to include the latter allegation in the complaint and the discharge case proceeds in due course to a hearing before an ALJ, during the hearing the union should present a piggy-back motion pursuant to Section 102.17 of the NLRB Rules and Regulations[56] in which it requests the ALJ to amend the complaint to include the refusal-to-bargain allegation; and appropriate evidence or offer of proof should be presented to make the necessary record. From then on, regardless of the action of the ALJ or the Board on this matter—and I would hope that either or both would find a separate violation of Sections 8(a)(1) and 8(a)(5)—the issue will have been joined and will thus eventually become ripe for a final order, which if adverse will be appealable by the union to a U.S. Court of Appeals.

Implementation through Substantive Administrative Rulemaking

A last-resort alternative means of securing implementation would be for the union to petition the NLRB for issuance of a substantive rule in accordance with the APA,[57] a rule declaring in essence that

> Pursuant to Sections 8(a)(1) and 8(a)(5) of the Act, where employees in an appropriate bargaining unit are not currently represented by a certified or recognized Section 9(a) exclusive/majority labor organization, the employer, upon request, has a duty to bargain with a minority labor organization on behalf of the employees who are its members, but not on behalf of any other employees.

I refer to this approach as a means of last resort because of the possibility that under this procedure the Board might inordinately delay its consideration and/or resolution of the issue.[58] Otherwise, it is a viable procedure.

This process calls for the filing of a rulemaking petition by "an interested person" within the meaning of Section 553(e) of the APA[59] and its corresponding NLRB procedural rule.[60] As the House Judiciary Committee explained with reference to that provision when the APA was passed, "[w]here such petitions are made, the agency must fully and promptly consider them [and] take such action as may be required. . . . "[61] And as Representative

Francis Walters cautioned prior to final passage of that Act, an *interested-person* petition must be given serious consideration, for

> No agency may receive such petition in a merely pro forma manner. . . .
> The right of petition is written into the Constitution itself. . . . This sub-
> section should be a most useful instrument of . . . protecting the public by
> affording interested persons a legal and regular means of securing the is-
> suance, change or revision of a rule.[62]

The reason this procedure has been rarely used at the NLRB is probably because the Board itself has been reluctant to engage in any APA substantive rulemaking,[63] and the labor-law community is generally unaware of this petitioning process. It has been attempted on several occasions, but thus far without notable success.[64] However, should an *interested-person* petition be submitted for issuance of a proposed rule on minority-union bargaining, I assume—or at least hope—that the Board will rise to the occasion and fulfill its statutory obligation to decide the issue without unreasonable delay. If not, the proponents of the proposed rule could resort to public pressure and/ or a mandamus-type action in federal district court to require the consideration of the issue.

11 *Union Organizing through Members-Only Collective Bargaining*

The National Labor Relations Act does not guarantee the right of representation, but it does—like the U.S. Constitution—guarantee the right of association.[1] Associations are as American as apple pie and baseball. Although the saga of American growth has glorified the role of rugged individualism, a key factor in the pioneering spirit and its aftermath was the recognized need of individuals to join together to help each other in the tedious process of building a stable and vigorous society. Associations were an integral part of that process. As Alexis de Tocqueville recognized more than a century and a half ago, associations are quintessentially American:

> Better use has been made of association and this powerful instrument of action has been applied to more varied aims in America than anywhere else in the world.
>
> Apart from permanent associations such as townships, cities, and counties created by law, there are a quantity of others whose existence and growth are solely due to the initiative of individuals.[2]

Faithful to this tradition, since the earliest days of union organizing individual workers have joined together in their workplaces to form trade unions in order to present a united front to their employer. As we have observed in Chapter 1, workers realized that only through such associations could they achieve a strong voice and some degree of power over their own wages and working conditions. Now, once again, for employees who desire union representation and for unions that hope to represent them and other unorganized workers, it will be appropriate to pursue those objectives by organizing through the formerly common—but now largely forgotten—method of recruiting for union members, which is not the same as soliciting for union supporters.

First, however, a digression to note another area of likely organizational development, but one that I shall not explore here. Although this chapter—indeed this book—focuses on the organization of conventional labor unions, I am well aware that recognition and acceptance of the minority bargaining process will probably spawn a variety of alternative forms of worker representation, including nontraditional labor organizations initiated both by employees and employers. And it is likely that many of these newly formed groups will simply be familiar unaffiliated independent labor unions—except that their promoters, using some of the methods discussed in this chapter, will now find such unions easier to organize. In addition, some even more innovative organizational forms are likely to develop. The prospective availability of novel employee-representational structures should be especially attractive to professional and highly skilled technical employees, for the absence of requirements for majority status and appropriate bargaining units ought to spur the creation of new types of employee groups that will facilitate the coupling of shared common interests and cooperative action among such employees. Some of these new organizations may even resemble the employee caucuses that already exist in a few American companies;[3] for these, the members-only process will now confer added legitimacy and enhanced legal status. Although these additional areas of potential organizational and representational development deserve serious attention and elucidation, such treatment would require further extensive research and analysis, which I suspect will eventually be forthcoming from other authors. Accordingly, this chapter focuses only on members-only organizing and bargaining vis-à-vis conventional labor unions.

Now to our exploration of these new—or renewed—procedures for organizing labor-union members. By such organizing I mean an unembellished process of workers actually *joining* unions—not just signing authorization cards or casting ballots for a union in a Labor Board election. This back-to-basics approach will mean that workers who are interested—from the very beginning—will have to join and become members of their union. The successful practice of members-only collective bargaining will require that employees make an affirmative commitment to that union *before* their associational rights can become effective. These new procedures, however, are in reality old procedures. Prior to unions becoming dependent on NLRB elections, they

> were free to organize in whatever manner they found most effective. Frequently, a union would build its membership in a shop by first organizing a small group of workers who had the fortitude to stand strong for the union. Upon the organization of such group, certain job improvements would be obtained for them from management. And this working example of the gains to be achieved through organization frequently formed the most potent organizational appeal to other workers in the shop, and they too would join to improve their conditions.[4]

By following that old-fashioned doctrine of membership-based bargaining—now rediscovered—the American labor movement will be returning to its roots.

Getting Started: A New Organizational Approach

What follows is in effect a procedural manual on how workers and unions can more efficiently reach the goal of mature, majority-based exclusive union representation, utilizing—as a stepping-stone—membership based minority-union collective bargaining. It is not my intent, however, to provide reasons why employees should join unions or arguments or information that might be useful in persuading them to do so. A vast amount of literature on that subject is already available,[5] and traditional unions and their organizational staffs are better qualified than I to present that message. My intention here is only to outline a few organizational guidelines that stem naturally from the legal recognition of a protected right to engage in members-only collective bargaining.

How does this less-than-majority organizational approach differ from a conventional-union organizational campaign that is usually designed to culminate in an election? The differences, which are significant, concern both form and substance. From the beginning, participants will emphasize the building of an organization, not the winning of an election. The process will call for a totally different mind-set. Both the old and the new approaches, however, depend largely on inside employee groups and the solicitation of employees. The traditional approach uses these informal employee committees to spread the organizational message, and virtually all employees in the unit are solicited to sign union authorization cards, because in order to obtain an election a petitioning union must show support from a minimum of 30 percent of the employees in the bargaining unit.[6] That showing is usually demonstrated by signatures on cards or, although less frequently, on employee petitions. Most unions, however, do not seek an election without first obtaining at least a card majority, for the anti-union campaign that the employer is expected to mount will often erode much of the union's potential support. In contrast to those familiar procedures, a membership-based organizational campaign concentrates from the outset on organizing a union, and any inside organizational committee of employees will probably be but one of several different committees. More important, however, a membership-based campaign will not seek or solicit union authorization cards—rather, it will seek and offer genuine union membership.

Just as unions organized before they became addicted to the election process, they will now solicit union membership as a prerequisite to union representation.[7] Thus, employees who join a developing minority union prior to their employer's extending recognition will know they are making a meaningful commitment to the labor organization of their choice. To accommodate the resulting new categories of membership, unions that engage in this member-based form of organizing may decide to adjust their dues structures accordingly, perhaps by instituting a multitiered plan. For example, only moderate dues (or initiation fees) might be charged when employees join at the first level, that is, at the organizational precontract stage; later, after the first members-only bargaining contract is signed, a mid-level or second-tier rate might apply; and when the employer agrees to exclusive majority-based recognition and begins bargaining—or alternatively when such a first exclusivity agreement is signed—the third level, full membership dues, might apply.

Payment of union dues, even though nominal in amount, will mean that pro-union workers will have "put their money where their mouth is." Having paid their dues, there will be no doubt as to their voluntary choice of union representation,[8] for they will be investing not only time and energy but also a modest sum of money, and this can only bring significant returns later when job improvements have been delivered through the collective bargaining process. But such a result may not occur until two conditions prevail: (1) that a substantial number of employees join with them in demonstrating solidarity with the union's campaign and (2) that the employer respond with good-faith bargaining. Achieving those conditions will not be easy, at least in the early years when employer opposition will undoubtedly be formidable,[9] but in the long run this new organizational strategy should prove infinitely more successful than the conventional election-bound approach that currently prevails.

Whether a members-only organizing drive is initiated by an outside union, by employees who seek help from an outside union early in the process, or by a group of employees who desire to create their own union without outside-union assistance, the following is a likely description of what may transpire during that drive. By word-of-mouth notice—although conceivably also through other means, such as telephone, leaflets, or e-mail—the union organizers will probably invite interested workers to a preliminary meeting where one of the first tasks will be to explain the novel concept of membership-based organizing and its goals. Inasmuch as this initial employee group will probably be predisposed to union representation, selling them on the membership idea may not be difficult, although it should be carefully explained how and why this approach will be different from other organizational drives with which they might be familiar. Because of the required payment of dues, it may be more difficult later to sell this new concept to other employees who may be less sympathetic to the idea of unions. Eventually, however, that difficulty might prove to be an advantage, for when the more-hesitant employees finally make their decision to join, their commitment will obviously be a serious one, and many of them will be more likely to become active participants—not just on-lookers—in the new union's organizational and decision-making process.

One way in which this membership-based approach need not differ from election-bound campaigns is in the use of union buttons and other identifying insignia. With membership being the critical factor in this new organizational and representational approach, the visibility of union members in the workplace becomes especially important. For both types of organizing, union buttons and other such insignia serve a threefold purpose: (1) They advertise the union to other employees, (2) they provide a sense of solidarity to the union's adherents, and (3) they apprise management of the identity of union employees, thus granting them some degree of protection against discharge or other economic discrimination, for the employer will be unable to claim lack of knowledge of an insignia-wearing employee's union activity.[10] Nevertheless, some new members may prefer not to advertise their union affiliation, which is understandable in view of the pervasive anti-union culture to which they may have been exposed. It is therefore to be expected that in workplaces where employees are afraid to make known their union sympathies, the decision to wear or not to wear union insignia may be respected as a purely personal choice.

When the fledgling union is large enough (and I make no effort to define "enough," for one size does not fit all), its first order of business will probably be to select temporary officers and adopt a temporary name. Although outside organizers, if available, will surely offer suggestions and assistance, the employee members should understand that the union is theirs, and they are the ones who ought to be actively involved in its decisions and proceedings. This new labor organization might be designated a "local union" or "branch" of an established union or given some other identification, possibly a name relationship with the employing company. Officers—who will probably be the activist members—should be selected as early as possible, perhaps on an interim basis. The president will probably have the usual executive duties, but she or he might also serve as the union's shop steward (or equivalent), at least during the organizational stage. In fact, a union steward should definitely be designated very early, perhaps as an appointed position. The secretary will of course keep written records, and the treasurer's duties may include maintaining a bank account that can serve as a visible repository for dues money. There might also be a board of directors.[11]

The Union Steward's Role and the *Weingarten* Rule for Nonunion Employees

The position of union steward is especially important, for that person will have an early role to play in dealing with the employer. Acting pursuant to the long-standing *Weingarten*[12] rule, which applies in workplaces where employees are represented by a union, the steward is available to assist an employee who is called in by management for an investigatory interview that he or she reasonably fears may result in disciplinary action. Until recently, the essence of that rule was also available in nonunion workplaces under the *Epilepsy Foundation*[13] decision, pursuant to which a nonunion employee could call on a coworker to provide such assistance. Shortly before this book went to press, however, that decision was overturned by the Labor Board in the *IBM Corporation*[14] case. As a consequence, the typical role of a union steward in a brand-new members-only union will now be more important than ever to the organizational process. A brief explanation of the *Weingarten* rule is thus in order, for that rule provides a remarkable and early opportunity for a start-up minority union to demonstrate how it can directly assist workers in dealing with management at the level of the individual employee.

The *Weingarten* decision, which the Supreme Court decided in 1975, upheld an NLRB rule that granted unionized employees a statutory right to refuse to submit to prospective disciplinary interviews without union representation. As the Board and the Court explained: "The representative is present to assist the employee, and may attempt to clarify the facts or suggest other employees who may have knowledge of them."[15] Justice Brennan, who wrote the Court's opinion, expounded further on the rationale for the rule:

> A single employee confronted by an employer investigating whether certain conduct deserves discipline may be too fearful or inarticulate to relate accurately the incident being investigated, or too ignorant to raise extenuating factors. A knowledgeable union representative could assist the employer by eliciting favorable facts, and save the employer production time by getting to the bottom of the incident occasioning the interview.[16]

Inasmuch as this rule is based on the right to engage in concerted activity for "mutual aid or protection" pursuant to Section 7 of the Act[17]—not on the duty to engage in collective bargaining under Section 8(a)(5)[18]—the Board in 2000 ruled in *Epilepsy Foundation*, as it had previously ruled twelve years earlier, that employees in nonunion workplaces are entitled to similar protection; this would be provided, however, by the presence of a coworker rather than a union representative. That decision was strongly affirmed by the Court of Appeals for the District of Columbia Circuit. Writing for that court, Judge Harry Edwards explained that "the presence of a coworker gives an employee a potential witness, advisor, and advocate in an adversarial situation, and, ideally, militates against the imposition of unjust discipline by the employer."[19]

As previously noted, that is no longer the law—the current Labor Board having reversed *Epilepsy Foundation* in *IBM Corporation*, holding that the *Weingarten* rule is inappropriate in the nonunion workplace. The majority in *IBM* explained that

> a union representative has a different status in his relationship with an employer than does a coworker. The union representative typically is accus-

tomed to dealing with the employer on a regular basis concerning matters other than those prompting the interview. Their ongoing relationship has the benefit of aiding in the development of a body of consistent practices concerning workplace issues and contributes to a speedier and more efficient resolution of the problem requiring the investigation. . . . A coworker is unlikely to bring such skills to an interview primarily because he has no experience as the statutory representative of a group of employees.[20]

To which the dissenting members of the Board responded: "The majority makes a powerful case for unionization."[21]

In fact, newly formed members-only minority unions will surely use the *Weingarten* rule to help make that case for unionization. Accordingly, with *Epilepsy Foundation* overruled, it is now more important than ever that the organizing union make known to all employees in the workplace—both union and nonunion—that its union steward is available to assist employees called in for investigatory interviews. That steward—who ideally will be an experienced and respected employee—will be the logical person whom a targeted employee will request for support and representation.

If the employer proceeds with the interview, the law requires that the employee's union representative be permitted to attend and participate. Although the employer will have no duty to bargain with that representative,[22] such person "must be accorded an opportunity to speak, for the rule contemplates meaningful representation,"[23] and the Supreme Court's decision in *Weingarten* makes clear that the representative's role at the investigatory interview is to provide assistance and counsel to the interrogated employee. To perform that function, the steward is entitled to consult with the employee in advance of the interview, though not on company time[24] unless the interview is so scheduled that there is not sufficient opportunity for consultation on the employee's own time prior to the interview.[25]

The *Weingarten* rule does not require the employer to give employees any notice of their right to representation—not even to the employee slated for an interview—for the "right arises only in situations where the employee *requests* representation."[26] Accordingly, it behooves the organizing union to make known to all employees—not just to union members—that this guaranteed right is readily available. Not only is it available to existing members, it can also be offered to prospective members. In order to accommodate a nonunion employee in immediate need of representation at an impending disciplinary interview, the union steward can proffer an instant membership card and, upon its execution, thereafter provide prompt *Weingarten* representation to the interviewee. Thus, notwithstanding the Board's regressive decision in IBM, *Weingarten* rights can be alive and well in the minority-union workplace.

When an employee insists on *Weingarten* representation, the employer may decide not to conduct the interview, which is its privilege.[27] Such a refusal, however, might sometimes benefit an employee who might otherwise be asked to provide embarrassing or incriminating information; and an employer's refusal to give the employee an opportunity to present an explanation as to the matter in question, unless he or she is willing to waive the right of representation,[28] might be perceived by other employees as grossly unfair. On the other hand, if the interview is held with the union representative present, the employer's investigatory effort will likely be viewed as fair and reasonable, for it will in fact represent a healthy example of due process in the workplace. The union steward's *Weingarten* role allows a nonmajority union to visibly demonstrate its importance by providing on-the-job worker representation.

Indeed, during the organizational stage, many services that a union might offer to both union and nonunion employees will likely involve the union steward. Such services will probably be of the kind previously defined as *second-track* Section 7 concerted activity for "mutual aid or protection."[29] There are many such activities involving familiar subject matter that can be offered by members-only unions to all employees, both union and nonunion. Accordingly, before discussing the minority union's primary role, which is to provide collective bargaining representation to its own members, I shall list some of these other services, for they represent additional contributions to a broadened role that a union—particularly one that is actively organizing— can fill superbly without reference to the collective bargaining process. A newly organized members-only union—especially with the help of outside representatives or other resource providers—can offer workers a variety of social and economic services that are not dependent on collective bargaining.[30] Such unions can, without involving the employer, provide information, advice, and assistance concerning many worker-related services, for example: health and safety issues under state and federal law, workers' compensation, unemployment compensation, legal minimum wage and overtime requirements, disability requirements and benefits, social security and welfare benefits, 401(k)[31] and other financial issues, vocational rehabilitation, and state and federal antidiscrimination laws. In other words, this new union can serve as an ideal clearinghouse for such information and action and also be an organizational link to a wide assortment of community[32] and political activities, which might range from informal efforts to obtain child care or educational training to formal participation in political campaigns. All of these and related activities—most of which fall within the rubric of "mutual aid or protection"—are ideally suited for the role of a new union that is seeking to prove its worth and expand its membership. These nonbargaining activities fit well into the pattern of social unionism that is currently gaining support in the American labor movement.[33] Some of these tasks may be coupled with the union's basic representational role, which is treated in the discussion that follows.

Notifying the Employer of the Union's Presence and Function

This now brings me to the crux of the collective bargaining function that distinguishes how a developing nonmajority union will operate in its organizational phase compared with the manner in which most unions presently conduct their organizing drives. Once this new union has achieved sufficient size and structure—and only good judgment and experience, or good luck in the absence of experience, will indicate when that has occurred—the union should formally notify the employer (1) of its existence, (2) of its representational status for its members, and (3) of any immediate requests for negotiations. This notice should preferably be in writing, most likely a hand-delivered or certified-return-receipt letter addressed to the company official in charge of employee relations, probably the human resources (HR) director. The following annotated example of a notice letter includes suggested generic language, in italics and quotation marks, which might serve as a useful model. Needless to say, however, this precise language is not essential, although its message is recommended as appropriate content.

"*This letter is to advise management that a substantial number of the employees of the* [named] *company—although not a majority—in* [a described category or location] *are currently members of this union. Therefore, inasmuch as these employees are not currently represented by an exclusive-majority representative pursuant to Section 9(a) of the National Labor Relations Act (NLRA), this union hereby requests that it be recognized as their representative for purposes of collective bargaining on a members-only basis regarding their wages (i.e., all forms of compensation), hours, and other terms and conditions of their employment. This is not a request to be recognized as the exclusive bargaining representative of all the employees in any appropriate bargaining unit.*" The letter might further advise the employer that "*in the event any matter should arise concerning a change or proposed change in any condition of employment applicable to one or more of our employee members, this union, as their bargaining agent, will provide appropriate representation. Therefore, in accordance with the requirements of the NLRA, the company should henceforth refrain from making any unilateral changes in those conditions*[34] *or negotiating directly with any such employee*[35] *without first providing an opportunity for union representation regarding such changes. When necessary or appropriate, it will be the responsibility of the employee involved or this union to advise the company of that employee's union membership.*"

With the sending of this letter, the union will need to make a soul-searching decision whether to reveal at this stage the identity of all or only a portion of its membership. If the decision is to reveal only a portion, presumably only the local officers will be revealed. This decision will call for a judgment based on strategic considerations that will vary from company to company. However, all members' names will eventually have to be presented to management, at least by the time the parties engage in comprehensive collective bargaining negotiations. In addition, as *ad hoc* bargaining situations arise affecting individual member-employees—such as disciplinary actions or matters involving individual compensation—the affected employees obviously must be identified as union members. However, regarding this initial-notice letter to the employer, it will probably suffice to provide only the names of the union officers, for they are likely to be the activists whose identity is already known to management—and if not, their identity should now be revealed for their own protection. In some workplaces—hopefully in most after the minority-union bargaining process becomes widely recognized—unions will not be afraid to provide employers with full membership lists at a relatively early stage. But this may represent only my own wishful thinking, for it probably underestimates the tenacity of American employers in their opposition to labor unions.

The initial letter may also introduce a request to bargain about a limited number of subjects that are deemed immediately urgent or worthy of prompt attention. These specific requests will be in addition to the previously included general request for members-only recognition. The following, or something similar, might be appropriate for inclusion: "*Inasmuch as there are several important matters that should be addressed promptly, the company is hereby requested to join us in setting up a meeting as soon as reasonably possible for the purpose of negotiating interim agreements concerning the following matters: (1) employee discipline and grievance and arbitration procedures,*[36] *(2) bulletin-board space,*[37] *and (3)* [list any other item or items that call for prompt attention or correction]. *Please note that this list is preliminary and relates only to matters that require immediate attention. In due course we shall request bargaining about other matters.*" An employer's refusal to extend the requested recognition will provide grounds for an NLRB refusal-to-bargain charge.

Needless to say, the notice letter should contain the full names of responsible persons to contact—including both outside-union representatives and employee-members who hold the various union offices, especially including the steward's position—with mailing addresses, telephone and fax numbers, and e-mail addresses.

A final comment—the tone of the letter should be positive and nonconfrontational; indeed, it ought to show strong and loyal support for the company and its business. And it might add (in what certainly should be an accurate statement) something to this effect: "*These employees have joined together in order to better serve both their own interests and that of the company. They sincerely believe that the company will benefit significantly from this opportunity for constructive employee participation and its resulting partnership for decision making concerning employment-related matters. We are confident that the union and collective bargaining can improve the morale of the employees and also the quality and quantity of their work, all of which will make for a better place to work and a better company for all concerned, including the management and owners* [or shareholders]."

From Ad Hoc Bargaining to Contract Bargaining

After the company has been notified of the union's representational status and its request for members-only recognition, the union's chief function will be simply to act like a union. That means concentrating on representing its members regarding a multiplicity of issues concerning their work. An important by-product of the union's dedicated efforts to speak up for its members and to negotiate on their behalf should be a favorable reaction among the nonunion employees. The union's efforts may convince many of them to join the organization. Employees who personally participate in the union will be its strongest advocates, and in a partially unionized workplace their enthusiasm can be contagious. Richard B. Freeman and Joel Rogers remind us that workers who experience union membership, especially current membership, overwhelmingly tend to favor union representation.[38]

To represent its members without inordinate delay, a new union should almost never wait idly until the scheduling or start of formal collective bargaining. Rather, it should proceed early to engage the company in interim negotiations regarding workplace problems as they arise. Although this same advice might also apply to any newly authorized union, including those that are election-certified, this disciplined approach is especially suitable for a members-only minority union because such a union is entitled to bargain even when its employee-membership base is relatively small. However, such a union will probably choose to delay full-contract negotiations until its membership is large enough to demonstrate a meaningful degree of bargaining power. Meanwhile, however, it will be the numerous changes in employment conditions that frequently arise in any workplace that will provide raw material for the minority union's initial forays into the collective bargaining process. These are the routine employment decisions that nonunion employers typically make unilaterally—although sometimes with nominal input from affected employees. In contrast, in workplaces where employees are represented by a union bargaining agent any such unilateral change in employment conditions or status will almost always represent a per se refusal to bargain.[39] These potential bargaining situations should now be actively addressed by the new union. However, before discussing how this ad hoc bargaining process might work in actual practice, it will be useful to examine a checklist of some of the most common mandatory subjects of bargaining likely to arise in any workplace where there has not been a recent history of collective bargaining. Here is such a list, with basic authorities cited in accompanying notes:

layoffs;[40] recalls;[41] work rules and discipline;[42] discharges;[43] grievance procedures;[44] arbitration;[45] material changes in work assignments;[46] work loads;[47] sick leave;[48] workplace rules;[49] union use of bulletin boards;[50] seniority;[51] promotions;[52] safety and health;[53] wage rates;[54] merit increases;[55] incentive-pay plans;[56] profit-sharing plans;[57] stock purchase plans;[58] compensation bonuses;[59] vacations and vacation pay;[60] holidays and holiday pay;[61] health insurance;[62] pension plans;[63] retirement eligibility;[64] food prices and paid lunch periods;[65] hours of work.[66]

As incidents arise concerning changes in any of these or other bargainable subjects that might affect one or more union members, it will be the new union's responsibility to provide assistance and voice to the person or persons affected, for, as the Supreme Court has reminded us, "[c]ollective bargaining is a continuing process"[67] that involves day-to-day adjustments in working conditions. It is not something that occurs only when a bargaining contract is being negotiated.

When the new union seeks to resolve these ad hoc bargainable occurrences, it will have available a variety of tactical measures to assist in the process. One of the most useful—and necessary—procedures will be to request information relevant to the issue in question. Not only might such information supply a convincing rationale for the union's position, it will also provide the union with positive visibility inside the workplace. If the union's position is perceived by interested employees to be more fair and reasonable than what the company is offering, it might also prove to be convincing to the company. If not, the company's intransigence might enhance the union's image, perhaps even increase its membership and thus ultimately strengthen its overall bargaining position. But what if the company refuses to produce the requested information? It is established law, with very few exceptions, that an employer's failure to supply information that a union requires for bargaining constitutes a refusal to bargain,[68] and *relevancy*—which has been liberally construed to be what is "reasonably necessary"—is the standard test of what is required.[69]

Another tactical advantage that might be available to the fledgling union is that time may often be on its side. While still building its membership, the union may not need to be in a hurry to quickly conclude every individual bargaining situation; whereas the employer, which will have initiated most of the issues in the first place, may be anxious to resolve them without delay. Inasmuch as good-faith bargaining ordinarily requires bargaining to impasse as a precondition to unilateral implementation,[70] time and patience might occasionally reward the union grievant.

For the most part, however, when a union has little or no means to pressure an employer—which may be the case for almost all minority unions at the organizational stage—its ultimate success at ad hoc bargaining will most likely depend on the reasonableness of its proposals and the persuasiveness of its spokesperson. That person, if possible, should be an outside representative, preferably one with a track record of representational experience. It should be noted that the very presence of an outside union representative *inside the workplace* during the time that grievances are being investigated or presented can convey a powerful pro-union message to wavering nonunion employees.[71] Bargaining while organizing may thus become a new union's most potent response to an employer's effort to communicate anti-union messages to employees through captive-audience contact. And with the employer no longer having the goal of an election—but having a continuing duty to bargain regardless of the union's lack of majority—anti-union presentations to captive audiences will undoubtedly be less effective. In fact, with union members in the audience, they may prove so counterproductive that they may eventually be abandoned.

To illustrate how the ad hoc bargaining process might function, I shall exercise a law professor's prerogative and pose a hypothetical. The scene begins with a grievance over a discharge, following which several other employment-related events occur. The setting is a company where the employees are not currently represented by a Section 9(a) majority union and management is aware of its legal responsibility to recognize and bargain with a minority union on a members-only basis. This employer relies primarily on its HR director to deal with the union regarding these occasional employment-related changes. Some companies, however—probably out of habit—might prefer to rely on their labor attorneys to handle these minibargaining situations. It should be noted, however, that one legally oriented bargaining pattern heretofore commonly favored by many companies, especially in first-contract negotiations following acrimonious NLRB-election campaigns, may now lose some of its appeal. That pattern is to delay negotiations and legalistically manipulate the process in order to achieve a strategic bargaining impasse that allows the unilateral implementation of management's proposals, thereby avoiding the reaching of an agreement. For ad hoc bargaining, however, this tactic may not yield the same advantage. Nevertheless, with that feature in mind, the reader should feel free to substitute "attorney" for "HR director" in the following scenario, although I doubt whether there would be any difference in the final outcome. Here is the hypothetical.

Ima Wyner, a member of a newly organized nonmajority union has just been fired for excessive absenteeism. She notifies Stu Helper, her union steward, who in turn calls on Grace Underfier, the outside-union representative. Grace immediately phones Johnny Onthespot, the company's HR director, and requests a meeting. Johnny assumes that if he refuses to discuss Ima's discharge Grace will file a refusal-to-bargain charge with the NLRB; he therefore reluctantly agrees to a meeting for the following day. That evening Stu and Grace interview Ima and learn that she was genuinely ill the last time she was absent, although some of her prior absences were indeed questionable. However, when they ask her about the frequency of those absences she replies that her record is not as bad as that of several other employees who are still working. The next day, Grace and Stu meet with Johnny and request to see the attendance records for Ima's department, although without discloser of the names of individual employees. Consistent with legal requirements for production of relevant information necessary for collective bargaining, previously noted, an employer must generally disclose facts that a union needs to process a grievance,[72] and the records now being requested are relevant to show the company's prior practice regarding employee attendance.[73] Johnny finally agrees to show the records, but he refuses to withdraw Ima's termination. Although Grace and Stu are disappointed, they feel they have no reasonable alternative but to accept the decision inasmuch as there is not yet a grievance procedure with third-party arbitration. An unreasonable alternative would be to call a strike, which would certainly be protected concerted activity[74] but of dubious value, for although the strikers could not be lawfully discharged[75] they could be replaced,[76] and Ima's case does not seem strong enough to garner wide support among her fellow employees.

A few weeks later another union member is fired, and the script is substantially repeated, except this time after prolonged negotiations Johnny agrees to change the termination to a one-week suspension. Although he has yielded graciously to the union's persistence, he is visibly annoyed at the perceived nuisance of having to spend so much time with ad hoc grievances. Stu then reminds him that the union's initial letter requested bargaining for a grievance and arbitration plan and that a written proposal for such a plan was later submitted. (The reader will here note that the due-process rationality of the union's proffered grievance procedure may serve as both a bargaining chip and an organizational chip, for if the company refuses to agree to a fair and reasonable grievance plan, its position may be viewed by most of the employees as arbitrary and unjust.) After the submission of several more grievances, the company agrees to negotiate about a grievance procedure, for Johnny finally admits that he is tired of holding minibargaining sessions for every grievance. He indicates, however, that the most the company will agree to is a procedure for notifying the union of impending disciplinary actions and a commitment to a loose schedule of penalties within a plan of progressive discipline, which will include written warnings, disciplinary layoffs, and, ultimately, termination. The union reluctantly agrees to accept that plan—although only on an interim basis—for it asserts that in due time it will seek a comprehensive grievance procedure containing several steps that culminate in binding third-party arbitration.

Continuing our hypothetical scenario, the company next announces a significant reduction in its paid-vacation plan. The union immediately responds with a protest, advising that the company must not unilaterally apply the altered plan to union members without first bargaining with the union. Several meetings are subsequently held on this subject, and some changes are finally agreed on, whereupon the company announces that it will also put these changes into effect for its nonunion employees. This begins a pattern whereby the company first reaches an agreement with the union applicable to union employees, and it then extends the same benefits to other employees. This radiation effect may appeal to employees who do not want to join the union, and the company may choose to point out to all its employees that union membership is thus not required in order to receive the economic benefits of collective bargaining. In turn, the new union will likely make an effort to persuade the nonunion employees not to be free-riders and to urge them to join in order to increase the employees' bargaining power.

These ad hoc bargaining procedures will likely continue until the parties decide to initiate serious negotiations for a comprehensive agreement or until at some point the union feels it has sufficient members—albeit fewer than a majority—to exercise enough bargaining clout to draw up a complete contract and present it for negotiations. In our hypothetical, Johnny has been spending so much time on the nitty-gritty of repetitive ad hoc bargaining that he is now able to convinces his colleagues in management that it would be preferable to have a written agreement that provides agreed answers to a multiplicity of bargainable issues. After several negotiating sessions and the threat of a strike, a collective bargaining contract containing a grievance procedure with third-party arbitration at its core is finally executed.

Here, then, in one hypothetical workplace, is a small part of Senator Wagner's vision of industrial democracy taking root. As Justice Douglas recognized in *Warrior & Gulf*,[77] the flagship decision of the Supreme Court's *Steelworker Trilogy* on labor arbitration, a "collective bargaining agreement is an effort to erect a system of industrial self-government,"[78] and "the grievance machinery under [such an] agreement is at the very heart of the system. . . ."[79]

Although this first agreement will be applicable to *union members only,* it will nevertheless be a legally enforceable contract.[80] But as we have been forewarned, the company announces that the same economic benefits will also be given to the nonunion employees. The grievance procedure, however, is applicable to union members only. Should the company decide to make another grievance procedure available to nonunion employees, the latter would not have the benefit of union representation or the union's expertise in handling grievances and arbitrations.

In our hypothetical, this first collective agreement carries a duration term of one year. If the new union progresses as it intends, at the end of that term its membership will have grown well in excess of a unit majority, at which time it will demand recognition as an exclusive Section 9(a) bargaining agent. Needless to say, however, considering the endemic nature of American employers' opposition to unions and the aversion that many nonunion employees have toward unions, some minority unions will not become majority unions, at least not promptly, and in many cases probably never. Even so, the employees in those unions will have exercised their right "to bargain collectively through representatives of their own choosing," notwithstanding that a majority of their coworkers have declined to join with them. These minority-group employees will at least have acquired some degree of union protection and benefits, albeit with limited bargaining power, although such status need not necessarily be viewed as either temporary or incomplete. Minority unionism is not uncommon in many other countries, especially in Europe.[81] Union members and nonmembers in the United States may likewise be able to work side by side without special problems, particularly if the employer does not interfere with the exercise of their freedom of choice to belong or not to belong to a labor union, and if the union in turn recognizes that its existence does not require absolute majority status.

It may be anticipated, however, that many, if not most, members-only unions will have no need to resort to elections or other external means to demonstrate their majority status when it is finally attained, for their obvious growth will likely have achieved a *fait accompli* that demonstrates to the employer that an election or other verification will serve no useful purpose. However, in some workplaces an election may be necessary to confirm a new union's majority. Nevertheless, a new union should not proceed to an election until it is actively operating as an established labor organization. When this occurs, the outcome of the election should not be in doubt because the union will have already established itself as a functioning representative of employees with a substantial majority of dues-paying members. As we have learned in Chapter 4, this was the election pattern that commonly occurred during the early years following passage of the Wagner Act, especially in the organization of the steel and automobile industries.[82] That pattern may now be repeated.

In our hypothetical, the company voluntarily agrees to grant exclusive recognition, for it now has no doubt that the union represents a majority of its employees in an appropriate bargaining unit.[83] On the other hand, if the company were to refuse such recognition, the union would have available several options to establish its majority bargaining status: it could offer to submit its membership records to an independent auditor, which would suffice if the company were to agree to that procedure; or it might petition for an NLRB election that it fully expects to win. And there is yet another option that might be appropriate in some situations, which is for the union to offer to verify its majority representation by membership records and the demonstrable fact that a majority of the employees in the unit have been paying union dues; whereupon, if the employer declines to confer exclusive recognition, the union could file a refusal-to-bargain charge with the NLRB. It is my considered opinion that such a charge would now be valid, for it would be based on verifiable memberships rather than on authorization cards; hence, the Supreme Court's holding in *Linden Lumber*[84] would not apply. This prospect should be worthy of serious attention.[85]

This brings to a conclusion my descriptive forecast of the organizational and initial bargaining process that nonmajority unions will be likely to follow. I reiterate, however, that I am not suggesting that once the law recognizes the right of minority unions to bargain for their members prior to establishment of Section 9(a) representation that union organizing will be easy. But it will be easier. And I am certainly not predicting that American employers will cease fighting unions and henceforth abandon their efforts to maintain a union-free environment. Nevertheless, when employers finally realize that under the NLRA workers require neither a majority union nor an election to entitled them to engage in collective bargaining, a major incentive for mounting aggressive anti-union campaigns will have vanished. Furthermore, employers will no longer have election targets with finite campaign timelines in which to persuade, promise, intimidate, or punish employees in order to discourage them from voting for union representation. Regardless, many employers will undoubtedly persist in discharging and otherwise discriminating against union adherents, many will continue to issue threats and promises of benefits to discourage unionization, and some will probably encourage or create inside labor organizations to compete with independent unions.[86] But there will be a difference. When charges alleging Section 8(a)(1)[87] interference and Section 8(a)(3)[88] discrimination are filed with the NLRB, they will probably be pursued more vigorously and prosecuted with greater efficiency, for there should be far fewer such cases to process. Even more important, however, the organizing union will remain on the employer's premises regardless of whether it represents a majority of the workers, and it will continue to have the right to bargain for its members while unfair-labor-practice charges are pending. And even when Section 8(a)(2) charges are being processed regarding an alleged company union, the members-only union will still be able to assert its presence in the workplace by representing and bargaining on behalf of its own members. Furthermore, some of the most time-consuming cases—those involving Section 8(a)(5) refusals to bargain—should no longer absorb so much of the Board's time and attention (at least after the establishment of the rudimentary parameters of minority-union bargaining) because a major incentive that previously motivated employers in many of those cases, to wit, the desire to eliminate the union's presence and the employer's obligation to bargain with it, will now have been removed. In other words, even if it should be proved that a union is no longer the exclusive representative because it does not represents a majority of the employees in the unit—either as a defense in a Section 8(a)(5) case or pursuant to an election—the employer will still have an enforceable obligation to bargain with that union for its employee-members only.

In this new industrial-relations atmosphere in which a union's right to bargain will no longer depend on majority authorization, an employer can only seek to weaken a union, not totally destroy its right to bargain. But if such weakening is achieved lawfully, the practice of industrial democracy may still be well served, for the mutual exercise of the rights of free speech and association are integral parts of the democratic process. The "right to form, join, or assist labor organizations [and] bargain collectively through representatives of their own choosing"[89]—whether exercised in minority or majority unions—may thus finally become a reality for those American workers who desire union representation under the National Labor Relations Act.

This newly discovered collective bargaining process will naturally require legal adjustments and fine-tuning, for certain features of members-only bargaining will differ from exclusivity bargaining. Those features and related prospective developments are examined in Chapter 12.

12 *Industrial Democracy at Work*

Turning Wagner's Vision into Reality

[A] long habit of not thinking a thing wrong, gives a superficial appearance of being right, and raises at first a formidable outcry in defense of custom. But the tumult soon subsides. Time makes more
converts than reason.

—THOMAS PAINE[1]

Habits are hard to break. Americans have long been in the habit of accept-
ing the feudal notion of the master-and-servant rule for governance of the
workplace. There was, however, a brief moment in cosmic time when that
archaic view was replaced by a vision of industrial democracy. As we have
learned in the early chapters, during the 1930s, both before and after passage of the Wagner Act, substantially everyone actively involved in American industry—including the many employers who opposed and resisted the
concept—understood that workers had both a legal and an accessible right
to join labor unions and to engage in collective bargaining. From the 1940s
through the 1960s, the American labor movement for the most part pros-
pered, and the fruits of collective bargaining contributed to a vibrant American economy. Yet it was during those "good times" that the long habit of
thinking that all minority-union bargaining was wrong began to evolve,
and—as Tom Paine's observation reminds us—it was that habit that eventually gave this erroneous view the superficial appearance of being right.

Now that we know what the law actually requires, what is likely to happen to American labor relations? What will probably happen in the beginning is that most of the employer community, together with their legal and

public relations representatives, will fiercely resist any reformation of the labor-law status quo. But inasmuch as no legislative change is required for the introduction of members-only bargaining, their campaign to oppose such bargaining will be directed, at least initially, to the Labor Board and to the courts, and it will surely be accompanied by a formidable outcry in defense of custom. Considering the dearth of valid legal arguments available to raise against premajority collective bargaining, I expect that we shall see an intensive effort to convince both the public and the decision makers that such bargaining is a bad idea, that it will not work, that it will adversely affect employer-employee relations, and that it will harm the economy. And such efforts will certainly include a charge that unions are attempting to alter a fair and democratic system that has withstood the test of time—after all, elections are supposed to be a part of the democratic process. But that Chicken-Little approach will ultimately be dispelled by reason and reality. That may take more than a while, however. Tom Paine was right—although the tumult may soon subside, time makes more converts than reason.

My objective in this final chapter is to present a comparative forecast of the labor-relations landscape as it is likely to appear following the introduction and acceptance of minority-union members-only collective bargaining. For this purpose, I bring neither a crystal ball nor any special talent for predicting the future. I bring only my life experience in labor law and industrial relations, plus the concentrated research and thought invested in the production of this book. But I warn the reader of two additional factors: (1) my own inveterate optimism might distort my judgment, although I endeavor to be as objective as possible, and (2) whatever the NLRB and the courts ultimately do to fine-tune the unfamiliar features of the duty-to-bargain obligation applicable to members-only bargaining may prove to be important variables. Having offered these disclaimers, what follows is my best estimate of what is likely to transpire.

Union Organizing in the Twenty-First Century

We begin with an examination of union organizing under the prospective new bargaining regime. We first view the big picture affecting large-company employers; this is followed by an assessment of the anticipated organizational process likely to be utilized when unions proceed to organize employees at smaller companies.

In order to better understand the new organizational protocol that I am outlining, it is appropriate first to examine the practices and procedures that currently prevail under the contemporary version of the duty to bargain. A prototypical example of such labor-law practices can be found in the current behavior of a single giant corporation—Wal-Mart and its Sam's Club division. A few insightful news articles and a number of NLRB case opinions by the Board and its ALJs regarding that company's activities provide reliable factual scenarios to view and compare with the prospects of union organizing under the members-only bargaining thesis advanced here. The data contained in these legal opinions and media sources offer a revealing glimpse at the real world of overwhelming obstacles that large nonunion employers commonly erect to discourage and prevent their employees from achieving union representation. Wal-Mart, the nation's largest employer—3,300 stores and more than 1 million workers[2]—is the elephant in the room that cannot be ignored.

We begin with two *Business Week* articles, the first under the heading "How Wal-Mart Keeps Unions at Bay," which examines Wal-Mart's anti-union strategy, exemplified by its actions at a Sam's Club in Los Vegas, Nevada, where the United Food and Commercial Workers (UFCW) was attempting to organize.[3] That article describes the "blistering counteroffensive" Wal-Mart was waging against those efforts, including sending in "a dozen labor-relations troops from its Bentonville (Ark.) headquarters, instructing local managers in a fierce anti-union campaign, including surveillance of employees and the firing of several union sympathizers. . . . "[4]

Wal-Mart executives, on the other hand, claim that "the company has been able to remain nonunion not because of unfair tactics but because the company keeps its employees happy and pays competitive wages";[5] however, according to analysts credited by *Business Week*, "unionized chains such as Kroger Co. and Safeway . . . shoulder labor costs at least 20% higher than Wal-Mart's."[6] And the other *Business Week* article, entitled "Is Wal-Mart Too Powerful?," notes that "this staunchly anti-union company, America's largest private employer, is widely blamed for the sorry state of retail wages in America."[7] Whereas the average wage for sales clerks in unionized supermarkets is $13 an hour, Wal-Mart clerks "average about $8.50 an hour, or about $14,000 a year, while the poverty line for a family of three is $15,060."[8] Indeed, Wal-Mart's low-wage costs are credited with being "the primary reason"[9] why the unionized supermarkets in Southern California felt the need to cut their labor costs, thereby precipitating a 20-week-long strike by 59,000 retail grocery employees.[10]

The executive vice-president of Wal-Mart's People Division, Coleman Peterson, makes it abundantly "clear that Wal-Mart doesn't want a union" and asserts that because its employees "feel free to communicate openly with their management, why would they need a third party to represent them?"[11] That *third-party* theme is often raised by the company and contrasted with its "open door policy," which—as the judge in one of the *Wal-Mart* NLRB cases observed—"is an integral part of [Wal-Mart's] corporate culture. It is also beyond doubt that the policy is intended, at least in part, to discourage employees from seeking union representation."[12]

In addition, however, it is now well-established that Wal-Mart has frequently engaged in illegal anti-union activity as a means of discouraging its employees from attempting to unionize. The *New York Times* noted in late 2002 that

> Over the last four years, the National Labor Relations Board has filed more than 40 complaints against Wal-Mart, accusing managers in more than two dozen stores of illegal practices, including improperly firing union supporters, intimidating workers and threatening to deny bonuses if workers unionized. Of those, the board found illegal practices in 10 cases; 8 cases were settled and the rest are pending. . . . Labor leaders said these cases represented a high percentage of the 90 stores where there has been organizing activity.[13]

Despite that extensive record of labor-law violations—which has continued, as shown by the more recent cases to be discussed shortly—Wal-Mart publicly insists that it does not condone violations of the law, with Peterson even contending that "there's no corporate support for illegal tactics."[14]

According to some former Wal-Mart managers, hardball tactics are typical company policy. For example, Jon M. Lehman, who had been a Wal-Mart store manager for seventeen years, reported that in 1997 when he found a union flyer in the bathroom of the store in Hillview, Kentucky, he called the Bentonville "hotline" and "[t]hree labor experts swooped in from Arkansas to show anti-union videos at mandatory employee meetings[,] scoured personnel files for dirt to use against union supporters . . . and the store trained surveillance cameras on suspect workers."[15] Summing up what he views as standard Wal-Mart practice, Lehman said that "[a]s soon as they determine you're pro-union, they go after you. . . . It's almost like a neurosurgeon going after a brain tumor: We got to get that thing out before it infects the rest of the store, the rest of the body."[16]

Wal-Mart's unyielding approach to remaining union-free is well known in corporate retail circles. Gary Wright, chief executive of a retail consulting firm, told the *New York Times:* "They would do anything they could to keep from becoming . . . union."[17] And Burt Flickinger III, managing director of Reach Management, another retail consulting firm, agreed that "Wal-Mart fights unions very aggressively."[18] In fact, Wal-Mart proudly admits that it has a program especially designed to prevent unions from gaining adherents among its employees, whom it euphemistically calls "associates." "It gives its managers a 56-page guide called 'The Manager's Toolbox to Remaining Union Free'"[19] which, as described by an NLRB judge,

> serves as a resource for managers in developing strategies for union avoidance [and] indicates that the managers are the "first line of defense against unionization." Managers are cautioned to be "alert for efforts by a union to organize" and are directed to call the "Union Hotline" when they become aware of union activity. . . . The flow of information back to store manages is referred to as the "Remedy System."[20]

That highly centralized control of labor relations was certainly evident in February 2000 when the small meat department (eleven employees) in Jacksonville, Texas, became the only Wal-Mart operation in the United States to vote successfully for union representation. Eleven days later, however, the company announced that it was eliminating meat-cutting operations entirely and would henceforth use prepackaged meat in that and 179 other stores.[21] Leonard Page, the Board's General Counsel at the time, commented that "Wal-Mart's timing was 'outrageous,'" but said he did not file charges because he was unable to gather enough evidence to prove that the timing was not coincidental."[22]

Notwithstanding that failure to allege that Wal-Mart's phasing-out of meat-cutting operations was designed to warn its employees nationwide about the perils of unionizing, three years later an ALJ found the company in violation of its duty to bargain about the *effects* of eliminating those Jacksonville meat-cutting jobs and reassigning the affected employees as meat stockers.[23] Accordingly, Wal-Mart was ordered to "restore the meatcutting duties performed by meat processors [prior to] implementation of its decision to eliminate meatcutting and sell only case-ready meat," which duties would continue until the conclusion of collective bargaining over the effects of that decision. Asserting that the judge had misapplied the law, Wal-Mart's lawyers indicated the company would challenge the ruling.[24] That appeal process will likely consume several more years before a final decision is reached.

Such delay is a prime factor in denying workers meaningful rights under the Act. As *The Nation* observed with reference to Wal-Mart,

> Faced with the inevitable litany of unfair-labor-practice charges from the union in response to its illegal maneuverings, Wal-Mart can count on the glacial pace of the labor board to stall [any union] campaign. If the board rules in the union's favor, the company suffers a slap on the wrist, posting a notice of the company malfeasance in the break room.[25]

Business Week agrees that Wal-Mart's activities that are found to be "illegal carry insignificant penalties."[26] And Fred Feinstein, former NLRB General Counsel, concurs, acknowledging that "even when the board charged companies like Wal-Mart with illegal actions, the remedies often could not salvage an organizing drive crippled by employer illegalities."[27] As I explain shortly, the Board's nonremedial remedies and the "glacial pace" of its adjudicatory and enforcement processes may turn out to be less significant after members-only bargaining becomes a recognized part of American labor law.

In the meantime, regardless of the Labor Board's perennial failure to achieve effective enforcement of workers' rights—whether at Wal-Mart or elsewhere—it is useful to examine specific Wal-Mart actions that have been described and ruled on by the NLRB and its ALJs in some recent and pending cases, for such activities offer valuable benchmarks for comparative evaluation of large-company conduct when the right of employees to bargain through minority unions is ultimately established. It is immaterial that some of these decisions are not final as of this writing. Inasmuch as our immediate concern is only with particular conduct that is illustrative of what many large employers engage in to remain union-free, it suffices for present purposes simply to document examples of anti-union and illegal actions committed by Wal-Mart as recognized by formal adjudication. What follows, therefore, are recent findings concerning its violations by Wal-Mart of Sections 8(a)(1) and 8(a)(3) of the NLRA as reported by the Labor Board in five decisions and by its judges in eight other decisions. The finding of a ninth judge, Judge Keltner W. Locke, Wal-Mart refused to bargain with a duly-elected majority union in Jacksonville, Texas, in violation of Section 8(a)(5), has already been noted.

We begin with the most recent of five Board decisions. This is a case out of a Wal-Mart store in Deland, Florida,[28] where the Board found that Wal-Mart had violated the Act by discharging employee Edward Egan (whom it had previously considered for a leadman position) because he had signed a union card.

In a case from a Wal-Mart store in Noblesville, Indiana,[29] the Board found that the company violated Section 8(a)(1) "by discriminatorily prohibiting Union agents from engaging in lawful handbilling of employees on its premises while allowing other organizations to engage in solicitation [and] by discriminatorily contacting the police and causing the police to warn the Union agents because they were engaged in lawful handbilling of the employees. . . . "

In a case from its store in Grand Rapids, Michigan,[30] the Board found Wal-Mart guilty of unlawfully: (1) "Telling employees that they are not permitted to discuss their wages and benefits among themselves and threatening them with termination if they do so," (2) "Telling its department managers who are not statutory supervisors that they cannot participate in union activities, that it would be unlawful for them to do so, and to report union activity to management," and (3) directing an "implicit threat to employee Deborah Hager that she would be fired for her union activity."

In a case from its store in Tahlequah, Oklahoma,[31] the Board found that Wal-Mart had (1) unlawfully removed employee Brian Shieldnight from its property because he wore a T-shirt with a union-related message during an off-duty visit to its store and (2) issued a written disciplinary "coaching" warning to employee Shieldnight because of his invitations to three coworkers to attend a union meeting.

In a case from its store in Lubbock, Texas,[32] the Board found that Wal-Mart had violated the Act when it (1) "interrogated an employee about the employee's union activities" and (2) "solicited an employee to submit grievances to the company in order to interfere with employee rights guaranteed by the Act."

In a case from its store in Kingman, Arizona,[33] NLRB Judge Gregory Z.

Meyerson found that Wal-Mart had (1) distributed to its employees nationally an employee-benefit book containing a clause that threatened employees who supported a labor union with loss of company benefits, (2) engaged in surveillance of its employees' union and other concerted activities—or created the impression of such surveillance, (3) granted benefits and improved working conditions to discourage its employees from supporting a union, (4) threatened employees with loss of merit raises if they supported a union, (5) discriminatorily and disparately applied and enforced its nonharassment policies to the detriment of employees who supported a union, and (6) discriminatorily discharged and denied extended-benefit coverage to employee Brad Jones in order to discourage union membership.

In a case from a Wal-Mart store in Las Vegas, Nevada,[34] Judge Albert A. Metz found that Wal-Mart had (1) disparaged employees' union activities and invited them to quit because they supported a union, (2) discriminatorily disciplined employees because they had engaged in union activities, (3) discriminatorily prevented employees from engaging in solicitations and distributions of union materials and promulgated and enforced no-solicitation and no-distribution rules that that were overly broad and discriminatory, (4) prevented and hindered employees from engaging in union activities on the sidewalks and parking lots in front of Wal-Mart's stores, (5) failed and refused to honor requests by employees for an employee witness during a *Weingarten*[35] interview that the employees reasonably believed might result in discipline, and continued to conduct such an interview after a targeted employee had requested an employee witness, (6) confiscated union literature from employees who were lawfully distributing such materials, (7) refused and failed to select employees for job positions because they had engaged in union activities, (8) created the impression among employees that their union activities were under surveillance, (9) interrogated employees concerning their union activities, (10) threatened employees with loss of benefits if they engaged in union activities, and (11) discriminatorily discharged employee Diana "Angie" Griego to discourage union membership.

In a case from a Wal-Mart's Sam's Club in Las Vegas,[36] Judge James L. Rose found that Wal-Mart had (1) denied employees their *Weingarten* rights of having an employee witness present at a meeting with management that the employee reasonably believed could result in discipline, (2) confiscated union pens and other union-related material, (3) prohibited employees from wearing union-logo lanyards, union pins, and name-badge backers that stated their *Weingarten* rights, (4) suspended merit raises pending a representation election without telling employees the raises would be reinstated after the election regardless of who won the election, (5) solicited employee signatures on letters stating the employee's opposition to the union, and (6) suspended an employee because she had invoked her *Weingarten* rights.

In a case from a Wal-Mart store in Wasilla, Alaska,[37] Judge Burton Litvack found that Wal-Mart (1) had required that employees who had a reasonable belief that matters to be discussed at an interview might result in discipline continue to participate in such an interview after denying their request for the presence of their own witness, and (2) had discharged employee Ken Stanhope for exercising his *Weingarten* rights.

In a case from a Wal-Mart's Sam's Club in Las Vegas,[38] Judge Thomas Michael Patton found that Wal-Mart had (1) coercively questioned employees about their protected concerted activities, (2) created the impression the company was engaging in surveillance of employees' protected concerted activities, (3) threatened employees with reprisals for engaging in protected concerted activities, (4) imposed a requirement that an employee not use channels outside the immediate employee-employer relationship to voice concerns about employees' conditions of employment or the need for a union, and (5) imposed a "D-Day" (third and final step of Wal-Mart's formal progressive discipline system) on employee Alan T. Peto to discourage union membership.

In a case from Wal-Mart's Stapleton, Denver, Colorado store,[39] Judge Clifford H. Anderson found that Wal-Mart had (1) created the impression among its employees that their activities on behalf of the union were under surveillance by the company and (2) engaged in harassing a pro-union employee by following him closely as he was shopping in the Wal-Mart store during nonworking time.

In a case from the Wal-Mart store in Aiken, South Carolina,[40] Judge John H. West found that Wal-Mart had (1) promised to improve employee wages to discourage union activity, (2) promulgated and enforced an unlawful no-talking rule to discourage union activity, (3) issued verbal warnings to employees because they had joined, supported, or assisted the union, and had engaged in protected concerted activity, and (4) increased the wages of ninety employees for the purpose of discouraging union activity.

In a case from a Wal-Mart store in Henderson, Nevada,[41] Judge Lana H. Parke found that Wal-Mart had unlawfully directed employees to destroy or disregard union literature and had taken away union literature from employees.

How will the foregoing examples of organizational activity by workers and unions seeking to obtain bargaining rights at large companies such as Wal-Mart and the companies' vigorous counteractions be affected following general recognition and acceptance of the concept that an employer has a duty to bargain with a minority union for its members-only where there is no certified or recognized Section 9(a) majority representative? In other words, what consequences can be anticipated with reference to the union-organizational process as a result of this prospective change in the parties' perception of the duty to bargain? As indicated in the preceding chapter, I do not suggest that organizing will now be easy—but it will be easier. The Wal-Mart model, with its documented scenarios of both legal and illegal anti-union activity, offers a basis for forecasting what might be expected from large non-union employers, especially from those that are aggressively anti-union. There is reason to believe that at such companies the prospective new labor-law regime will make a meaningful and positive difference in the ability of employees to achieve union representation, notwithstanding their employers' reluctance to abide by either the letter or spirit of the law.

As *Business Week* noted, "[i]nterest in unionization has surged in the U.S., in part as a result of corporate scandals and the troubled economy. Fully half of all nonunion U.S. workers say they would vote yes if a union election were held at their company today, up from about 40% throughout the 1990s. . . ."[42] Eliminating the need for bitterly contested NLRB elections will make it possible for interested nonunion workers to obtain union representation despite the predictable efforts of their employers to deny them such rights. And if employers comply—either voluntarily or by force of law—with the original intent of the National Labor Relations Act by allowing their employees to engage in collective bargaining while they are still in the process of building their union—even though other employees may not yet be ready for union representation or prefer not to be represented by a union—these organized employees will now have a practical means to participate in decisions affecting their employment.

Can this objective be achieved at a mega-company such as Wal-Mart? It should be noted, as Coleman Peterson of Wal-Mart's People Division confirmed, that Wal-Mart boasts that it does not support illegal tactics.[43] In fact, Wal-Mart proudly points to the respect it gives to all its "associates." For example, immediately following the Supreme Court's invalidation of the Texas sodomy law,[44] Wal-Mart expanded its antidiscrimination policy to protect gay and lesbian employees;[45] Mona Williams, Wal-Mart's vice-president for communications, explained: "We want all our associates to feel they are valued and treated with respect—*no exceptions.* And it's the right thing to do for our business."[46] Wal-Mart should be taken at its word. As its employees proceed with their efforts to organize a union and to seek to negotiate about bargainable matters, they will have the opportunity to remind the company that under federal law workers have the "fundamental right"[47] "to form [and] join labor organizations [and] to bargain collectively through representatives of their own choosing,"[48] that it is the official policy of the United States to encourage "the practice and procedure of collective bargaining,"[49] and that the right of workers to join unions and engage in collective bargaining is recognized as a basic human right under international law to which the United States is a party.[50] Accordingly, if Wal-Mart is to be believed, its unionizing employees should have reason to anticipate that they too will be "treated with respect—*no exceptions,*" which would mean that Wal-Mart will expand its antidiscrimination policy to include protection of its pro-union "associates" from discrimination. But as we know too well from its prior conduct, that is unlikely. If Wal-Mart acts with the same disregard for employee rights as it has in the past, it will refuse to deal with the newly organized union and will continue to discriminate against any union or concerted activity; whereupon the organizing union will respond by promptly filing charges with the Labor Board and by publicizing the company's hypocritical position on employee rights.

So what will have changed? There will now be a difference. The new organizational process will be unlike the organizational campaigns referred to in the aforementioned news articles and NLRB decisions. From the beginning, the emphasis will center on employees who desire to join a union and become union members, not on the solicitation of authorization cards or the seeking of votes for a union election some day in the distant future. Under this approach, as soon as a cohesive group of union-minded employees can come together, they will organize themselves—despite the company's opposition—into a functioning labor union. From then on, every one of these union members will be advised to channel all issues relating to job performance or compensation through the medium of their union.

The new union will stress that it consists of Wal-Mart—or other named company—employees, that "we" are the union and that "we" are not a third party, even when—as will likely be the case—the new union is part of or assisted by an established outside union, such as the UFCW or the Teamsters.[51] Although such assistance will be freely acknowledged, the emphasis will appropriately be on the local makeup of the membership, for that factor will ultimately determine the essence of the organization and its bargaining strength. Members and prospective members will need to understand that it is *they* who compose the union and that the union is not a third-party outsider. Such an appraisal ought to be credible as well as accurate, because from the earliest stage of its visible presence, this fledgling union will be a membership-participatory body. Its primary function will be to provide united—and hopefully effective—representation of its member-employees in their dealings with management, and the union's presence should be felt immediately when an employee joins.

This concept of union solidarity must begin early, and it should be nurtured as part of the organizational process. Nevertheless, the new members' expectations of improved employment benefits must be realistic, for benefits will largely depend on the extent of the union's growth, the unity of its membership, the rationality of its activity, and the degree and nature of the employer's resistance or cooperation. What will be different, however, is that these expectations will not be based on the uncertain prospect of an election. This is not to say that elections will become a thing of the past, for they will continue to fulfill a proper—but more limited—role, which will be either (1) to prove to a doubting employer that a union that has already achieved solid majority membership and now seeks exclusive representation does in fact represent a majority of the bargaining-unit employees or (2), in those rare instances when more than one union is claiming exclusive representation, to determine which union represents the employees.[52] Until a majority and exclusive union is designated, however, the minority union and its members will rely on the law's guarantee of the right of employees to bargain collectively through a union of their own choosing. But such bargaining will be for members only, not for any other employees.

Initially, this members-only bargaining will probably seem strange to both employers and traditional unions, for no one today remembers that this type of bargaining was not uncommon in earlier years, before and after passage of the Act. As explained in the previous chapter, this rediscovered process will simply mean that whatever is negotiated and agreed on by a nonmajority union will become binding only as to union members,[53] but employers will probably extend to similarly situated nonunion employees whatever economic benefits the union negotiates—for which the union will obviously be entitled to assume credit. In the long run, this should be helpful to the organizational process.

Can bargaining really occur while a union is still struggling at an early stage in its organizational development? Such efforts at bargaining—and they are likely to be only efforts in the beginning—should be thought of as part of the organizational process. But whenever employment-related issues involving union members arise, the union spokesperson—usually the shop steward—will be expected to accompany the affected member, or members, to meetings with management; and wherever an alleged "open-door" policy exists—such as at Wal-Mart—the union should use it or at least test it. Acting through their union, employees will now be able to legally insist that the union represent them for any work-related matter in dispute. And—to the extent possible—the union should follow the ad hoc bargaining procedures outlined in the previous chapter,[54] including requests for information required for handling grievances or other matters to be negotiated.[55] And at some point in time it will be strategically appropriate for nonemployee union representatives to seek entry into the workplace to represent member-employees in the handling of their grievances.[56] The physical presence of a union professional inside the company's premises will not go unnoticed by other employees who have yet to join the union. Needless to say, in the beginning, legal action to enforce this right will undoubtedly be required.

If an employer is intent on violating the law, such as refusing to meet with minority-union representatives or refusing to deal with employees except on an individual basis,[57] then ad hoc bargaining efforts will probably need to be repeated, perhaps frequently; and, if they are unsuccessful, they should become the subject of unfair-labor-practice charges at the Labor Board. What if, however, the employer also engages in the kind of hardball tactics previously ascribed to Wal-Mart, such as denying promotions or pay increases, engaging in surveillance of union activity, accelerating progressive disciplinary steps, terminating employment, or issuing threats of such actions, in order to discourage union membership? And what if it denies workers their *Weingarten* rights or discharges or threatens termination or other discipline if they exercise those rights? As to each such incident the union should not only file NLRB charges under Sections 8(a)(1) and/or 8(a)(3), it should also seek to bargain about such matters, for when an employer denies workers collective representation and voice and refuses to meet and discuss mandatory subjects of bargaining with their union, such conduct becomes grounds for additional refusal-to-bargain charges under both 8(a)(1) and 8(a)(5).[58] The absence of exclusive-bargaining status will no longer shield the employer from its duty to bargain in good faith, and the percentage of union employees in a bargaining unit will be legally irrelevant to members-only bargaining.

The extent of a union's membership, however, will obviously have a direct bearing on its bargaining strength. But whatever its membership, changing the anti-union culture at such companies as Wal-Mart will be extremely difficult—which is probably an understatement. Nevertheless, the establishment of minority-union bargaining in the organizational context here described is bound to produce significant gains for employees, especially in terms of their dignity and their sense of meaningful participation in decision making that affects their employment. Although resulting employee benefits may be only incremental at the early developmental stages, those gains will be meaningful, for they will be the product of democratic participation in a partnership with the employer—despite the latter's reluctance and probable necessity of NLRB enforcement. Indeed, in the beginning of this new age of minority-union bargaining the Labor Board will undoubtedly be quite busy with an anticipated flood of new unfair-labor-practice cases.

With this prospect of a resurgence in union activity and the resulting heavy reliance on the NLRB, I am hopeful that the Board and its General Counsel will endeavor to make better and more expeditious use of the statute's available enforcement authority, particularly the utilization of Section 10(j)[59] injunctions to restrain the commission of serious unfair labor practices.[60] But even if the Board continues to drag its feet, workers' ability to achieve effective collective bargaining may henceforth be less dependent on the Board, for unions will be functioning from an improved position to engage in self-help. In particular, unions will have authority to bargain without an election, which in turn should discourage many employers from engaging in excessive anti-union activity, for such conduct will no longer guarantee a union-free environment.

I want to stress again that although majority and exclusive representation will remain its goal, an organizing union should not be obsessed with obtaining majority status, certainly not until after its members have demonstrated their solidarity and the union has become a functioning labor organization actively representing its members. However, if the employer is adamantly unreasonable in its dealings with a union that speaks for a significant number of its workforce, albeit less than a majority, that union may choose to resort to traditional lawful economic pressure to obtain bargaining concessions. Accordingly, should such a union deem it advisable to appeal directly to the public and to members of organized labor, it will probably publicize the employer's recalcitrant conduct with conventional leaflets and/or picket signs; and those messages might be coordinated with other lawful economic activity, including corporate campaigns that appeal particularly to stockholders and directors. In addition, this members-only union may have an opportunity to engage in protected activity that will yield an important legal advantage, which is that if the employer's refusal to meet or bargain causes the employees to strike, the result will be an unfair-labor-practice strike—not an economic strike. The workers will thus be protected from permanent replacement, in which event the possibility of escalating back-pay liability following an unconditional offer to return to work could provide significant economic leverage to encourage a settlement.[61]

When applied to large employers, the foregoing organizational methodology should produce significant increases in union membership. To what extent might similar organizational changes and results be expected among employees of smaller companies? Most of the changes will be applicable, but I expect there will be some differences of scale, which I shall highlight. The legal principles will of course be the same, although the factors of time and size may lead to different scenarios in different places.

Established unions are usually not inclined to expend limited organizational capital on small employers. Thus, union organizers will be more likely to be concentrated at large-company workplaces, just as they have been in the past. Consequently, I would not expect to see any appreciable increase in organizational activity among affiliated unions at small workplaces—at least not in the near future. This is not to say, however, that the changed bargaining requirements will have no impact on small employers. But their impact, which is likely to appear in a variety of settings, will probably result mainly from the spontaneous efforts of the employees themselves, many of whom will be eager to organize once they learn that unionizing no longer requires a tedious and elaborate struggle to obtain an NLRB election. Education about employee rights in the workplace will thus be essential for an early and widespread realization of those rights. Unfortunately, the NLRB in the past has done virtually nothing to apprise the public in general and workers in particular about the law that it administers. I hope that will change, for the Board ought to follow the example of other federal administrative agencies concerning their work-related statutes[62] and require the posting of notices about NLRA rights on employee notice-boards within all establishments subject to NLRB jurisdiction.[63] Yet, regardless of what the Labor Board does—or fails to do—about adequately notifying its constituency, interested workers will eventually learn that they have a right to an attainable organizational process that will enable them to interact as a group with their employer. This newly found right will probably spur employees in a number of small and medium-size companies to create many different forms of labor organizations, and outside affiliated unions will probably be available to assist some of those self-generated efforts. Although this book has concentrated on traditional and conventional unions, I am pleased to recognize that the organizational structures that will now be available in a variety of workplaces may prove to be infinitely more diverse than the familiar union patterns discussed herein. Achieving dignity at work through shared decision making is an objective that ought to be available to all employees in a free society, whether in conventional labor unions or in nontraditional democratic associations.

Most employers will probably not welcome this unexpected renaissance of workers and unions organizing, and many will undoubtedly attempt to vigorously suppress any rumblings in the workplace even slightly suggestive of union activity. But inasmuch as groups of union-minded employees will no longer be required to convince a specified number of their coworkers in order to make up a majority, they will now be able to insist that their less-than-majority voices be heard by their employer as a coherent entity—which previously was impossible. As a consequence, illegal employer opposition against union organizing may not be as effective as it has been in the past. We must acknowledge, however, that there is nothing undemocratic about an employer's legal expression of opposition to union organizing, for free speech in the workplace should really be free. But if an employer crosses the line with unlawful threats or promises—however veiled—or discriminates against union membership, or refuses to deal in good faith with the employees' union, the NLRB must be relied upon to enforce the law.

Nevertheless, hope springs eternal that the day will finally come when the NLRA will require no more enforcement than most regulatory statutes, with voluntary compliance the norm and violations the exception. Conceivably, employers might increasingly discover that this newly found collective bargaining protocol is not something to be feared or fought, that the existence of an independent organization of employees, aside from the obvious benefit to the employees themselves, can also be of benefit to the enterprise. If so, such an enlightened approach to collective bargaining might provide an unparalleled opportunity for a continuing and constructive dialogue between management and workers—a course that could produce a mutually advantageous means for the resolution of work-related problems and innovation of improvements in the work process. I expound on this prospect later in this chapter.

This concludes my forecast of changes in union organizational behavior that might be expected in the new era of minority-union bargaining. Obviously, the broad-brushed generalizations that I have painted into selected scenarios will not be universally applicable to the infinite variety of American workplaces. Whether in manufacturing, extraction, construction, telecommunication, or service industries—whether in large, medium, or small establishments—whatever the type of employing enterprise subject to NLRB jurisdiction, one size will not fit all. I shall therefore leave further prognostications about union organizing in particular work situations to the imagination and ingenuity of the reader or—perhaps more appropriately—to the parties who will be shaping the parameters of this renewed unionization process.

Members-Only Collective Bargaining

How will bargaining for union members only differ from the familiar practice of bargaining for all employee in a bargaining unit? Before attempting to answer that question, I want to stress again that in most cases members-only bargaining will be an interim stage that will ultimately be followed by conventional exclusivity bargaining. I recognize, however, that there will be some workplaces where minority unions will never achieve majority status, and there will be others—although perhaps not many—where more than one labor organization will represent different groups of employees, at least temporarily. I shall address those situations separately. As to the two most important kinds of bargaining—single-union members-only and exclusive— the differences are not as great as some might have assumed.

Inasmuch as Chapter 11 has outlined a suggested sequence of premajority bargaining options,[64] I shall not repeat here the anticipated mechanics of such bargaining. But I note some of its possible legal implications, beginning with an examination of the consequences that members-only agreements might have on other, (i.e., nonunion) employees. When a minority union succeeds in negotiating economic benefits for its members—as distinguished from noneconomic benefits, such as grievance procedures—it may be indirectly negotiating those same benefits on behalf of others, for the employer may choose to extend them to nonunion workers similarly situated.[65] A nonmajority union must be careful not to urge that such benefits be applicable to union members only, for it will want to avoid being charged with having caused the employer to discriminate against nonunion employees.[66] On the other hand, if the employer on its own chooses not to extend the same benefits to nonunion employees, this would not violate the Act unless it can be shown that its purpose was to discriminate against those employees in order to encourage their joining the union, which normally would be unlikely. The employer's purpose might simply be to save money, in which event, however, many nonunion workers would undoubtedly hasten to join the union to obtain the negotiated benefits. The more likely scenario is that the employer will extend those benefits to the other employees, but this will nevertheless represent a gain for the union in that it can now properly claim credit for the employer's action while exhorting the recipients of the windfall not to be free-riders. Significantly, as previously noted, such extended benefits will not be part of the collective agreement, hence not enforceable thereunder, either by arbitration or court action.[67]

Regarding the employer's behavior at this unfamiliar bargaining table— and probably in some cases its refusal even to come to the table—the NLRB may have to confront new and unfamiliar examples of obstructive conduct. These scenarios will require careful and well-reasoned evaluations to determine whether the employer is "bargaining collectively" as the Act requires, that is, whether it is meeting "at reasonable times" and conferring in "good faith"[68] about mandatory bargaining subjects.[69] I can foresee no reason, however, for any major alteration in the Board's tests of good-faith bargaining. An established body of law on this subject is readily available to guide the parties in their bargaining conduct.[70] Although Taft-Hartley added the words "good faith" to the express language in the Act,[71] the requirement of *good faith* had long been recognized even prior to passage of the Wagner Act. Senator Wagner had confirmed to his Senate colleagues that his bill, like its predecessor, Section 7(a) of the NIRA as construed in the *Houde*[72] case, obligated the employer "to negotiate in good faith with his employees' representatives . . . and to make every reasonable effort to reach an agreement."[73] That concept of *intent to reach an agreement* became the established legal standard of "good faith." In point of fact, shortly after enactment of the NLRA, the Supreme Court in *Consolidated Edison*[74] provided its first strong expression of the bargaining obligation required by the Act. The reader will recall that this was the case that affirmed the legality of members-only and minority-union collective bargaining agreements.[75] The Court there emphasized that the "making of contracts with labor organizations . . . is the manifest objective in providing for collective bargaining," and the contracts there in issue were *members-only* contracts. Clearly, the test of good faith in members-only bargaining should be no different from what it has always been under the NLRA—basically a determination of whether the party in question is honestly seeking to reach an agreement. The familiar test articulated by the Fourth Circuit in *Highland Park Manufacturing,*[76] that the parties "negotiate in good faith with the view of reaching an agreement if possible,"[77] will surely remain the standard. In other words, an employer dealing with a members-only bargaining union should simply be required to accept the legal reality of the collective bargaining relationship. Senator Wagner correctly characterized that relationship as a *"partnership,"*[78] for once employees have chosen to engage in collective bargaining the terms and conditions of their employment must be determined *jointly* through the bargaining process and, unless a legal impasse occurs, those terms and conditions may not be altered unilaterally by the employer.[79]

Despite the similarities between members-only bargaining and exclusivity bargaining, it is to be expected that the NLRB will be faced with some novel bargaining situations. Accordingly, in its efforts to shape this newly found duty to bargain to conform with the Act's collective bargaining policy, the Board will be called on to exercise its administrative expertise, probably on a case-by-case basis. Although most issues likely to arise are not presently predictable, one example that may be reasonably expected is a defense an employer might raise to justify its refusal to grant certain requested benefits to minority-union employees, to wit, the impact that such a collective grant would—or could—have on nonunion employees in the same workplace. It is my opinion that the Board would most likely and properly decide that such defense is irrelevant, absent the presence of an issue under Section 8(a)(3).[80] Nevertheless, the Board might give some consideration to the relative size of the minority union's membership in relation to the total number of similarly situated employees in the potential bargaining unit, or to the possibility that the employer could extend the same benefits to the nonunion employees, or it might consider other alternatives available to the employer; and notice will naturally be taken of the employer's good faith or absence thereof as demonstrated by other conduct. There is no point, however, in trying to anticipate exactly how the Board will or should rule on such an issue, especially when facts unique to the situations might prove to be controlling. What will be important is that the Board carefully weigh the evidence in these new cases and arrive at decisions consistent with the Act's express policy of encouraging the practice and procedure of collective bargaining. At this predevelopment stage, it suffices to note that deciding such issues is the Board's normal statutory function.

Another area of uncharted law will be the employer's bargaining obligation when more than one union represents employees in the same workplace. Although this condition may not often occur, it can and undoubtedly will develop in some establishments. The consequent pluralistic bargaining,[81] to which the NLRB gave its blessing over half a century ago in the *Hoover*[82] case, will result when competing unions organize among the same complement of employees prior to the designation of majority representation. These multiple unions may choose to bargain separately or agree to bargain jointly. The latter generally occurs in those European countries where multiple unions are common, particularly in Belgium[83] and the Netherlands.[84] In the event that multiple members-only unions in America choose to bargain separately, the employer, because of the constraints of Section 8(a)(2), must deal with them equally, without discrimination.[85]

In his presentation favoring pluralistic bargaining, Professor Matthew W. Finkin projects that

> the sequential ripening of nonmajority bargaining obligations would not seem to differ materially from the situation a company—say, Woolworth—would face as various bargaining units—say, each of its food counters—proceed to unionize over time. The bargain struck with one organization representing either only its members or a bargaining unit would be binding upon those it covers; and the terms agreed to might be extended unilaterally by the employer to nonrepresented employees. But whatever the existing employment terms are, they constitute the status quo to which the unilateral action rule would apply as new organizations secure bargaining rights, just as they do now.[86]

Here is how Professor Roger Blanpain describes the joint-bargaining process in Belgium between the Socialist Trade Union Movement (FGTB) and the Christian Trade Unions (CSC), that country's two principal unions:

> There are no jurisdictional disputes between the parallel organizations of CSC and FGTB; rather they present a common front to the employers or employers' associations. This means that the unions will bargain with the employer on the basis of a "common" programme. Firstly the several unions will draft their separate programmes; they will meet together and formulate a "common" programme to be presented jointly to the employer(s). Both organizations are equally recognized by the employer side of the bargaining table, although of course each movement will be seeking to attract as many members as possible.[87]

The prospect of pluralistic bargaining in the United States offers interesting possibilities for workplaces where multiple unions might develop. Members-only bargaining will certainly provide workers with a wide choice of opportunities regarding the selection of bargaining representatives and differing bargaining formats. Although the representatives in multiple-bargaining workplaces may choose to continue their separate identities, it is more likely that representation-election procedures under Section 9 will be pursued to determine, by majority vote, which labor organization will represent all the employees in an appropriate bargaining unit.[88] Even that process, however, might produce a joint council, consisting of two or more unions that choose to represent employees on a combined basis, for if a labor organization, regardless of how composed, claims or seeks to represent a majority in an appropriate unit, the NLRB will provide an election. Needless to say, however, in the event of the continued presence of two or more hostile unions in the same potential bargaining unit, each seeking to bargain for its respective members, a variety of unforeseen problems might arise. Although I readily admit to not having answers to many of the hypothetical questions that could thus be posed, I am confident that such problems will not be insoluble. The NLRB will address such issues on a case-by-case basis and exercise its normal function of weighing factual and policy considerations to achieve resolutions consistent with the Act.

Whether as a result of having lost a representation election or never having sufficient members to warrant a claim of majority representation, it is conceivable that some members-only unions will never attain majority status. Unlike the present state of affairs, however, such a condition will not deprive union workers of their right to engage in collective bargaining through a union of their own choosing.[89] It will simply mean that minority employees who want union representation will have it for themselves, but those who do not want such representation—in those cases the majority of the employees—will not have it. But both groups will have their preferences satisfied. Although such a minority union may not possess great bargaining strength, its members will still maintain the advantages of representation, and their economic benefits will perhaps appear to be satisfactory because the employer may be actively—and lawfully—demonstrating to its employees that they can obtain good benefits without belonging to a union. Whatever the reason for the union's minority status, democracy at work will have been functioning.

One other aspect concerning the legal status of members-only unions to be noted is that such unions are not likely be bound by the duty of fair representation (DFR)[90]—at least under the current rationale for that duty—inasmuch as that doctrine is based entirely on the statutory grant of exclusive representation of employees, including nonpaying nonmembers and reluctant payers of minimal costs of collective bargaining.[91] As the Supreme Court wrote in the initial decision that established the DFR doctrine, with the grant of exclusivity

> the representative is clothed with power not unlike that of a legislature, which is subject to constitutional limitations on its power to deny, restrict, destroy or discriminate against the rights of those for whom it legislates and which is also under an affirmative constitutional duty equally to protect those rights.[92]

Members-only unions, however, unlike exclusive-representation unions, derive their agency authority from conventional agency law based on voluntary union membership.

Democracy in the Workplace

The Collectivization of Capital and Labor

It is now time to assess the prospective outcome of the implementation of members-only bargaining—which means evaluating the anticipated proliferation of mature collective bargaining expected to result from this change in the mandatory bargaining process. Such an extraordinary escalation of unionized workplaces will represent a major example of governmental action designed to protect basic rights in a democratic free-enterprise economy. The federal government's ongoing role in this process is not unique. The role of protecting workers' rights under the National Labor Relations Act is virtually the same as the role government commonly plays in the protection of shareholders' rights in the American system of corporate ownership and governance. In both roles, it is the government's function to provide the requisite legal authority to prevent abuses of important rights that evolved over many years in the ordering of our nation's system of democratic capitalism.

American capitalism, under the restraining influence of the federal antitrust laws for more than a century[93] and under the regulations of the federal Securities Acts for the better part of a century,[94] has flourished, producing the largest and strongest economy in world history. Through those statutes, government provided the market economy with the essential instruments for the maintenance of competition and protection of investors. Indeed, government—both state and federal—has always played a critical role in the development of commerce and industry in this country. Relevant to our present concern, it should be noted that it was early governmental acquiescence and action in England and the United States that produced the essential ingredients for the acceptance of the concept of *collective* ownership of capital that would dramatically accelerate our economy during the industrial revolution and eventually lift it to the soaring heights we now take for granted. Society and law recognized such collective ownership in the form of the *limited-liability corporation*. Each such corporation was an engine of collective action that multiple owners of capital could employ to pursue their common economic interest.

It is thus fitting to remind the reader that collective economic action is not confined to the labor movement—it is very much a part of the world of business and commerce. Inasmuch as members-only collective bargaining will generally represent an early stage in a union's development, it is appropriate to compare it with the early developmental stage of a limited liability corporation. For this purpose there is no better illustration of how collectivization of ownership capital began than the story of the origin and growth of America's first important manufacturing enterprise, the Boston Manufacturing Company of Waltham, Massachusetts. That company began with eleven stockholders in 1813; by 1830 there were 76, and by 1850 there were 123. (Unlike the conventional-wisdom view that a labor union must begin large rather than small, that corporation—as would be typical—began small with a few shareholders and then steadily grew larger.) Boston Manufacturing was the earliest of the large New England textile firms; Professors Adolf A. Berle and Gardiner C. Means considered it "in many ways the prototype of the corporations of later date."[95] They described its growth as follows:

> The size of the industrial plant was . . . large in relation to those of competing concerns, and for the first time, all the textile processes, from breaking open the bale of cotton to shipping the finished cloth were brought under a single direction. . . . By "selling out to the public," to use the modern phrase, the original organizers freed themselves and a large part of their capital from the fortunes of their first investment and were enabled to go on to organize further similar corporate units. This they did, forming a succession of large textile concerns, all corporate in form. . . .[96]

This example from the early growth of limited liability corporations is not unlike the early history of trade unions. Although unions trace their roots to the craft-guild system of the Middle Ages, and their presence was evident in England in the late seventeenth century, [97] it was the industrial revolution that spurred their development and shaped their growth. As Sidney and Beatrice Webb concluded:

> the earliest durable combinations of wage-earners in England precede[d] the factory system by a whole century[,[98] but] the cardinal example of the conception of Trade Unionism with the divorce of the worker from the instruments of production is seen in the rapid rise of trade combinations on the introduction of the factory system."[99]

Trade unions have thus been around for a long time, although their presence in the United States was never as strong as in Europe.[100] However, it was not until early in the twentieth century that the federal government began to provide some degree of protection for the right of workers to organize into trade unions.[101] By contrast, the collective-ownership status of employer companies had long been legally protected by corporation laws, mostly state laws. However, following the stock market crash of 1929, it was federal legislation enacted during the New Deal period that provided shareholders with the protections they sorely needed.

Accordingly, the collective organization of shareholders, which is supported and encouraged by corporate law with rights protected by a federal agency—the Securities and Exchange Commission pursuant to the federal Securities Acts[102]—parallels the collective organization of workers, which is also supported and encouraged by law, with rights protected by a similar federal agency—the National Labor Relations Board. Federal governmental protection of organizational freedom for management and labor—enacted for both during the New Deal period—provided the ideal springboard from which the labor-management partnership envisioned by Senator Wagner could take off. The Securities Acts of 1933 and 1934, in juxtaposition with Section 7(a) of the NIRA[103] of 1933 and the Wagner Act of 1935, should thus be viewed as interrelated regulatory enactments, for they were commonly designed, on the one hand, to protect individual and collective owners of capital in corporations and, on the other, to protect individual workers and their collective bargaining organizations. For the most part, those same workers would be employed by those same corporations. This was a promising start for the building of a democratic partnership between workers and their employers.

That partnership idea—which had achieved its first mandatory legislative incarnation under the symbolism of the Blue Eagle in Section 7(a) of the NIRA—was uppermost in Senator Wagner's mind when he embarked on the passage of the NLRA. His bill—the pertinent parts of which, as we have seen, are still contained in the law today—was expressly written to permit workers to use their collective strength as a countervailing force to achieve a balance against the power of their employers, thus allowing them to engage in collective bargaining as an equal partner. Several excerpts from Wagner's prepassage statements to the Senate highlight his partnership concept of industrial democracy. Here is a medley of his expressions of legislative intent which—except for the gender references—ring as true today as when they were spoken:

> [R]eadjustments necessary to strike a fair balance between industry and labor . . . can be accomplished only by cooperation between employers and employees, which rests upon equality of bargaining power and the freedom of either party from restraints imposed by the other.[104]
>
> . . . Major questions of self-expression and democracy are involved. At a time when politics is becoming impersonalized and when the average worker is remote from the processes of government, it is more imperative than ever before that industry should afford him real opportunities to participate in the determination of economic issues.[105]
>
> . . . A partnership is the result of agreement and presupposes equality of bargaining. . . . Thus it becomes fair to describe the relationship as a partnership only after an agreement has been entered into by the parties from some equality of bargaining power. [The bill is] primarily intended to bring about by collective bargaining that true partnership of which I have spoken. . . . But free men hate charity as much as they cherish independence. So that collective bargaining has come to mean industrial freedom to American workmen.[106]
>
> I do not underestimate racketeering in organized labor. It exists, unfortunately, as it exists in politics, in industry, among lawyers, and with bankers and brokers.[107] Leadership is a crying need in this field as in the others. And I am convinced that there are today in our country employers who have some vision of the new industrial democracy that is bound to come, that is growing, here at our feet, inexorably; who will, perhaps be leaders side by side with the leaders of labor. For with power grows responsibility. Democratic traditions cannot be built on the fear of consequences. It must be grounded in faith and courage and patience. If the faith is not justified, our institutions are, indeed, of no value. For ultimately men and not theories determine the achievements of our civilization.[108]
>
> . . . This process of economic self-rule must fail unless every group is equally well represented. In order that the strong may not take advantage of the weak, every group must be equally strong. Not only is this common sense; but it is also in line with the philosophy of checks and balances that colors our political thinking. It is in accord with modern democratic concepts which reject the merger of all group interests into a totalitarian state.[109]

Without an independent union voice, employees' interests are indeed unilaterally merged with their employer's interests, which—however benevolent—represents "totalitarian" control at the workplace. As a remedy, Congress crafted a collectively based bargaining model that was premised on equality between the parties, which the Supreme Court subsequently recognized. As we noted earlier in *City Disposal Systems*,[110] the Court found and expressly endorsed "a congressional intent to create an *equality in bargaining power* between the employee and the employer throughout the *entire process of labor organizing, collective bargaining*, and enforcement of collective bargaining agreements."[111] This coupling of "labor organizing" with "collective bargaining" as part of the "equality" contemplated by the Act underscores the significant role that such bargaining is expected to play during a union's organizational stage, prior to its achieving mature majority-exclusive representational status. Realization of Senator Wagner's version of industrial democracy, in which bargaining equality is a major component, is long overdue.

Workplace Democracy under Conventional Collective Bargaining

In their well-named book, *Working in America, A Blueprint for the New Labor Market*,[112] Professors Paul Osterman, Thomas A. Kochan, Richard M. Locke, and Michael J. Piore of the Massachusetts of Technology (hereinafter the MIT Four) aptly define the nature of work and what Americans expect from government regarding the environment in which they work. Their definition and expression of ultimate societal goal provide an ideal introduction to our examination of the democratic potential of American collective bargaining. They explain that

> work is a social as well as an economic process [and] involves important moral values and power relationships that are not always reflected in the unregulated workings of market forces. In short, Americans expect their government to provide a policy environment that reflects their moral values and their sense of fairness, but to do so efficiently, leaving the greatest possible amount of control in the hands of those closest to the problem.[113]

Although the MIT Four present a sensible plan to achieve that admirable goal, their plan, as presently conceived, is unworkable because its indispensable element of labor-law reform[114] requires congressional action, which will not and cannot occur in the foreseeable future. It is a known fact of political life that serious labor legislation is too controversial to survive a Senate filibuster and/or presidential veto. Nevertheless, the laudable objectives posed by the MIT Four can be pursued by means already at hand. As this book has demonstrated, the NLRA, despite its flaws, is a simply worded statute whose basic democratic provisions are currently capable of delivering substantial labor-law reform without legislation.

As explained earlier in this and the preceding chapter, the rediscovery of members-only bargaining offers a viable means to restart a program of union organizing that could lead to the widespread establishment of democratic worker-participation plans throughout the country. Most such plans will probably be based on the time-tested formula that has long existed at numerous American companies operating under conventional union contracts. That familiar model, despite the alarming decline in the size of unionized workforces, has shown remarkable resiliency in its adaptability to the changing conditions of work and new demands of the global economy.

I recognize, however, that there are some alternative plans that may also be attractive,[115] although most contain an inherent drawback. Although employers and employees will always have substantial interests in common, and cooperation between them should be encouraged, it is an inescapable fact that certain fundamental conflicts of interest inhere in the typical employment relationship. Accordingly, in most workplaces a modern outside union is better able to address workers' interests than an unaffiliated inside labor organization, which is more likely to yield too easily to pressure from the employer.

As countless unionized workplaces have demonstrated over the years, conventional collective bargaining is a form of private government that usually works exceedingly well. The written collective bargaining contract, about which the parties negotiate regularly every few years, becomes the law of the workplace. It assumes a *statutory* status that provides a mutually recognized standard for resolving disputes, almost all of which are usually settled by discussion and negotiation. The few grievances that cannot be so resolved are disposed of by neutral third-party arbitration. Although a collective bargaining contract is judicially enforceable in federal district court,[116] almost all labor-arbitration awards are final and binding, as the Supreme Court decided long ago in the *Steelworker Trilogy*[117] (although it has since retreated a bit from such finality[118]).

Democracy under collective bargaining, like most democratic forms of government, is primarily representative democracy, with some representatives elected directly and others appointed in accordance with democratic protocol. Union spokespersons for day-to-day employee representation, such as shop stewards, generally provide the representation at the earliest stages of the grievance procedure;[119] others, perhaps business agents or national or international representatives, may handle the later stages; and still others—who probably will also include some of the foregoing—handle contract negotiations with their counterpart management representatives. Such collective bargaining negotiations represent the *legislative* phase of workplace democracy, just as the aforementioned institution of third-party arbitration, which is a key part of virtually every bargaining contract, represents the *judicial* phase, or more accurately the *quasi-judicial* phase. Such arbitration, which has a long and highly acclaimed history of due process and fairness in American labor jurisprudence,[120] plays a prominent role in unionized workplaces. Its presence sharply distinguishes the union workplace from the nonunion, where decision making, however benevolent and however camouflaged, must inevitably be one-sided and controlled by management. In the typical union workplace, except perhaps under unusual circumstances, such as in a bitter strike, there is usually both an informality and an orderliness that pervades the entire relationship, including all stages of grievance handling and contract negotiations. Democracy at work, whatever its imperfections, is basically a civilized process that almost always treats both workers and managers with dignity.

No less an authority than the World Bank provides the reader with a checklist that aptly summarizes the benefits that routinely prevail in unionized workplaces. Here is that description:

> Unions are institutions with a collective voice operating within internal labor markets. The union's role within this framework is to communicate worker preferences directly to the management, as well as to participate in the establishment of work rules and seniority provisions in the internal labor market. This changes the exit-voice tradeoff of workers by providing a channel through which they can express their grievances without having to leave the firm. This reduces turnover (voting with the feet), increases the incentive of employers to provide firm-specific training, and facilitates long-term working relationships that benefit all parties. In addition, unions can help to establish seniority provisions, which lessen the rivalry between experienced and inexperienced workers, among other things. This can increase the amount of informal, on-the-job training that the former is willing to provide to the latter.
>
> Unions facilitate procedural arrangements and other agency services that help to reduce the likelihood of costly disputes about wage and employment conditions.
>
> Unions help to enforce contracts between workers and management. For example, if the market demand for a product is uncertain, workers may be reluctant to acquire firm-specific skills unless the firm can promise not to fire them if demand turns out to be low. Without a credible enforcement mechanism, the firm cannot make such a promise and workers acquire too few firm-specific skills. However, a union can help to enforce the promise if the firm prefers to honor the implicit agreement rather than to become embroiled in a strike.
>
> Unions can increase productivity by providing a channel through which labor can draw management's attention to changes in working methods or reduction techniques that may be beneficial to both parties. This channel also offers a mechanism by which the union can "shock" management into better practices (reduce X-inefficiency).[121]

In fact, despite the general reluctance of American management to give organized labor credit where credit is due, occasionally some enlightened members of management do publicly attest to the value of labor unions, such as when Peter J. Pestillo, Ford Motor Company's executive vice-president of corporate relations, told the Dunlop Commission that

> If management wants unions to help make companies more competitive and to be an ally in the struggle with foreign competitors, management must accept the validity of employee chosen unions as a legitimate institution in our society. Management must accept this union role, must honor it, must value it, must work with it. A strong alliance requires two strong members.[122]

The record demonstrates that conventional collective bargaining can indeed provide a policy environment reflective of high moral values and a sense of fairness, which are objectives that can be achieved "efficiently, leaving the greatest possible amount of control in the hands of those closest to the problem."[123]

Employee Involvement to Enhance Productivity

As previously noted, easy access to minority-union bargaining will probably spawn not only an increase in traditional labor unions but also various innovative employee-representation plans that will also meet the statutory definition of a labor organization.[124] Some of these—provided they are not the product of illegal employer creation or domination (i.e., company unions)[125]—may prove to be useful entities that can make positive contributions to increased productivity, such as many traditional unions have already accomplished in recent years.

During the latter part of the twentieth century, significant sectors of American industry experienced a major change in concept as to how their workplaces should function. There was growing recognition that in order to realize higher productivity, workers should be extensively and genuinely involved in decision making concerning a wide range of matters that affect their work. This process came to be known as *employee involvement* (EI). Notwithstanding the imprecision of the term, employee involvement became the hallmark of the popular conception of the ideal American workplace.[126] Despite the absence of consensus as to the distinguishing features of this participatory process, and despite the proliferation of widely different kinds and degrees of employee involvement, the EI concept has gained remarkable acceptance in the industrial-relations community. Employers, both union and non-union, sing its praises and many labor unions join in the chorus.[127] And apparently most workers agree, for the Freeman and Rogers study concludes that "[e]mployees want greater workplace participation as individuals and as part of a group as well. [They] want cooperative relations with management [and] the vast majority think that a workplace organization can only be effective if it enjoys management participation and support."[128]

Although EI programs exist in various shapes and forms in both union and nonunion establishments, there is considerable evidence that for a participatory program to achieve its greatest potential the employees must share in a broad range of decision-making activities concerning both production methods and other work-related subjects, such as "conditions of work."[129] Where employees are represented by an independent labor organization, shared decision making can lawfully relate both to methods of productions and to conditions of work, including compensation plans and due-process grievance procedures. But because the latter topics are mandatory-bargaining subjects under the NLRA,[130] they can legally be dealt with *jointly* only by an employer and a labor organization voluntarily selected by the employees, not with an employee entity selected or controlled by the employer.[131] As an astute researcher has observed, on the shop floor "it may be difficult to separate discussions of process improvements from discussions of job assignments and conditions of work, or discussions of quality training from discussions of pay for skills and compensation;"[132] thus, nonunion EI plans—at least the legal ones—must focus almost exclusively on methods of production, leaving the employees with no meaningful voice in the determination of matters of compensation and other working conditions. It is therefore not surprising that substantial empirical data support the conclusion that high-performance work programs functioning in labor-management partnerships under traditional collective bargaining are among the most successful examples of such programs.[133]

Whether through traditional collective bargaining or some other form of employee representation, the development of legal EI plans is likely to be encouraged under the rediscovered program of members-only bargaining. If this happens, the resulting enhancement of employee productivity could strengthen the competitiveness of American products in the global marketplace.

Social Capital inside and outside the Workplace

Another benefit to be expected after union representation and collective bargaining become standard operating procedure is that the critical social fabric of community involvement will be strengthened substantially. This should hold true not only inside the workplace but also outside, for the values and habits acquired in democratic participation at work are bound to carry over and reinforce citizen involvement in other walks of community and political life. Democratic interaction among workers, plus the resulting two-way dialogue between workers and employers, can thus help counteract the alarming drift from the sense of community that Robert D. Putnam discerns and decries in *Bowling Alone*.[134] I am appreciative of his reminder of the importance of *social capital*—as distinguished from *physical capital,* which concerns physical objects, and *human capital,* which refers to the properties of individuals—and also of his observation that "'social capital' calls attention to the fact that civic virtue is most powerful when embedded in a dense network of reciprocal social relations."[135] Although Putnam acknowledges the historical decline in union membership—therefore a decline in what he refers to as "networks of reciprocity" in the workplace[136]—he fails to grasp the full potential of the workplace as a major situs of communal interchange. However, Professor Cynthia L. Estlund superbly fills that gap when she points out "that the workplace is the single most important site of cooperative interaction and sociability among adult citizens outside the family."[137] She notes that at work, "citizens acquire 'social capital,' participate in forms of democratic discourse and develop ties of empathy and solidarity with their fellow citizens; they do all of these things within what is often a relatively diverse group of coworkers."[138] Recognizing that the typical workplace is "undemocratic, unequal, and unfree,"[139] she endeavors to bring its presence into the discourse about democracy and civil society, for, as she emphasize, "[t]he law is deeply and broadly implicated in the structure of the workplace and working relationships. The law has given the workplace a unique and important function in democratic society."[140] I join with her in underscoring the importance of law in the workplace and with her urging "that both unions and management must adjust their strategies, build mutual trust, and learn to collaborate in constructing more flexible and fluid work practices."[141] But I am convinced that such a civilized state of affairs is unobtainable under the conventional approach to unionization and the duty to bargain, for the ease with which employers are currently able to thwart their employees' efforts to unionize, plus the polarized attitudes that routinely prevail in the workplace, discourage the building of nonthreatening cooperative relationships.

Professor Estlund views the decline in union representation as "a major loss for the mediating function of the workplace," for, as she points out, "unions actively cultivate solidarity, egalitarian values, and democratic practices, and they multiply opportunities for constructive interaction among coworkers through the vehicles of union governance and collective bargaining."[142] In the main, that is a valid description of how unions function. Noting both its present reality and its potential, she asserts that the American workplace "as thus constituted—with rudimentary elements of democracy, liberty, and equality superimposed on a basically undemocratic foundation of private ownership and management—can serve democracy in ways that are underappreciated."[143] I hope that those ways will now be better appreciated, for the workplace, which is where people are most connected on a daily basis, can indeed become the common denominator in the overall scheme of a democratic society.

Reclaiming the Right of Association in the American Workplace

The anticipated change in the industrial-relations community's perception of the collective bargaining obligation might also bring about a change—or at least a softening—in the mutual hostility that too often characterizes labor-management relations in the United States. Considering the bitter atmosphere generated by employers' union-avoidance tactics—whether displayed at shop levels through professionally organized election campaigns or at regional or national levels through repetitive anti-union media relations and lobbying—to which the unions add countermeasures loaded with anti-employer rhetoric and militant activity, it is little wonder that employers and unions too often treat one another as enemies. The current system breeds adversity, which is anomalous inasmuch as mainstream American unions—unlike most European unions—have not been class-oriented[144] and have sought to work within the private-enterprise system rather than to destroy it.

Not surprisingly, however, the prevailing labor-relations system has produced paranoiac manifestations in both labor and management. To generalize—but with recognition that there are significant exceptions—it is safe to conclude that American unions and their leaders, from local levels to national and international levels, tend to be insecure in their positions and unsure of their role in society. Even allegedly "powerful" union officials—whom the media frequently refer to generically as "union bosses"—have reason to feel they are not accepted. It is therefore not surprising that at times some unions and their leaders pursue policies of pure self-interest in order to survive. And management tends to be just as paranoically inclined, although not because of any real feeling of insecurity. Rather, many employers—and much of the public—seem to believe and behave as if unions are the very embodiment of evil in the economic system. Some employers are literally afraid of unions, which might only be a fear of the unknown. Regardless, the nation will surely be better served when there is no longer basis for such mutual institutional paranoia. If and when employers lose their fear of unions and unions attain a sense of security and are accepted as legitimate partners in the economy, these natural partners will be in a better position to confront the many serious economic problems that affect the national well-being.

It is my belief that both communal and economic life in America will benefit when collective bargaining becomes the norm and employers and unions shed their paranoiac attitudes toward each other. Other things being equal, the reappearance of countervailing union power ought to produce a countervailing economic effect[145] on the nation's grossly skewed distribution of income. As Kevin Phillips reported in *Wealth and Democracy,* "[t]he top one fifth of American households with the highest incomes now earns half of all the income in the United States. Their share has risen since 1977, while the share of the one-fifth with the lowest incomes has fallen."[146] A down-to-earth illustration of how union countervailing power might eventually help ameliorate the economic plight of low-wage earners was touched upon by Bernie Hesse of UFCW Local 789 of the Twin Cities. With reference to his union's efforts to organize Wal-Mart employees,[147] he observed that "[i]f these retailers are going to be the jobs of the future, if we've really switched from a production to a service economy, then what is so revolutionary about insisting that they pay a living wage."[148] Organized labor may now have the power to so insist. Union organization of service employees—especially those whose jobs are not exportable—and the collective bargaining that will inevitably follow, can produce a positive effect on their incomes, hence on the health of the economy. Perhaps we shall witness a renaissance in the re-building of union countervailing power, which would be reminiscent of the unionization of the employees in mass-production industries that prevailed during the third quarter of the twentieth century, when millions of well-paid union workers swelled the ranks of the American middle class. The same might again hold true for employment sectors likely to be covered by col-lective bargaining when labor organizing is revitalized.

This is not to suggest, however, that the expected increase in unionized workplaces will provide easy answers to the nation's economic problems, particularly those relating to globalization and the concurrent exporting and outsourcing of both blue- and white-collar jobs to the world's lowest-wage bidders. But democratizing a greater number of American workplaces, thereby providing these workers with a meaningful voice, will surely create a more level playing field from which such problems can be addressed.

Members-only minority-union collective bargaining can be the gateway to democracy at work. Through the medium of collective bargaining, dem-ocratic procedures can become the norm for employment-related decision making and, consequently, a viable means for building working arrange-ments characterized by fairness, reasonable job security, high productivity, and economic competitiveness. Statutory empowerment begun in 1933 un-der the Blue Eagle can thus be revived, with collective bargaining restored to a potential that has lain dormant for almost half a century. By embracing these measures, the United States will be joining with other democratic in-dustrial nations in recognizing that the right to join a union and engage in collective bargaining is a valuable human right entitled to effective protec-tion, and Senator Wagner's dream of industrial democracy can thereby be turned into reality. When that occurs, meaningful democratic rights will have been reclaimed in the American workplace. The Blue Eagle is not extinct—its labor law is alive and ready to fly.

Appendix to Chapter 2

Relevant Provisions in Drafts of 1934 "Labor Disputes" Bill and "National Adjustment Bill" Substitute, S. 2926

Draft 1[1]

This draft is fragmentary. It contains only brief, general language, none of which is directly applicable here.

Draft 2(a)[2]

This draft contains the earliest relevant references, which appear in the following provisions:

[Section I]:

Section 5 . . . . It is hereby declared to be the policy of Congress to equalize the bargaining power of employers and employees, to encourage the making of collective bargaining agreements, and to discourage the use of strikes, lockouts and similar weapons of industrial strife, as means of composing industrial disputes.[3]

Section III:

First: **Employees shall have the right** to organize and to join labor organizations, and **to bargain collectively through representatives of their own choosing,** and to engage in concerted activities for the purpose of choosing and designating representative, for the purpose of collective bargaining and for other mutual aid or protection.[4]

* * *

Fourth: (a) If any dispute shall arise between an employer and its employees, or between two groups of employees employed by the same employer, as to who are the duly chosen representatives of such employees, it shall be the duty of the National Labor Board, upon the request of either party to the dispute, to investigate such dispute and to certify to both parties, in writing, within thirty days after the invocation of its services, the name or names of the individuals or organizations that have been designated and authorized to represent the employees involved in the dispute. In such an investigation, the National Labor Board shall be authorized to take a secret ballot of the employees, or to utilize any other appropriate method of ascertaining the names of their duly chosen representatives in such a manner as shall insure the choice of representatives by the employees without interference, influence, restraint or coercion exercised by the employer.

(b) **Representatives chosen by the majority** of the employees eligible to participate in the choice of representatives, **shall,** for the purposes of this Act, **be the sole representatives of all of the employees** who were eligible to participate in such choice. In case of any dispute arising as to whether such eligibility shall be determined on the basis of employer unit, craft unit or plant unit, the National Labor Board, upon the request of any of the parties to the dispute, shall decide such disputed question.[5]

Draft 2(b)[6]

This is the draft reputedly authored by Charles E. Wyzanski, Jr.[7] It mostly contains procedural and administrative provisions. However, it also contains, in Section 307, text similar to Section III, Fourth (a) in Draft 2(a), but with the addition of bargaining-unit language. This clause reads as follows:

Section 307. The Board shall have power in any dispute that may arise between an employer and his employees, or between two groups of employees employed by the same employer, as to who are the properly chosen representatives of such employees to investigate such dispute and to certify to both parties, in writing, the name or names of the individuals or organizations that have been designated and authorized to represent the employees involved in the dispute. In such proceedings the Board shall be authorized to take a secret ballot of the employees, in such form as it may see fit, or to utilize any other appropriate method to ascertain the names of their duly chosen representatives. The Board shall determine whether eligibility to participate in elections shall be determined by employers [sic] unit, craft unit, plant unit, or other appropriate grouping.[8]

Draft 3[9]

In this draft the relevant language in the Declaration of Policy, previously contained in Section 5, is now contained in the following provision:

Section 8 .... It is hereby declared to be the policy of Congress to remove obstructions to the free flow of interstate commerce by removing the obstacles which prevent the organization of labor for the purpose of cooperative action in maintaining their standards of living, by encouraging the equalization of the bargaining powers of employers and employees, and by providing agencies for the peaceful settlement of industrial disputes.[10]

The basic text from NIRA Section 7(a) that initially appeared in Section III, First, is now contained in renumbered Section 10,[11] with the language slightly changed:

Section 10. **Employees shall have the right to engage in concerted activities,** either in labor unions or otherwise, **for the purposes of** organizing and **bargaining collectively through representatives of their own choosing** or for other purposes of mutual aid or protection.[12]

A new Section 11(a) is added. This represents the genesis of the broad, unfair-labor-practice-type provision that ultimately became Section 8(1) in the Act as finally enacted in 1935:

Section 11. (a) **No employer shall by interference,** influence, **restraint,** favor, **coercion,** or in any other manner **attempt to abrogate or modify the right of employees guaranteed in Section 10.**[13]

A new Section 12(a) introduces an affirmative duty of employers to recognize and bargain with employee representatives, whether or not they are employees:

Section 12 (a) **It shall be the duty of employers to recognize and to bargain collectively with the representatives designated by employees,** and with the organizations to which these representatives belong, **whether these representative are or are not employees.**[14]

The former Section III, Fourth (b) (from Draft 2(a)) is changed to read as follows in Section 12(b):

[Section 12] (b) **Representatives** agreed upon and **selected by the majority** of employees participating in the choice of representative **shall,** for the purposes of dealing with employers, **be the sole representatives of employees who are eligible to participate in the choice:** *Provided,* that a quorum for the purpose of making a choice shall be not less than 60 percent of the employees eligible to participate in such choice; and *Provided* further, that no organization which imposes inequitable restrictions upon membership shall be entitled to represent employees who are not members thereof.[15]

Draft 4 *(Changes only.)*[16]

A new paragraph (c) of Section 12 is added that specifically refers to minority representation:

Section 12. (c) **Where no representatives have been selected by the majority** as provided in the above paragraph, the **representatives chosen by any group of two or more employees shall represent such group for the purpose of dealing with employers.**[17]

Draft 5 *(Changes only.)*[18]

Section 10 is changed to read as follows:

Section 10. **Employees shall have the right** to organize and join labor organizations, and **to engage in concerted activities,** either in labor organizations or otherwise, **for** the purposes of organizing and **bargaining collectively through representatives of their own choosing** or for other purposes of mutual aid or protection.[19]

Section 12(a) is changed to read as follows:

Section 12 (a) **Every employer shall recognize the representatives designated by employees,** and shall make every reasonable effort to make and maintain agreements with such representatives concerning wages, hours, rules and other conditions of employment. **When such representative are acting as the agents of any organization, the employer shall recognize such organization.**[20]

Section 12(b) is changed to read as follows:

[Section 12] (b) **Whenever representatives are agreed upon and selected either (1) by the majority of the employees eligible to participate in the choice or (2) by the majority of employees participating in the choice when such majority constitute not less than 40 per cent of those eligible to participate, such representatives shall, for the purposes of dealing with employers, be the sole representatives of employees eligible to participate in the choice and of employees who subsequently fall within the classification upon which eligibility was based at the time of the choice:** *Provided,* that no organization which imposes inequitable restrictions upon membership shall be entitled to represent employees who are not members thereof.[21]

Section 12(c) (from Draft 4) is deleted.[22]

Draft 6 *(Changes only.)*[23]

The relevant provision in Section 8 is changed to read as follows:

It is hereby declared to be the policy of Congress to remove obstructions to the free flow of interstate commerce *and* to provide for the national welfare by removing the obstacles which prevent the organization of labor for the purpose of cooperative action in maintaining their standards of living, by encouraging the equalization of the bargaining powers of employers and employees, and by providing agencies for the peaceful settlement of industrial disputes.[24]

This draft introduces the device of unfair labor practices, with Section 11 changed to read as follows:

Section 11. **It shall be an unfair labor practice for**

(a) **An employer** or any person acting in his interest to attempt **by interference,** influence, **restraint,** favor, **coercion,** or in any other manner, **to impair the right of his employees guaranteed in Section 10.**[25]
(b) **An employer to refuse to recognize and/or deal with the representatives of (his) employees** or to fail to exert every reasonable effort to make and maintain agreements with such representatives concerning wages, hours, rules and other conditions of employment.[26]

Section 12(a) (from Drafts 4 and 5) is deleted and Section 12(b) (from Draft 5) is retained as the entire Section 12.[27]

Draft 7[28]

There are no changes affecting the matters in issue.

Draft 8[29]

The Declaration of Policy that formerly appeared in Section 8 (Drafts 6 through 7) now appears unchanged in Section 2.[30] *The basic rights that formerly appeared in Section 10 (Drafts 3 through 7) now appear in Section 4. The language there is identical with that of Section 10 in Drafts 5 through 7 except that the word "unions" is substituted for "organizations":*

Section 4. **Employees shall have the right** to organize and join labor organizations, and **to engage in concerted activities,** either in labor unions or otherwise, **for the purposes of** organizing and **bargaining collectively through representatives of their own choosing** or for other purposes of mutual aid or projection.[31]

Slight changes are made in the relevant parts of Section 11, now renumbered as Section 5, which now reads as follows:

Section 5. **It shall be an unfair labor practice for an employer,** or anyone acting in his interests, directly or indirectly

(a) **To attempt, by interference,** influence, **restraint,** favor, **coercion,** lockout or in any manner, **to impair the right of employees guaranteed in Section [4].**

(b) **To refuse to recognize and/or deal with the representatives of his employees** or to fail to exert every reasonable effort to make and maintain agreements with such representatives concerning wages, hours, and other conditions of employment.[32]

* * *

Section 12 is renumbered as Section 7 with slight, generally nonsubstantive changes in some of the wording ("choice" now becomes "selection," and "dealing with employers" becomes "collective bargaining") reading; it now reads as follows:

Section 7. **Whenever representatives are agreed upon and selected either (1) by the majority of the employees eligible to participate in the selection or (2) by the majority of employees participating in the selection when such majority constitute not less than 40 per cent of those eligible to participate, such representatives shall, for the purposes of collective bargaining, be the sole representatives of employees eligible to participate in the selection and of employees who subsequently fall within the classification upon which eligibility was based at the time of the selection:** *Provided,* that no organization which imposes inequitable restrictions upon membership shall be entitled to represent employees who are not members thereof.[33]

This draft includes a Title II that incorporates much of the language from Draft 2(b) for the creation of a National Labor Board (not relevant here). This draft also includes Section 207(a), which is derived primarily from Section 307 of Draft 2(b), that spells out certification and election options available to the Board and also the concept of appropriate bargaining units:

Section 207. (a) In any disputes that may arise between an employer and his employees, or between groups of employees, as to who are the representatives of such employees the Board, if the dispute might burden or affect commerce, or obstruct the free flow of commerce, may investigate such dispute and certify to both parties, in writing, the name or names of the individuals or organizations that have been designated and authorized to represent the employees involved in the dispute. In such an investigation, the Board shall be authorized to take a secret ballot of employees, or to utilize any other appropriate method to ascertain their representatives. The Board shall decide whether eligibility to participate in elections shall be determined on the basis of employer unit, craft unit, plant unit, or other appropriate grouping.[34]

Ninth and Final (Wagner/Keyserling) draft, *introduced in the Senate on March 1, 1934, as S. 2926.*[35]

The relevant language in the Declaration of Policy is contained in Section 2 as follows:

Sec. 2 .... It is hereby declared to be the policy of Congress to remove obstructions to the free flow of commerce, to encourage the establishment of uniform labor standards, and to provide for the general welfare, by removing the obstacles which prevent the organization of labor for the purpose of cooperative action in maintaining its standards of living, by encouraging the equalization of the bargaining power of employers and employees, and by providing agencies for the peaceful settlement of industrial disputes.

Section 7 (formerly Section 12) providing exclusivity for majority representation is deleted entirely.[36]

Section 207(a) is changed slightly to read in pertinent part as follows:

Section 207. (a) In any dispute as to who are the representatives of such employees, the **Board,** if the dispute might burden or affect commerce, or obstruct the free flow of commerce, **may investigate** such dispute **and certify** to the parties, in writing, **the name or names of the individuals or labor organizations that have been designated and authorized to represent employees.** In any such investigation, the Board shall be authorized to take a secret ballot of employees, or to utilize any other appropriate method to ascertain their representatives. The Board shall decide whether eligibility to participate in elections shall be determined by employer unit, craft unit, plant unit, or other appropriate grouping.[37]

Draft of S. 2926 (Walsh Bill), *as reported from Senate Committee on Education and Labor, May 26, 1934.*[38]

This draft was prepared by Charles Wyzanski, Solicitor of the Department of Labor, at the request of Senator David Walsh, Chairman of the Senate Committee on Education and Labor.[39] *It had wide support from key figures in the Roosevelt administration, including the President and Senator Wagner.*[40]

The Declaration of Policy is now moved to Section 1, reading as follows:

Section 1. It is hereby declared to be the policy of the United States to remove unnecessary obstructions to the free flow of commerce, to encourage the establishment of uniform labor standards, and to provide for the general welfare, by establishing agencies for the peaceful settlement of labor disputes, and by protecting the exercise by the worker of **complete freedom of association,** self-organization, and **designation of representatives of his own choosing, for the purpose of negotiating the terms and conditions of his employment or other mutual aid or protection.**[41]

The unfair-labor-practice section (formerly Section 5), is now renumbered as Section 3 and contains the following relevant provision:

Sec. 3. It shall be an unfair labor practice—

(1) For an employer to attempt, by interference or coercion, to impair the exercise by employees of the right to form, or join labor organizations, to designate representatives of their own choosing, and to engage in concerted activities for the purpose of collective bargaining or other mutual aid or protection.[42]

The former subsection (2) relating to "refusal to recognize and/or deal" is deleted.

* * *

The following provision gave the Board discretion to authorize proportional representation or majority-exclusive representation:

Sec. 10. (a) In any dispute as to who are the representatives of employees, **the Board,** if the dispute might burden or affect commerce or obstruct the free flow of commerce **may investigate** such dispute and certify to the parties, in writing, the name or names of the individuals or labor organizations that have been designated and authorized to represent employees. In any such investigation, the Board shall hold an appropriate hearing, and the Board shall be authorized to take a secret ballot of employees, or to utilize any other suitable method to ascertain by whom or by what labor organization they desire to be represented. The Board shall decide whether eligibility to participate in a choice of representatives shall be determined on the basis of employer unit, craft unit, plant unit, or other appropriate unit. **Each unit may be given representation in proportion to its membership. The Board may determine that representatives agreed upon by the majority of employees in an appropriate unit shall represent the entire unit** for the purpose of negotiating agreements concerning terms and conditions of employment. Provided, That nothing in the Act shall be construed to prohibit an employer from discussing grievances with an employee or groups of employers at any time.[43]

Appendix to Chapter 3

Relevant Provisions in 1935 Drafts of "National Labor Relations Act," S. 1958

First NLRA Draft[1]

"November, 1934 Modified from last Wagner version of Labor Disputes Act, May 5, 1934."[2]

Section 1 . . . . It is hereby declared to be the policy of the United States to remove unnecessary obstructions to the free flow of commerce, to encourage the establishment of uniform labor standards, and to provide for the general welfare, by establishing agencies for the peaceful settlement of labor disputes, and by protecting the exercise by the worker of full freedom of association, self-organization, and **designation of representatives of his own choosing, for the purpose of negotiating the terms and conditions of his employment** or other mutual aid or protection.[3]

* * *

SEC. (7) [Note by Keyserling: to be dictated][4]

SEC. (8) **It shall be an unfair labor practice for an employer—**

(1) **To attempt, by interference, restraint, or coercion, to impair the exercise by employees of the rights guaranteed in section 7.**[5]

* * *

(3) By discrimination in regard to hire or tenure of employment or any term or condition of employment, or by contract or agreement, to encourage or discourage the exercise by employees of the rights guaranteed in Section 7: *Provided,* that nothing in this Act, or in the National Industrial Recovery Act or in any code or agreement approved thereunder, or in any other statute of the United States, shall preclude an employer from making an agreement with a labor organization to require as a

condition of employment membership in such labor organization **if the agreement is sought by the majority of the employees in a unit covered by it when made.**[6]

* * *

(5) To refuse to bargain collectively with the representatives of his employees.[7]

* * *

Sec. 9(a) **Representatives designated or selected for the purposes of collective bargaining by the majority of the employees in the unit appropriate for such purposes, shall be the exclusive representatives of the entire unit** for the purposes of collective bargaining in respect to rates of pay, hours of employment, and other basic conditions of employment: *Provided,* however, that any minority group of employees in an appropriate unit shall have the right to bargain collectively through representatives of their own choosing when no representatives have been designated or selected by a majority in such unit: and Provided further, that nothing in this section shall prevent any individual or minority group of employees at any time from having representatives of their own choosing to present grievances to their employer, or from engaging in self-organization for their mutual protection or benefit.[8]

(b) In any dispute affecting commerce as to who are the representatives of employees, the Board may investigate such dispute and certify to the parties, in writing, the name or names of the representatives that have been designated or selected. In any such investigation, the Board shall hold an appropriate hearing, either in conjunction with a proceeding under section 9 or otherwise, and the Board shall be authorized to take a secret ballot of employees, or to utilize any other suitable method to ascertain such representatives. The Board shall decide whether, in order the effectuate the purposes of this Act, the appropriate unit for the purposes of collective bargaining shall be the employer unit, craft unit, plant unit, or other appropriate unit.[9]

Second NLRA Draft[10]

Draft bill introduced in the Senate on February 21, 1935, as S. 1958.

Sec. 1 . . . . It is hereby declared to be the policy of the United States to remove obstructions to the free flow of commerce and to provide for the general welfare by encouraging the practice of collective bargaining, and by protecting the exercise by the worker of full freedom of association, self-organization, and **designation of representatives of his own choosing, for the purpose of negotiating the terms and conditions of his employment** or other mutual aid or protection.[11]

* * *

Sec. 7. **Employees shall have the right** to self-organization, to form, join, or assist labor organizations, **to bargain collectively through representatives of their own choosing,** and to engage in concerted activities, for the purpose of collective bargaining or other mutual aid or protection.[12]

Sec. 8. It shall be an unfair labor practice for an employer—

(1) **To interfere with, restrain, or coerce employees in the exercise of the rights guaranteed in section 7.**[13]

* * *

(3) By discrimination in regard to hire or tenure of employment or any term or condition of employment to encourage or discourage membership in any labor organization: *Provided,* that nothing in this Act, or in the National Industrial Recovery Act (U.S.C., title 15, secs. 701–712), as amended from time to time, or in any code or agreement approved or prescribed thereunder, or in any other statute of the United States, shall preclude an employer from making an agreement with a labor organization (not established, maintained, or assisted by any action defined in this Act as an unfair labor practice) to require as a condition of employment membership therein, **if such labor organization is the representative of the majority of the employees in the appropriate collective bargaining unit covered by such agreement when made.**[14]

* * *

Sec. 8(5) is deleted.

* * *

Sec. 9. (a) **Representatives designated or selected for the purposes of collective bargaining by the majority of the employees in a unit appropriate for such purposes, shall be the exclusive representatives of all the employees in such unit for the purposes of collective bargaining** in respect to rates of pay, hours of employment, and other conditions of employment: Provided, That any individual employee or group of employees shall have the right at any time to present grievances to their employer through representatives of their own choosing.[15]

(b) The Board shall decide whether, in order to effectuate the policies of this Act, the unit appropriate for the purposes of collective bargaining shall be the employer unit, craft unit, plant unit, or other appropriate unit.[16]

(c) Whenever a question affecting commerce arises concerning the representation of employees, the Board may investigate such controversy and certify to the parties, in writing, the name or names of the representatives that have been designated or selected. In any such investigation, the Board shall provide for an appropriate hearing, either in conjunction with a proceeding under section 10 or otherwise, and may take a secret ballot of employees, or utilize any other suitable method to ascertain such representatives.[17]

Third NLRA Draft[18]

Proposed Amendments to S. 1958 marked up between February 21 and March 1 and considered by Senate Committee on Education and Labor prior to May 2, 1935.[19]

Section 1 . . . . It is hereby declared to be the policy of this Act **to encourage the practice of negotiating terms and conditions of employment through collective bar-**

gaining, and to protect the exercise by the worker of full freedom of association, self-organization, and **designation of representatives of his own choosing, for the purpose of collective bargaining** or other mutual aid or protection.[20]

* * *

Section 3. By discrimination in regard to hire or tenure of employment or any term or condition of employment to encourage or discourage membership in any labor organization: *Provided,* that nothing in this Act, or in the National Industrial Recovery Act (U.S.C., title 15, secs. 701–712), as amended from time to time, or in any code or agreement approved or prescribed thereunder, or in any other statute of the United States, shall preclude an employer from making an agreement with a labor organization (not established, maintained, or assisted by any action defined in this Act as an unfair labor practice) to require as a condition of employment membership therein, **if such labor organization is the representative of employees** *as provided in Section 9(a)* in the appropriate collective bargaining unit covered by such agreement when made.[21]

* * *

Section 8(5) [NLRB Chairman Biddle added][22]

* * *

(5) **To refuse to bargain collectively with the representatives of his employees, subject to the provisions of Section 9(a).**[23]

or, (5) **To refuse to bargain collectively with employees through their representatives, chosen as** *provided in Section 9(a).*[24]

Fourth NLRA Draft[25]

This draft was the version of the bill reported out of the Senate Committee on Education and Labor on May 2, 1935, which, as to all relevant substantive provisions,[26] was passed by the Senate on May 16, 1935,[27] and by the House on June 19, 1935.[28] The only change in the relevant provisions was the following:

Section 3. By discrimination in regard to hire or tenure of employment or any term or condition of employment to encourage or discourage membership in any labor organization: *Provided,* that nothing in this Act, or in the National Industrial Recovery Act (U.S.C., title 15, secs. 701–712), as amended from time to time, or in any code or agreement approved or prescribed thereunder, or in any other statute of the United States, shall preclude an employer from making an agreement with a labor organization (not established, maintained, or assisted by any action defined in this Act as an unfair labor practice) to require as a condition of employment membership therein, **if such labor organization is the representative of employees** *as provided in Section 9(a)* in the appropriate collective bargaining unit covered by such agreement when made.[29]

* * *

Section 8(5), reading as follows, was added:

(5) to refuse to bargain collectively with the representatives of his employees, subject to the provisions of section 9(a).[30]

Fifth and Final NLRA Draft[31]

This is the draft approved by the Senate and House on June 27, 1935,[32] following a conference committee report.[33] It was signed by the President on July 5, 1935.[34] The only change from the relevant provisions in Drafts 3 and 4 are language changes in the pertinent public-policy paragraph of Section 1 that emphasizes the plural nature of the protected concerted activities as follows:

Sec. 1 . . . . It is hereby declared to be the policy of the United States to eliminate the causes of certain substantial obstructions to the free flow of commerce and to mitigate and eliminate these obstructions when they have occurred by encouraging the practice and procedure of collective bargaining and by protecting the exercise by workers of **full freedom of association,** self-organization, and **designation of representatives of their own choosing, for the purpose of negotiating the terms and conditions of their employment** or other mutual aid or protection.[35]

Notes

Foreword

1. Professor Morris puts the emphasis on employees' rights and employers' duties. I shall do the same. But of course these rights and duties are reciprocal. The extension of bargaining rights to minority unions would also convey valuable rights to employers to demand good-faith bargaining on the part of the unions.

2. Clyde Summers, *Unions without Majority — A Black Hole,* 66 CHI.-KENT L. REV. 531 (1990).

3. *Id.* at 540.

4. 49 Stat. 449, 452 (1935), 29 U.S.C. § 157 (2000).

Introduction

1. A program of the San Diego Labor Council Extension Fund, Inc.

2. *See* Hi Tech Honeycomb, Inc., NLRB Case No. 21-CA-22262, filed on June 4, 1999, and closed pursuant to a settlement agreement on Jan. 25, 2001. References herein to the facts of that case are based on affidavits and other documents contained in the official case records.

3. National Labor Relations Act. 49 Stat. 449 (1935), 29 U.S.C. §§ 151–69 (as amended).

4. Clyde Summers, *The Kenneth M. Piper Lecture: Unions without Majority — A Black Hole?,* 66 CHI-KENT. L. REV. 531 (1990) (hereinafter Summers).

5. *See* E. G. Latham, *Legislative Purpose and Administrative Policy under the National Labor Relations Act,* 4 GEO. WASH. L. REV. 433 (1936) (hereinafter Latham), discussed *infra* at notes 25 & 26.

6. Summers, *supra* note 4 at 539.

7. *Id.* at 538.

8. *See* Alan Hyde, *After Smyrna: Rights and Powers of Unions that Represent Less than a Majority,* 45 RUTGERS L. REV. 637, 639 n. 8 (1993); Matthew W. Finkin, *The Road Not Taken: Some Thoughts on Nonmajority Employee Representation,* 69 CHI.-KENT. L. REV. 195, 198 n. 18 (1993).

9. Charles J. Morris, *A Blueprint for Reform of the National Labor Relations Act,* 8 AD-MIN. L.J. AM. U. 517, 554 (1994).

10. *Id.* at 555 and nn. 163 & 168.

11. The following were the employees involved: Ly Mey, Phat Tran, Billy Sar, Quy Tran, Chunna Touch, Soth Hor, Vincent Delrosario, Firas Juwaideh, Tan Le, Tien Le, Luis Mata, Jesse Tran, Bory Keo, Phal Cheang, Khmay Lun, Khauv Yin, and Sokha Chit.

12. §7. 29 U.S.C. §157.

13. Senator Robert F. Wagner, 1 Legislative History of the NLRA, 1935 (1949) (hereinafter 1 Legis. Hist.), at 1318.

14. NLRB v. Washington Aluminum Co., 370 U.S. 9 (1962). *See* Ch. 9 *infra* at notes 73–76.

15. *See* Ch. 9 *infra* at note 84.

16. §2(5). 29 U.S.C. §152(5).

17. *See* Ch. 9 *infra* at notes 77, 81, & 87.

18. George Gershwin (libretto by DuBose Heyward), Porgy and Bess, Act II, Scene 2 (1934).

19. *See* Ch. 3 *infra.*

20. Irving Bernstein, Turbulent Years, A History of the American Worker 1933–1941 458, 466 (1971). Emphasis added. *See* Ch. 4 *infra* at notes 10–11.

21. Steelworkers Organizing Committee of the Congress of Industrial Organizations (CIO).

22. United Automobile Workers of the CIO.

23. American Federation of Labor.

24. *See* Ch. 4 *infra* at notes 5–33.

25. Latham, *supra* note 5 at 453. Emphasis in original.

26. *Id.* at 456, n. 65. Emphasis added.

27. 29 U.S.C. §159(a).

28. §7. 29 U.S.C. §157. *See* Ch. 5 *infra.*

29. *See* Ch. 9 *infra.*

30. *See* Ch. 5 *infra* at notes 7–38.

31. *See* Ch. 4 *infra* at notes 34–44.

32. Act of June 23, 1947, ch. 120, §1ff, 61 Stat. 136.

33. Milton Derber, The American Idea of Industrial Democracy, 1865–1965 6 (1970), *citing* Profit Sharing Trends (Chicago: Council of Profit Sharing Industries, March–April 1959), p. 3.

34. Final Report of the Industrial Commission, Vol. xix of the Commission reports, 57th Cong., 1st Sess., H.R. Doc. No. 380 at 805.

35. U.S. Commission on Industrial Relations, Final Report and Testimony 8:7659–7662 (1916).

36. Irving Bernstein, The New Deal Collective Bargaining Policy 28 (1950), quoted from Leon H. Keyserling, *Why the Wagner Act?* in Louis G. Silverberg, ed., The Wagner Act: After Ten Years 12–13 (1945).

37. 1 Legis. Hist. at 1319.

38. *The Ideal Industrial State—As Wagner Sees It,* New York Times Magazine, May 9, 1937, at 23, quoted in Leon H. Keyserling, *The Wagner Act: Its Origin and Current Significance,* 29 Geo. Wash. L. Rev. 199 (1960).

39. §1. 29 U.S.C. §151.

40. *See* Ch. 5 *infra* at notes 49–53.

41. "Everyone has the right to freedom of peaceful assembly and association. . . . Everyone has the right to form and to join trade unions for the protection of his interests." Universal Declaration of Human Rights, Arts. 20 & 23 (1948). *See* Ch. 8 *infra* at notes 28–29.

42. International Covenant on Civil and Political Rights, S. Exec. Doc. E, 95–2 (1978), 999 U.N.T.S. 171 (adopted in 1966, entered into force in 1976, ratified by U.S. in 1992); 42 U.S.C. §1983 (1994). *See* Ch. 8 *infra* at notes 6 & 37–73. International Labor Organization Declaration on Fundamental Principles and Rights at Work, International Labour Conf., 86th Sess. (June 1998). *See* Ch. 8 *infra* notes 7 & 74–89 at §2(9).

43. U.S. Bureau of Labor Statistics, Union Membership 2001 (2002), available at ftp//ftp.bls.gov/pub/special.requests/lf/aat42.txt.

44. *See* Lance Compa, Human Rights Watch, Unfair Advantage: Workers' Freedom of Association in the United States under International Human Rights Standards 17–39 (2000) (hereinafter Human Rights Watch).

45. Annual poll by Peter Hart Associates for AFL-CIO reported in Czarneki's Labor Education Newsletter, Sept. 9, 2002.

46. Human Rights Watch, *supra* note 44 at 16.

47. *See* Patrick Hardin & John E. Higgins, Jr., eds. The Developing Labor Law: The Board, the Courts, and the National Labor Relations Act 67–69 (4th ed. 2001), for a

description of the 1978 labor law reform effort that had majority support in both houses of Congress but failed the Senate filibuster test.

48. 44 Stat. 577 (1926).

49. Ch. 90, §7(a), 48 Stat. 195 (1933) (declared unconstitutional in Schecter Poultry Corp. v. United States, 295 U.S. 495 (1935)). *See* Ch. 1 *infra* at note 3.

50. *See* Ch. 1 *infra* at notes 29–31.

51. 29 U.S.C. §§ 101–115.

52. 281 U.S. 548 (1930).

53. *Id.* at 570, *citing* American Steel Foundries v. Tri-City Central Trades Council, 257 U.S. 184, 209 (1921) ("Labor unions are recognized by the [1915] Clayton Act [15 U.S.C. §§ 12 et seq.] as legal when instituted for mutual help and lawfully carrying out their legitimate objects. They have long been thus recognized by the courts. They were organized out of the necessities of the situation. A single employee was helpless in dealing with an employer. . . . Union was essential to give laborers opportunity to deal on equality with their employer. . . . The right to combine for such a lawful purpose has in many years not been denied by any court.")

54. The vote in the Senate was 63 to 12, with 19 not voting. 2 Legislative History of the NLRA, 1935 (1949), at 2414 & 3267. The vote in the House, with 232 present, was 132 to 45. *Id.* at 3267.

55. §§7 & 8(a)(1), 29 U.S.C. §§ 157 & 158(a)(1).

56. 1 Legis. Hist. at 1312.

57. 1 Legis. Hist. at 1406 (Mr. 11, 1935).

58. *See* Ch. 3 *infra* at notes 36–48 and Ch. 5 *infra* at notes 97–99.

59. *See* Ch. 6 *infra.*

60. 42 U.S.C. § 1982, Ch. 31, §1, at 14 Stat. 27I (1866).

61. 392 U.S. 409 (1968).

62. *Id.* at 437, repeating with approval what the Attorney General of the United States had stated at oral argument.

63. *See* NLRB v. J. Weingarten, Inc., 420 U.S. 251 (1975); Epilepsy Foundation of Northeast Ohio, 331 NLRB No. 92, *aff'd in pertinent part,* 268 F.3d 1095 (D.C. Cir. 2001), overruled by IBM Corporation, 341 NLRB No. 148 (June 9, 2004). *See* Ch. 7 *infra* at note 50 and Ch. 11 *infra* at notes 12–28.

64. *I.e.,* providing assistance concerning a variety of worker-related problems and services, for example, regarding health and safety issues, workers' compensation, minimum wage and overtime requirements, disability requirements and benefits, vocational rehabilitation, state and federal antidiscrimination laws, and various financial matters. *See* Ch. 11 *infra* at notes 30–31.

65. *See* Ch. 11 *infra* at note 31.

66. These nonbargaining activities also fit well into the pattern of social unionism that is gaining support in the American labor movement. *See, e.g.,* Lowell Turner et al., *Revival of the American Labor Movement: Issues, Problems, Prospects,* in Rekindling the Movement at 1 and 9 (Lowell Turner et al. eds., 2001); Samuel B. Bacharach et al., Mutual Aid and Union Renewal: Cycles of Logics of Action (2001).

67. *See* Ch. 11 *infra* at notes 34–80.

68. *See* Ch. 11 *infra* at note 80.

69. *See* Ch. 12 infra at notes 6–10.

70. Paul Osterman, et al., Working in America: A Blueprint for the New Labor Market 152 (2001).

71. *Id.*

72. The substantive text of the original Wagner Act contained in the present statute consists of only 344 words (§7, 42 words; §8(a), 223 words; §9(a), 79 words).

73. *See generally* John Kenneth Galbraith, American Capitalism: The Concept of Countervailing Power (1952, 1956).

Chapter 1

1. National Labor Relations Act. 49 Stat. 449 (1935), 29 U.S.C. §§ 151–69; §7, 29 U.S.C. §157.

2. 29 U.S.C. §§ 101–115.

3. Ch. 90, §7(a), 48 Stat. 195 (1933) (the entire statute was declared unconstitutional in Schecter Poultry Corp. v. United States, 295 U.S. 495 (1935), on grounds that it represented an unconstitutional delegation of legislative power and that its application to intrastate activities exceeded the commerce power).

4. National Industrial Conference Board, Inc., INDIVIDUAL AND COLLECTIVE BARGAINING UNDER THE N.I.R.A.—A STATISTICAL STUDY OF PRESENT PRACTICE 6 (1933) (hereinafter CONFERENCE BOARD); R. W. Fleming, *The Significance of the Wagner Act,* in LABOR AND THE NEW DEAL 126 (Milton Derber & Edwin Young eds., 1961).

5. U.S. BUREAU OF LABOR STATISTICS, BULLETIN NO. 287, NATIONAL WAR LABOR BOARD 32 (1918), quoted in Raymond S. Rubinow, SECTION 7(A): ITS HISTORY, INTERPRETATION AND ADMINISTRATION (Office of National Recovery Administration, Div. of Review, Labor Studies Section), 11 (1936) (hereinafter Rubinow).

6. §8(1) of the Wagner Act is the present §8(a)(1). All of the provisions with which we are concerned in this book are provisions contained in the original Wagner Act, for none of the substantive language in issue was changed or affected by either the Taft-Hartley amendments of 1947 (Labor Management Relations Act, ch. 120, §101, 61 Stat. 136 (1947)) or the Landrum-Griffin amendments of 1959 (Labor-Management Reporting and Disclosure Act, Pub. L. No. 86–257, 73 Stat. 519 (1959)). However, as a result of the Taft-Hartley amendments, the statutory designations for the original §8 employer unfair labor practices were redesignated as subsections of §8(a); therefore, to avoid confusion here and in other parts of the book that refer to legislative history, identification of those provisions, where deemed appropriate, will be made according to their Wagner Act designations, such as §8(1) and §8(5) instead of §8(a)(1) and §8(a)(5), respectively. The reader should also bear in mind that other references to the NLRA here and in other sources, and also in the case law, will ordinarily carry the appropriate §8 or §8(a) designation, depending on the time reference—whether pre- or post-1947—to which they refer.

7. Boldface and italicized emphasis added.

8. 29 U.S.C. §102. Boldface and italicized emphasis added.

9. Boldface and italicized emphasis added.

10. Boldface emphasis added. The final print of the bill that was passed on July 5, 1935, contained the comma after "*other concerted activities. . . .* " That comma later disappeared, which was a grammatical improvement that obviously had no adverse effect on the meaning of the clause.

11. Boldface italicized emphasis added.

12. The day the NIRA became effective.

13. The day the Supreme Court decided Schecter Poultry Corp. v. United States, *supra* note 3.

14. *See* Minier Sargent, *Majority Rule in Collective Bargaining under Section 7(a),* 29 ILL. L. REV. 275, 280 (1934) (hereinafter Sargent) ("For many years it has been customary for each employee to select his own union or organization to act for him in collective bargaining").

15. Louis August Rufener, PRINCIPLES OF ECONOMICS 399 (1927).

16. Dale Yoder, LABOR ECONOMICS AND LABOR PROBLEMS 443 (1933). Emphasis added. This and the Rufener reference in the preceding note were cited by Justice Stone in NLRB v. Pennsylvania Greyhound Lines, Inc., 303 U.S. 261, 267, n. 2 (1938), concerning the significance of recognition to the collective bargaining process. *See also* Matthew W. Finkin, *The Road Not Taken: Some Thoughts on Nonmajority Employee Representation,* 69 CHI.-KENT L. REV. 195, 197 (1993) ("[T]he tradition of American 'trades unions' throughout the nineteenth and the early twentieth century was to bargain only for their members; but this was coupled to the demand that employers hire union members exclusively. . . . ").

17. For example, as noted in the REPORT OF THE UNITED STATES INDUSTRIAL COMMISSION, H. DOC. 7, V73 No. 179, 830, 861–64, 898–900 (1902), the Iron Molders Union's agreements in the stove industry contained members-only provisions, as did agreements in the glass industry.

18. Milton Derber, THE AMERICAN IDEA OF INDUSTRIAL DEMOCRACY, 1865–1965 (1970) (hereinafter Derber).

19. *Id.* at 94.

20. THE TWENTIETH CENTURY FUND, HOW COLLECTIVE BARGAINING WORKS: A SURVEY

OF EXPERIENCE IN LEADING AMERICAN INDUSTRIES (Harry A. Millis, Research Director) 689 (1942) (hereinafter TWENTIETH CENTURY FUND).

21. "Early collective bargaining agreements took two forms: exclusive and nonexclusive. In nonexclusive agreements, *employers agreed to recognize a union as representative only for employees who were members of the union*. . . . In exclusive agreements, on the other hand, an employer agreed to recognize a union as the exclusive representative for all the employees in a defined unit. [However, a] union shop provision was the only practical way of guaranteeing a union's exclusive control over bargaining, and thus in the pre-Wagner Act era exclusive recognition of a union was synonymous with a union shop." Richard R. Carlson, *The Origin and Future of Exclusive Representation in American Labor Law*, 30 DUQ. L. REV. 779, 804 (1992). Emphasis added. *See also* conclusions derived from a 1933 survey by the National Industrial Conference Board *infra* at notes 86–88.

22. Contracts that obligated employees "to agree that they would not join any union." Foster Rhea Dulles, LABOR IN AMERICA, 3ʳᵈ ed. 194 (1966) (hereinafter Dulles).

23. *See generally* Dulles, *Id.*; Irving Bernstein, A HISTORY OF THE AMERICAN WORKER — THE LEAN YEARS, 1920–1933 (1960); Harry A. Millis & Royal E. Montgomery, ORGANIZED LABOR 76–187 (1945); E.E. Cummins, THE LABOR PROBLEM IN THE UNITED STATES 260–352, 443–79 (1932); Samuel Yellen, AMERICAN LABOR STRUGGLES 1877–1934 (1936); Felix Frankfurter & Nathan Greene, THE LABOR INJUNCTION (1930); TWENTIETH CENTURY FUND, *supra* note 20 at 476.

24. Dulles, *supra* note 22 at 247.

25. There was no mention of majority rule in the reports of either the Industrial Commission of 1902, FINAL REPORT OF THE INDUSTRIAL COMMISSION, HR Document No. 380 (1902), or the U.S. Commission on Industrial Relations of 1916, TESTIMONY AND FINAL REPORT (1916). *See* Derber, *supra* note 18 at 177.

26. Herbert Schreiber, *The Origin of the Majority Rule and the Simultaneous Development of Institutions to Protect the Minority: A Chapter in Early American Labor Law*, 25 RUTGERS L. REV. 237, 296–97 (1971) (hereinafter Schreiber).

27. 44 Stat. 577 (1926).

28. Schreiber, *supra* note 26 at 296–97. *See also* Dana E. Eischen, *Chap. II, Representation Disputes and Their Resolution in the Railroad and Airline Industries*, in THE RAILWAY LABOR ACT AT FIFTY, 24–26 (Charles M. Rehmus ed., 1977); *cf.* Sargent, *supra* note 14 at 280.

29. In § 2, Ninth, 45 U.S.C. §§152, Ninth.

30. *Id.* Emphasis added. "Craft or class" is the term for *appropriate bargaining unit* under the RLA.

31. § 2, Fourth, 45 U.S.C. §§152, Fourth.

32. *See infra* at notes 91–95.

33. 29 U.S.C. §102.

34. Felix Frankfurter & Nathan Greene, THE LABOR INJUNCTION 212 (1930).

35. *Id.*

36. Dulles, *supra* note 22 at 263 (1966).

37. *Cf. infra* at notes 69–70.

38. Lewis L. Lorwin & Arthur Wubnig, LABOR RELATIONS BOARDS 22 (Brookings Institution, 1935) (hereinafter Lorwin & Wubnig). Emphasis added.

39. H.R. No. 243 & S. D. No. 76, 73ʳᵈ Cong., 1ˢᵗ Sess. (1933).

40. *See* Irving Bernstein, THE NEW DEAL COLLECTIVE BARGAINING POLICY 29–33 (1950) (hereinafter Bernstein NEW DEAL).

41. *Id.* at 28 & 31.

42. *Id.* at 28, quoted from Leon H. Keyserling, *Why the Wagner Act?* in Louis G. Silverberg, ed., THE WAGNER ACT: AFTER TEN YEARS 12–13 (1945).

43. *Id.*

44. Derber, *supra* note 18. *See also* Raymond L. Hogler, *Worker Participation, Employer Anti-Unionism, and Labor Law: The Case of the Steel Industry, 1918–1937*, 7 HOFSTRA LAB. L. J. 1, 5–14 (1989).

45. Derber, *id.* at 6, citing PROFIT SHARING TRENDS (Chicago: Council of Profit Sharing Industries, March–April 1959), p. 3.

46. Prepared in accordance with an 1898 Act of Congress. *See* FINAL REPORT OF THE IN-

DUSTRIAL COMMISSION, Vol. xix of the Commission reports, 57th Cong., 1st Sess., H.R. Doc. No. 380.

47. *Id.* at 805.

48. U.S. COMMISSION ON INDUSTRIAL RELATIONS, FINAL REPORT AND TESTIMONY 8:7659–7662 (1916). Also quoted in Derber, *supra* note 18 at 136.

49. Bernstein NEW DEAL, *supra* note 40 at 32.

50. CONFERENCE BOARD, *supra* note 4 at 6. "The principal draftsman [of §7(a)], Donald Richberg, has said that the substance of the paragraph came from his familiarity with the Railway Labor Act of 1926, the Norris-LaGuardia Act of 1932, and the 1933 amendments to the Federal Bankruptcy Act." R. W. Fleming, *The Significance of the Wagner Act,* in LABOR AND THE NEW DEAL 126 (Milton Derber & Edwin Young eds., 1961). *See also* Lorwin & Wubnig, *supra* note 38 at 22, n. 26.

51. Ch. 90, §7(a), 48 Stat. 195 (1933). Emphasis added for comparison with §7 of the Wagner Act, with the basic fourteen-word phrase highlighted in bold face.

52. Kenneth Casebeer, *Holder of the Pen: An Interview with Leon Keyserling on Drafting the Wagner Act,* 42 U. MIAMI L. REV. 285, 297 (1987).

53. NEW YORK TIMES, June 17, 1933.

54. Testimony in support of his Labor Disputes bill, S. 2926, 1 LEGISLATIVE HISTORY OF THE NLRA, 1935 (1949) (hereinafter 1 LEGIS. HIST.) at 38.

55. James A. Gross, THE MAKING OF THE NATIONAL LABOR RELATIONS BOARD 11 (1974) (hereinafter Gross). Emphasis added.

56. NRA Release No. 28, July 3, 1933, quoted in Rubinow, *supra* note 5 at 55.

57. Bernstein NEW DEAL, *supra* note 40 at 57.

58. *Industrial Disputes,* 37 MONTHLY LAB. REV. 869 (1933), *quoted in* Bernstein, *id.* at 58. The average monthly worker-days lost during the first half of 1933 was under 603,000. *Id.* Most of these strikes were for recognition. *See* note 66 *infra.*

59. Rubinow, *supra* note 5 at 67.

60. Lorwin & Wubnig, *supra* note 38 at 92–93.

61. Gross, *supra* note 55 at 15.

62. Lorwin & Wubnig, *supra* note 38 at 93.

63. *See infra* at notes 111–12.

64. Rubinow, *supra* note 5 at 70.

65. Secretary of Labor Frances Perkins explained to the Senate Committee on Education and Labor following the introduction of Senator Wagner's S. 1958 in 1935, that "the first steps of the original Labor Board which was appointed rather hastily, to solve questions under Section 7(a), was along the line of conciliation. . . . " 1 LEGIS. HIST. at 1434. *See also* Lloyd K. Garrison, THE NATIONAL LABOR BOARDS, 184 Annals Am. Acad. Pol. & Soc. Sci. 138, 139 (1936) (hereinafter Garrison).

66. *See* CONFERENCE BOARD, *supra* note 4 at 11 (1933) (reference to "statement of the National Labor Board that in 70% of the labor controversies coming under its jurisdiction the question of representation has in some way been involved.")

67. On October 22, 1933, Senator Wagner, the Board's chairman, expressed that self-governing approach in the following letter to the chairman of a newly established regional board:

> The recent surge of strikes and similar industrial disturbances has been due almost entirely to misunderstandings and misconceptions of the new rights and obligations conferred and imposed upon industry and labor alike in the program to make America safe for industrial democracy. Out of confusion which must necessarily accompany the beginning of any new scheme of so vast a scope, have risen cross-currents of distrust and antagonism between labor and industry, which have no substantial basis in fact. The very brief experience of the National Labor Board has already demonstrated that practically all of the recent industrial conflicts can be amicably settled when the parties have been brought together to discuss their differences in an atmosphere of calmness and disinterestedness and with a clearer knowledge of their respective rights and duties. Cooperation based on mutual trust and understanding must be the keynote henceforward.

Letter from Senator Robert F. Wagner to Marion Smith, October 22, 1933. National Archives, Record Group 25, records of the National Labor Relations Board, National Labor Board, and National Labor Relations Board I: office of the executive secretary, correspondence and reports relating to regional boards, 1933–35, Region VI, Atlanta, quoted in Gross, *supra* note 55 at 16.

68. "The original personnel of the Board, numbering seven, was as follows: For industry: Walter C. Teagle (Chairman of the Industrial Advisory Board), Louis Kirstein, Gerard Swope, for labor: Dr. Leo Wolman (Chairman of the Labor Advisory Board), William Green, John L. Lewis; as impartial chairman, Senator Robert F. Wagner. The board was reorganized in February 1934 and its number increased to thirteen, as follows: Senator Wagner, Chairman, Clay Williams and L. C. Marshall, Vice-Chairman; Henry S. Dennison, Ernest Draper, Pierre S. du Pont, Louis E. Kirstein, Walter C. Teagle, for industry; George L. Berry, William Green, Dr. Francis Haas, John L. Lewis, Dr. Leo Wolman, for labor." Rubinow, *supra* note 5 at 69, n. **.

69. *See* text accompanying notes 71–88 *infra*.

70. Sargent, *supra* note 14 at 278.

71. Presently known as "The Conference Board." The organization was founded in 1916. Here is its website description of its founding and continued purpose: "A group of concerned business leaders, representing a variety of major industries, concluded that the time had arrived for an entirely new type of organization. Not another trade association. Not a propaganda machine. But a respected, not-for-profit, nonpartisan organization that would bring leaders together to find solutions to common problems and objectively examine major issues having an impact on business and society. . . . The Conference Board is a non-partisan, non-advocacy organization." http://www.conference-board.org/whoweare.

72. CONFERENCE BOARD, *supra* note 4.

73. The first such requirement was issued on March 1, 1934, when Denver Tramway Corp., 1 NLB 64 (1934), was decided. *See infra* at notes 124–36. No such requirement was contained in the *Reading formula* of August 11, 1933. *See infra* at note 94.

74. The survey thus did not cover shipping, truck transportation, nonmanufacturing warehousing, private utilities, and sales and service industries. Although construction was also excluded, union organization and bargaining in that industry has traditionally been *sui generis* and not greatly affected by any labor legislation until the Taft-Hartley and Landrum-Griffin amendments of 1947 and 1959, respectively. *See* 29 U.S.C. §§158(b)(4), 158(b)(7), 158(e), & 158(f). Railroads likewise were not included in the survey, for they were covered by the Railway Labor Act.

75. The following is the monograph's description of the Conference Board's selection process (Conference Board, *supra* note 4 at 11–12), which is included here in full to demonstrate the reliability of the data:

> . . . The best available source of a representative list of companies seemed to be a commercial register, and accordingly Thomas' Register was selected. Since it was manifestly impracticable to address inquiries to all of the 221,094 concerns in these two fields, it was necessary to adopt some basis of selection that limit the number, while preserving the representative character of the list selected. Approximate capitalization of companies is indicated in the register by ratings. It was estimated that, if all companies with an AAA, $500,000, rating or higher were taken, the list would total about 10,000, a number large enough to provide a fairly representative cross-section of industry. This plan was followed, and it resulted in inquiries being addressed to 10,335 companies, in the selection of which a minimum size, as judged by capitalization, was the only qualification.
>
> That this basis of selection secured the breadth of coverage desired is indicated by the distribution of the companies that replied to the inquiry according to size, as shown in Table 3 [not here reproduced] in this report. Companies employing fewer than 100 wage-earners constitute 24.3% of the total number that furnished information, and 48.2% employ between 100 and 500 workers. If concerns employing fewer than 100 wage-earners may be classified as small, those employing between 100 and 1,000 as medium-size, and those employing over 1,000 as large, it is found that 24.3% of he companies covered by this study are small, 62.3% are medium size, and 13.4% are large. This would seem to indicate a generally representative sample.

76. According to a 1935 research study, Alfred L. Bernheim & Dorothy Van Doren, eds. (Published for Twentieth Century Fund, Inc.) LABOR AND THE GOVERNMENT—AN INVESTIGATION OF THE ROLE OF THE GOVERNMENT IN LABOR RELATIONS 65 (1935), "'*Employee repre-*

sentation plan' is [a term] favored by employers" rather than the term *company union.* Emphasis added.

77. *See* CONFERENCE BOARD, *supra* note 4 at 12. Several other supplementary questions, not pertinent to this analysis, were also asked.

78. *Id.* at 13.

79. *Id.* at 16. Permission to reproduce tables 1 and 2 provided by the Conference Board.

80. *See* note 76 *supra.*

81. *See* Ch. 2 *infra* at notes 99, 112–13, & 116.

82. Table 2, second and fifth columns.

83. Table 2 (second column) shows 147 companies with a combination of individual and union bargaining; 21 with a combination of employee representation (company union) and union bargaining; and 18 with a combination of individual bargaining, union, and employee representation (company union)—a total of 186 companies.

84. Table 2 (fifth column): the sum of 39,240 + 8,140 + 3,730.

85. *See* columns three, four, and five in Table 2.

86. For further evidence of the coexistence of company-union and independent-union bargaining during the NIRA period, *see* Ch. 2 *infra* at notes 114–15.

87. In fact, Senator Wagner was well aware of the Conference Board study, for he referenced it in a *New York Times* article on March 11, 1934, that was made a part of the *Congressional Record* during consideration of his Labor Disputes bill, S. 2926, March 12, 1934. 1 LEGIS. HIST. 22.

88. Sargent, *supra* note 14 at 285. Emphasis added.

89. Christopher L. Tomlins, THE STATE AND THE UNIONS: LABOR RELATIONS, LAW, AND THE ORGANIZED LABOR MOVEMENT IN AMERICA, 1886–1960 113 (1985) (hereinafter Tomlins). As William M. Leiserson, the NLB's secretary, responded to an early inquiry:

> Section 7 of the Recovery Act gives the employees the right to organize and choose their own representatives. [A]s to what steps are necessary, we can only say that that is a matter for the employees to decide for themselves. They may call a meeting and elect these representatives in any way they desire.

Id., from *RG* 25, Box 81 (U.S. Archives) "NLB General Correspondence File K."

90. *Supra* notes 65–67.

91. Gross *supra* note 55 at 18–21.

92. Emily Clark Brown, *Selection of Employees' Representatives,* 40 MONTHLY LAB. REV. 1, 15 (1935) (hereinafter Brown).

93. BERKELY WOOLEN MILLS, 1 NLB 5–6 (1933). *See also* National Lock Co., 1 NLB (Part 2) 16 (1934) ("Representation is not restricted under the statute to fellow employees. . . . Organization and representation are matters which concern the employees exclusively." *Id.* at 19).

94. Irving Bernstein, TURBULENT YEARS, A HISTORY OF THE AMERICAN WORKER 1933–1941 174 (1971) (hereinafter Bernstein TURBULENT YEARS). Emphasis added. For the full text of the Reading settlement agreement, *see* NRA Release No. 285, Aug. 11, 1933, reproduced in Rubinow, *supra* note 5 at 166. *Cf.* H. W. Anthony Mill, 1 NLB 1 (1933) (holding that written agreements were part of the bargaining process contemplated by the Reading formula).

95. Bernstein TURBULENT YEARS, *id.* at 174.

96. *Eg., see* Edward G. Budd Mfg. Co., 1 NLB 58 (1933), and *infra* at notes 98–104.

97. Bernstein NEW DEAL, *supra* note 40 at 59.

98. *Supra* note 96.

99. *Id.* at 59.

100. *Id.* at 60. *See* Bernstein NEW DEAL, *supra* note 40 at 59.

101. 1 NLB at 60. Emphasis added.

102. *Id.*

103. Bernstein TURBULENT YEARS, *supra* note 94 at 179–80.

104. *See* Lloyd K .Garrison's reference to the "open defiance on the part of the Weirton Steel Company, the Budd Manufacturing Company, and others." Garrison, *supra* note 65 at 139, *and also* Rubinow, supra *note* 5 at 71, n*.

105. 1 NLB 26 (1933).

106. *Id.* at 26.

107. *Id.* at 27. The NLB's frustration concerning its lack of enforcement authority was ev-

ident in its remedial order. It held that because "the strike was precipitated by the company's refusal to deal with the *duly selected representative of the workers,* the striking employees are entitled to priority over those who have been employed since the strike." However, because an election was deemed the only remedy available, it ordered that an election be held that would include all strikers who desired reinstatement. *Id.* Emphasis added.

108. *See* notes 121–22 *infra* and accompanying text.

109. From Aug. 5, 1933, to its dissolution and replacement by the National Labor Relations Board (old) on Jul. 9, 1934.

110. Brown, *supra* note 92 at 5–6.

111. Exec. Order No. 6511, Dec. 16, 1933, 1 NLB vi (1933).

112. *Id.*

113. Exec. Order No. 6580, Feb. 1, 1934, 1 NLB vii (1933).

114. *Id.* Emphasis added.

115. For a comprehensive list of President Roosevelt's different positions on this issue, *see* Garrison, *supra* note 65 at 143–44.

116. "Notably the Iron and Steel Institute and the National Association of Manufacturers." Lorwin & Wubnig, *supra* note 38 at 109 & n. 44.

117. *Id.* at 191.

118. *Id.*

119. *Id.* at 192.

120. *Id.* and n. 26 as follows:

In all, the NLB and its regional boards held 183 elections, comprising 546 industrial units. . . . Trade unions polled 69.4 per cent of the valid votes and won by a majority in 74.7 per cent of the units. Employee representation plans [company unions] polled 28.4 per cent of the valid votes and won by a majority in 28.5 per cent of the units. No representation, voted for by 2.2 per cent of the workers casting valid ballots, prevailed in 2.1 per cent of the plants. . . . In 69 of the unit elections, no alternative to trade union representation was started [*sic*]. Here trade union representation was chosen by 77.8 per cent of the voters in 82.6 per cent of the units. In 449 of the unit elections, the workers had a straightforward choice between trade or company union. Trade union representation was here chosen by 67.0 per cent of the workers in 71.9 per cent of the units.

Citing Brown, *supra* note 92 at 5, particularly Tables 2 & 3. *See* Ch. 2 *infra* at notes 111–12.

121. NRA General Counsel. It will be recalled that Richberg was the principal author of §7(a). *See* note 50 *supra* and accompanying text.

122. NRA Release No. 3125, Feb. 4, 1934 (i.e., three days after the Executive Order), quoted in full in Rubinow, *supra* note 5 at 167–68. Emphasis added.

123. 1 NLB (Part 2) 15 (1934).

124. 1 NLB 64 (1934).

125. *Bee Bus Line Co.*, 1 NLB (Part 2) 24 (1934).

126. *Eagle Rubber Co.*, 1 NLB (Part 2) 31 (1934).

127. *Id.* at 64.

128. The Amalgamated Association of Street and Electric Railway Employees, Division 1001.

129. A company union that had previously represented the employees.

130. 1 NLB at 64. Emphasis added.

131. Lorwin & Wubnig, *supra* note 38 at 194.

132. 1 NLB at 64–65.

133. Gross, *supra* note 55 at 57. *See also* Tomlins, *supra* note 89 at 115, noting that this "transition from mediation to majority rule early in 1934 was a decisive step in the evolution of federal labor relations policy."

134. 1 NLB 65.

135. He wrote that the two unions "shall represent respectively the numbers of said employees favoring them. With respect to the . . . employees who cast no ballot, the [employer] shall bargain with them individually until such time as all or part of them shall choose representatives for collective bargaining." *Id.* Professor Gross adds an instructive gloss: "[M]ember duPont . . . maintained in the unpublished portion of his written dissent that General Johnson's interpretations of Section 7(a) and Executive Order Number 6580 were correct." Gross, *supra*

note 55 at 57. "The informal file in the *Denver Tramway* case contains a 6-page type-written analysis by duPont . . . , [only] a portion of which was printed in [1 NLB 64, 65 (1934)]. In the unpublished portions of his dissent duPont noted that the word 'majority was not used in Section 7(a). . . . Under a law confirming to employees the "right to organize and bargain collectively through representatives of their own choosing" how can we deny that right to over half of the employees of the Denver Tramway Corporation.'" *Id.* at n. 83.

136. *See* Lorwin & Wubnig, *supra* note 38 at 191–92; TWENTIETH CENTURY FUND, *supra* note 20 at 344; Gross, *supra* note 67 at 92; Cornelius W. Wickersham, *The NIRA from the Employers' Viewpoint* 48 HARV. L. REV. 954, 973 (1935). *See also* Ch. 2 *infra* at notes 74–94.

137. *See* Ch. 3 *infra* at note 68.

138. *Labor Board Rejects Minority Appeal in Real Silk Case*, NATIONAL RECOVERY ADMINISTRATION, NATIONAL LABOR BOARD, Press Release No. 4647, Ap. 27, 1934. Emphasis added.

139. It is unfortunate that historian Irving Bernstein presented a misleading report of the *Real Silk* case, which he cited for the proposition that "[t]he majority rule obtained even when the union asked to represent only its own members or a minority," implying that minority bargaining would not have been countenanced by the NLB under any circumstances. He failed to note the critical factor in the case, that the Hosiery Workers' Union was seeking to represent its members *after* it had lost an election to another union, which under *Denver Tramway,* which had already been decided, would have violated the concept of majority exclusivity. *Real Silk* had no bearing on a minority union's right to bargain for its members *prior* to the selection of a majority representative.

Real Silk was also a case in which employer Board members recorded their opposition to the majority-rule principle. *See* Tomlins, *supra* note 100, quoting Board Member Draper: "[T]he law states quite clearly that workers may have the privilege [*sic*] of being represented for purposes of bargaining by representatives of their own choosing. To rule, then, that a minority group must be represented by representatives of the majority—the very representatives whom the minority particularly object to—is to make a ruling that defeats rather than carries out the clear meaning of he law." Draper to Miller, April 30, 1934, April 30, 1934, in RG25 Box 85.

140. Houde Engineering Corp., 1 NLRB (old) 35 (1934). *See* Ch. 2 *infra* at notes 62–91.

141. "The transition from mediation to majority rule early in 1934 was the decisive step in the evolution of federal labor relations policy." Tomlins, *supra* note 89 at 115,

142. *See* WASHINGTON POST, March 26, 1934, reprinted in Congressional Record at 1 LEGIS. HIST. at 1067.

143. *See* Bernstein NEW DEAL, *supra* note 40 at 60; Bernstein TURBULENT YEARS, *supra* note 94 at 181–85; Gross, *supra* note 55 at 61; Rubinow, *supra* note 5 at 73. That agreement originally had the support of the AFL; however, as Lloyd K. Garrison recorded, "The A. F. of L. soon repented, and later withdrew from this agreement. But the President, in extending the automobile code on Jan. 31, 1935, incorporated the principles of the agreement into the code. . . . " Garrison, *supra* note 65 at 143 & n. 9. Those principles governed labor relations in the automobile industry for the duration of the National Recovery Administration. *See generally* Sidney Fine, *Proportional Representation of Workers in the Auto Industry, 1934–1935,* 12 INDUS. & LAB. REL. REV. 182 (1959); *see also* Sidney Fine, THE AUTOMOBILE UNDER THE BLUE EAGLE (1963).

144. Gross, *supra* note 55 at 61–64; Bernstein NEW DEAL, *supra* note 40 at 60.

145. *Supra* note 123.

146. *Supra* note 125.

147. *Supra* note 126.

148. 1 NLB (Part 2) at 15.

149. *Id.* at 16.

150. *Id.* The Board indicated that this would require further investigation, including testimony under oath.

151. *Id.* at 19. "In the published decision, the wording is that given above. An examination of the original decision, signed by Senator Wagner, indicates that the phrase was intended to read ' . . . involves a *duality* of obligation . . . '. Through a typographical error the word 'duality' appeared as 'quality'." Rubinow, *supra* note 5 at 81, n. ****.

152. *Id.* Emphasis added

153. 1 NLB (Part 2) at 31.

154. *Id.* Emphasis added

155. *Id.* at 32.

156. *Id.* at 32–33.

157. The Executive Order of Feb. 1, 1934, *supra* note 125, empowered the NLB to hold elections when requested by "a substantial number of employees." *See also* Rubinow, *supra* note 5 at 83.

158. Gross *supra* note 55 at 46–53 & 63.

159. *See, e.g., Harriman Hosiery Co. Loses the Blue Eagle,* AMERICAN FEDERATION OF LABOR WEEKLY NEWS SERVICE, April 28, 1934, at 1, reporting a telegram from General Hugh S. Johnson to Harriman Hosiery advising that the NLB had "recommended that your Blue Eagle be withdrawn" for violations of the employees' rights under §7(a) of the NIRA, whereupon, the company was advised: "I hereby direct you to surrender all your Blue Eagles to the postmaster at Harriman and to refrain thereafter from using the Blue Eagle at your plant or in advertising or in any other manner."

Chapter 2

1. *See* Ch. 1 *supra* at notes 90–137.

2. James A. Gross, THE MAKING OF THE NATIONAL LABOR RELATIONS BOARD 63 (1974) (hereinafter Gross); Irving Bernstein, THE NEW DEAL COLLECTIVE BARGAINING POLICY 62 (1950) (hereinafter Bernstein NEW DEAL).

3. Lloyd K. Garrison, *The National Labor Boards,* 184 ANNALS AM. ACAD. POL. & SOC. SCI. 138, 139, 145 (1936) (hereinafter Garrison).

4. *See* Ch. 1 *supra* at notes 111–15 & 142–44.

5. Kenneth M. Casebeer, *Holder of the Pen: An Interview with Leon Keyserling on Drafting the Wagner Act,* 42 U. MIAMI L. REV. 285, 302, 323, 349 (1987) (hereinafter Casebeer *Holder of the Pen*); Kenneth Casebeer, *Drafting Wagner's Act: Leon Keyserling and the Precommittee Drafts of the Labor Disputes Act and the National Labor Relations Act,* 11 INDUS. REL. L. J. 73, 73 (1989) (hereinafter Casebeer *Keyserling Drafts*).

6. Casebeer *Holder of the Pen, id.* at 302.

7. Bernstein NEW DEAL, *supra* note 2 at 62.

8. *Id.* at 63.

9. *Id., citing* "Proposals for National Labor Board, Jan. 31, 1934, Keyserling papers; Disputes Act, n.d., Wkyzanski papers."

10. *Id.* at 63, 88.

11. As recounted by Keyserling in Casebeer *Holder of the Pen, supra* note 5 at 302–303.

12. *Id.* at 361.

13. *Id.* at 295, 303, 343; Casebeer *Keyserling Drafts, supra* note 5 at 76; Bernstein NEW DEAL, *supra* note 2 at 112; Irving Bernstein, TURBULENT YEARS, A HISTORY OF THE AMERICAN WORKER 1933–1941 340 (1971); Gross, *supra* note 2 at 139.

14. Casebeer *Holder of the Pen, supra* note 5 at 341–42. *See also* Leon H. Keyserling, *The Wagner Act: Its Origin and Current Significance,* 29 GEO. WASH. L. REV. 199, 215 (1960).

15. Specifically from William M. Leiserson (its Executive Secretary), Milton Handler (its General Counsel), and from William G. Rice, Jr. and Benedict Wolf. Bernstein NEW DEAL, *supra* note 2 at 58, 62.

16. As S. 2926. 1 LEGISLATIVE HISTORY OF THE NLRA, 1935 (1949) (hereinafter 1 LEGIS. HIST.), at 1. This was the same day the NLB issued its decision in *Denver Tramway, see* Ch. 1 *supra* at notes 124 & 141.

17. Casebeer *Keyserling Drafts, supra* note 5 at 102–120. Eight drafts are definitely the work of Kerserling, but one, labeled Draft 2(b), which covers administration and procedure, may have been written by Wyzanski. *Id.* at 75–77, 80. Notwithstanding the ambiguity regarding Draft 2(b), for present purposes I am treating the Wagner drafts as a package of nine drafts.

18. 1 LEGIS. HIST. at 1.

19. *Id.* at 1070.

20. References to those drafts in this chapter will identify relevant provisions by sections and subsections and not by reference to pages in either the Casebeer *Keyserling Drafts* or in the official LEGISLATIVE HISTORY volumes.

21. *See* Ch. 1 *supra* at notes 121–22 & 142–43.

22. *See* Ch. 1 *supra* at notes 21 & 71–88.

23. The incomplete drafts are Draft 1, which is only fragmentary, containing only brief, general language, and Draft 2(b), which contains mostly procedural and administrative provisions.

24. Draft 2(a) in §III, First; Drafts 3 & 4 in §10; Drafts 5,6, & 7 in §10; Drafts 8 & 10 in §4. Emphasis added.

25. They thus relied on language guaranteeing the right to bargain collectively as it had been construed by the NLB in several cases. *Eg.,* S. Dresner & Son, 1 NLB 26 (1933); National Lock Co., 1 NLB (Part 2) 15 (1934); Eagle Rubber Co., 1 NLB (Part 2) 31 (1934). *See* Ch. 1 *supra* at notes 105–106, 123, 126, 145, 147–52, & 153–54. *See also* Raymond S. Rubinow, SECTION 7(A): ITS HISTORY, INTERPRETATION AND ADMINISTRATION (Office of National Recovery Administration, Div. of Review, Labor Studies Section, 81–83 (1936) (hereinafter Rubinow); William H. Spencer, COLLECTIVE BARGAINING UNDER SECTION 7(A) OF THE NATIONAL INDUSTRIAL RECOVERY ACT 19–21 (1935).

26. Draft 2(a), §III, Fourth (b). Emphasis added.

27. Draft 3, §12(a).

28. *E.g.,* Berkley Woolen Mills, 1 NLB 5 (1933); A. Roth and Co., 1 NLB 75 (1934). *See* Ch. 1 *supra* at note 93.

29. Emphasis added.

30. That was the U.S. Supreme Court's later reading of "dealing with" contained in §2(5) of the NLRA, 29 U.S.C. §2(5). NLRB v. Cabot Carbon Co., 360 U.S. 203 (1959).

31. *See* note 25 *supra* and accompanying text.

32. Emphasis added. *See* §2, First, of the Railway Labor Act, 45 U.S.C. §152, First.

33. The deleted Section read as follows: "Whenever representatives are agreed upon and selected either (1) by the majority of the employees eligible to participate in the selection or (2) by the majority of employees participating in the selection when such majority constitute not less than 40 per cent of those eligible to participate, such representatives shall, for the purposes of collective bargaining, be the sole representatives of employees eligible to participate in the selection and of employees who subsequently fall within the classification upon which eligibility was based at the time of the selection: *Provided,* that no organization which imposes inequitable restrictions upon membership shall be entitled to represent employees who are not members thereof."

34. Draft 8 was sent to the committee on Feb. 27, 1934. Casebeer *Keyserling Drafts, supra* note 5 at 116.

35. Former §11(b) was renumbered §5(b). *See* text of the provision at note 32 *supra*.

36. For such coverage, however, *see* Gross, *supra* note 2 at 64–88; Bernstein NEW DEAL, *supra* note 2 at 57–72.

37. Bernstein, *id.,* at 67.

38. *Id.* "After the bill was introduced in 1934, it had tremendous opposition from industry and universal opposition from the press, including Walter Lippman [who] wrote violent editorials against [it]." Keyserling in Casebeer *Holder of the Pen, supra* note 5 at 303–304.

39. Bernstein NEW DEAL, *supra* note 2 at 68.

40. *Id.* at 71, and *see* Ch. 1 *supra* at notes 142–43.

41. Bernstein, *id.* at 69–71.

42. *Id.* at 71.

43. *Id.* at 72, *citing* Alfred L. Bernheim & Dorothy Van Doren, eds. (Published for Twentieth Century Fund, Inc.) LABOR AND THE GOVERNMENT — AN INVESTIGATION OF THE ROLE OF THE GOVERNMENT IN LABOR RELATIONS 126–27 (1935) (hereinafter TWENTIETH CENTURY FUND); *Industrial Disputes,* 39 MONTHLY LAB. REV. 1140 (1934).

44. 1 LEGIS. HIST. at 1070, where the full text is reported. In 1986, Keyserling referred to the product as "this greatly mutilated bill." Casebeer *Holder of the Pen, supra* note 5 at 304.

45. For a summary of the bill, *see* Bernstein NEW DEAL, *supra* note 2 at 73–74.

46. *See* Appendix to Ch. 2 at notes 38–43,

47. *Id.*

48. Bernstein NEW DEAL, *supra* note 2 at 74, *citing* N.Y. HERALD TRIBUNE, May 24, 1934, & N.Y. TIMES, May 26, 1934.

49. *Id.* at 74.

50. *Id.* at 74–75.

51. *Id.* at 75.

52. *Id.*

53. *Id., citing* N.Y. HERALD TRIBUNE, June 6, 1934.

54. *Id.* at 76–77. Wyzanski proposed a National Labor Board centered in the Labor Department authorized to interpret Section 7(a), hold elections, and provide mediation, conciliation, and arbitration services. *Id.* at 77 (citing *Wyzanski's Proposal,* June 11, 1934, Wyzanski papers.) Richberg's draft provided for the right to organize without interference, although neither employees nor employers were required to bargain; it authorized the President to create boards to investigate labor controversies, determine their merits, act as arbitrators, and provide a means to settle representation disputes, including holding elections; penalties were provided for violations. *Id.* (citing *Richberg's Proposal,* June 11, 1934, Wyzanski papers).

55. *Id.* at 77–78.

56. The House adopted the resolution without a roll call. The Senate moved more slowly. Several progressive Republican senators, Robert M. La Follette, George W. Norris, Gerald P. Nye, and Bronson Cutting, had sought approval for S. 2926 with improvements provided by Senator Wagner. Wagner, however, declined to join them; whereupon La Follette, who had introduced the progressives' motion, withdrew their proposal. La Follette, however, succeeded in adding a provision to Resolution 44 that expressly protected the right to strike. With that amendment, the resolution passed the Senate unanimously and the House immediately accepted the amendment. *Id.* at 79–80.

57. Resolution No. 44, 73rd Cong., H.J. Res. 375, 48 Stat. 1183 (1934). The resolution can also be found at 1 NLRB (old) v and at 1 LEGIS. HIST. 1255B.

58. Bernstein NEW DEAL, *supra* note 2 at 81.

59. *Id.*

60. Exec. Order No. 6073, June 29, 1934.

60. 1 NLRB (old) 35 (1934).

61. When Chairman Garrison resigned after several months to return to his university, he was replaced by Philadelphia attorney Francis Biddle.

62. 1 NLRB (old) 35 (1934).

63. Gross, *supra* 2 at 89.

64. 1 NLRB (old) at 38.

65. *Id.* at 39.

66. *See* Ch. 1 *supra* at notes 142–44.

67. 1 NLRB (old) at 40.

68. *Id.* This was consistent with the prior ruling of the NLB in Denver Tramway, 1 NLB 64 (1934). *See* Ch. 1 *supra* at notes 124 & 127–38.

69. The case was also important for its reaffirmation of the basic requirements of an employer's duty to bargain. The latter issue, however, is only indirectly germane to the theme of this book. The extent of that relevance, with reference to the specific holding in *Houde,* is discussed in Ch. 3 *infra* at notes 82–87.

70. 1 NLRB (old) at 44. Italic and boldface emphasis added.

71. *See* Ch. 3 *infra* at notes 71–72.

72. Clyde Summers, *The Kenneth M. Piper Lecture: Unions without Majority—A Black Hole?,* 66 CHI-KENT. L. REV. 531, 539 (1990).

73. AFL President William Green characterized the ruling as the "only safe guide which can be followed in the development of human relations in industry." Gross, *supra* note 2 at 91–92, quoting telegram from Green to L. K. Garrison, Sept. 3, 1934.

74. *Id.* at 92–93.

75. Louis Stark, *Labor Breaks with the New Deal,* N.Y. Times, Feb. 3, 1935, §4 at 6E, quoted in Gross, *supra* note 2 at 93.

76. Minier Sargent, *Majority Rule in Collective Bargaining under Section 7(a),* 29 Ill. L. Rev. 275, (1934). Emphasis added.

77. *Id.* at 278.

78. *Id.* at 280.

79. *Id.* at 278.

80. *Id.* at 279.

81. *Id.* at 286, n. 19; NRA Release No. 3125, Feb. 4, 1934. *See* Ch. 1 *supra* at notes 121–22 for the pertinent text of the Johnson-Richberg statement.

82. *Id.* at 286–87. *See* Ch. 1 *supra* at notes 142–44.

83. *See* Ch. 3 *infra* at note 29.

84. Raymond S. Smethurst, *Effect of Administrative Interpretation of the Powers of the National Labor Relations Board,* 3 GEO. WASH. L. REV. 141 (1935) (hereinafter Smethurst).

85. Cornelius W. Wickersham, *The NIRA from the Employers' Viewpoint,* 48 HARV. L. REV. 954, 973 (1935) (hereinafter Wickersham).

86. *E.g., see* Ch. 1 *supra* at note 116.

87. Smethurst, *supra* note 84 at 145.

88. *Id.* at 147.

89. Wickersham, *supra* note 85 at 971, *citing* U.S. NEWS, Nov. 26, 1934, at 12, 13.

90. *Id.* at 973.

91. *Id.*

92. *See* Ch. 1 *supra* at notes 124 & 127–37.

93. *See* Ch. 1 *supra* at notes 116–21.

94. *See* Ch. 1 *supra* at notes 135–36.

95. Gross, *supra* note 2 at 103, *citing* memorandum to NLRB(old) of Oct. 17, 1934.

96. Bernstein NEW DEAL, *supra* note 2 at 72. *See also Industrial Disputes,* 40 MONTHLY LAB. REV. 101–103, (1935).

97. Harry A. Millis & Royal E. Montgomery, ORGANIZED LABOR 843 (1945) (hereinafter Millis & Montgomery).

98. BUREAU OF LABOR STATISTICS, U.S. DEP'T OF LABOR, BULLETIN NO. 634, CHARACTERISTICS OF COMPANY UNIONS 1935 28 (1937) (hereinafter BLS No. 634). "Of all the company unions in existence in 1935, nearly two-thirds were established during the N.R.A." *Id.*

99. Millis & Montgomery, *supra* note 97 at 841, Table 17, *citing* TWENTIETH CENTURY FUND, *supra* note 43 at 79–80 (1935); Leo Wolman, EBB AND FLOW IN TRADE UNIONISM (National Bureau of Economic Research pub. No. 30) 34 (1936); National Industrial Conference Board, Inc., INDIVIDUAL AND COLLECTIVE BARGAINING UNDER THE N.I.R.A.—A STATISTICAL STUDY OF PRESENT PRACTICE 16 (1933).

100. Millis & Montgomery, *id.*

101. *Id.* at 840–41.

102. In the opening moments of Wagner's speech to the Senate introducing his 1934 bill, he said: "The greatest obstacles to collective bargaining are employer-dominated unions, which have multiplied with amazing rapidity since the enactment of the recovery law. Such a union makes a sham of equal bargaining power. . . . " 1 LEGIS. HIST. at 15.

103. Emily Clark Brown, *Selection of Employees' Representatives,* 40 MONTHLY LAB. REV. 1 (1935) (hereinafter Brown). This study examined the results of elections conducted by the NLB from July 9, 1934, to August 5, 1953, the period of its existence. *See* Ch. 3 *infra* at notes 77–80.

104. See Ch. 3 *infra* at note 28.

105. TWENTIETH CENTURY FUND, *supra* note 43.

106. A preliminary report was published in October 1935: *Extent and Characteristics of Company Unions: Preliminary Report,* 40 MONTHLY LAB. REV. 865 (1935). The final report was published in 1937: BLS No. 634, *supra* note 98.

107. BLS No. 634, *supra* note 98 at 81.

108. *Id.* at 85. Regarding the other 20 percent: "Where an employee or a group of employees took the first step in organizing a company union, the next step was almost invariably to ask the management's approval. Not only was this approval forthcoming in almost all instances but in most of the cases under consideration the company took an active part in the organizing work." *Id.* at 90.

109. *Id.* at 67.

110. 1 LEGIS. HIST. at 24.

111. Brown *supra* note 103 at 4–6, Tables 1–4. Based on elections conducted in a total of 546 units, she found that: "Much the largest group, 429 unit elections, were those in which there was a choice between trade-union representation and some form of nonunion employee representation, however informal. Among these 449 cases, 323 or 71.9 percent were won by trade unions, while 61,231 or 67 percent of the 91,326 votes were union." *Id.* at 5–6. *See also* note 120 in Ch. 1 *supra.*

112. Ch. 1 *supra* at notes 83–100.

113. BLS No. 634, *supra* note 98 at 203.

114. *Id.* at 191. The BLS mail questionnaire did not inquire as to the extent of trade-union coverage for employees represented by a trade union. It asked only whether the employer dealt with a trade union, and it did not inquire as to the nature of such dealing other than to ask if there was a union agreement. These limitations are understandable, however, for the study was about company unions, not trade unions. *Id.* at 284.

115. *See* Ch. 1 *supra* at notes 97–98.

116. *See* Ch. 4 *infra* at notes 5–30.

Chapter 3

1. Irving Bernstein, THE NEW DEAL COLLECTIVE BARGAINING POLICY 88 (1950) (hereinafter Bernstein NEW DEAL)

2. *Id.* at 88, N. Y. TIMES, Nov. 7, 1934: "The election for practical purposes eliminated the right-wing of the Republican Party."

3. *Id.*; Kenneth Casebeer, *Drafting Wagner's Act: Leon Keyserling and the Precommittee Drafts of the Labor Disputes Act and the National Labor Relations Act,* 11 INDUS. REL. L. J. 73, 120 (1989) (hereinafter Casebeer *Keyserling Drafts*); Kenneth M. Casebeer, *Holder of the Pen: An Interview with Leon Keyserling on Drafting the Wagner Act,* 42 U. MIAMI L. REV. 285, 349 (1987) (hereinafter Casebeer *Holder of the Pen*).

4. Casebeer *Keyserling Drafts, id.,* at 120; James A. Gross, THE MAKING OF THE NATIONAL LABOR RELATIONS BOARD 171 (1974) (hereinafter Gross).

5. 1 LEGISLATIVE HISTORY OF THE NLRA, 1935 (1949) (hereinafter 1 LEGIS. HIST.) at 1295.

6. The first and third drafts are to be found in Professor Casebeer's 1989 publication, Casebeer *Keyserling Drafts, supra* note 3 at 120–131; the second draft is in 1 LEGIS. HIST. at 1295, and the fourth and fifth drafts are in 2 LEGISLATIVE HISTORY OF THE NLRA, 1935 (1949) (hereinafter 2 LEGIS. HIST.), at 2285 and 3270, respectively. For the text of all relevant portions of those drafts, *see* Appendix to Ch. 3 *infra.*

7. References to those drafts in this chapter will, in most instances, identify relevant provisions by sections and subsections and not by reference to pages in either the Casebeer *Keyserling Drafts* or in the official LEGISLATIVE HISTORY volumes.

8. *E.g., see generally* Bernstein NEW DEAL, *supra* note 1; Irving Bernstein, TURBULENT YEARS, A HISTORY OF THE AMERICAN WORKER 1933–1941(1971) (hereinafter Bernstein TURBULENT YEARS); Gross, *supra* note 4; Harry A. Millis & Royal E. Montgomery, ORGANIZED LABOR (1945).

9. *See* Appendix to Ch. 3 *infra* at notes 1–9. The date of May 5, 1934, is interesting because whatever was prepared for Wagner at that time was never filed as an amendment to S. 2926; instead the Walsh bill was substituted on May 26, 1934. *See* discussion in Ch. 2 *supra* at notes 44–53.

10. *See* Appendix to Ch. 2 *infra* at note 41.

11. *See* Final (Wagner/Keyserling) Draft, *id.* at note 35.

12. *See* note 87 *infra* and accompanying text.

13. Casebeer *Keyserling Drafts, supra* note 3 at 124.

14. *Id.* at 85.

15. *See* Casebeer *Holder of the Pen* 303, *supra* note 3 at 303.

16. *See* notes 38–48 *infra* and accompanying text.

17. *See* Appendix to Ch. 3 *infra* at notes 30–31.

18. See §12(a) in *Drafts 3 & 4*; *§12(a)* in *Draft 5*; *§11(b)* in *Drafts 6 & 7*; *§ 5(b)* in *Draft 8*; Appendix to Ch. 2 *infra.*

19. *See* text at notes 71 & 77 *infra,* for Wagner's positions, and Casebeer *Holder of the Pen, supra* note 3 at 229–330, for Keyserling's positions.

20. Either as originally introduced or as amended. *See* Ch. 2 *supra* at notes 32 & 46–47.

21. Emphasis added.

22. *See* notes 28–29 in Ch. 2 *supra* and accompanying text.

23. *Id.* Emphasis added.

24. Emphasis added.

25. Emphasis added. *See infra* at note 118.

26. Bernstein NEW DEAL, *supra* note 1 at 88. *See* Appendix to Ch. 3 *infra* at notes 10–17.

27. *Id.* Emphasis added.

28. *See* Ch. 1 *supra* at notes 6–11.

29. Emphasis added.

30. *Memorandum Comparing S. 1958, 74ᵗʰ Cong., 1ˢᵗ Sess., A Bill Introduced by Senator Wagner on Feb. 21, 1935, To Create a National Labor Relations Board, and for Other Purposes, with the Bill Reported by Senator Walsh on May 26, 1934, as a Substitute for S. 2926, 73ʳᵈ Cong., also introduced by Senator Wagner*, dated March 11, 1935, 1 LEGIS. HIST. 1319 (hereinafter *Comparison Memorandum*), at 1322.

31. Former Executive Secretary of the National Labor Board, then Chairman of the National Mediation Board under the Railway Labor Act. *See* Ch. 2 *supra* at note 15.

32. 1 LEGIS. HIST. at 1350. Emphasis added.

33. §8(2) prohibited company unions, a main area of contention. §8(3) prohibited employment discrimination to discourage or encourage union membership, but included a caveat defining an allowable exception for closed-shop agreements, which was another area about which there was considerable contention and debate. §8(4) provided protection for employees who filed charges or gave testimony under the Act.

34. *See infra* at notes 49–52.

35. 1 NLRB (old) 35 (1934). *See infra* at notes 71 & 81–87.

36. *See* Appendix to Ch. 3 *infra* at notes 18–24. The original of this draft is in the collection of the Leon Keyserling papers in the Lauinger Library of Georgetown University, which graciously provided me with a photocopy for use in the preparation of this book.

37. *See* Casebeer *Keyserling Drafts, supra* note 3 at 86, 130.

38. *Comparison Memorandum, supra* note 30 at 1319.

39. *See* Report of Senate Committee on Education and Labor, Rep. No. 573, May 2, 1935, 2 LEGIS. HIST. at 2300, and Bill S. 1958 of same date, *id.* at 2285.

40. Casebeer mistakenly identifies this document as "*NLRA Draft 2*," which it obviously was not, for it is superimposed on the printed version of the second draft introduced in the Senate on February 21. *See* Appendix to Ch. 3 *infra* at note 19. This nonsubstantive error, however, does not detract from the accuracy of the publication of the draft as contained in Casebeer *Keyserling Drafts, supra* note 3. Indeed, the academic, legal, and industrial relations communities are deeply indebted to Professor Casebeer for having made this and the other Keyserling drafts available to the public.

41. Sometimes designated with "Frey."

42. *Keyserling Drafts, supra* note 3 at 130–31.

43. *E.g.*, Secretary Perkins's proposal to delete §11, providing for district court injunctions, and NLRB Compliance Chief Davis's proposal to delete §12, providing for arbitration, were adopted by the committee and these sections accordingly were deleted from the final bill.

44. *See* discussion in Ch. 5 *infra* at notes 89–99.

45. Emphasis added.

46. *Comparison Memorandum, supra* note 30 at 1331.

47. *See* discussion *infra* at notes 91–93.

48. The rejection of that second version was also consistent with Biddle's original §8(5) proposal contained in the *First NLRA Draft*, thus reinforcing the conclusion that Biddle himself never intended that the bargaining required by §8(5) would be confined only to majority representatives. *See supra* at note 13.

49. *See* Appendix to Ch. 3 *infra* at notes 6, 14, 21, 29.

50. *E.g.*, the final Senate committee report provided as its first justification for the proviso the following:

> The assertion that the bill favors the closed shop is particularly misleading in view of the fact that the proviso . . . actually narrows the now extant law regarding closed-shop agreements. While today an employer may negotiate such an agreement even with a minority union, the bill provides that an employer shall be allowed to make a closed-shop contract only with a labor organization that represents the majority of employees in the appropriate collective-bargaining unit covered by such agreement when made.

2 LEGIS. HIST. at 2311.

51. Emphasis added.

52. *See* Appendix to Ch. 3 *infra* at notes 19 & 22–24 and either the original or photocopy of the draft (*see* note 36 *supra*).

53. As Professor Gross reported, "the Wagner forces remained in 'effective control of the legislation at all times.'" Gross *supra* note 4 at 139. "[T]he Senator insisted upon keeping control over the drafting process of virtually all legislation that he introduced." Casebeer *Keyserling Drafts, supra* note 3 at 76. "In the Senate Labor Committee Chairman Walsh had reversed his 1934 position and had delegated full responsibility to prepare the report to Wagner, who was again assisted by Keyserling." Bernstein TURBULENT YEARS *supra* note 8 at 340. *See also* Casebeer *Holder of the Pen, supra* note 3 at 310; Bernstein NEW DEAL, *supra* note 1 at 88.

54. Bernstein NEW DEAL, *id.*; Gross *supra* note 4 at 131.

55. The expiration date was June 16, 1935. *See* 1 LEGIS. HIST. at 1557.

56. Bernstein TURBULENT YEARS, *supra* note 8 at 322; Gross, *supra* note 4 at 63, 122–30, 135. Francis Biddle, Chairman of the old NLRB under Public Resolution No. 44, reported to the President that compliance had been obtained in only 46 of the 158 cases in which compliance had been directed; he testified in a Senate committee hearing that the NLRB's failure to obtain enforcement amounted "to a complete nullification of the law." 1 LEGIS. HIST. at 1472. Senator Wagner articulated the problem when he argued on behalf of S.1958 that "the greatest difficulty with Section 7(a) has been that the present National Labor Relations Board has not been vested with enforcement powers." 2 LEGIS. HIST. at 2330.

57. Lloyd K. Garrison, *The National Labor Boards,* 184 ANNALS AM. ACAD. POL. & SOC. SCI. 138, 145 (1936). *See also* Ch. 1 *supra* at notes 158–59.

58. Bernstein TURBULENT YEARS, *supra* note 8 at 326.

59. This concept of the intent behind the Wagner bill has been widely recognized. *E.g., see* Melvyn Dubofsky, THE STATE AND LABOR IN MODERN AMERICA 127 (1994) (the bill was "designed to clarify Section 7(a) and create a permanent NLRB with enforcement powers. Wagner stressed that his proposal was not new; instead it perfected the bill introduced the previous year"). Indeed, on the day of introduction, Wagner told the Senate, "The national labor relations bill which I now propose is novel neither in philosophy nor in content. It creates no new substantive rights." 1 LEGIS. HIST. at 1312.

60. The "Borrowed statute" rule. William N. Eskridge, Jr., DYNAMIC STATUTORY INTERPRETATION, *Appendix 3, The Rehnquist Court's Cannons of Statutory Construction, 323, 324,* (1994), *citing* Molzof v. United States, 112 S. Ct. 711, 716 (1992); Metropolitan Life Ins. Co. v. Taylor, 481 U.S. 58 (1987).

61. Lloyd K. Garrison at March 15, 1935, hearing before Senate Committee on Education and Labor, 1 LEGIS. HIST. at 1507–08.

62. *Id.* at 1553.

63. *Id.* at 1553–62. Boldface and italic emphasis added, with some paragraphs consolidated.

64. As distinguished from issues of enforcement procedures and constitutionality, which were also subjects of much legislative discussion.

65. *See* Ch. 1 *supra* at notes 82–101 (Senator Wagner's personal knowledge of the Conference Board study is shown at note 87 therein). *See also* Ch. 2 *supra* at notes 113–17. The practice was also noted in the Senate committee by the testimony of Walter Gordon Merritt, representing the League for Industrial Rights, an employers' association. 2 LEGIS. HIST. 1706.

66. *See* Bernstein NEW DEAL, *supra* note 1 at 109 ("Business attacked the majority rule for denying the rights of minorities. . . . "). *See also* Ch. 1 *supra* at note 135 and Ch. 2 *supra* at 84–91.

67. 1 LEGIS. HIST. 1419. Professor Clyde Summers accurately points out that "[t]he history of the majority rule principle shows that its purpose was not to limit the ability of a nonmajority union to represent its own members, but to protect a majority union's ability to bargain collectively." Clyde Summers, *The Kenneth M. Piper Lecture: Unions without Majority—A Black Hole?,* 66 CHI-KENT. L. REV. 531, 539 (1990) (hereinafter Summers.)

68. Bernstein NEW DEAL, *supra* note 1 at 109. *See also* the following typical illustrations of the position of the business community: Statement of C. S. Craigmile representing Electric Industry of Illinois to the Senate committee, 2 LEGIS. HIST. 1911 ("[The majority rule] principle takes away the right of a minority group, even though it be 49.9 percent of the total, to select representatives of their own choosing for collective bargaining. . . . "); the proposed amendment to §9(a) by Walter Gordon Merritt (*see* note 65 *supra*) to change the majority ba-

sis for exclusive bargaining to a "pro rata" basis, *id.* at 1335; and his statement to the Senate committee ("[W]hat I object to is that substantial minorities here are barred from the very negotiations of bargaining." *Id.* at 1707). The position of the vocal employer community regarding minority-union bargaining thus remained consistent throughout the New Deal period. *See* Ch. 1 *supra* at notes 117–18 & 135–37 and Ch. 2 *supra* at notes 84–94.

69. 2 LEGIS HIST. at 2336. Emphasis added.

70. 2 LEGIS. HIST. at 2313. Emphasis added. The comparable passage in the House report read: "As a necessary corollary it is an act of interference (under sec. 8(1)) for an employer, *after* representatives have been so designated by the majority, to negotiate with individuals or minority groups in their own behalf on the basic subjects of collective bargaining." *Id.* at 2974. Emphasis added.

71. *Supra* note 35.

72. 2 LEGIS. HIST. at 2252. Emphasis added. For a full discussion of *Houde, see* Ch. 2 *supra* at notes 62–91.

73. As Professor Summers observes: "In the reports and legislative debates, preceding the Wagner Act, the arguments for majority rule were made in the context of competing unions and the necessity that the majority union have exclusive authority to negotiate for all employees. The purpose of an election was to determine which, if any, union was to be given exclusive representation rights, thereby empowering it to represent nonconsenting employees. There is no suggestion that a majority, by preferring individual bargaining, could deprive a minority of their right to bargain collectively for themselves thorough representatives of their own choosing." Summers, *supra* note 67 at 539.

74. 2 LEGIS. HIST. at 2312. Emphasis added.

75. *Id.* at 2976.

76. 1 LEGIS HIST. at 1496. Emphasis added.

77. *See* note 73 *supra.*

78. *See* Emily Clark Brown, *Selection of Employees' Representatives,* 40 MONTHLY LAB. REV. 1, 5 (1935). *See also* Ch. 2 *supra* at notes 103 & 111–12.

79. *Id., citing* National Labor Board, press release No. 6295, July 7, 1934.

80. *Id.* at 15. Emphasis added.

81. As Keyserling recalled in the Casebeer interview: "'Is a refusal to bargain collectively on the part of the employer a denial of the right of a worker to organize the [*sic*] bargain collectively?' And I certainly would have answered with an emphatic 'Yes,' because that would be the only answer I could give. . . . I think the Biddle amendment merely specifically incorporated the actual intent." Casebeer *Holder of the Pen supra* note 3 at 330.

82. 1 LEGIS. HIST. at 1419. Emphasis added. Several weeks later Wagner reaffirmed that position. *See* 2 LEGIS. HIST. at 2102.

83. *Supra* note 71.

84. 1 LEGIS. HIST. at 1419.

85. *See* Lewis L. Lorwin & Arthur Wubnig, LABOR RELATIONS BOARDS 32–33 (Brookings Institution, 1935), for discussion of the collective bargaining principles contained in 17 cited cases decided by the NLB and NLRB (old) during 1934.

86. *In the matter of Eagle Rubber Company and United Rubbers Workers' Federal Labor Union No. 18683* (decided May 16, 1934); *In the matter of National Aniline & Chemical Company and Allied Chemical Workers' Local #18705* (decided May 25, 1934); *In the matter of Connecticut Coke Company and United Coke & Gas Workers' Union, No. 18829* (decided June 30, 1934). Footnote 1 in the original.

87. 1 NLRB (old) at 35.

88. Gross, *supra* note 4 at 137.

89. *Supra* at notes 13–17 & 42–48.

90. 1 LEGIS. HIST. at 1455; 2 LEGIS. HIST. at 2649.

91. Gross *supra* note 4 at 139.

92. *See* Appendix to Ch. 3 at notes 25–30. *See also* Russell A. Smith, *The Evolution of the "Duty to Bargain" Concept in American Labor Law,* 39 MICH. L. REV. 1065, 1085 (1941): "[T]here was little discussion of the bargaining concept at the committee hearings. Even the suggestion of Chairman Biddle of the old board that an express duty to bargain be inserted in the bill failed to stimulate discussion, though the suggestion was adopted." *See supra* notes 43–45 and accompanying text regarding wording of the amendment.

93. 2 LEGIS. HIST. at 2348.

94. *Supra* at notes 45–48.

95. 1 LEGIS. HIST. at 1455.

96. 2 LEGIS. HIST. at 2649.

97. *Id.* at 2309. Emphasis added. This nonlimiting feature of the specific unfair labor practices was ingrained in the original concept of S. 1958. *See* William M. Leiserson's Mr. 11, 1935, comparison of that bill with the prior S. 2926 in which he indicated that the unfair labor practice subdivisions "are not exclusive, and, furthermore do not limit the general scope of subdivision (1)." 1 LEGIS. HIST. at 1352.

98. *Id.* at 2971. Emphasis added.

99. 2 LEGIS. HIST. at 2333. Emphasis added.

100. *Id.* at 2974. Emphasis added.

101. See notes 71–72 *supra* and Ch. 2 *supra* at note 70.

102. 1 LEG. HIST. 1455.

103. *Id.*

104. *See* Appendix to Ch. 3 at notes 31–35 for full text of the change.

105. *See* Ch. 2 *supra* at notes 10–14.

106. Casebeer, *Holder of the Pen, supra* note 3 at 343. *See also* Gross *supra* note 4 at 139; Bernstein NEW DEAL *supra* note 8 at 112; Bernstein TURBULENT YEARS *supra* note 8 at 340.

107. Presented on March 11, 1935. 1 LEGIS. HIST. at 1419.

108. *Id. Emphasis added.*

109. *See supra* at note 68; Ch. 1 *supra* at notes 129–34 & 154–58; Ch. 2 *supra* at 84–91.

110. *See* Ch. 1 *supra* at notes 82–100 and Ch. 2 *supra* at notes 113–17.

111. 1 LEGIS. HIST. at 1419.

112. Chairman of the Senate Committee on Education and Labor.

113. *Id.* at 1420. Emphasis added.

114. Under §9(b), bargaining units can be defined only by the Board. *See* Patrick Hardin & John E. Higgins, Jr., eds., THE DEVELOPING LABOR LAW: THE BOARD, THE COURTS, AND THE NATIONAL LABOR RELATIONS ACT, 589–90 (4th ed. 2001).

115. 2 LEGIS. HIST. at 2313. Emphasis added.

116. "It is well nigh universally recognized that it is practically impossible to apply two or more sets of agreements to one unit of workers at the same time, or to apply the terms of one agreement to only a portion of the workers in a single unit. For this reason, collective bargaining means majority rule." *Id.* at 2336.

117. *Id.* at 2313 & 2336 respectively.

118. *See* text at note 25 *supra*.

119. *Id.* at 2974. Emphasis added.

120. *Id.* Emphasis added.

121. *See* Ch. 2 *supra* at note 70 and the text following.

122. The nature of such bargaining, which will naturally be different in several respects from *exclusivity* bargaining, is discussed in Chs. 11 and 12. This House report also emphasized, as previously noted, that §8(5) and the other specific unfair labor practices "are not intended to limit in any way the interpretation of the general provisions" of §§7 and 8. 2 LEGIS. HIST. at 2971.

123. See Ch. 4 *infra*.

124. For comprehensive discussion and legal analysis of the final text of the statute relevant to this book's major thesis, *see* Ch. 5 *infra*.

Chapter 4

1. Employer critics began their legal assault immediately after the Act's passage. A total of 95 injunction suits were brought against the fledgling Labor Board. 2 NLRB ANN. REP. 31 (1937). The constitutional challenge was led by a group of 58 nationally prominent lawyers and public figures operating as the "Liberty League," which "pronounced the Act an affront to the Constitution." Irving Bernstein, TURBULENT YEARS, A HISTORY OF THE AMERICAN WORKER 1933–1941 349 (1971) (hereinafter Bernstein). *See* Charles Fahy, *The NLRB and the Courts,* in THE WAGNER ACT: AFTER TEN YEARS 43, 44 (Louis G. Silverberg ed., 1945) (hereinafter Sil-

verberg); James A. Gross, THE MAKING OF THE NATIONAL LABOR RELATIONS BOARD 183–88 (1974); Patrick Hardin & John E. Higgins, Jr., eds., THE DEVELOPING LABOR LAW (4ᵗʰ ed.) 30–31 (2001). (hereinafter DEVELOPING LABOR LAW).

2. 301 U.S. 1 (1937), decided on April 12, 1937.

3. Affiliated trade union membership had been 2,497,000 in 1932; by 1935 it had risen to 3,317,000. Leo Wolman, EBB AND FLOW IN TRADE UNIONISM (National Bureau of Economic Research pub. No. 30) 147 (1936). But by 1938 union membership reached "the all-time peak to that time of about 8,200,000." Royal E. Montgomery, *Evolution of American Labor,* 274 ANNALS AM. ACAD. POL. & SOC. SCI. 1, 7 (1951), *citing* National Resources Committee, THE STRUCTURE OF THE AMERICAN ECONOMY; Proceedings of AFL conventions; and various releases of the U.S. Bureau of Labor Statistics.

4. Most of the traditional unions remained within the framework of the AFL, whereas most of the newly organized and some of the refurbished industrial unions coalesced with the United Mineworkers under the leadership of John L. Lewis into the new federation, the CIO. The latter had emerged from the tumultuous internal organizational conflicts that surrounded its earlier incarnation as the AFL's Committee for Industrial Organization, which had also included such established industrial unions as the International Ladies Garment Workers Union and the Amalgamated Clothing Workers Union. *See* Bernstein, *supra* note 1 at 351–431 & 682–714.

5. 1-A LRRM (BNA) 781 (1938).

6. *Id.*

7. *Id.* at 783–87.

8. Robert R. R. Brooks, AS STEEL GOES, . . . : UNIONISM IN A BASIC INDUSTRY, 166–67 (1940) (hereinafter Brooks). *See also* Raymond L. Hogler, *Worker Participation, Employer Anti-Unionism, and Labor Law: The Case of the Steel Industry, 1918–1937* 26–36, 7 HOFSTRA LAB. L. J. 1 (1989).

9. A holding company with some 200 operating subsidiaries with approximately 200,000 employees. Bernstein, *supra* note 1 at 457–59.

10. Bernstein, *supra* note 1 at 458 & 466. *See: It Happened in Steel,* 15 FORTUNE 91 (May 1937). *See also* THE TWENTIETH CENTURY FUND, HOW COLLECTIVE BARGAINING WORKS: A SURVEY OF EXPERIENCE IN LEADING AMERICAN INDUSTRIES (Harry A. Millis, Research Director) 522–24 (1942) (hereinafter TWENTIETH CENTURY FUND).

11. *Id.* Emphasis added.

12. Bernstein, *supra* note 1 at 465.

13. *See generally,* DEVELOPING LABOR LAW, *supra* note 1 at 501, 730.

14. According to Philip Murray, SWOC's Chairman. Bernstein, *supra* note 1 at 465.

15. *Id.* at 466.

16. For discussion of the reasons motivating Taylor, *see* Bernstein, *supra* note 1, at 467–70; TWENTIETH CENTURY FUND, *supra* note 10 at 523–24; Harry A. Millis & Royal E. Montgomery, ORGANIZED LABOR 224–25, n. 4 (1945).

17. *Id.;* 1-A LRRM (BNA) 829 (1938). The typical U.S. Steel recognition clause, in pertinent part, read as follows:

> The Corporation recognizes the Steel Workers Organizing Committee, or its successors, as the collective bargaining agent for those employees of the Corporation who are members of the Amalgamated Association of Iron, Steel and Tin Workers of North America (hereinafter referred to as the Union). The Corporation recognizes and will not interfere with the right of its employees to become members of the Union, or its successors.

Union Recognition as Shown in Contracts. 1-A LRRM (BNA) 781, 783–84 (1938).

18. The recognitional process at "Little Steel," however, proved to be anything but easy. For a discussion of the bitter strikes at the Bethlehem, Republic, Inland, and Youngstown Sheet & Tube companies during the summer of 1937, *see* Bernstein, *supra* note 1 at 474–98.

19. *Collective Bargaining Contracts and Industrial Practices: Bargaining in the Steel Industry,* 3 LRRM (BNA) 553 (1939).

20. *Id.*

21. Brooks, *supra* note 8 at 166. The total number of SWOC contracts increased from 593 in June, 1939, to 638 in January 1940; however, U.S. Steel contracts still continued to be "for members only." *Id.* at 248.

22. TWENTIETH CENTURY FUND, *supra* note 10 at 24. Emphasis added.

23. Bernstein, *supra* note 1 at 516.

24. *Id.* at 541.

25. Sidney Fine, SIT-DOWN: THE GENERAL MOTORS STRIKE OF 1936–1937 266–312, 328 (1969) (hereinafter Fine). The UAW had sought exclusive recognition, but lacking majority support required for NLRB exclusivity it considered the members-only recognition an historic victory. *Id.* at 306. As Fine noted, "What the UAW, like other unions at the time, understood by the term 'recognition' had always been rather nebulous, but the union believed, and it had reason to, that it had been accorded a status of legitimacy in GM plants that it had never before enjoyed. It was confident that it would be able to consolidate its position. . . . " *Id.*

26. James B. Atleson, VALUES AND ASSUMPTIONS IN AMERICAN LABOR LAW 196, n. 43 (1983).

27. *Bargaining in the Automobile Industry,* 2 LRRM 952, 953 (1938). Typical of the UAW members-only recognition provisions was the following:

> It is agreed that the International Union, United Automobile Workers of America, will be recognized as the bargaining agent for its members and for those who voluntarily desire to avail themselves of its services, and not otherwise. The company will negotiate at all times necessary with the chosen accredited representatives of the employees, for determining any disputes which may arise between them and the company, as to wage rates, working conditions, discriminations, or dismissals, and will consider any grievances and complaints which may now exist or which may arise in the future. *Id.*

28. *See* text at notes 5–8 *supra.*

29. 305 U.S. 197 (1938).

30. *See* Ch. 5 *infra* at notes 13–16 for discussion of this case.

31. 5 NLRB ANN. REP. 18–19, 141, 151 (1941). *See also* Fine, *supra* note 25 at 329.

32. W. H. McPherson, *Automobiles,* in TWENTIETH CENTURY FUND, *supra* note 10 at 571 & 595.

33. McQuay-Norris Mfg. Co. v. NLRB, 116 F.2d 748 (7th Cir. 1940), *cert. denied,* 313 U.S. 565 (1941).

34. Until the 1947 Taft-Hartley amendments, §9(c) (29 U.S.C. §159(c)) allowed the Board, in addition to holding secret-ballot elections, to "utilize any other suitable method to ascertain such representatives."

35. Of 265 elections held, independent unions won 214 (company unions were still competing at that time and were so listed); voluntary recognition of independent unions was obtained in 194 cases following the filing of representation petitions; the Board granted such unions certification in six cases based on "clearly proven majorities." 2 NLRB ANN. REP. 25–26 (1937).

36. Of 1,152 elections, unions won 945; voluntary recognition was obtained in 603 cases; certifications were granted based by payroll checks in 241 cases. 3 NLRB ANN. REP. 39, 49 (1939).

37. Of 746 elections, unions won 574; voluntary recognition was obtained in 257 cases; certification by card check was granted in 241 cases; in 112 cases the Board was convinced of majority status and granted certification without an election. 4 NLRB ANN. REP. 43, 53 (1940).

38. Exact figures are not obtainable for this year because in some instances more than one election was held in a single case. 5 NLRB ANN. REP. 18, n. 6 (1941).

39. Some representation and statistical methods were changed in the 1940 Annual Report. Unions won 921 of 1,192 elections conducted; they also apparently obtained recognition by nonformal procedures in 793 cases. *Id.* at 17, 18, 29.

40. 6 NLRB ANN. REP. 37, Table 19 (1942). The number of informal settlements in which unions obtained recognition was not reported.

41. 7 NLRB ANN. REP. 90, Table 18 (1943).

42. 8 NLRB ANN. REP. 37, 38, 90, Table 18 (1944).

43. 9 NLRB ANN. REP. 88, Table 13 (1944).

44. 10 NLRB ANN. REP. 4 (1946); 11 NLRB ANN. REP. 3 (1947).

45. Paul R. Hutchins, *Effect on the Trade Union,* in Silverberg, *supra* note 1 at 72–73.

46. §9 of the Act.

47. §10 of the Act.

48. *See generally,* Charles Fahy, *The NLRB and the Courts,* in Silverberg, *supra* note 1 at 43 & 54–59.

49. *See* Ch. 3 *supra* at notes 65–76.

50. Illustrative of that short memory and the way in which the Act was now viewed, Paul R. Hutchins, the union official quoted at note 45 *supra,* complained in 1945 that "the Act and its administration have brought about a substantial change in emphasis within the organized labor movements. . . . Now, trade unions must conform their organization activities to the appropriate bargaining unit patterns laid down by the Board." Silverberg, *supra* note 1 at 73. Hutchins then opined that "employers are prevented, *in effect,* from recognizing and bargaining with any labor union unless such organization represents a majority of the workers in an 'appropriate bargaining unit.' As a consequence, today the employer who negotiates with the union without first requiring that the union prove its majority status does so at his peril." *Id.* at 74 (emphasis added.) Hutchins was undoubtedly referring to such cases as the early NLRB "false majority" decisions identified in Ch. 9 *infra* at notes 35–39, in which the Board had found that the employers had no obligation to bargain because the unions were demanding recognition as *exclusive* representatives when in fact they did not represent a majority of the employees, as they had claimed. Although Hutchins perceived this to be "in effect" a bar to minority unions engaging in collective bargaining, those cases only barred such unions from bargaining as *exclusive* representatives in units where they did not represent a majority, which is what the plain language of §9 requires for *exclusive* representation. (*See* Ch. 5 *infra,* before and following note 82.) In none of those cases, however, did the union seek to bargain for its members only, and there is no indication from NLRB cases of any employer having refused such bargaining. Notwithstanding, here was Hutchins, a union official, assuming in 1945 that a union would be wasting its time if it sought to bargain before it represented a majority of the employees in an appropriate unit. That would certainly have been true if the minority union was seeking to bargain for all the employees, which was the case in the false-majority decisions, as we see later in Ch. 9. By that time, unions were viewing NLRB elections and card checks as an essential part of the standard organizational process.

51. For an excellent description of that period, *see* James B. Atleson, Labor and the Wartime State: Labor Relations and Law during World War II (1988). *See also* Melvin Dubofsky, The State and Labor in Modern America 169–95 (1944).

52. Foster Rhea Dulles, Labor in America, 3rd ed. 349 (1966).

53. *Id.* at 53.

54. *Id.* at 208–209.

55. In particular, in the telephone, marine, shipbuilding, and airline industries. *Id.*

56. Labor-Management Relations Act, June 23, 1947, c. 120, §§1ff, 61 Stat. 136.

57. Foremost among those actions were secondary-boycott injunctions under §10(l), 29 U.S.C. §160, and damage suits under §301, 29 U.S.C. §185. *See generally* Developing Labor Law, *supra* note 1 at 39–45.

58. For a general description of the Taft-Hartley changes, *see* Developing Labor Law, *supra* note 1 at 34–47.

59. *Id.* at 546.

60. These occasional expressions were only untested assumptions, however, for there were never any NLRB holdings validating the conventional wisdom. *See* Ch. 9 *infra* at notes 68–102.

61. *E.g.,* 94 (BNA) LRRM 1396 (1977). *See* Ch. 9. *infra* at *note* 99.

Chapter 5

1. *See* Ch. 3 *supra* at notes 32 & 57–60, including reference to the *borrowed statute* rule.

2. 29 U.S.C. §158(a)(1) and §158(a)(5). It is again noted that references to §8(a) here and in the cited cases may sometimes appear as §8—*e.g.,* either §8(a)(5) or §8(5), depending on the applicable pre- or post-Taft-Hartley frame of reference. For further clarification, *see* note 6 in Ch. 1 *supra.*

3. Chevron U.S.A., Inc. v. Natural Resources Defense Council, Inc., 467 U.S. 837, 843 n. 9 (1984).

4. *See* William N. Eskridge, Jr., Dynamic Statutory Interpretation 323 , Appendix 3 (1994) (hereinafter Eskridge Dynamic) ("*Rehnquist Court's Canons of Statutory Construction.* . . . 'Plain meaning rule: follow the plain meaning of the statutory text, except when text

suggests an absurd result or a scrivener's error,'" *citing* Estate of Coward v. Nicklos Drilling Co., 112 S. Ct. 2589 (1992); United States v. Providence Journal Co., 485 U.S. 693 (1988); Holmes v. SIPC, 112 S. Ct. 1311 (1922); United States v. Wilson, 112 S. Ct. 1351 (1992); Green v. Bock Laundry Machine Co., 490 U.S. 504 (1989).); Tennessee Valley Authority (TVA) v. Hill, 437 U.S. 153, 56 n. 29 (1978) ("When confronted with a statute which is plain and unambiguous on its face, we ordinarily do not look to legislative history as a guide to its meaning, " *citing* Ex parte Collett, 337 U.S. 55, 61 (1949)); Eskridge DYNAMIC at 219–20; Antonin Scalia, *The Rule of Law as a Law of Rules*, 56 U. CHI. L. REV. 1175 (1989); William N. Eskridge, *The New Textualism*, 37 UCLA L. REV. 621 (1990).

5. Bernard W. Bell, *Legislative History without Legislative Intent: The Public Justification Approach to Statutory Interpretation*, 60 Ohio St. L.J. 1, 52 (1999) (hereinafter Bell), *citing* Mertens v. Hewitt Assocs., 508 U.S. 248, 257–58 (1993) (Scalia, J.); Church of Scientology v. IRS, 792 F.2d 153, 156–57 (D.C. Cir. 1986) (Scalia, J.), *aff'd*, 484 U.S. 9 (1987).

6. Eskridge DYNAMIC, *supra* note 4 at 34. For further discussion and references concerning the often competing roles of "legislative history," "new textualism," and "plain meaning," *see* Ch. 7 *infra* at notes 1–26.

7. 301 U.S. 1 (1937).

8. *Citing* American Steel Foundries v. Tri-City Central Trades Council, 257 U.S. 184, 209 (1921). Emphasis added.

9. 301 U.S. at 33. Emphasis added. One of the cases cited was Virginia Ry Co. v. Sys. Fed'n No. 40, 300 U.S. 515 (1937), in which the Court had approved the government's recognition under the RLA of premajority bargaining. *Id.* at 548–49 & n. 6.

10. *See* Chs. 6 & 8 *infra*, which deal, respectively, with applicable constitutional and international-law and human-rights perspectives.

11. *See* Lance Compa, Human Rights Watch, UNFAIR ADVANTAGE: WORKERS' FREEDOM OF ASSOCIATION IN THE UNITED STATES UNDER INTERNATIONAL HUMAN RIGHTS STANDARDS (2000); Charles J. Morris, *A Tale of Two Statutes: Discrimination for Union Activity under the NLRA and RLA*, 2 EMPLOYEE RTS. & EMPL. POL'Y J. 317, 321–33 (1998); Paul C. Weiler, *Promises to Keep: Securing Workers' Rights to Self-Organization under the NLRA*, 96 HARV. L. REV. 1769 (1983). *See also Introduction supra* at notes 44–46, Ch. 6 *infra* at note 46, and Ch. 12 *infra* at notes 2–40.

12. 305 U.S. 197 (1938). The commonality of members-only agreements in the public utility industry at the time was demonstrated in the Bureau of National Affairs report *cited* in Ch. 4 *supra* at note 7.

13. Consolidated Edison Co. of New York, Inc., 4 NLRB 71, 92, n. 3 (1937).

14. *Id.* at 108. *See also* Solvay Process Co., 5 NLRB 330 (1938), at note 31 *infra,* another case where the Board made the same determination, that members-only collective bargaining did not violate §8(2).

15. 305 U.S. at 236–37. Emphasis added.

16. *Id.*

17. International Ladies Garment Workers v. NLRB (Bernhard-Altmann Texas Corp.), 366 U.S. 731 (1961).

18. Ch. 9 *infra* at notes 42 & 57.

19. 366 at 741, *citing Consolidated Edison, supra* note 12; Virginia Ry. v. Sys. Fed'n, 300 U.S. 515 (1937); NLRB v. Drivers Local 639, 362 U.S. 274 (1960).

20. *Id.* at 742–43.

21. *Id.* at 743, n. 3.

22. 366 U.S. at 736. Emphasis added.

23. 369 U.S. 17 (1962).

24. 29 U.S.C. §185(a).

25. *Citing Consolidated Edison, supra* note 12, 369 U.S. at 29.

26. NLRB v. Washington Aluminum Co., 370 U.S. 9 (1962). *See also* Ch. 9 *infra* at notes 73–75.

27. *See* Ch. 9 *infra* at notes 11–22.

28. Such a strike is also protected by Section 13 of the Act, 29 U.S.C. §163: "Nothing in this Act, except as specifically provided for herein, shall be construed so as either to interfere with or impede or diminish in any way the right to strike, or to affect the limitations or qualifications on that right."

29. 465 U.S. 822 (1984).

30. *Id.* at 835. *Compare with* the Court's *Jones & Laughlin* language at note 9 *supra*.

31. 5 NLRB 330 (1938).

32. 90 NLRB 1614 (1950).

33. 99 NLRB 972 (1952).

34. NLRB v. Lundy Mfg. Corp., 316 F.2d 921 (2d Cir. 1963), *cert. denied,* 375 U.S. 895 (1963), *enforcing* 136 NLRB 1230 (1962). *See* Ch. 9 *infra* at notes 59–57.

35. *Supra* note 12.

36. Midwest Piping Co., 63 NLRB 1060 (1945) (holding that it is an unfair labor practice under §8(2) for an employer to recognize one of two competing unions after a representation petition had been filed with the Board).

37. 90 NLRB at 1618.

38. 99 NLRB at 975, n. 5.

39. *See* Ch. 9 *infra* at notes 59–67.

40. *See, e.g.,* TVA v. Hill, *supra* note 4 at 184 ("[T]he *totality of congressional action* makes it abundantly clear that the result we reach today is wholly in accord with both the words of the statute and the intent of Congress. The plain intent of Congress in enacting this statute was to halt and reverse the trend toward species extinction, whatever the cost. This *is reflected not only in the stated policies of the Act, but in literally every section of the statute.*" Emphasis added).

41. *See* Kenneth M. Casebeer, *Holder of the Pen: An Interview with Leon Keyserling on Drafting the Wagner Act,* 42 U. MIAMI L. REV. 285, 308, 311 (1987); Irving Bernstein, THE NEW DEAL COLLECTIVE BARGAINING POLICY 88 (1950) (hereinafter Bernstein NEW DEAL) ; Irving Bernstein, TURBULENT YEARS, A HISTORY OF THE AMERICAN WORKER 1933–1941 325 (1971) (hereinafter Bernstein TURBULANT YEARS). *See also* Ch. 4 *supra* at note 1.

42. 29 U.S.C. §151.

43. *Id.*

44. *See* Ch. 1 *supra* at notes 1–13 and following.

45. Emphasis added.

46. Emphasis added.

47. Agricultural labor, domestic service workers, and members of an employer's family, however, were excluded from the Act's coverage. 29 U.S.C. §152(3). *See* Bernstein TURBULENT YEARS, *supra* note 40, at 326.

48. *See* Bell, *supra* note 5 at 97, where he postulates that "The public justification approach [to statutory interpretation] provides a basis for asserting that legislatures have a duty not merely to enact statutes, but to explain them as well, and that accordingly legislators have a duty to respond to the institutional explanations of those statutes. The public justification approach allows courts to examine legislative history without conceiving of the interpretive task as a factual inquiry into subjective intent and provides something of a guide to distinguishing documents that should be given weight in the interpretive process from those documents that should not." *See also* Susan Rose-Ackerman, RETHINKING THE PROGRESSIVE AGENDA: THE REFORM OF THE AMERICAN REGULATORY STATE, 44, 51–52 (1992); Susan Rose-Ackerman, *Progressive Law and Economics and the New Administrative Law,* 98 YALE L. J. 341, 355 (1988).

49. Pub. L. No. 101, 80th Cong., 1st Sess., 1947.

50. *See* Landrum-Griffin Act, Pub. L. No. 257, 86th Cong., 1st Sess., 1959; Health Care coverage, Pub. L. No. 360, 93rd Cong., 2nd Sess., 1974.

51. The committee only added the word "some" before the two opening references to "employers" who deny employees the right to organize and refuse to accept the process of collective bargaining; and it inserted a separate provision relating to union unfair labor practices; none of these changes had any effect on the original declaration concerning the centrality of collective bargaining.

52. 2 LEGISLATIVE HISTORY OF THE LABOR MANAGEMENT RELATIONS ACT, 1947 (1948), at 1007. Emphasis added.

53. *Id.* at 1653. Emphasis added.

54. 29 U.S.C. §158(a)(2) (generally outlawing company unions).

55. 29 U.S.C. §158(a)(3) (outlawing employment discrimination that encourages or discourages union membership, with a caveat regarding union-shop agreements).

56. 29 U.S.C. §158(a)(4) (outlawing discrimination for filing charges or testifying under the Act).

57. 29 U.S.C. §158(a)(5) (outlawing refusal to bargain collectively, subject to the provisions of §9(a), 29 U.S.C. §159(a)).

58. However, the *union-shop* proviso to §8(a)(3) (*i.e.*, the *closed-shop* proviso in the original Act) contains an indirect reference supportive of minority-union bargaining. *See* Ch. 3 *supra* at notes 49–52.

59. The full text of §7 currently reads as follows:

Employees shall have the right to self-organization, to form, join, or assist labor organizations, to bargain collectively through representatives of their own choosing, and to engage in other concerted activities for the purpose of collective bargaining or other mutual aid or protection, *and shall also have the right to refrain from any or all of such activities except to the extent that such right may be affected by an agreement requiring membership in a labor organization as a condition of employment as authorized in section 8(a)(3).*

29 U.S.C. §157. The Taft-Hartley amendment is printed in italics.

60. *Id.* Emphasis added.

61. Especially from §7(a) of the NIRA. *See* Ch. 1 *supra* at notes 1–13.

62. *See* Mallard v. United States Dist. Ct. for So. Dist. of Iowa, 490 U.S. 296 (1989).

63. *See* Will v. Michigan Dept. of State Police, 491 U.S. 58 (1989) (Supreme Court relied upon "common usage" to define a statutory term).

64. See Ch. 3 *supra* at notes 81–87.

65. §2. 29 U.S.C. §152.

66. Houde Engineering Corp., 1 NLRB (old) 35 (1934). *See* Ch. 2 *supra* at notes 62–95 and Ch. 3 *supra* at notes 83–87. *See particularly* Connecticut Coke Co., 1 NLB (Part 2) 88 (1934); National Aniline & Chem. Co., 1 NLB (Part 2) 38, 39–40 (1934); Eagle Rubber Co., 1 NLB (Part 2) 31, 33 (1934); National Lock Co., 1 NLB (Part 2) 15, 19 (1934).

67. 1 LEGISLATIVE HISTORY OF THE NLRA, 1935 (1949) at 1419. *See* Ch. 3 *supra* at notes 82–84.

68. 1 NLRB (old) at 35.

69. *Id.*

70. Alfred L. Bernheim & Dorothy Van Doren, eds. (Published for Twentieth Century Fund, Inc.) LABOR AND THE GOVERNMENT—AN INVESTIGATION OF THE ROLE OF THE GOVERNMENT IN LABOR RELATIONS 5–6 (1935). The parenthetical phrase is a footnote in the original; the emphasis is added.

71. *See* St. Francis College v. Al-Khazraji, 481 U.S. 604 (1987).

72. WEBSTER'S NEW INTERNATIONAL DICTIONARY OF THE ENGLISH LANGUAGE, 2nd ed. Unabridged, 525 (1934) (hereinafter WEBSTER'S). Emphasis added. *See* further discussion in Ch. 9 *infra* at notes 2–10.

73. *See* Ch. 9 *infra* at notes 24–34 for further treatment of the essential role of "organization" in the concept of collective bargaining contemplated by Section 7.

74. NLRB v. Jones & Laughlin Steel Corp., *supra* note 7 at 33. Emphasis added. *See* notes 7–11 *supra*. *See also* Ch. 8 *infra* for application of fundamental international human-rights concepts to union membership and collective bargaining and Ch. 6 *infra* for implications under the U.S. Constitution.

75. The word "own" was thus not surplusage. *See supra* at note 5 regarding the judicial presumption that all words in a statutory provision have an intended meaning.

76. The indirect exception contained in §8(a)(3) for a "union" shop ("closed" shop prior to Taft-Hartley) by its terms cannot be activated until after selection of a "§9(a)" representative.) *See* note 84 *infra*.

77. I am aware of no express and relevant legislative history concerning this plural reference other than the fact that the plural expression "representatives" was commonly used throughout the New Deal period under §7(a) of the NIRA and was often carried over into legislative discussion and statutory text regarding the Wagner Act. Regardless of its origin, the plural reference is not inconsistent with my thesis.

78. Clyde Summers, *The Kenneth M. Piper Lecture: Unions without Majority—A Black Hole?*, 66 CHI-KENT. L. REV. 531, 534 (1990) (hereinafter Summers).

79. *See* 1938 NLRB Ann. Rep. 52 (1939). *See also* Patrick Hardin & John E. Higgins, Jr., eds. THE DEVELOPING LABOR LAW: THE BOARD, THE COURTS, AND THE NATIONAL LABOR RELATIONS ACT 82 (4th ed. 2001).

80. Senate Report: 2 Legislative History of the NLRA, 1935 (1949) (hereinafter 2 Legis. Hist.) at 2309; House Report: 2 Legis. Hist. at 2971. *See* Ch. 3 *supra* at notes 97–99.

81. *See* discussion *infra* preceding note 103 & continuing through note 111.

82. Summers, *supra* note 78 at 538.

83. *See* discussion *infra* preceding note 103 and continuing through note 111.

84. The only other related limitation is the one contained in the union-shop (originally "closed"-shop) proviso to §8(a)(3), which limits such contracts to §9(a) majority unions. As explained in Ch. 3 *supra* at notes 49–52, this passage supports the minority-union bargaining thesis.

85. Summers. *supra* note 78 at 539.

86. *See* discussion in Ch. 3 *supra* at notes 35–36, 51, 69–72, & 118–20.

87. *Id.* at notes 67–80. *See also* Ch. 2 *supra* at notes 64–65.

88. *Id. and see* the following cases wiith discussion therein of collective bargaining pluralism: Denver Tramway Corp., 1 NLB 64 (1934), at notes 136–49 in Ch. 1 *supra,* and Houde Engineering Corp., 1 NLRB (old) 35 (1934) at notes 62–91 in Ch. 2 *supra.*

89. *See* Ch. 3 *supra* at notes 13–23 & 44–48.

90. *See* text at notes 107–11 *infra* and Ch. 3 *supra* at notes 92–93 & 97–103.

91. *See* Ch. 3 *supra* at notes 89–91.

92. *Id.* at notes 81–84.

93. *See* Ch. 3 *supra* at notes 89–93.

94. Houde Engineering Corp., *supra* note 88. *See* Ch. 2 *supra* at notes 62–91 and Ch. 3 *supra* at notes 71–72.

95. " . . . *Provided,* That any individual employee or a group of employees shall have the right at any time to present grievances to their employer and to have such grievances adjusted without the intervention of the bargaining representative, as long as the adjustment is not inconsistent with the terms of a collective-bargaining contract or agreement then in effect: *Provided further,* that the bargaining representative has been given opportunity to be present at such adjustment." *See* Emporium Co. v. Western Addition Community Organization, 420 U.S. 50 (1975), and Ch. 9 *infra* at note 64.

96. Eskridge Dynamic, *supra* note 4 at 324, *citing* United States v. Ron Pair Enterprises, Inc., 489 U.S. 237, 241–42 (1989); San Francisco Arts & Athletics, Inc. v. United States Olympic Comm., 483 U.S. 522, 528–29 (1987).

97. *See* notes 45–48 in Ch. 3 *supra* and accompanying text.

98. *Id.* at note 45. *See* Kenneth Casebeer, *Drafting Wagner's Act: Leon Keyserling and the Precommittee Drafts of the Labor Disputes Act and the National Labor Relations Act,* 11 Indus. Rel. L. J. 73, 130–31 (1989), and photocopy of draft of bill in the author's files supplied by Georgetown University, Lauinger Library, from its collection of Leon Keyserling's papers. Emphasis added.

99. *See* Almendarez-Torres v. United States, 523 U.S. 224 (1998). (Comparison with an earlier version of a statutory provision is well recognized as a "legitimate tool of construction." Scalia, J. in dissenting opinion, *Id.* at 73.)

100. E. G. Latham, *Legislative Purpose and Administrative Policy under the National Labor Relations Act,* Geo. Wash. L. Rev., 433 (1936). E. G. Latham was a fellow of the Social Science Research Council.

101. *Id.* at 453. Emphasis in original.

102. *Id.* at 453–54, n. 65. Emphasis added. Latham cited the Senate Committee statement that: "Another protection for minorities is that the right of a majority group through its representative to bargain for all is confined by the bill to cases where the majority is actually organized 'for the purposes of collective bargaining.' . . . " U.S. Senate Committee on Education and Labor, 74th Cong. 1st Sess, Rep. on S. 1958, p, 14 [2 Leg. Hist. 2313]. From this, he drew the conclusion that "[p]resumably where a majority is not actually organized for such purposes, the right of minorities to bargain for themselves is reserved. It is reasonable to suppose that where there is no majority organization at all, such minority rights are similarly reserved." *Id.,* n. 65.

103. Which provides that it is an unfair labor practice for an employer "by discrimination in regard to hire or tenure of employment or any term or condition of employment to encourage or discourage membership in any labor organization. . . . "

104. *E.g.,* NLRB v. Burnup & Sims, 379 U.S. 21 (1964); Washington Aluminum Co., *supra* note 26.

105. NLRB v. Burnup & Sims, *id.*
106. *E.g., id.*; NLRB v. City Disposal Systems, *supra* note 29; NLRB v. Caval Tool Div., Chromalloy Gas Turbine Corp., 262 F.3d 184 (2nd Cir. 2001), Every Woman's Place, Inc. v. NLRB, 833 F.2d 1012 (6th Cir. 1987); Jeannette Corp. v. NLRB, 532 F.2d 916 (3rd Cir. 1976); NLRB v. Guernsey-Muskigum Elec. Co-op, Inc., 285 F.2d 8 (6th Cir. 1960); American Red Cross Blood Services, Johnson Region, 322 NLRB 590 (1996); Imaging and Sensing Technology Corp., 302 NLRB 531 (1991); Salisbury Hotel, Inc., 283 NLRB 685 (1987).
107. 2 LEGIS. HIST. at 2309.
108. *Id.* at 2971.
109. *Id.*
110. *Id.* at 2309.
111. *See* Thornberg v. Gingles, 478 U.S. 30, 43–44 nn. 7–8 (1986) (noting that committee reports are considered the most "authoritative source for legislative intent . . . ").
112. 458 U.S. 566 (1982).
113. *Id.* at 570, *citing* Consumer Product Safety Commission v. GTE Sylvania, Inc., 447 U.S. 102, 108 (1980).
114. Proof of such failure has been extensively documented. *E.g., see* note 11 *supra.*

Chapter 6

1. International Covenant on Civil and Political Rights, S. Exec. Doc. E, 95–2 (1978), 999 U.N.T.S. 171 (adopted in 1966, entered into force in 1976, ratified by U.S. in 1992); 42 U.S.C. §1983 (1994); 6 I.L.M. 368. *See* Ch. 8 *infra* at notes 37–73.
2. INTERNATIONAL LABOUR ORGANIZATION DECLARATION ON FUNDAMENTAL PRINCIPLES AND RIGHTS AT WORK, International Labour Conf., 86th Sess. (June 1998). *See* Ch. 8 *infra* at notes 74–89.
3. *See* Crowell v. Benson, 285 U.S. 22 (1932).
4. *Id.* at 62.
5. NLRB v. Catholic Bishop of Chicago, 440 U.S. 490 (1979) (the Supreme Court found that construction of the Act to permit NLRB jurisdiction over bargaining at Catholic high schools would raise a serious constitutional question under the First Amendment).
6. Edward J. DeBartolo Corp. v. Florida Gulf Coast Bldg. & Constr. Trades Council, 485 U.S. 568 (1988) (the Supreme Court found that determining the legality of handbill distribution at a shopping center under §8(b)(4) of the Act posed serious questions under the First Amendment, which were avoided by holding the handbills legal under the statute). *See* notes 8 & 142–45 *infra*.
7. Communication Workers v. Beck, 487 U.S. 735 (1988). *See* notes 62–63 *infra*.
8. *Id.* at 575. *See infra* at note 141.
9. Alexis de Tocqueville, DEMOCRACY IN AMERICA 203 (P. Bradley ed. 1954).
10. 458 U.S. 886 (1982).
11. *Id.* at 933.
12. §1. *See* Ch. 5 *supra* at notes 41–48.
13. *E.g.,* Dred Scott v. Sandford, 60 U.S. 393 (1856).
14. *See generally* Charles O. Gregory, LABOR AND THE LAW 1–104 (2nd rev. ed. 1961).
15. 38 Stat. 730 (1914), 15 U.S.C. §12 et sec.
16. *Id.* at §6.
17. *E.g.,* Adair v. United States, 208 U.S. 161 (1908) (invalidated federal prohibition of yellow-dog contracts); Coppage v. Kansas, 236 U.S. 1 (invalidated state prohibition of yellow-dog contracts 1915); Duplex Printing Press Co. v. Deering, 254 U.S. 443 (1921) (interpreted labor exemption in §20 of Clayton Act to apply only to employees in proximate relationship to controversy); Bedford Cut Stone Co. v. Journeymen Stone Cutters' Association, 274 U.S. 37 (1927) (held refusal to work on "unfair" stone violated Sherman Antitrust Act, 26 Stat. 209 (1890), 15 U.S.C. §§1–7 (as amended)).
18. 257 U.S. 184 (1921).
19. *Id.* at 209.
20. *Id.*
21. Texas & New Orleans R.R. v. Brotherhood of Ry. & S. S. Clerks, 281 U.S. 548 (1930).

22. *Id.* at 570.

23. 29 U.S.C. §§101–15.

24. *Id.* §2 (§102). Previously, in 1926, Congress passed the Railway Labor Act, 44 Stat. 577 (1926); 45 U.S.C. §§151–88 (as amended).

25. United States v. Hutcheson, 312 U.S. 219 (1940).

26. *See infra* at notes 97–106.

27. NLRB v. Jones & Laughlin Steel Corp., 301 U.S. 1 (1937). *See* Ch. 5 *supra* at notes 7–10.

28. *Id.* at 33. Emphasis added. *See* Ch. 8 *infra* for application of fundamental human-rights concepts under international law to the current issue.

29. The Supreme Court has recognized two distinct types of protected associations: *intimate* associations and *expressive* associations. *See* Roberts. v. U.S. Jaycees, 468 U.S. 609, 617–23 (1984). A labor organization is clearly an expressive association, for its primary purpose is to express to the employer the wants of its employee members.

30. Laurence H. Tribe, AMERICAN CONSTITUTIONAL LAW 1010 (2nd ed. 1988) (hereinafter Tribe). *See generally, id.* at 1010–22.

31. *Supra* note 29.

32. Later-enacted national constitutions have generally included specific protection of the right of association. *E.g., see* §2(d) of the Canadian Charter of Rights and Freedoms, referred to *infra* at notes 113–121.

33. *Id.* at 618. Emphasis added. *See* Citizens against Rent Control v. Berkeley, 454 U.S. 290, 294 (1981) (the Court traced the history of the right of association to the long-established "practice of persons sharing common views banding together to achieve a common end. . . . The tradition of volunteer committees for collective action has manifested itself in myriad community and public activities. . . .)."

34. *See* Ch. 8 *infra* at notes 70–73 for discussion of NLRA state action applicable to the private sector as assumed by the Truman, Jimmy Carter, and George H.W. Bush administrations in relation to treaty obligations. For a description of the constitutional significance of state action, *see* Tribe, *supra* note 30 at 1688: "Nearly all of the Constitution's self-executing, and therefore judicially enforceable, guarantees of individual rights shield individuals only from government action. Accordingly, when litigants claim protection of such guarantees, courts must first determine whether it is indeed government action—state or federal—that the litigants are challenging." It "is elementary constitutional doctrine that the First Amendment only restrains action undertaken by the Government." Buckley v. Television & Radio Artists, 496 F.2d 305, 309 (2nd Cir.), *cert. denied,* 419 U.S. 1093 (1974). It should be further noted that in the issue here under consideration, state action is *federal* congressional and administrative action, hence subject to direct First Amendment application, whereas action by a state that is violative of any of the Bill of Rights provisions passes through the *due process* clause of the Fourteenth Amendment. *See generally,* Donald E. Lively, et al, CONSTITUTIONAL LAW: CASES, HISTORY, AND DIALOGUES 245–359 (2nd ed. 2000); Gerald Gunther, CONSTITUTIONAL LAW 394–600 (12th ed. 1991).

35. Lugar v. Edmondson Oil Co., Inc., 457 U.S. 922, 937 (1982).

36. 357 U.S. 449 (1958).

37. 361 U.S. 516 (1960).

38. 357 U.S. at 460.

39. *Id.* at 463.

40. 361 U.S. at 524.

41. 357 U.S. at 463.

42. This is comparable to other proscribed governmental action that has "an obvious chilling effect on free speech." Reno v. American Civil Liberties Union, 521 U.S. 844, 872 (1997). *See also* Keyishian v. University of New York Bd. of Regents, 385 U.S. 589 (1967); Bartnicki v. Vopper, 532 U.S. 514 (2001). It is certainly similar to the chilling effect that the NLRB and the courts commonly find in unfair-labor-practice cases, particularly as justification for extraordinary relief. See, *e.g.,* Pye v. Excel Case Ready, 238 F. 3d 69, 73 (1st Cir. 2001) (discharge of employees "had a 'substantial, chilling effect on Union activity' [such that the] unionization effort has ground to a halt.")

43. 431 U.S. 209 (1977).

44. International Association of Machinists v. Street, 367 U.S. 740 (1961) (RLA union-

shop provision, in accordance with First Amendment requirements, was construed to deny unions the power, over an employee's objection, to use his exacted funds under a union-shop agreement to support political causes that he opposes).

45. *Id.* at 777 (concurring opinion). Justice Douglas was the author of Railway Employees' Dept. v. Hanson, 351 U.S. 225 (1956), which upheld the constitutionality of the provision in the RLA authorizing the union shop.

46. As the study conducted by Human Rights Watch concluded: "Firing a worker for organizing is illegal but commonplace in the United States." Lance Compa, Human Rights Watch, UNFAIR ADVANTAGE: WORKERS' FREEDOM OF ASSOCIATION IN THE UNITED STATES UNDER INTERNATIONAL HUMAN RIGHTS STANDARDS 18 (2000). *See also* Introduction, *supra* at notes 44–46, Ch. 8 *infra* at notes 67 & 87–89, and Ch. 12 *infra* at notes 20–40. Based on official NLRB reports from 1968 through 1997 regarding the relationship between §8(a)(3) cases that found employment discrimination to discourage union representation and the incidence of §9 NLRB elections, it was conservatively demonstrated that on average during those years "one of every eighteen employees in union election campaigns was subject to discharge or other employment discrimination to discourage union representation." Charles J. Morris, *A Tale of Two Statutes: Discrimination for Union Activity under the NLRA and RLA*, 2 Employee Rts. & Emp. Pol'y J. 317, 330 (1998). A different statistical approach that yielded similar results was reported in Paul C. Weiler, *Promises to Keep: Securing Workers' Rights to Self-Organization under the NLRA*, 96 HARV. L. REV. 1769, 172–73 (1983). *See also* discussion in Ch. 12 *infra*, at notes 2–40, of the current organizational scene at Wal-Mart and Sam's Club stores.

47. 530 U.S. 640 (2000).

48. *Id.* at 648, quoting from Roberts v. United States Jaycees, *supra* note 29 at 623.

49. *Supra* note 35 at 937.

50. *Id.* at 937. Emphasis added.

51. *Id.* at 939.

52. *Id.* at 941. Emphasis added.

53. *Id.* at 942.

54. *Id.*

55. *See* Linden Lumber Div., Summer & Co. v. NLRB, 419 U.S. 301 (1974), discussed in Ch. 11 *infra* at notes 84–85.

56. *See* discussion *infra* at notes 97–107.

57. 29 U.S.C. § 158(b)(4).

58. 29 U.S.C. § 160(l).

59. *See* NLRB v. Mackay Radio & Tel. Co., 304 U.S. 333 (1938). *See also* note 84 in Ch. 9 *infra*.

60. §7 of the NLRA.

61. *Supra* note 44.

62. *Supra* note 7.

63. *Street*, *supra* note 44, 367 U.S. at 749, *citing* Crowell v. Benson, *supra* note 3 at 62. *See also* notes 3–7 *supra* and note 141 *infra*. The *Beck* Court declined to address the constitutional issue of state action directly, for it piggybacked on the *Street* case, which had already avoided the constitutional issue by its interpretation of the RLA provision that was deemed not only "fairly possible but entirely reasonable." 487 U.S. at 762. The *Beck* Court concluded that *Street* was controlling because the NLRA and RLA provisions "are in all material respects identical." 487 U.S. at 745.

64. *E.g.*, Buckley v. Valeo, 424 U.S. 1 (1976) (federal statute limiting campaign expenditures); Keyishian v. Board of Regents, *supra* note 42 (New York statute that barred employment on the basis of membership in "subversive" organizations).

65. National Industrial Recovery Act. *See generally* Chs. 1 and 2 *supra*.

66. *See generally*, James M. Landis & Marcus Manoff, CASES ON LABOR LAW (1934).

67. *See supra* at notes 15 & 23.

68. *See infra* at notes 124–39.

69. 377 U.S. 1 (1964).

70. 389 U.S. 217 (1967).

71. 401 U.S. 576 (1971).

72. 377 U.S. at 5–6.

73. 389 U.S. at 222.

74. *Id.*
75. 401 U.S. at 580.
76. *Id.* at 584. Emphasis added.
77. *Supra* note 18.
78. *Supra* note 21.
79. *Supra* at notes 14–18.
80. Consolidated Edison Co. v. NLRB, 305 U.S. 197 (1938). *See* Ch. 5 *supra* at notes 12–16.
81. International Brotherhood of Electrical Workers and its local unions.
82. 305 U.S. at 236.
83. *Id.* at 237. Emphasis added.
84. *Id.* at 238.
85. *Id.* at 239.
86. 29 U.S.C. §158(b)(4),(i)(ii)(A) & (B), added by the Taft-Hartley Act in 1947.
87. 29 U.S.C. §158(b)(7), added by the Landrum-Griffin Amendments in 1959.
88. *But see* note 114 *infra*.
89. Added by the Taft-Hartley Act in 1947.
90. 29 U.S.C. §187, added by the Taft-Hartley Act in 1947.
91. *See* Ch. 1 *supra* at notes 17–18, 22, 33, 68–70, 82–88, 121–157 and Ch. 2 *supra* at notes 62–117.
92. §7(a). *See* Ch. 3 *infra* at notes 85–88.
93. National Lock Company, NLB (Part 2) 15 (1934); *Bee Bus Line Co.*, 1 NLB (Part 2) 24 (1934); Eagle Rubber Co., 1 NLB (Part 2) 31 (1934). *See* discussion in Ch. 1 at notes 157–69.
94. *Supra* note 25.
95. 1 NLB (Part 2) at 31.
96. *See* Ch. 1 *supra* at note 168.
97. Most of the strikes occurring during that period were for recognition. *See* Ch. 1 *supra* at note 66.
98. 312 U.S. 219 (1941).
99. United Brotherhood of Carpenters and Joiners of America.
100. International Association of Machinists.
101. They also distributed literature requesting union members and others to refrain from buying Anheuser-Busch beer.
102. 15 U.S.C. §§1–8.
103. 2 U.S.C. §101–15.
104. 15 U.S.C. §§12–27.
105. The Court provided the following rationale for its decision: "The Norris-LaGuardia Act removed the fetters upon trade union activities, which according to judicial construction §20 of the Clayton Act had left untouched. . . . More especially, the Act explicitly formulated the 'public policy of the United States' in regard to the industrial conflict and by its light established that the allowable area of union activity was not to be restricted, as it had been in the Duplex case, to an immediate employer-employee relation. Therefore, whether trade union conduct constitutes a violation of the Sherman Law is to be determined only by reading the Sherman Law and §20 of the Clayton Act and the Norris-LaGuardia Act as a harmonizing text of outlawry of labor conduct." 312 U.S. at 231. In Duplex Printing Press Co. v. Deering, *supra* note 17, the Court had narrowly construed §20 of the Clayton Act, which exempted a broad range of union activity from Sherman Act antitrust coverage by restricting the scope of that provision to trade union activities directed against an employer by its own employees.
106. 312 U.S. at 232.
107. Relating to union membership.
108. Felix Frankfurter & Nathan Greene, The Labor Injunction 212 (1930). Emphasis added.
109. NLRB v. Peter Cailler Kohler Swiss Chocolates Co., 130 F.2d 503, 506 (1942). *Cf.* Bakery Drivers v. Wagshal, 333 U.S. 437, 442 (1948).
110. The statutory proscription in §8(b) applies to all "labor organizations," which, pursuant to the definition in §2(5), 29 U.S.C. §152(5), is all-inclusive. *See* note 43 in Ch. 7 *infra*.
111. 456 U.S. 212 (1982).

112. 394 U.S. 369 (1969) (involving picketing of a railroad terminal that was not a party to the primary dispute).

113. *Id.* at 378. Emphasis added. He also noted that "[n]o cosmic principles announce the existence of secondary conduct, condemn it as an evil, or delimit its boundaries. These tasks were first undertaken by judges, intermixing metaphysics with notions of social and economic policy." *Id.* at 386.

114. On the other hand, §8(b)(7), as is noted in Ch. 10 *infra* at notes 40–52, does not apply to picketing for member-only recognition—as distinguished from picketing for exclusive recognition—but some might assume that it does apply.

115. 2001 SCC 94 (2001).

116. Part I of the Charter provides in its §1 that: "The Canadian Charter of Rights and Freedoms guarantees the rights and freedoms set out in it subject only to such reasonable limits prescribed by law as can be democratically justified in a free and democratic society." §2 provides: "Everyone has the following fundamental freedoms: . . . (d) freedom of association."

117. 2001 SCC 94 at ¶ 23.

118. *Id.* at ¶ 36.

119. *Id.* Part (ii) at ¶ 38. Capital letters in original.

120. *Id.* at ¶ 43.

121. *See supra* at notes 36–42.

122. *Id.* at ¶ 45. Emphasis added.

123. *Id.* at ¶ 46.

124. NAACP v. Button, 371 U.S. 415, 438 (1963).

125. NAACP v. Claiborne Hardware Co., 458 U.S. 886, 912 (1982).

126. NAACP v. Alabama, *supra* note 36 at 460–61. Emphasis added. *See also* Bates v. Little Rock, *supra* note 37; Trainmen v. Virginia, *supra* note 69; Mineworkers v. Illinois State Bar Ass'n, *supra* note 70; United Transportation Union v. State Bar of Michigan, *supra* note 71; NAACP v. Button, *supra* note 124.

127. 431 U.S. 209 (1977). The Court *cited* Emporium Capwell Co. v. Western Addition Community Org., 420 U.S. 50, 62–63 & 67–70 (1975); NLRB v. Allis-Chalmers Mfg. Co., 388 U.S. 175, 180 (1967); Medo Photo Supply Corp. v. NLRB, 321 U.S. 678, 684–85 (1944); Virginia Ry Co. v. Sys. Fed'n No. 40, 300 U.S. 515, 545–49 (1937).

128. 431 U.S. at 220–21.

129. See Ch. 3 *supra* at notes 67 and 120.

130. *See, e.g.,* Ch. 3 *supra* at notes 28–32 & 44–52 and Ch. 5 *supra* at notes 97–102.

131. For general treatment of the overbreadth doctrine *see* Tribe, *supra* note 30 at 1022–39. Professor Tribe points out that the constitutional challenge arises "when (1) the protected activity is a significant part of the law's target, and (2) there exists no satisfactory way of severing the law's constitutional from its unconstitutional applications so as to excise the later clearly in a single step from the law's reach." *Id.* at 1022.

132. *Supra* note 80, 305 U.S. at 236.

133. Virginia Ry Co. v. Sys. Fed'n, *supra* note 127, 300 U.S. at 848–49 & n. 6; International Ladies Garment Workers v. NLRB (Bernhard-Altmann Texas Corp.), 366 U.S. 731, 736, 742–43 (1961); Retail Clerks v. Lion Dry Goods, Inc., 369 U.S. 17 (1962). See Ch. 5 *supra* at notes 12–25.

134. In *Consolidated Builders, Inc.,* 99 NLRB 972, 975, n. 5 (1952), it pointed out that because "an employer may grant recognition to each of two rival unions on a members-only basis [citing *The Hoover Company,* 90 NLRB 1614 (1950),] a fortiori, therefore, an employer may grant recognition on a nonexclusive basis to a minority union where, as here, there is no rival union claim." *See also The Solvay Process Company,* 5 NLRB 330 (1938). *See* Ch. 5 *supra* at notes 31–38. In NLRB v. Lundy Mfg. Corp., 316 F.2d 921 (2d Cir. 1963), *cert. denied,* 375 U.S. 895 (1963), *enforcing* 136 NLRB 1230 (1962), the Board held that a group of unorganized employees had a right to deal with their employer as a group regarding their grievances. *See* Ch. 5 *supra* at note 39 and Ch. 9 *infra* at notes 59–67.

135. *See* notes 77 & 87 in Ch. 9 *infra.*

136. *See generally* Ch. 4 *supra.*

137. International Ladies Garment Workers v. NLRB (Bernhard-Altmann Texas Corp.), *supra* note 133.

138. *Id.* at 742,

139. Bates v. Little Rock, *supra* note 37, 361 U.S. at 525.
140. DeBartolo Corp. v. Florida Gulf Coast Bldg. & Constr. Trades Council, *supra* note 6 at 575. *See also* Crowell v. Benson, *supra* note 3; NLRB v. Catholic Bishop of Chicago, *supra* note 5; Communication Workers v. Beck, *supra* note 7.
141. *Murray v. The Charming Betsy,* 2 Cranch 64, 118 (1804). *See* Ch. 8 *infra* at notes 61–64.
142. Edward J. DeBartolo Corp. v. Florida Gulf Coast Bldg. & Constr. Trades Council, *supra* note 6.
143. Section 8(b)(4)(ii)(B).
144. 485 U.S. at 577.
145. *Id.* at 578.
146. 395 U.S. 575 (1969).
147. The "free speech" provision of the Act, 29 U.S.C. § 158(c).
148. *Id.* at 616. Emphasis added.
149. *See* the *Jones & Laughlin* case, *supra* at notes 27–28.
150. For a different but consistent approach, *see* Clyde W. Summers, *The Privatization of Personal Freedoms and Enrichment of Democracy: Some Lessons from Labor Law,* 1986 U. ILL. L. REV. 689 (1986).

Chapter 7

1. Chevron U.S.A. Inc. v. Natural Resources Defense Counsel, Inc., 467 U.S. 837 (1984).
2. *Id.* at 842–43.
3. 467 U.S. 843, n. 9.
4. *Id.* Emphasis added.
5. 467 U.S. 843.
6. *Id.,* n. 11.
7. Richard J. Pierce, Jr., *The Supreme Court's New Hypertextualism: An Invitation to Cacophony and Incoherence in the Administrative State,* 95 COLUM. L. REV. 749, 750 (1995) (hereinafter Pierce).
8. Food and Drug Administration v. Brown & Williamson Tobacco Corp., 529 U.S. 1200 (2000).
9. *Id.* at 132.
10. *Id.* at 133.
11. Here is a sampler: William N. Eskridge, Jr., DYNAMIC STATUTORY INTERPRETATION, 161–73 (1994) (hereinafter Eskridge DYNAMIC); Ronald Dworkin, LAW'S EMPIRE, 313–54 (1986); Einer Elhauge, *Preference-Estimating Statutory Default Rules,* 102 COLUM. L. REV. 2027 (2002) (hereinafter Elhauge); Thomas W. Merrill & Kristin E. Hickman, *Chevron's Domain,* 89 GEO. L.J. 833 (2001); Bernard W. Bell, *R-E-S-P-E-C-T: Respecting Legislative Judgments In Interpretive Theory,* 78 N. C. L. Rev. 1254 (2000); Ernest Gellhorn & Paul Verkuil, *Delegation: What Should We Do About It? Controlling Chevron-Based Delegations,* 20 Cardozo L. Rev. 989 (1999); Bernard W. Bell, *Legislative History without Legislative Intent: The Public Justification Approach to Statutory Interpretation,* 60 OHIO ST. L. J. 1 (1999) (hereinafter Bell); John F. Manning, *Textualism as a Nondelegation Doctrine,* 97 COLUM. L. REV. 673 (1997); Ronald M. Levin, *The Anatomy of Chevron: Step Two Reconsidered,* 73 CHI.-KENT L. REV. 1253 (1997); Gregory E. Maggs, *Reconciling Textualism and the Chevron Doctrine: In Defense of Justice Scalia,* 28 CONN. L. REV. 393 (1996); Pierce, *supra* note 7; Charles Tiefer, *The Reconceptualism of Legislative History in the Supreme Court,* 95 COLUM. L. REV. 749 (1995); Ernest Gellhorn, *Justice Breyer on Statutory Review and Interpretation,* 8 AM. U. ADMIN. L. J. 755 (1995); Muriel Morisey Spence, *The Sleeping Giant: Textualism as Power Struggle,* 67 S. CAL. L. REV. 585 (1994); Thomas W. Merrill, *Textualism and the Future of the Chevron Doctrine,* 72 WASH. U. L. Q. 351 (1994); Thomas W. Merrill, *Judicial Deference to Executive Precedent,* 101 YALE L. J. 969 (1992); Stephen Breyer, *On the Uses of Legislative History in Interpreting Statutes,* 65 CAL. L. REV. 845 (1992) (hereinafter Breyer); Daniel B. Rodriguez, *Statutory Interpretations and Political Advantages,* 12 INT'L REV. L. & ECON. 217 (1992); William N. Eskridge, Jr., *Overriding Supreme Court Statutory Interpretation Decisions,* 101 YALE L. J. 331 (1991); Maureen B. Callahan, *Must Federal Courts Defer to Agency Interpretations of Statutes?: A New Doctrinal Basis for Chevron U.S.A. v. Natural Resources Defense*

Council, 1991 WIS. L. REV. 1275 (1991); William N. Eskridge, Jr. & Philip P. Frickey, *Statutory Interpretation as Practical Reasoning,* 42 STAN. L. REV. 321 (1990); William N. Eskridge, Jr., *The New Textualism,* 37 U.C.L.A. L. REV. 621 (1990) (hereinafter Eskridge *New Textualism*); Nicholas S. Zeppos, *Legislative History and the Interpretation of Statutes: Toward a Fact-Finding Model of Statutory Interpretation,* 76 VA. L. REV. 1295 (1990); Cass R. Sunstein, *Law and Administration after Chevron,* 90 COLUM. L. REV. 2071 (1990); Cass R. Sunstein, *Interpreting Statutes in the Regulatory State,* 103 HARV. L. REV. 405 (1989); Antonin Scalia, *Judicial Deference to Administrative Interpretations of Law,* 1989 DUKE L. J. 511 (1989); Daniel A. Farber, *Statutory Interpretation and Legislative Supremacy,* 78 GEO. L. J. 281 (1989); Antonin Scalia, *The Rule of Law as a Law of Rules,* 56 U. CHI. L. REV. 1175 (1989); Richard J. Pierce, Jr., *Chevron and Its Aftermath: Judicial Review of Agency Interpretations of Statutory Provisions,* 41 VAND. L. REV. 301 (1988); Daniel A Farber & Philip P. Frickey, *Legislative Intent and Public Choice,* 74 VA. L. REV. 423 (1988); Kenneth W. Starr, *Observations about the Use of Legislative History,* 1987 DUKE L. J. 371 (1987); Abner J. Mikva, *A Reply To Judge Starr's Observations,* 1987 DUKE L. J. 380 (1987).

12. NLRB v. United Food & Commercial Wkrs, 484 U.S. 112, 123 (1987).
13. Eskridge *New Textualism, supra* note 11.
14. Pierce, *supra* note 7.
15. Eskridge DYNAMIC, *supra* note 11 at 158, 222, & 304.
16. Pierce, *supra* note 7.
17. Bell, *supra* note 11.
18. *Id.*
19. Elhauge, *supra* note 11.
20. Immigration and Naturalization Service v. Cardoza-Fonseca, 480 U.S. 421 (1986).
21. *See generally* Ch. 5 *supra* and its references to statutory construction at notes 3–6.
22. 480 U.S. at 452–53.
23. *See* Ch. 5 *supra* at notes 103–106.
24. *See* Chs. 1 through 3 *supra.*
25. Breyer, *supra* note 11 at 845 & 848.
26. *See* Ch. 3 *supra.*
27. *E.g., compare* Republic Aviation Corp. v. NLRB, 324 U.S. 793 (1945), where the Court approved the Board's presumption that an employer's rule prohibiting solicitation on its premises outside of working hours interfered with employees' §7 rights, *with* Lechmere, Inc. v. NLRB, 502 U.S. 527 (1992), where the Court reversed the Board's construction of §7 allowing nonemployee union organizers to solicit employees on an employer's customer parking lot. In *Lechmere,* however, the Court relied primarily on its prior decision in NLRB v. Babcock & Wilcox Co., 351 U.S. 105 (1956), in which it had recognized a distinction under §7 between an employer's own employees and outside union organizers. Regarding the issue herein, there is no comparable prior decision that would diminish employees' rights to union representation of their own choosing, notwithstanding the absence of majority membership.
28. 322 U.S. 111 (1944).
29. *Id.* at 131.
30. 484 U.S. 113 (1987).
31. *Id.* at 123 (emphasis added), *citing* Fall River Dyeing & Finishing Corp. v. NLRB, 482 U.S. 27, 42 (1987); Ford Motor Co. v. NLRB, 441 U.S. 488, 495, 497 (1979); Beth Israel Hospital v. NLRB, 437 U.S. 483, 501 (1978).
32. 494 U.S. 775 (1990).
33. *Id.* at 787, *citing* NLRB v. J. Weingarten, Inc., 420 U.S. 251, 265–66 (1975) ("The use by an administrative agency of the evolutionary approach is particularly fitting. To hold that the Board's earlier decisions froze the development of this important aspect of the national labor law would misconceive the nature of administrative decisionmaking"). *Accord,* NLRB v. Iron Workers, 434 U.S. 335, 350 (1978).
34. Holly Farms Corp. v. NLRB, 517 U.S. 392 (1996).
35. *Id.* at 399. Emphasis added.
36. 467 U.S. at 843–44. Emphasis added.
37. *See* especially Ch. 5 *supra* at notes 40–58.
38. *E.g., see* Ch. 3 *supra* at notes 44–48, 57–60, & 85–103.
39. *See* Consolidated Edison Co. v. NLRB, 305 U.S. 197 (1938), discussed in Ch. 5 *supra*

at notes 12–16; International Ladies Garment Wkrs v. NLRB (Bernhard-Altmann Texas Corp.), 366 U.S. 731 (1961), discussed in Ch. 5 *supra* at notes 17–22. *Cf.* Retail Clerks v. Lion Dry Goods, Inc., 369 U.S. 17 (1962), discussed in Ch. 5 *supra* at notes 23–25.

40. *See* The Solvay Process Co., 5 NLRB 330 (1938); The Hoover Co. 90 NLRB 1614 (1950); Consolidated Builders, Inc., 99 NLRB 972 (1952). *Cf.* NLRB v. Lundy Mfg. Corp., 316 F.2d 921 (2d Cir. 1963), *cert. denied,* 375 U.S. 895 (1963), *enforcing* 136 NLRB 1230 (1962). These cases are discussed in Ch. 5 *supra* at notes 31–37.

41. §8(a)(2). *See* Professor Millis's discussion of the ban on company unions in "Paragraph 2 of section 8" in Ch. 3 *supra* at note 63.

42. *See* Ch. 4 *supra.*

43. 29 U.S.C. §152(5):

The term "labor organization" means any organization of any kind, or any agency or employee representation committee or plan, in which employees participate and which exists for the purpose, in whole or in part, of dealing with employers concerning grievances, labor disputes, wages, rates of pay, hours of employment, or conditions of work.

44. *See* Introduction *supra* at notes 1–2 & 11–15, and Ch. 9 *infra* at notes 68–102.

45. *See* expanded discussion of this process in Chs. 11 and 12.

46. *Supra* note 27.

47. NLRB v. Weingarten, Inc., 420 U.S. 251 (1975). *See* Ch. 11 *infra* at notes 12–15.

48. Epilepsy Foundation of Northeast Ohio, 331 NLRB 676, *aff'd in pertinent part,* 268 F. 3d 1095 (D.C. Cir. 2001), *cert. denied,* 536 U.S. 904 (*infra* 2002). See Ch. 11 at notes 13 & 16–21.

49. *Id.,* 268 F.3d at 1102.

50. 341 NLRB No. 148 (June 9, 2004). For a comprehensive discussion of the cases that forerun *Epilepsy Foundation, see* Charles J. Morris, *NLRB Protection in the Nonunion Workplace: A Glimpse at a General Theory of Section 7 Conduct,* 137 U. Pa. L. Rev. 1673, 1730–50 (1989) (hereinafter Morris). For further discussion of *Weingarten* rights, *see* Ch. 11 *infra* at notes 12–28.

51. 331 NLRB at 678. Emphasis added.

52. Introduction, *supra* at notes 10–15.

53. *See* Morris, *supra* note 50 at 1678–86.

54. *See* note 43 *supra.*

55. Even as to informal groups that do not qualify as labor organizations but only attempt to discuss grievances on a group basis without seeking to engage in traditional collective bargaining, such meetings and discussions with management should—in my opinion—be recognized as protected concerted activity for "mutual aid or protection." (*See* discussion of this *second-track* §7 concerted activity in Ch. 9 *infra* at notes 11–34.) Four previous NLRB General Counsels sought such a determination from the Board; however, for various reasons, that issue never reached a decision on the merits. *Id.* at notes 68–101. *See also* Administrative Law Judge's position, *id.* at note 91. Yet in an earlier case, NLRB v. Lundy Mfg. Corp., 316 F.2d 921 (2d Cir. 1963), *cert. denied,* 375 U.S. 895 (1963), *enforcing* 136 NLRB 1230 (1962)—a decision that has not been relied on but has never been overruled—the Board recognized that a group of unorganized employees had the protected right to deal with their employer concerning grievances on a group basis. *See* Ch. 9 *infra* at notes 59–67.

56. 331 NLRB at 679, n. 12. Emphasis added.

57. *Id.* at 678, n. 11 (with reference to Member Brame's dissenting opinion). Emphasis added.

58. *Id.*

59. Holly Farms Corp. v. NLRB, *supra* note 34 at 398.

60. NLRB v. United Food & Commercial Wkrs, *supra* note 30 at 123.

61. *See* note 39 *supra.*

62. See generally Ch. 10 *infra* for treatment of the mechanics of obtaining a Board decision.

Chapter 8

1. *See* Ch. 5 *supra.*

2. *See* Chs. 1–3 *supra.*

3. *See* Ch. *6 supra.*
4. Chevron U.S.A. Inc. v. Natural Resources Defense Counsel, Inc., 467 U.S. 837 (1984).
5. *See* Ch. *7 supra.*
6. International Covenant on Civil and Political Rights, S. Exec. Doc. E, 95–2 (1978), 999 U.N.T.S. 171 (adopted in 1966, entered into force in 1976, ratified by United States in 1992); 42 U.S.C. §1983 (1994); 6 I.L.M. 368; available at http://www.unhchr.ch/pdf/report.pdf *and/ or* http://www.unhchr.ch/html/menu3/b/a_ccpr.htm (5/8/2003).
7. INTERNATIONAL LABOUR ORGANIZATION DECLARATION ON FUNDAMENTAL PRINCIPLES AND RIGHTS AT WORK, International Labour Conf., 86th Sess. (June 1998); reprinted in 144 Cong. Rec. S6909–10 (daily ed. June 23, 1998) (with statement of Sen. Moynihan); available at http://www.ilo.org/public/english/standards/decl/declaration/text (hereinafter Declaration).
8. *Declaration Affirms ILO Principles,* DAILY LAB. REP. (BNA) Jul. 6, 1998, at D-23; *Who Abstained from Voting?,* DAILY LAB. REP. (BNA) Jul. 6, 1998, at D-24.
9. *See generally* Allan Flanders, *Great Britain, in* COMPARATIVE LABOR MOVEMENTS 1, (Walter Galenson ed., 1952); Walter Galenson, *Scandinavia, in* COMPARATIVE LABOR MOVEMENTS 1, (Walter Galenson ed., 1952); Philip Taft, *Germany, in* COMPARATIVE LABOR MOVEMENTS 1, (Walter Galenson ed., 1952); Walter Galenson, *Scandinavia, in* COMPARATIVE LABOR MOVEMENTS 1, (Walter Galenson ed., 1952); Everett M. Kassalow, TRADE UNIONS AND INDUSTRIAL RELATIONS: AN INTERNATIONAL COMPARISON, 5–82 (1969); Foster Rhea Dulles, LABOR IN AMERICA, 1–241 (3rd ed. 1966); Norman J. Ware, THE LABOR MOVEMENT IN THE UNITED STATES 1860–1890: A STUDY IN DEMOCRACY (1929, reprinted 1964).
10. *See generally id.*; WRITINGS AND SPEECHES OF EUGENE V. DEBS (1948).
11. *See generally* Daniel Rogers, ATLANTIC CROSSINGS: SOCIAL POLITICS IN A PROGRESSIVE AGE (1998); Harry W. Arthurs, *Where Have You Gone, John R. Commons, Now that We Need You So,* 21 COMP. LAB. L. & POL. J. 373 (2000) (hereinafter Arthurs).
12. David L. Gregory, *The Right to Unionize as a Fundamental Human and Civil Right,* 9 MISS. COL. L. REV. 135, 151–53 (1988) (hereinafter Gregory). *See also infra* at notes 14–18.
13. Arthurs, *supra* note 11 at 386.
14. Gregory, *supra* note 12 at 152.
15. Pope Leo III, *Rerum Novarum (On the Condition of Labor),* in SEVEN GREAT ENCYCLICALS 1 (W. Gibbons ed. 1963).
16. See G. Baum, THE PRIORITY OF LABOR (1982). *See also* David L. Gregory, *Catholic Labor Theory and the Transformation of Work,* 45 WASH. & LEE L. REV. 119 (1988).
17. Pope John Paul II, SOLLICITUDO REI SOCIALIS (1987).
18. Gregory, *supra* note 12 at 152.
19. James A. Gross, *A Human Rights Perspective on United States Labor Relations Law: A Violation of the Right of Freedom of Association,* 3 EMPLOYEE RTS. & EMP. POL'Y J. 65, 71 (1999) (hereinafter Gross). *See also* his more recent essay, *A Logical Extreme: Proposing Human Rights as the Foundation for Workers' Rights in the U.S.* in WORKERS' RIGHTS IN THE U.S. (Richard N. Block et al eds., forthcoming 2005, Cornell University Press/ILR.) (hereinafter WORKERS' RIGHTS) ("Human rights are standards more fundamental than statutory or even constitutional standards").
20. Roy J. Adams, *Choice or Voice? Rethinking American Labor Policy in Light of the International Human Rights Consensus,* 5 EMPLOYEE RTS. & EMPL. POL'Y J. 521, 526 (2001) (hereinafter Adams). *See generally* James A. Gross ed., WORKERS' RIGHTS AS HUMAN RIGHTS (2003).
21. *See* Edward C. Lorenz, DEFINING GLOBAL JUSTICE: THE HISTORY OF U.S. INTERNATIONAL LABOR STANDARDS POLICY, 69–74 (2002); Richard McIntyre & Matthew M. Bodah, *The US and ILO Conventions No. 87 and No. 98: The Freedom of Association and Right to Bargain Collectively* in WORKERS' RIGHTS, *supra* note 19 (hereinafter McIntyre & Bodah).
22. *Id.*; John E. Lawyer, *The International Labor Organization and Freedom of Association,* 15 J. BAR ASS'N D.C. 141, 150 (1948) (hereinafter Lawyer). In fall 1946, the ILO entered into an agreement with the United Nations in which it was recognized as a specialized agency with the responsibility of performing functions entrusted to it by the governments of its member states pursuant to its constitution. *Id.* at 148. In 1977, the United States withdrew from the ILO because of that organization's alleged sympathy with the Soviet-block nations, but two years later it rejoined. McIntyre & Bodah, *supra* note 21. *See also* Lorenz, *supra* note 21 at 123–29.

23. *See* Lawyer, *supra* note 22 at 146; ILO CONSTITUTION, ANNEX, available at http://www.ilo.org/public/english/about/iloconst.htm. (5/8/2003).

24. Art. I

25. Art. III. Emphasis added.

26. Art V.

27. *See infra* at notes 74–89.

28. G.A. Res. 217A, U.N. GAOR, 3d Sess., Supp. No. 1, at 135, U.N. Doc. A/810 (1948), available at http://www.un.org/Overview/rights.html. (5/8/2003)

29. *Id.*, Arts. 20(1) & 23(4), respectively.

30. International Labour Organization, 31ˢᵗ Sess. (1948), INTERNATIONAL LABOUR CONVENTIONS & RECOMMENDATIONS 435 (1992).

31. International Labour Organization, 32ⁿᵈ Sess. (1949), INTERNATIONAL LABOUR CONVENTIONS & RECOMMENDATIONS 524 (1992).

32. *Supra* note 30, Art. 2.

33. *Id.*, Art. 11.

34. *Supra* note 31, Art. 4.

35. *See* Edward E. Potter, FREEDOM OF ASSOCIATION, THE RIGHT TO ORGANIZE AND COLLECTIVE BARGAINING: THE IMPACT ON U.S. LAW AND PRACTICE OF RATIFICATION OF ILO CONVENTIONS NO. 87 & NO. 98 (1984). For a contrary view, *see* McIntyre & Bodah, *supra* note 21. *See also* Gross, *supra* note 19. The United States "lags far behind others in ratifying ILO conventions. To date the US has ratified only fourteen of the 184 Conventions adopted by the ILO since its inception. . . . Only 23 of the 175 ILO member nations have ratified fewer, and none are western or industrialized." McIntyre & Bodah, *supra* note 21. Of the other large industrialized "Group of Eight," the numbers ratified: Canada 30, France 116, Germany 77, Italy 109, Japan 46, Russia 58, and the UK 85. *Id.*

36. *But see* references to a pertinent constitutional feature that surfaced during that debate, *infra* at note 73.

37. For citations and history, *see* note 6 *supra*.

38. For a summary of these conditions, *see* Kristen D. A. Carpenter, *The International Covenant on Civil and Political Rights: A Toothless Tiger?* n. 17, 26 N.C. J. INT'L L. & COM. REG. 1 (2000) (hereinafter Carpenter).

39. U.S. Const., art. VI, §2 ("This Constitution, and the Laws of the United States which shall be made in Pursuance thereof; and all Treaties made, or which shall be made, under the authority of the United States shall be the supreme Law of the Land. . . . "). A treaty, duly ratified by the Senate, must thus "be regarded in courts of justice as equivalent to an act of the legislature. . . . " Foster v. Neilson, 27 U.S. (2 Pet.) 253, 315 (Marshall, C.J.). *See* Laurence H. Tribe, AMERICAN CONSTITUTIONAL LAW 643–48 (3ʳᵈ ed. 2000). *See also* notes 51–56 *infra*.

40. Senate Comm. on Foreign Relations, REPORT ON THE INT'L COVENANT ON CIVIL AND POLITICAL RIGHTS, S. Exec. Rep. No. 102–23, at 1 (1992); 31 I.L.M. 645, 648 (hereinafter SENATE REPORT).

41. *Id.* at 2; 31 I.L.M. 649.

42. Emphasis added.

43. Emphasis added.

44. *See Reservation (1)* specifying that Art. 20 "does not authorize or require . . . action . . . that would restrict the right of free speech and association protected by the Constitution and laws of the United States."

45. *See Reservations (2)* and *(3)*, which refer to constitutional restrains relating to capital punishment and to cruel and unusual treatment and punishments.

46. *E.g., see generally* writings cited in notes 51 & 53 *infra*.

47. *E.g.*, Maria v. McElroy, 68 F. Supp. 2d 206 (E.D.N.Y. 1999), *aff'd sub nom.* Pottinger v. Reno, 242 F.3d 367 (2ⁿᵈ Cir. 2000); Beharry v. Reno, 183 F. Supp. 2d 584 (E.D.N.Y. 2002), *rev'd and remanded sub nom.* Beharry v. Ashcroft, 2003 U.S. App. LEXIS 8279 2003 (without decision on ICCPR issue).

48. Emphasis added.

49. Emphasis added.

50. Emphasis added.

51. *E.g., see* John J. Paust, INTERNATIONAL LAW AS LAW OF THE UNITED STATES 67–98,

361–93 (2nd ed. 2003) (hereinafter Paust); John Henry Stone, *The International Covenant on Civil and Political Rights and the United States Reservations: The American Conception of International Human Rights*, 7 U.C. DAVIS J. INT'L L. & POL'Y 1 (2001); Carpenter, *supra* note 38; Curtis A. Bradley & Jack L. Goldsmith, *Treaties, Human Rights, and Conditional Consent*, 149 U. PA. L. REV. 399 (2000); David Sloss, *The Domestication of International Human Rights: Non-Self-Executing Declarations and Human Rights Treaties*, 24 YALE J. INT'L L. 129 (1999) (hereinafter Sloss); John Quigley, *The International Covenant on Civil and Political Rights and the Supremacy Clause*, 42 DEPAUL L. REV. 1287 (1993) (hereinafter Quigley); M. Cherif Bassiouni, *Reflections on the Ratification of the International Covenant on Civil and Political Rights by the United States Senate*, 42 DEPAUL L. REV. 1169 (1993).

52. *See* Paust, *supra* note 51 at 78–79 ("Although [NSE] treaties cannot operate directly as domestic law to create a cause of action [they] are still law of the United States and can be used . . . indirectly as a means of interpreting relevant constitutional, statutory, common law or other legal provisions"). Carlos Manuel Vazquez, *Treaty-Based Rights and Remedies of Individuals*, 92 COLUM. L. REV. 1082, 1143 (1992) ("a treaty that does not itself confer a right of action . . . is not for that reason unenforceable in the courts. . . . If the treaty expressly entitles the individual to a remedy, he is entitled to that remedy by virtue of the Supremacy Clause."). *See also* Sloss, *supra* note 51 at 152 ("the fact that a treaty provision is not self-executing, in the sense that it does not create a private cause of action, does not preclude direct judicial application of the provision in all cases."), and *id.* at 146, n. 97 ("subject to a few narrow exceptions, non-self-executing treaty provisions are the 'Law of the Land' under the Supremacy Clause, even if courts cannot apply them directly."), *citing, inter alia*, Louis Henkin, FOREIGN AFFAIRS AND THE UNITED STATES CONSTITUTION 203 (2nd ed. 1996) ("Whether a treaty is self-executing or not . . . it is supreme law of the land."); Yuji Iwasawa, *The Doctrine of Self-Executing Treaties in the United States: A Critical Analysis*, 26 VA. J. INT'L L. 627, 645 (1986) (hereinafter Iwasawa) ("U.S. courts have consistently recognized that provisions of constitutions and statutes are the law of the land, whether or not they are self-executing. Non-self-executing treaty provisions should not be treated any differently.")

53. *Id. See also, e.g.*, John H. Jackson, *Status of Treaties in Domestic Legal Systems: A Policy Analysis*, 86 AM. J. INT'L L. 310 (1992); Jordan J. Paust, *Self-Executing Treaties*, 82 AM. J. INT'L L. 760 (1988); Iwasawa, *supra* note 52; Stefan A. Riesenfeld, *The Doctrine of Self-Executing Treaties and U.S. v. Postal: Win at Any Price?*, 74 AM. J. INT'L L. 892 (1980).

54. Senate Report, *supra* note 38, 31 I.L.M. at 657. Emphasis added. *See* John Quigley, *The Rule of Non-Inquiry and Human Rights Treaties*, 45 CATH. U.L. REV. 1213, 1230, n. 118 (1996).

55. *See* note 52 *supra*. *See also* Carpenter, *supra* note 38 at 12 ("[the NSE declaration] should not . . . preclude a party raising the covenant either defensively or through an existing enabling law.").

56. Following ratification of the ICCPR, the United States assured the U.N Human Rights Committee that "[n]otwithstanding the non-self-executing declaration of the United States, American courts are not prevented from seeking guidance from the Covenant in interpreting American law." CONCLUDING OBSERVATIONS OF THE HUMAN RIGHTS COMMITTEE: UNITED STATES OF AMERICA, U.N. GAOR Hum. Rts. Comm., 53d Sess., 1413th mtg. at ¶ 276, U.N. Doc. CCPR/C/79/Add.50 (1995). *See* Sloss, *supra* note 51 at 145 & n. 92.

57. *Understanding No. (5)*.

58. Art. 2, ¶ 1.

59. Art. 2, ¶ 3(a). Emphasis added.

60. Art. 2, ¶3(c).

61. 456 U.S. 25, 32 (1982).

62. *Murray v. The Charming Betsy*, 2 Cranch 64, 118 (1804).

63. McCulloch v. Sociedad Nacional de Marineros, 372 U.S. 10 (1962). For an application of this same principle to the ICCPR, *see* Maria v. McElroy, *supra* note 47 ("An act of Congress should be construed in accordance with international law where it is possible to do so without distorting the statute. . . . The retroactive deprivation [of plaintiff's] statutory right to humanitarian relief from deportation would arguable be contrary to both the International Covenant on Civil and Political Rights ('ICCPR') and customary international human rights law." *Id.* at 231).

64. DeBartolo Corp. v. Florida Gulf Coast Bldg. & Constr. Trades Council, 485 U.S. 568 (1988). *See also* Crowell v. Benson, 285 U.S. 22 (1932); NLRB v. Catholic Bishop of Chicago, 440 U.S. 490 (1979), discussed in Ch. 6 *supra* at notes 4–7 & 141.

65. 265 U.S. 332 (1924) (holding a city ordinance to be in violation of a treaty that mandated equality between American citizens and Japanese citizens residing in the United States).

66. *Id.* at 342.

67. See *infra* at notes 87–89, Introduction *supra* at notes 43–46, Ch. 6 *supra* at note 46, and Ch. 12 *infra* at notes 2–40 (where this phenomenon is illustrated by a review of conditions prevailing at Wal-Mart and Sam's Club retail stores).

68. *See* SENATE REPORT, *supra* note 40, at XI, Appendix B.

69. *Id.*

70. *Id.* Emphasis added.

71. *See* Ch. 6 *supra* at note 34.

72. Senate Report, *supra* note 40 at II, *Background*.

73. That reliance on the First Amendment in support of the right of private-sector workers to join trade unions and engage in collective bargaining was not unique to the Bush Administration in 1992. The Truman and Carter administrations had expressed the same position. When President Truman submitted ILO Convention No. 87 in 1949 to the Senate for approval, it was accompanied by a letter from Secretary of State Dean Acheson noting "that the Convention affirms the guaranties provided under the first, fifth, tenth, and fourteenth Amendments to the Constitution of the United States." *The United States and the International Labor Organization: Hearing on Examination of the Relationship between the United States and the International Labor Organization before the Senate Committee on Labor and Human Resources,* 99ᵗʰ Cong., 1ˢᵗ Sess. 49, 53 (Sept. 11, 1985) (U.S. Dept. of Labor Briefing Paper, ILO Convention Concerning Freedom of Association, Oct. 1980). This represented an early recognition that the rights of workers to join labor unions, contained in Section 7, were also protected by the Constitution. That same position was repeated in a 1976 *memorandum of law* submitted by the Solicitor of the U.S. Department of Labor in the Carter Administration, which asserted that the rights spelled out in Convention No. 87 "are inherent in the First, Fifth, and Fourteenth Amendments to the Constitution. . . . " *Id.* at 62–63.

74. Declaration, *supra* note 7.

75. *Id.* Emphasis added. The *citation* is to the 1969 *Comparative Analysis of the International Covenants on Human Rights and International Labor Conventions and Recommendations* in the Official Bulletin of the International Labor Office, referring to identical original-source language in the 1948 Universal Declaration of Human Rights, Art. 23(4). *See* notes 28–29 *supra*.

76. *See supra* at notes 30–34.

77. *Workplace Human Rights Focus of '98 Int'l Labor Conference,* ILO Focus (published by the Washington branch office of the ILO), Vol. 11, No. 2 (1998), at 1.

78. *ILO Meets Trade Challenge with New Message on Core Labor Standards, id.* at 1, 6.

79. *See* notes 23–27 *supra*.

80. Declaration, *supra* note 7 at ¶1(a). Emphasis added.

81. *Id.* at ¶2 & 2(a). Emphasis added. (The other "principles" concern "(b)," elimination of forced or compulsory labor, "(c)," abolition of child labor, and "(d)," elimination of discrimination in employment and occupation.)

82. The ILO's enforcement responsibility is confined to publicity, for which a *Follow-Up Annex* to the Declaration makes provision for the preparation and filing of annual reports designed to publicize the extent of member states' compliance with the Declaration. *E.g., see infra* at notes 84–85.

83. *USCIB Applauds ILO's Breakthrough in Campaign to Respect Workers' Rights,* PR NEWSWIRE ASSOCIATION, INC. June 19, 1998. Emphasis added.

84. *See* note 82 *supra*.

85. ANNUAL REPORTS UNDER THE FOLLOW-UP TO THE ILO DECLARATION ON THE FUNDAMENTAL PRINCIPLES AND RIGHTS AT WORK (2000), available at http://www.ilo.org/dyn;declaris/Show_ARHTML. Emphasis added. This admission elicited acclaim from the ILO Panel of Experts "for its open recognition of difficulties still to be overcome . . . relevant to achieving full respect for the principles and rights in the Declaration." REVIEW OF 1999 ANNUAL REPORTS BY ILO EXPERT-ADVISORS REGARDING COMPLIANCE WITH THE *Declaration,* ¶44, *id.* That the 1999

U.S. statement was later deleted, without explanation, from the 2002 U.S. report submitted by the George W. Bush Administration, *id.*, does not detract from its original honesty and significance.

86. *See supra* at note 67.

87. U.S. Department of Labor and U.S. Department of Commerce, Commission on the Future of Worker-Management Relations, REPORT AND RECOMMENDATIONS xviii (Dec. 1994).

88. Lance Compa, Human Rights Watch, UNFAIR ADVANTAGE: WORKERS' FREEDOM OF ASSOCIATION IN THE UNITED STATES UNDER INTERNATIONAL HUMAN RIGHTS STANDARDS 17 (2000).

89. *Id.* at 9.

90. *I.e.,* "encouraging the practice and procedure of collective bargaining and by protecting the exercise by workers of full freedom of association, self-organization, and designation of representatives of their own choosing. . . . " §1 of the Act.

91. *See generally* Ch. 5 *supra.*

92. *See generally* Adams, *supra* note 20 at 529–31; Hoyt N. Wheeler, THE FUTURE OF THE AMERICAN LABOR MOVEMENT 21–22 & 159–71 (2002). For a recent example of American judicial recognition of relevant international authority, *see* Lawrence v. Texas, 539 U.S. 558, 123 S. Ct. 2472, 2481 (2003), (declaring the Texas sodomy law unconstitutional) in which the Supreme Court cited a decision of the European Court of Human Rights that held a law of Northern Ireland that prohibited consensual homosexual conduct to be in violation of the European Convention on Human Rights. Dudgeon v. United Kingdom, 45 Eur. Ct. H.R. (1981) p. 52. The Court's opinion also noted with approval that "[t]he right the petitioners seek in [the Texas] case has been accepted as an integral part of human freedom in many other countries." 123 S. Ct. at 2483.

Chapter 9

1. Patrick Hardin & John E. Higgins, Jr., eds. THE DEVELOPING LABOR LAW: THE BOARD, THE COURTS, AND THE NATIONAL LABOR RELATIONS ACT (4th ed. 2001) (hereinafter DEVELOPING LABOR LAW).

2. *See* Ch. 5 *supra* following note 73.

3. §2(5) 29 U.S.C. §152(5). *See* text at note 43 in Ch. 7 *supra.*

4. 29 U.S.C. 158(a)(2). This is known as the company-union provision; it prohibits employer domination and undue interference with the organization or administration of labor organizations. In contrast to the definition of "labor organization" contained in §2(5) of the final statute (*see infra* this note), Senator Wagner's 1934 bill (S. 2926) contained the following definition:

> (5) The term "labor organization includes any individual or *labor organization, association, corporation, or society* of any kind in which employees participate to any degree whatsoever, which exists for the purpose, in whole or in part, of dealing with employers concerning grievances, labor disputes, wages, or hours of employment.

1 LEGISLATIVE HISTORY OF THE NLRA, 1935 (1949), at 32. Emphasis added. However, as a result of the hearings on S. 2926, particularly the testimony of Professor Edwin E. Witte of the University of Wisconsin, it became apparent that the foregoing language—which applied to traditionally organized company unions but not to the more informal types of employee plans that employers were creating in ever-greater numbers—needed to be broadened. As Professor Witte testified, "there is danger that your language [in S. 2926] does not include this most prevalent form of company unionism that we now know, the employee representation committee. . . . " *Id.* at 272. Accordingly, the definition was revised in the 1935 bill, S. 1958, to include in §2(5) "any agency or employee representation committee or plan in which employees participate. . . ," which is the language in the present Act. For discussion of the company-union problem to which the provision was directed, *see* Ch. 2 *supra* at notes 97–117.

5. *See* Ch. 5 *supra* at notes 63–73.

6. *See* NLRB v. Kennametal, Inc., 182 F.2d 817 (3rd Cir. 1950) (work stoppage and movement of a group of employees to employer's offices to present grievances held to be the activity of a labor organization). *But see* notes 10 & 100–101 *infra.*

7. §2(5). Emphasis added. *Id.* at 818.

8. NLRB v. Cabot Carbon Co., 360 U.S. 203 (1959),

9. *Id.* at 211, n. 7, quoting from the 1935 Senate Report on S. 1958, S. Rep. No. 573, 74th Cong., 1st Sess. 2 LEGISLATIVE HISTORY OF THE NLRA, 1935, at 2306 (1935). *See* E. I. du Pont de Nemours, 311 NLRB 893, 894 (1993), for a definition of "dealing" ("ordinarily entails a pattern or practice in which a group of employees, over time, makes proposals to management, management responds to these proposals by acceptance or rejection by word or deed, and compromise is not required").

10. *See* Charlston Nursing Center, 257 NLRB 554 (1981); Walker Methodist Residence & Health Care Center, Inc., 227 NLRB 1630 (1977); and discussion *infra* at notes 100–101. *See also* RANDOM HOUSE DICTIONARY OF THE ENGLISH LANGUAGE, 2nd ed. 1364 (1987) (an organization is "something that is organized").

11. *See* Introduction *supra* at notes 2 & 11–13, Ch. 11 *infra* at note 3, and Ch. 12 *infra* following note 63.

12. For an analysis of the nature of these non–collective bargaining activities, *see generally* Charles J. Morris, *NLRB Protection in the Nonunion Workplace: A Glimpse at a General Theory of Section 7 Conduct*, 137 U. PA. L. REV. 1673 (1989) (hereinafter Morris).

13. *Eg.,* NLRB v. Mike Yurosek & Son, Inc., 53 F.3d 261 (9th Cir. 1995); K Mart Corp., 297 NLRB 80 (1989).

14. *E.g.,* Delta Health Center, Inc., 310 NLRB 26 (1993).

15. *E.g.,* Boese Helburn Elec. Service Co., 313 NLRB 372 (1993).

16. *E.g.,* NLRB v. Main St. Terrace Care Center, 218 F.3d 531 (6th Cir. 2000).

17. *E.g.,* NLRB v. Washington Aluminum Co., 370 U.S. 9 (*see* discussion at notes 73–76 *infra*); Leslie Metal Arts Co., 208 NLRB 323 (1974), *enforced,* 509 F.2d 811 (6th Cir. 1975) (protest of supervisor's failure to protect employees from aggressions of other employees); Lanape Prods., 283 NLRB 178 (1987) (protest of failure to control excessive fumes and rat infestation); Magic Finishing Co., 323 NLRB 234 (1997) (protesting unbearable heat).

18. Vought Corp. MLRS Systems Div., 273 NLRB 1290, *enforced,* 788 F.2d 1378 (8th Cir. 1986).

19. Arrow Elec. Co., Inc. v. NLRB, 155 F.3d 762 (1998); NLRB Guernsey-Muskigum Elec. Co-op, Inc., 285 F.2d 8 (6th Cir. 1960).

20. 437 U.S. 556 (1978).

21. *Id.* at 565. Emphasis added.

22. Compuware Corp. v. NLRB, 134 F.3d 1285, 1288 (6th Cir. 1998), echoing the Supreme Court's rationale in *Washington Aluminum, supra* note 17 at 14 (1962).

23. More accurately, *alleged,* because the references to collective bargaining appear only in dicta, as will become apparent in our review of those cases.

24. *See* Chs. 2 , 3, & 5 *supra.*

25. Chevron U.S.A. Inc. v. Natural Resources Defense Counsel, Inc., 467 U.S. 837 (1984).

26. *Id.* at 843.

27. Holly Farms Corp. v. NLRB, 517 U.S. 392, 398 (1996) ("When the legislative prescription is not free from ambiguity, the administrator must choose between conflicting reasonable interpretations. Courts, in turn, must respect the judgment of the agency empowered to apply the law 'to varying fact patterns'. ... ")

28. *Chevron, supra* note 25 at 843.

29. NLRB v. United Food & Commercial Wkrs., 484 U.S. 112 (1987). See Ch. 7 *supra* at notes 28–35.

30. *Chevron, supra* note 25 at 843.

31. *United Food & Commercial Wkrs., supra* note 29 at 123.

32. *But see* note 55 in Ch. 7 *supra,* which provides further comment on the group-grievance issue.

33. *See generally* Morris, *supra* note 12.

34. *Id.* at 1704–1708; DEVELOPING LABOR LAW, *supra* note 1 at 204–15.

35. 1 NLRB 749 (1936).

36. 2 NLRB 952 (1937), *enforced as modified,* 94 F.2d 61 (4th Cir. 1938) (modification unrelated to issue).

37. 2 NLRB 1081 (1937).

38. 13 NLRB 191 (1939), *enforced,* 119 F.2d 359 (8th Cir. 1941).

39. 48 NLRB 171 (1943).

40. 86 NLRB 203 (1949), *enforced,* 191 F.2d 613 (5th Cir. 1951), *cert. denied,* 343 U.S. 970 (1952).

41. 81 NLRB 1262 (1949).

42. 366 U.S. 731 (1961).

43. 1 NLRB at 749.

44. *Id.* at 758. Emphasis added.

45. 2 NLRB at 952. Emphasis added.

46. That a majority of the unit supported the union during a strike that the union had called—approximately 1,000 of the employees had engaged in the strike—did not retroactively establish the union's majority *prior* to the strike, which was the critical time when the employer was alleged to have refused to bargain. *Id.* at 955.

47. *Id.* at 954.

48. *Id.* at 955.

49. *Id.* at 955.

50. 2 NLRB at 1082. Emphasis added.

51. 48 NLRB 171 (1943).

52. 48 NLRB at 173. Emphasis added.

53. *Formerly* 29 U.S.C. §§159(f), (g), & (h). These provisions were added by the Taft-Hartley Act in 1947 and were directed at regulating union internal affairs, including a requirement for filing non-Communist affidavits. They were repealed by the Landrum-Griffin amendments in 1959, Pub. L. 86–257, 86th Cong. Title VII (1959).

54. 86 NLRB at 206. *See id.* at 237 for details of the union's written demands.

55. 81 NLRB at 1264–65.

56. The Board made that clear by expressly noting that because "the union did not represent a majority of the employees [it] was therefore not their exclusive bargaining representative." *Id.* at 1264.

57. 366 U.S. at 736. Emphasis added. *See* further discussion of this case in Ch. 5 *supra* at notes 17–22.

58. *See* discussion *supra* at notes 25–32.

59. NLRB v. Lundy Mfg. Corp., 316 F.2d 921 (2d Cir. 1963), *cert. denied,* 375 U.S. 895 (1963), *enforcing* 136 NLRB 1230 (1962).

60. The company had previously recognized and signed a collective bargaining agreement with a union that the Board in an earlier decision had found to be a company union in violation of Section 8(a)(2), Lundy Mfg. Corp.,125 NLRB 1188 (1959); that finding was not enforced, however, for the court of appeals remanded the case because the issue was barred by the six-month statute of limitations under §10(b), 29 USC §160(b). 286 F.2d 424 (2nd Cir. 1960).

61. 136 NLRB at 1244. Emphasis added.

62. *Id.* at 1245.

63. Alan Hyde, *After Smyrna: Rights and Powers of Unions that Represent Less than a Majority,* 45 RUTGERS L. REV. 637, 646, n. 32 (1993) (hereinafter Hyde). *See* Introduction *supra* at note 8 highlighting a difference between my views and that of Professor Hyde.

64. 420 U.S. 50 (1975).

65. *Id.* at 61, n. 12

66. Inasmuch as the interpretation is rational and consistent with the Act. *See* discussions *supra* at notes 24–33 and in Ch. 7 *supra.*

67. Hyde, *supra* note 63 at 647.

68. 227 NLRB 228 (1976), *enforced in part, denied in part,* 568 F.2d 458 (5th Cir. 1978).

69. 244 NLRB 536 (1979).

70. *Supra* note 10.

71. The principal exception is to be found in the building and construction industry, where §9 representation procedures were rarely ever used. To meet the special problems in that industry, Section 8(f) was added to the Act by the Landrum-Griffin amendments of 1959. 29 U.S.C. §158(f). This provision permits unions and employers in this industry to enter into prehire agreements—hence, nonmajority-union agreements—thus bypassing the issue of majority representation. *See generally,* DEVELOPING LABOR LAW, *supra* note 1 at 958–66.

72. *See* BLACK'S LAW DICTIONARY, 7th ed. 1100 (1999), *and see infra* at note 102.

73. NLRB v. Washington Aluminum Co., *supra* note 17. *See* discussion of distinction between first and second track concerted activity at notes 12–22 *supra.*

74. Morris, *supra* note 12 at 1696.

75. 370 U.S. at 14.

76. "Strikers who have been engaged in an unfair-labor-practice strike are entitled to re-instatement to their former jobs upon an unconditional offer to return to work." DEVELOPING LABOR LAW, *supra* note 1 at 1472 & n. 92 and cases cited therein.

77. The complaint had been issued by Acting General Counsel John C. Miller. The prose-cution of the case before the ALJ, the Board, and the Fifth Circuit Court of Appeals was con-ducted under the direction of General Counsel John S. Irving, Jr. Miller, a Republican, had a long and distinguished career as an attorney with the NLRB, including the positions of Chief Coun-sel to the Chairman, Solicitor, and Acting Chairman. Following his service with the NLRB, Pres-ident Ronald Reagan appointed him General Counsel to the Federal Labor Relations Authority. *See* http.//www.nlrb.gov/gcs.html, *Periods of Service of NLRB General Counsels;* DAILY LAB. REP. (BNA), No. 13, at A-2 (Jan. 20, 1982); DAILY LAB. REP. (BNA), No. 79, at A-3 (Ap. 22, 1983). Irving, also a Republican, was appointed General Counsel by President Richard Nixon and served in that office from Dec. 1, 1975, until Nov. 19, 1979. *See* http.//www.nlrb.gov/gcs.html, *Periods of Service of NLRB General Counsels.* gcs.html, *Periods of Service of NLRB General Counsels;* DAILY LAB. REP. (BNA), No. 13, at A-2 (Jan. 20, 1982); DAILY LAB. REP. (BNA), No. 79, at A-3 (Ap. 22, 1983). Since leaving the Board, John Irving has been a manage-ment labor attorney in Washington, D.C., with the firm of Kirkland & Ellis.

78. Seeking to discuss the grievances, Ordaz, the group's spokesperson, obtained a meet-ing with Haines, the company's director of employee relations, who testified that he told Ordaz that he could not recognize him as a spokesman and that he was refusing to discuss the com-plaints of any employee other than Ordaz himself. That position was consistent with the com-pany's new employees' handbook, which provided for the processing of individual complaints only, whereas the prior handbook had provided for processing complaints with "employee-group representatives." 227 NLRB at 231. Notwithstanding Haines's assertion, Ordaz testified that he "continued to speak for the employees, and Haines did not shut him up, but listened to him." The meeting ended when Haines said he did not want to cut him off but he had to go to another meeting, to which Ordaz responded, "so far I feel you haven't told me anything to tell the people." Haines then replied, "Well, you do what you can, and that's all you can do." Or-daz reported to the other employees that he "had gotten the runaround," whereupon they de-cided to walk out. The twenty-four employees in the group obviously felt that the employer's conduct represented a refusal to deal with them as a group, which was also the General Coun-sel's position as expressed in the complaint. The ALJ, however, based on a credibility determi-nation, made a fact-finding to the contrary. He specifically found that the employer "did not refuse to listen to the complaints voiced by Ordaz as the spokesman for the group." *Id.* at 236.

79. *Id.* Emphasis added. Apparently the ALJ was not familiar with the *Lundy* case, *supra* notes 59–67.

80. Swearingen Aviation Corp., *supra* note 68. *See* discussion *infra* at notes 97–99.

81. We may assume that General Counsel Irving did not file an exception to the ALJ's cred-ibility finding that rejected Haines's assertion that he had refused to entertain a discussion of the group's grievances, for such finding had no bearing on the ultimate decision in the case; fur-thermore, it would have been futile to do so, for, as the Board noted regarding Respondent's ex-ceptions to the ALJ's credibility findings, it was the Board's established policy not to overrule such credibility determinations "unless the clear preponderance of all the relevant evidence con-vinces us that the resolutions are incorrect. Standard Dry Wall Products, Inc., 91 NLRB 544 (1950), *enforced*, 188 F.2d 362 (3rd Cir. 1951)." *Cf.* Universal Camera Corp. v. NLRB, 340, 474 (1951).

82. Unfortunately, the ALJ who originally heard the case died before ruling on a motion for which he had adjourned the hearing *sine die*. The case was then assigned to a replacement ALJ who—without holding a new hearing—issued a report containing, among the various is-sues addressed, some new dicta on the subject of group-grievance bargaining.

83. 244 NLRB at 538. Emphasis added.

84. 244 NLRB at 538. The ALJ then explained the stark reality of the law applicable to employees who strike in frustration in order to obtain an employer's attention to their griev-ances: "When employees withhold their services to enforce economic demands collectively, and give no indication of any intent to return until they win their objectives, the employer has a right to replace them and to pay them off." *Id.* It has long been accepted that an employer may law-

fully hire permanent replacements for economic strikers. NLRB v. Mackay Radio & Tel. Co., 304 U.S. 333 (1938). *See* DEVELOPING LABOR LAW, *supra* note 1 at 1478–79.

85. 244 NLRB at 537. Emphasis added.

86. 257 NLRB at 561, n. 29.

87. *Id.* The case was filed by Acting General Counsel Norton J. Come and presented and argued during the term of General Counsel William A. Lubbers. Come, a Democrat, was one of the Board's most distinguished and knowledgeable attorneys. He began his service with the NLRB in 1948 and for most of his career was Deputy Associate General Counsel for Supreme Court litigation. In 1996 he was awarded the President's Award for exceptional public service. *See* http.//www.nlrb.gov/gcs.html, *Periods of Service of NLRB General Counsels;* DAILY LAB. REP. (BNA), No. 102, at d26 (May 28, 1996). Lubbers, a Democrat, was appointed General Counsel by President Carter and served in that office from Dec. 24, 1979, to April 4, 1984. *See* http.//www.nlrb.gov/gcs.html, *Periods of Service of NLRB General Counsels.*

88. Lewis Carroll, ALICE'S ADVENTURES IN WONDERLAND, (hereinafter ALICE'S ADVENTURES) Ch. 2, at opening.

89. 257 NLRB at 554.

90. *Id.* at 561.

91. *Id.* Emphasis added.

92. *Id.* at 555.

93. *Id.*

94. *Id.* at 555. Emphasis added.

95. ALICE'S ADVENTURES, *supra* note 88, in Ch. 12.

96. 257 NLRB at 555.

97. *Supra* at notes 68 & 76–81.

98. 257 NLRB at 555.

99. 568 F.2d at 464. Emphasis added. We can only speculate as to how such serious inaccuracies in this and the preceding part found their way into the Board's opinion. Perhaps the erroneous citations stemmed from a junior attorney's reliance on unchecked headnotes (such as the headnote to the *Swearingen* case at 94 (BNA) LRRM 1396 that erroneously attributed to the Board's decision that the Act does not require the employer to meet with its "unorganized employees' spokesman [where] there is no collective bargaining contract requiring it to entertain and adjust grievances"), or perhaps there was a stretching of casual dictum in an effort to verify conventional wisdom, or perhaps senior attorneys did not sufficiently check the resulting product when it coincided with their own view of conventional wisdom, which they might have assumed had legal support somewhere. Or, inasmuch as the dictum assertions had no effect on the real issues in the case, the unreliable citations might simply have resulted from carelessness that survived unchallenged.

100. That holding was made in response to the employer's claim that the employees' strike was an unlawful violation of §8(g), 29 U.S.C. §158(g), which requires that a "labor organization" shall give a ten-day written notice of any strike at a health-care institution.

101. Walker Methodist Residence & Health Care Center, *supra* note 10.

102. BLACK'S LAW DICTIONARY, 7th ed. 1100 (1999).

103. Especially including Shepards, Lexis, and Bureau of National Affairs (BNA) services, together with conventional hardcopy volumes of court and NLRB decisions.

104. However, the dictum in *Charlston* was picked up in an unrelated context in a strange decision decided by the Board under Chairman Dotson in 1985, *Sears, Roebuck and Company,* 274 NLRB 230, 231 (1985), which was overruled in Epilepsy Foundation of Northeast Ohio, 331 NLRB No. 92, n. 8 (2000). *See* Morris, *supra* note 12 at 1730–50, *also* Ch. 7 *supra* at notes 49–58, and Ch. 12 *infra* at notes 13 & 16–21.

105. *Supra* note 41.

106. 416 U.S. 267 (1974).

107. Swift & Co., 115 NLRB 752, 753–54 (1956); Curtiss-Wright Corp., 103 NLRB 458, 464 (1953); American Locomotive Co., 92 NLRB 115, 116–17 (1950); Denton's, Inc., 83 NLRB 35, 37 (1949); Palace Laundry Dry Cleaning, 75 NLRB 320, 323 n. 4 (1947); Denver Dry Goods, 74 NLRB 1167, 1175 (1947).

108. George Gershwin (libretto by DuBose Heyward), PORGY AND BESS, Act II, Scene 1 (1934).

Chapter 10

1. *See* Ch. 11 *infra* at notes 5–33.
2. *See* Ch. 11 *infra* at note 3.
3. §3(d), 29 U.S.C. §153(d).
4. *See infra* at note 11.
5. *See generally* Patrick Hardin & John E. Higgins, Jr., eds. THE DEVELOPING LABOR LAW: THE BOARD, THE COURTS, AND THE NATIONAL LABOR RELATIONS ACT 2466–79 (4th ed. 2001).
6. *See* Chevron U.S.A. Inc. v. Natural Resources Defense Counsel, Inc., 467 U.S. 837 (1984), *and* Ch. 7 *supra* for comprehensive discussion of the doctrine. *See also* Ch. 9 *supra* at notes 25–32.
7. *See* Ch. 7 *supra* at notes 59–62.
8. 29 U.S.C. §158(b)(7).
9. 29 U.S.C. §160(l).
10. §10(f), 29 U.S.C. §160(f), provides in pertinent part: "Any person aggrieved by a final order of the Board granting or denying in whole or in part the relief sought may obtain a review of such order in [an appropriate United States Court of Appeals]."
11. *See* NLRB v. United Food & Commercial Wkrs, 408 U.S. 112, 126 (1987); NLRB v. Sears, Roebuck & Co., 421 U.S. 132, 138–39 (1975); Vaca v. Sipes, 386 U.S. 171, 182 (1967).
12. 308 U.S. 401 (1940).
13. 358 U.S. 184 (1958).
14. 376 U.S. 473 (1964).
15. 470 U.S. 821 (1985).
16. 401 U.S. 402 (1971).
17. 308 U.S. at 412.
18. 358 U.S. at 190, quoting from Switchmen's Union v. National Mediation Board, 320 U.S. 297 (1943).
19. Terminal Freight Handling Co. v. Solien, 444 F.2d 699, 703 (8th Cir. 1971), *cert. denied,* 405 U.S. 996 (1972) (holding that the district court had subject-matter jurisdiction in a mandamus-type action against a Regional Director for failure to file a secondary-boycott §10(l) injunction petition). *See also* Templeton v. Dixie Color Printing Co., 444 F.2d 1064 (5th Cir. 1971); Miami Newspaper Printing Pressmen's Union Local 46 v. McCulloch, 322 F.2d 993 (D.C. Cir. 1963).
20. Terminal Freight Handling Co. v. Solien, *Id.*
21. 5 U.S.C. §§701–706.
22. The constitutional issue is treated generally in Ch. 6 *supra. See also infra* at notes 31–32 & 35.
23. 5 U.S.C. §§701(a)(2). The Court's opinion addressed the relevant review provisions of the APA, which it succinctly framed as follows: "Any person 'adversely affected or aggrieved' by agency action . . . including a 'failure to act,' is entitled to 'judicial review thereof,' as long as the action is a 'final agency action for which there is no other adequate remedy in court,'" 470 U.S. at 828, *citing* 5 U.S.C. §§702 & 704, and further noting that "before any review at all may be had, a party must first clear the hurdle of §701(a)," which provision expressly states that such review is not applicable where "(1) statutes "preclude judicial review; or (2) agency action is committed to agency discretion by law." *Id.*
24. The Court refused to hold reviewable the refusal of the Food and Drug Administration to issue a finding that certain drugs were "safe and effective" for human executions before they could be distributed; however, it carefully articulated the limits of that holding.
25. 470 U.S. at 832. Emphasis added.
26. *Id.* at 832–33. Emphasis added.
27. *Id.* at 829.
28. *Id.* at 830.
29. *Citing* Abbott Laboratories v. Gardner, 387 U.S. 136, 141 (1967).
30. *Citing* S. Rep. No. 752, 79th Cong., 1st Sess., 26 (1945). 401 U.S. 410 (footnote omitted). Emphasis added.
31. 470 U.S. at 838.
32. Fay v. Douds, 172 F.2d 720, 723 (2nd Cir. 1949). This constitutional principle has been acknowledged in numerous federal cases. *E.g.,* Lubbers v. Machinists, 689 F.2d 598 (9th Cir.

1982); Baker v. IATSE, 629 F.2d 1291 (9th Cir. 1982); Braden v. Herman, 468 F.2d 592 (8th Cir. 1972); Balanyi v. Local 1031, IBEW, 374 F. 723 (7th Cir. 1967); Miami Newspaper Printing Pressmen's Local 46 v. McCulloch, *supra* note 19, McLeod v. Local 476, United Brotherhood of Industrial Wkrs, 288 F.2d 198 (2nd Cir 1961).

33. 5 U.S.C. §706(2).
34. 5 U.S.C. §706(2)(A).
35. 5 U.S.C. §706(2)(B).
36. §§10(e) & (f), 29 U.S.C. §§160(e) & (f).
37. *Supra* note 10.
38. Named after Associated Provincial Picture Houses, Ltd. v. Wednesbury Corp., [1948] 1 K.B. 223. *See* Council of Civil Serv. Unions v. Minister for the Civil Serv., [1984] 3 W.L.R. 1174, 1196, 1200. (Footnote in original.)
39. Bernard Schwartz, ADMINISTRATIVE LAW 495 (3rd ed. 1991).
40. Inclusion of §8(b)(7) coverage was added to §10(l) of the Act in 1959 when §8(b)(7) was added.
41. *See* NLRB v. International Rice Milling Co., 341 U.S. 665 (1951). To avoid violating §8(b)(4), 29 U.S.C. §158(b)(4), secondary locations should not be picketed.
42. §8(b)(7)(C).
43. *Id.* Emphasis added.
44. §10(l).
45. *See infra* at notes 46–51.
46. The provision was the favorable response of Congress to item 12 of President Eisenhower's twenty-point program of proposed labor-management legislation. 1 LEGISLATIVE HISTORY OF THE LABOR-MANAGEMENT REPORTING AND DISCLOSURE ACT OF 1959 (1959) (hereinafter 1 LMRDA LEGIS. HIST.) at 81. The proponents of this proposed amendment cited the facts of *Curtis Brothers* (Teamsters Local 639 (Curtis Bros.), 119 NLRB 232 (1957), *rev'd*, 274 F.2d 551 (D.C. Cir. 1958), *aff'd*, 362 U.S. 274 (1960)), as the prime example of conduct they sought to prohibit. They described the problem as follows: "Organizing from the top rather than persuasion of the employees has become the standard organizing procedure of many unions—in particular the racket-ridden Teamsters Union. The union seeks to bring economic pressure directly upon the employees to force them to join the union in order to protect their jobs. . . . Such picketing also has the purpose of coercing the employer into recognizing the union and signing a contract with it. . . . " 1LMRDA LEGIS. HIST. at 472–73.
47. NLRB v. Local 103, Iron Workers (Higdon Contracting Co.), 434 U.S. 335 (1977).
48. *Id.* at 344. Emphasis added.
49. *Id.* at 342–43.
50. *Id.* at 343, *citing* Building and Constr. Trades Council of Santa Barbara County (Sullivan Elec. Co.), 146 NLRB 1086 (1964); Bay Counties Dist. Council of Carpenters (Disney Roofing & Material Co.), 14 NLRB 1598, 1605 (1965).
51. *See* Building & Constr. Trades Council (Houston) (Claude Everett Constr. Co.) 136 NLRB 321 (1962).
52. Alan Hyde, *After Smyrna: Rights and Powers of Unions That Represent Less than a Majority,* 45 RUTGERS L. REV. 637, 655 (1993), *citing* Douds v. Local 1250, Retail Wholesale Dep't Store Union, 173 F.2d 764, 769–71 (2nd Cir. 1949), a decision by Judge Learned Hand, joined by Judges Swan and Clark, which held, regarding the earlier statutory provision, §8(b)(4)(C), 29 U.S.C. §158(b)(4)(C), that "members-only" recognition was not the recognitional objective reached by the Act.
53. 29 U.S.C. §158(a)(3).
54. *See* Ch. 11 *infra* at note 7.
55. *See* National Licorice Co. v. NLRB, 309 U.S. 350 (1940). *See also* Ch. 11 *infra* at notes 39, 43, & 67–70.
56. "Any such complaint may be amended upon such terms as may be deemed just . . . at the hearing and until the case has been transferred to the Board . . . upon motion, by the administrative law judge. . . . " NLRB RULES AND REGULATIONS AND STATEMENT OF PROCEDURE, Series 8, 29 C.F.R. §102.17, available at htp://www.nlrb.gov/rr/rrl.htm. (6/7/2003).
57. 5 U.S.C. §§551–559. The general requirements for *notice-and-comment rulemaking,* as this procedure is called, are contained in the following excerpt from 5 U.S.C. §553(c): "After notice required by this section, the agency shall give interested persons an opportunity to

participate in the rule making through submission of written data, views, or arguments with or without opportunity for oral presentation. After consideration of he relevant matter presented, the agency shall incorporate in the rules adopted a concise general statement of their basis and purpose. . . . "

58. *E.g., see* note 64 *infra* and note 63 in Ch. 12 *infra.*

59. 5 U.S.C. §553(e). ("Each agency shall give an interested person the right to petition for the issuance, amendment, or repeal of a rule.")

60. 29 C.F.R. §102.124 ("Any interested person may petition the Board, in writing, for the issuance, amendment, or repeal of a rule or regulation [which] shall state the rule or regulation proposed to be issued, amended, or repealed, together with a statement of grounds in support of such petition.")

61. Legislative History, Administrative Procedure Act, 79th Cong. 233, 260 (1946).

62. *Id.* at 359

63. Although the Supreme Court gave the Board a green light to proceed with substantive rulemaking in American Hosp. Ass'n v. NLRB, 499 U.S. 606 (1991), it has not completed any of its rulemaking efforts since that decision, and there is no indication of any present inclination to embark on further rulemaking efforts. The scene I described in 1987 thus remains valid. *See* Charles J. Morris, *The NLRB in the Dog House — Can an Old Board Learn New Tricks?,* 24 San Diego L. Rev. 9, 29–42 (1987).

64. *But see* Ch. 12 *infra* at note 63 regarding a pending "interested person" rulemaking petition. Such a petition was also attempted in 1996 in an effort to extend *Weingarten* rights (NLRB v. J. Weingarten, Inc., 420 U.S. 251 (1975)) to non-union employees. In re Rulemaking Proceeding Regarding Weingarten-Like Rights in the Nonunion Workplace, petition of Charles J. Morris, Joseph R. Grodin, Clyde W. Summers, and Ellen J. Dannin, *interested persons,* NLRB, Nov. 25, 1996. *See* Bernard Mower, *Professors Seek Expansion of Employee Rights at Disciplinary Interview,* 242 Daily Lab. Rep. (BNA) A-4, E-3 (Dec. 17, 1996). The Board held this petition for several years, until it considered the appeal from the ALJ's decision in the *Epilepsy Foundation* case (Epilepsy Foundation of Northeast Ohio et al, NLRB Cases No. 8-CA-28169 & 28264, ALJ Decision, Jan. 2, 1998), whereupon the petition was dismissed because of the pendency of that case. In its *Epilepsy Foundation* decision, the Board granted the relief that had been requested in the rulemaking petition, but without referencing the petition; it thus acted in accordance with its usual practice of announcing substantive rules in adjudicated cases, a practice the Supreme Court had validated in NLRB v. Bell Aerospace Co., 416 U.S. 267 (1974). *See* Epilepsy Foundation of Northeast Ohio, 331 NLRB 676, *aff'd in pertinent part,* 268 F.3d 1095 (D.C. Cir. 2001), *cert. denied,* 536 U.S. 904 (2002). *See* Ch. 7 *supra* at notes 48–51 and Ch. 11 *infra* at notes 13–28.

Chapter 11

1. §7 of the NLRA, 29 U.S.C. 157; U.S. Const. Amend. I. *See* Ch. 6 *supra* for treatment of the constitutional dimension of minority-union collective bargaining.

2. Alexis de Tocqueville, Democracy in America 174 (J. Mayer & M. Lerner eds. 1966).

3. *See* Alan Hyde, *Employee Caucus: A Key Institution in the Emerging System of Employment Law,* 69 Chi-Kent. L. Rev. 149 (1993); Ruben J. Garcia, *New Voices at Work: Race and Gender Identity Caucuses in the U.S. Labor Movement,* 54 Hastings L. J. 79 (2002).

4. Paul R. Hutchings, *Effect on the Trade Union,* in The Wagner Act: After Ten Years 72, 73 (Louis G. Silverberg ed., (1945), also quoted in Matthew W. Finkin, *The Road Not Taken: Some Thoughts on Nonmajority Employee Representation,* 69 Chi.-Kent L. Rev. 195, 198 (1993). *See* Ch. 4 *supra* at notes 2–32.

5. *E.g.,* Gary Chaison & Barbara Bigelow, Unions and Legitimacy (2002); Rekindling the Movement (Lowell Turner et al. eds., 2001) (hereinafter Rekindling the Movement); Paul F. Clark, Building More Effective Unions (2000); Organizing to Win (Kate Bronfenbrenner et al. eds., 1998); Restoring the Promise of American Labor (Sheldon Friedman et al. eds., 1994); Arthur B. Shostak, Robust Unionism: Innovations in the Labor Movement (1991).

6. NLRB Rules and Regulations and Statement of Procedure, Series 8, 29 U.S.C. §101.18.

7. Our Canadian neighbors have long recognized that union representation requires union membership. "The usual method of which trade unions establish representativeness in order to acquire bargaining rights is through evidence of membership." H. W. Arthurs, D. D Carter, H. J. Glasbeek, LABOUR LAW AND INDUSTRIAL RELATIONS IN CANADA 189 (2nd ed. 1984). "Generally it must be established that the employee has unequivocally applied for union membership and paid a certain sum of money to the union as either an initiation fee or as dues." *Id.* at ¶ 456, n. 3.

8. *See* discussion of Linden Lumber Div., Summer & Co. v. NLRB, 419 U.S. 301 (1974), *infra* at notes 84–85.

9. *See* Ch. 12 *infra* at notes 2–63 for discussion of some of those obstacles, including examples drawn from Wal-Mart and Sam's Club anti-union activities.

10. Wearing of union buttons and other emblems such as badges and T-shirts is protected concerted activity. Republic Aviation Corp. v. NLRB, 324 U.S. 793 (1945); NLRB v. Autodie Int'l, Inc., 169 F.3d 378 (6th Cir. 1999); Caterpillar Inc., 321 NLRB 1178 (1996). In order to establish discrimination under §8(a)(3), 29 U.S.C. §158(a)(3), proof of the employer's knowledge of union activity is normally required. NLRB v. GATX Logistics, 160 F.3d 353 (7th Cir. 1998) (employer's knowledge shown by employee's wearing of union jacket three days before discharge).

11. And this might be an appropriate time for the new union or its outside affiliate to file an LM-1 form indicating labor-union status with the U.S. Department of Labor, Office of Labor-Management Standards. *See* 29 U.S.C. §402(i) & (j)(2) and §431. For general treatment of internal union proceedings, *see* Mike Parker & Martha Gruelle, DEMOCRACY IS POWER: REBUILDING UNIONS FROM THE BOTTOM UP (1999).

12. NLRB v. J. Weingarten, Inc., 420 U.S. 251 (1975). *See* Ch. 7 *supra* at note 47.

13. Epilepsy Foundation of Northeast Ohio, 331 NLRB 676, *aff'd in pertinent part,* 268 F.3d 1095 (D.C. Cir. 2001), *cert. denied,* 536 U.S. 904 (2002), overruled Sears, Roebuck & Co., 274 NLRB 230 (1985). In 1982, in Materials Research Corp., 262 NLRB 1010 (1982), the Board had held the *Weingarten* rule applicable to the nonunion workplace, but three years later a different Board in the *Sears* case overruled that holding. *Epilepsy Foundation* was thus a reinstatement of the holding in *Materials Research. See* Ch. 7 *supra* at notes 48–58.

14. 341 NLRB No. 148 (June 9, 2004).

15. 420 U.S. at 259.

16. *Id.* at 263.

17. *See* Ch. 9 *supra* at notes 11–21.

18. 29 U.S.C. §158(a)(5).

19. 268 F.3d at 1100.

20. *Supra* note 14, slip op. at. 5.

21. ". . . but a weak one for refusing to recognize the rights of nonunion workers." *Id.* at 21 (dissenting opinion of Members Wilma B. Liebman and Dennis P. Walsh).

22. *Weingarten, supra* note 12 at 259.

23. Patrick Hardin & John E. Higgins, Jr., eds. THE DEVELOPING LABOR LAW: THE BOARD, THE COURTS, AND THE NATIONAL LABOR RELATIONS ACT 198 (4th ed. 2001) (hereinafter DEVELOPING LABOR LAW).

24. Climax Molybdenum, 227 NLRB 1189 (1977), *enforcement denied,* 584 F.2d 360 (10th Cir. 1978) (while refusing to require employer to provide preinterview opportunity on company time, the court declared that "we do believe that Weingarten requires that the employer set investigatory interviews at such a future time and place that the employee will be provided the opportunity to consult with his representative in advance thereof on his own time.")

25. U.S. Postal Serv., 288 NLRB 864 (1982).

26. *Weingarten, supra* note 12 at 256. Emphasis added.

27. *Id.* at 258. ("The employer has no obligation to justify his refusal to allow union representation, and despite refusal, the employer is free to carry on his inquiry without interviewing the employee, and thus leave to the employee the choice between having an interview unaccompanied by his representative, or having no interview and forgoing any benefits that might be derived from one.")

28. *Id.* ("As stated in Mobil Oil [196 N. L. R. B. 1052 (1972)]: 'The employer may, if it wishes, advise the employee that it will not proceed with the interview unless the employee is willing to enter the interview unaccompanied by his representative. The employee may then re-

frain from participating in the interview, thereby protecting his right to representation, but at the same time relinquishing any benefit which might be derived from the interview. The employer would then be free to act on the basis of information obtained from other sources.'")

29. *See* Ch. 9 *supra* at notes 11–22.

30. *See* Alan Hyde, *After Smyrna: Rights and Powers of Unions That Represent Less than a Majority*, 45 RUTGERS L. REV. 637, 663–64 (1993); Charles Hecksher, *Living with Flexibility, in* REKINDLING THE MOVEMENT, *supra* note 5 at 59, 66–69.

31. 26 U.S.C. §401(k).

32. Paul Osterman, et al., WORKING IN AMERICA: A BLUEPRINT FOR THE NEW LABOR MARKET 12 (2001), remind us that "unions are not the only institutions that provide workers with a collective voice. Community and identity groups also play this role in certain contexts."

33. *See e.g.*, Lowell Turner et al., *Revival of the American Labor Movement: Issues, Problems, Prospects, in* REKINDLING THE MOVEMENT, *supra* note 5 at 9; Samuel B. Bacharach, et al., MUTUAL AID AND UNION RENEWAL: CYCLES OF LOGICS OF ACTION (2001).

34. *See* note 39 *infra*.

35. *See* General Elec. Co., 150 NLRB 192 (1964), *enforced,* 418 F.2d 736 (2nd Cir. 1969), *cert. denied,* 397 U.S. 965 (1970); Leisure Knoll Ass'n. Inc., 327 NLRB 470 (1999).

36. *See infra* at notes 42–45.

37. Clearly a bargainable issue. *See* note 50 *infra. See also* Reed & Prince Mfg., 205 F.2d 131 (1st Cir. 1953); Arizona Portland Cement Co., 302 NLRB 36 (1991).

38. Their study revealed that nearly 90 percent of current union members indicated they would vote in favor of their union if an election were held tomorrow. That strong support stands in sharp contrast to the weak support expressed by nonunion employees, of whom only 32 percent indicated their readiness for union representation. Richard B. Freeman & Joel Rogers, WHAT WORKERS WANT 69 (1999).

39. NLRB v. Katz, 369 U.S. 736 (1962). *See also* Litton Fin. Printing Div. v. NLRB, 501 U.S. 190 (1991) ("[A]n employer commits an unfair labor practice if, without bargaining to impasse, it effects a unilateral change in an existing term or condition of bargaining." *Id.* at 198).

40. *E.g.,* Odebrecht Contractors of Cal., 324 NLRB 396 (1997).

41. *See* Quality Packaging, 265 NLRB 1141 (1982).

42. *E.g.*, Dynatron/Bondo Corp., 324 NLRB 572 (1997), *enforced in part and denied in part,* 176 F.3d 1310 (11th Cir. 1999).

43. *See* National Licorice Co. v. NLRB, 309 U.S. 350 (1940).

44. *See* NLRB v. Independent Stave Co., 591 F.2d 443 (8th Cir. 1979), *cert. denied,* 444 U.S. 829 (1979).

45. *See* Electrical Workers (Star Expansion Indus. Corp.) v. NLRB, 409 F.2d 150 (D.C. Cir. 1969).

46. *E.g.*, A.M.F. Bowling Co., 303 NLRB 167 (1991), *enforced in pertinent part,* 977 F.2d 141 (4th Cir. 1992).

47. *E.g.*, Beacon Piece Dyeing & Finishing Co., 121 NLRB 953 (1958).

48. *See* NLRB v. Katz, *supra* note 39.

49. *E.g.*, Dynatron/Bondo Corp, *supra* note 42; Pepsi Cola Bottling Co. of Fayetteville, Inc., 330 NLRB 900 (2000), *aff'd in pertinent part,* 2001 U.S. App. LEXIS 22594, 24 Fed. Appx. 104 (4th Cir. 2001).

50. *E.g.*, NLRB v. Proof Co., 242 F.2d 560 (7th Cir. 1957), *cert. denied,* 355 U.S. 731 (1957).

51. *E.g.*, Johns-Manville Sales Corp., 282 NLRB 182 (1986).

52. *E.g.,* Transit Union v. Donovan, 767 F.2d 939 (D.C. Cir. 1985) *cert. denied sub nom.* Metropolitan Atlanta Rapid Transit Auth. v. Transit Union, 475 U.S. 1046 (1986).

53. *See* Fibreboard Paper Prods. Corp. v. NLRB, 379 U.S. 203 (1964); NLRB v. Gulf Power Co., 384 F.2d 822 (5th Cir. 1967).

54. The term "wages" appears in the statutory specifications in §§8(d) & 9(a).

55. *E.g.*, J. H. Allison & Co., 110 NLRB 356 (1954)

56. *E.g.*, C&S Indus., 158 NLRB 454 (1966).

57. *E.g.*, Kroger Co. v. NLRB, 401 F.2d 682 (6th Cir. 1968).

58. *E.g.*, Richfield Oil Corp., 110 NLRB 356 (1954), *enforced,* 231 F.2d 717 (D.C. Cir.), *cert. denied,* 351 U.S. 909 (1956).

59. *E.g.,* Southern States Distrib., 264 NLRB 1 (1982).

60. *E.g.,* Jimmy-Richard Co., 210 NLRB 802, *enforced,* 527 F.2d 803 (D.C. Cir. 1975).

61. *E.g.,* Singer Mfg. Co., 24 NLRB 444 (1940), *enforced as modified,* 119 F.2d 131 (7th Cir. 1941).

62. *See* Allied Chem. & Alkali Workers Local 1 v. Pittsburgh Plate Glass Col, 404 U.S. 157 (1971).

63. *See* Inland Steel Co., 77 NLRB 1 (1948), *enforced,* 170 F.2d 247 (7th Cir. 1948).

64. *Id.*

65. *See* Ford Motor Co. v. NLRB, 441 U.S. 488 (1979); Van Dorn Plastic Mach Co., 286 NLRB 1233 (1987).

66. The term "hours" appears in the statutory specifications in §§8(d) & 9(a). *See also* Local No. 189, Amalgamated Meat Cutters v. Jewel Tea Co., 381 U.S. 676, 691 (1965).

67. *Conley v. Gibson,* 355 U.S. 41, 46 (1957).

68. NLRB v. Truitt Mfg. Co., 351 U.S. 149 (1956) ("Good-faith bargaining necessarily requires that claims made by either bargainer should be honest claims. . . . If . . . an argument is important enough to present in the give and take of bargaining, it is important enough to require some sort of proof of its accuracy." *Id.* at 153).

69. NLRB v. Item Co., 220 F.2d 956 (5th Cir.), *cert. denied,* 350 U.S. 836 (1955); J.I. Case Co. v. NLRB, 253 F.2d 149 (7th Cir. 1958); Otis Elevator Co., 170 NLRB 395 (1968).

70. "Upon impasse, the employer may make unilateral changes in working conditions, but unilateral changes implemented before a genuine impasse has been reached violate the Act." DEVELOPING LABOR LAW, *supra* note 23 at 926.

71. The employer should have no right to deny a union representative entry for such purposes at reasonable times. General Elec. Co. v. NLRB, 412 F.2d 512, 516 (2nd Cir. 1969) ("right of employees . . . to choose whomever they wish to represent them in formal labor negotiations is fundamental to the statutory scheme. . . . " *Id.* at 516).

72. *See* NLRB v. Acme Industrial Co., 385 U.S. 432 (1967) (affirmed the Board's requirement that the employer disclose information that will enable the union to make an informed decision about processing grievances; it also endorsed the "discovery-type," i.e. *relevancy* standard, applied by the Board). *See also* note 68 *supra.*

73. *See* Beverly California Corp., 326 NLRB 232 (1998), *aff'd in pertinent part,* 227 F.3d 817 (7th Cir. 2000), *cert. denied,* 533 U.S. 950 (2001).

74. *See* NLRB v. Washington Aluminum Co., 370 U.S. 9 (1962) (discussed in Ch. 9 *supra* at notes 73–75); *cf.* Auto Workers Local 259 (Fanelli Ford Sales), 133 NLRB 1468 (1961).

75. *See* NLRB v. U.S. Cold Storage Corp., 203 F.2d 924 (5th Cir.) *cert. denied,* 346 U.S. 818 (1953).

76. *See* NLRB v. Mackay Radio & Tel. Co., 304 U.S. 333 (1938).

77. United Steel Workers v. Warrior & Gulf Navigation Co., 363 U.S. 574 (1960).

78. *Id.* at 578.

79. *Id.* at 580.

80. *See* Retail Clerks v. Lion Dry Goods, Inc., 369 U.S. 17 (1962), discussed in Ch. 5 *supra* at note 23.

81. *See* Ch. 12 *infra* at notes 71, 72, & 75.

82. *See* Ch. 4 *supra* at notes 20–22 & 31–32.

83. For purposes of the hypothetical, I am assuming a common bargaining unit based on established NLRB precedent.

84. Linden Lumber Div., Summer & Co. v. NLRB, *supra* note 8.

85. There is a vast difference between a card majority and a membership majority. In *Linden Lumber,* where the employer had not committed other unfair labor practices, a Nixon-appointed Labor Board upheld the employer's refusal to accept a majority of authorization cards as evidence of the union's majority status, holding that the union was required to go forward with an election for certification. Although §9(a) requires only a "majority," without specifying how that majority must be established, the Supreme Court ruled that the Board's action was not "arbitrary and capricious or an abuse of discretion." *Id.* at 310. In other words, in language the Court later used in Chevron U.S.A. Inc. v. Natural Resources Defense Council, Inc., 467 U.S. 837 (1984), this was a "permissible construction of the statute," *id.* at 843, although not a mandatory requirement (*see* Ch. 7 *supra* at notes 1–6 and Ch. 9 *supra* at notes 25–29). The

Board is thus free to return to its earlier construction of the Act should it choose to do so. That earlier state of the law, as the Court explained in NLRB v. Gissel Packing Co., 395 U.S. 575 (1969), was that

> Almost from the inception of the Act . . . it was recognized that a union did not have to be certified as the winner of a Board election to invoke a bargaining obligation; it could establish majority status by other means under the unfair labor practice provision of §8(a)(5). *Id.* at 595–96.
> [W]e hold that the 1947 amendments did not restrict an employer's duty to bargain under §8(a)(5) solely to those unions whose representative status is certified after a Board election. *Id.* at 600.

Reversal of *Linden Lumber,* however, would not even be necessary in order to require bargaining where majority status is established not by solicited signatures on authorization cards but by proof of voluntary and active dues-paying union membership; hence, there would be no basis to doubt the authenticity of the union's majority. Indeed, it would seem that any other interpretation would clearly violate the Act.

86. For discussion of company-sponsored labor unions in relation to §8(a)(2), 29 U.S.C. §158(a)(2), *see* Charles J. Morris, *A Dialogue with the Chairman of the Labor Board: Challenging Conventional Wisdom on the Impact of Current Law on Alternative Forms of Employee Representation,* 15 Hofstra Lab. & Empl. L. J. 319 (1998).

87. 29 U.S.C. §158(a)(1).

88. 29 U.S.C. §158(a)(3).

89. §7 of the Act.

Chapter 12

1. Thomas Paine, Common Sense, *Introduction* (1776). Emphasis added.

2. Steven Greenhouse, *Trying to Overcome Embarrassment, Labor Opens a Drive to Organize Wal-Mart,* N.Y. Times, Nov. 8, 2002, at A-28 (hereinafter Greenhouse 2002).

3. Wendy Zellner, *How Wal-Mart Keeps Unions at Bay,* Bus. Wk., Oct. 28, 2002, at 94 (hereinafter Zellner).

4. The latter is credited to union sources. Two NLRB decisions and six ALJ NLRB decisions in pending cases confirm the widespread existence of these and other egregious unlawful practices. *See infra* at notes 13 & 29–40.

5. Greenhouse 2002, *supra* note 2.

6. Zellner, *supra* note 3.

7. Cover Story, *Is Wal-Mart Too Powerful?,* Bus. Wk., Oct. 6, 2003, at 100.

8. Steven Greenhouse, *Wal-Mart, Driving Workers and Supermarkets Crazy,* N.Y. Times, Oct. 19, 2003, at §4 (Week in Review) at 3.

9. Frank Green, *Labor Conflict Clouded: Wal-Mart's Plans for Stepped-up Arrival Complicate Grocery Negotiations,* San Diego Union Trib., Oct. 18, 2003, at C1; Greenhouse, *supra* note 8. (The fears of California's three largest supermarket chains "of fierce competition from Wal-Mart and their related drive to cut costs are widely seen as the main reason behind the . . . strike . . . at 859 supermarkets in Southern California."); Steven Greenhouse & Charlie LeDuff, *Grocery Workers Relieved, if Not Happy, at Strike's End,* N.Y. Times, Feb. 28, 2004, at A-8.

10. Frank Green, *The Grocery Strike: Smaller Stores Gain Customers from Big Chains,* San Diego Union Trib., Oct. 15, 2003, at A-1, A-20.

11. *Id.*

12. Wal-Mart Stores, Inc. and UFCW and its Local Union 99R, NLRB cases 28–16823 et al, 2003 NLRB LEXIS 86, Feb. 28, 2003 (hereinafter Wal-Mart/Kingman).

13. Greenhouse 2002, *supra* note 2.

14. *Id.*

15. Zellner, *supra* note 3. Lehman reported that he left Wal-Mart on good terms but now works for the UFCW.

16. Greenhouse 2002, *supra* note 2.

17. *Id.*

18. *Id.*

19. *Id.*

20. Judge Gregory Z. Meyerson, in *Wal-Mart/Kingman, supra* note 12 at n. 4.

21. Steven Greenhouse, N.Y. TIMES, June 19, 2003, at A-16 (hereinafter Greenhouse 2003). *See infra* at note 19.

22. This was an example of the inability of the NLRB General Counsel's office to properly investigate a suspected unfair labor practice because the Board does not use conventional pretrial discovery. Written interrogatories and/or oral depositions directed to key Wal-Mart officials in Bentonville, accompanied by subpoenas duces tecum for relevant internal documents, might have yielded positive results. I make this point here because vigorous enforcement of the Act will be important after members-only bargaining rights are confirmed. For criticism of the NLRB's reluctance to use or make available pretrial and precomplaint discovery, *see* Charles J. Morris, *Renaissance at the NLRB — Opportunity and Prospect for Non-Legislative Procedural Reform at the Labor Board,* 23 STETSON L. REV. 101, 130–31 (1993) (hereinafter Morris).

23. Keltner W. Locke, ALJ, in Wal-Mart Stores, Inc. and UFCW, NLRB cases 16-CA-20291 et al, 2003 NLRB LEXIS 302, June 10, 2003.

24. Greenhouse 2003, *supra* note 21.

25. John Dicker, *Union Blues at Wal-Mart: Attempts to Organize Are Squelched by a Flying Column of Unionbusters,* THE NATION, Jul. 8, 2002, at 14 (hereinafter Dicker).

26. Zellner, *supra* note 3.

27. *Id.*

28. Wal-Mart Stores, Inc., 341 NLRB No 111 (Ap. 30, 2004).

29. Wal-Mart Stores, Inc., 340 NLRB No. 144 (Nov. 28, 2003).

30. Wal-Mart Stores, Inc., 340 NLRB No. 31 (Sept. 17, 2003).

31. Wal-Mart Stores, Inc., 340 NLRB No. 76 (Sept. 30, 2003).

32. Wal-Mart Stores, Inc., 335 NLRB 1310 (2001)

33. Wal-Mart/Kingman, *supra* note 12.

34. Wal-Mart Stores, Inc. and UFCW, NLRB cases 28–16831 et al, 2002 NLRB LEXIS 462, Sept. 24, 2002.

35. NLRB v. J. Weingarten, Inc., 420 U.S. 251 (1975). *See* Ch. 11 *supra* at notes 12–28.

36. Sam's Club, a Division of Wal-Mart Stores, Inc. and UFCW, NLRB cases 28-CA-17057 et al, 2002 NLRB LEXIS 606, Nov. 29, 2002.

37. Wal-Mart Stores, Inc. and UFCW, NLRB case 19-CA-27720, 2002 NLRB LEXIS 579, Nov. 8, 2002.

38. Sam's Club, a Div. of Wal-Mart Corporation and Al Peto and UFCW, NLRB cases 28-CA-16669 et al, 2001 NLRB LEXIS 959, Dec. 6, 2001.

39. Wal-Mart Stores, Inc. and UFCW, NLRB cases 27-CA-18206 et al, 2003 NLRB LEXIS 418, July 22, 2003.

40. Wal-Mart Stores, Inc. and UFCW, NLRB cases 11-CA-19105 et al, 2003 NLRB LEXIS Sept. 10, 2003.

41. Wal-Mart Stores, Inc. and UFCW, NLRB Cases 28-CA-18255 et al, 2004 NLRB LEXIS 231, Ap. 26, 2004.

42. Zellner, *supra* note 3, *citing* polls by Peter D. Hart Research Associates, Inc. For comparison, *see* Ch. 11 *supra* at note 38.

43. *Supra* note 10.

44. Lawrence v. Texas, 539 U.S. 558 (2003).

45. Sarah Kershaw, *Wal-Mart Sets a New Policy That Protects Gay Workers,* N.Y. TIMES, July 2, 2003, at A-1.

46. *Id.* Emphasis added.

47. NLRB v. Jones & Laughlin Steel Corp., 301 U.S. 1, 33 (1937).

48. §7 of the Act.

49. §1 of the Act. *See* Ch. 5 *supra* at notes 39–53.

50. *See generally* Ch. 8 *supra.*

51. *See* Dicker, *supra* note 25, for discussion of Teamster efforts to organize Wal-Mart drivers and distribution-center employees.

52. An NLRB election was not intended to be a contest between a union and an employer. *See* Ch. 3 *supra* at notes 73–80 and Ch. 11 *supra* at notes 82–84.

53. *See* Ch. 11 *supra* at note 80.

54. *See* Ch. 11 *supra* at notes 38–78.

55. *See* Ch. 11 *supra* at notes 68–69.

56. *See* Ch. 11 *supra* at note 71.

57. The reader will recall *Hi-Tech Honeycomb's* insistence on meeting with employees individually regarding their grievances. *See* Introduction *supra* at notes 12–13.

58. *See* Ch. 11 *supra* at notes 39, 42, 43, 72, & 73.

59. 29 U.S.C. §160(j).

60. *See* Charles J. Morris, *A Tale of Two Statutes: Discrimination for Union Activity under the NLRA and RLA*, 2 EMPLOYEE RTS. & EMP. POL'Y J. 317 (1998); Charles J. Morris, *The NLRB in the Dog House—Can an Old Board Learn New Tricks?*, 24 SAN DIEGO L. REV. 9 (1987).

61. *See* Patrick Hardin & John E. Higgins, Jr., eds. THE DEVELOPING LABOR LAW: THE BOARD, THE COURTS, AND THE NATIONAL LABOR RELATIONS ACT 1471–78 (4ᵗʰ ed. 2001) (hereinafter DEVELOPING LABOR LAW).

62. Fair Labor Standards Act, 29 U.S.C. §§201–219; Occupational Safety and Health Act, 29 U.S.C. §§651–678; Title VII of the 1964 Civil Rights Act, 42 U.S.C. §§2000e–2000e-17; Americans with Disabilities Act, 42 U.S.C. §§12101–12213; Age Discrimination in Employment Act, 29 U.S.C. 621–634; Family and Medical Leave Act, §§2601–2654; Employee Polygraph Protection Act, 29 U.S.C. §§2001–2009. *See* Peter D. DeChiara, *The Right to Know: An Argument for Informing Employees of Their Rights under the National Labor Relations Act*, 32 HARV. J. ON LEGIS. 431, 433 nn. 8–14 (1995) (hereinafter DeChiara).

63. A petition to that effect, long dormant, is now actively pending before the Board. In 1993 I filed an *"interested person"* rule-making petition (later joined by Professor Samuel Estreicher of New York University School of Law) that proposed the adoption of such a notice-posting rule. *See Labor Law Professor Asks NLRB to Issue General Notice of Rights*, DAILY LAB. REP. (BNA) No. 28, at A-1 (Feb. 12, 1993); *See also* Morris, *supra* note 22 at 110–12; DeChiara, *supra* note 62. On Sept. 11, 2003, the AFL-CIO, by letter from its general counsel, Jonathan P. Hiatt, endorsed that petition and urged issuance of the proposed notice-posting rule. *See* Susan McGolrick, *AFL-CIO General Counsel Urges NLRB to Require Notices Describing NLRA Rights*, DAILY LAB. REP. (BNA) No. 192, at A-10 (Oct. 3, 2003).

64. *See* Ch. 11 *supra* at notes 38–79.

65. *Id.* following note 80. Such extension may be compared to the common European practice of extending the terms of collective bargaining to a wide range of employees and employers, regardless of the extent of union membership in their establishments. *See* Clyde W. Summers, *Exclusive Representation: A Comparative Inquiry into a "Unique" American Principle*, 20 COMP. LAB. L. J. 47, 50–53 (1998); Efren Cordova, *Chapter 10, Collective Bargaining*, in COMPARATIVE LABOUR LAW AND INDUSTRIAL RELATIONS 236 (Roger Blanpain ed., 1982).

66. *See* §8(b)(2), 29 U.S.C. §158(b)(2), which declares that it is an unfair labor practice for a union "to cause or attempt to cause an employer to discriminate against an employee in violation of subsection (a)(3)," i.e., to discriminate "to encourage or discourage membership in a labor organization." §8(a)(3), 29 U.S.C. §158(a)(3).

67. *See* Ch. 11 *supra* at note 80.

68. §8(d), 29 U.S.C. §158(d).

69. *See* Ch. 11 *supra* at notes 40–66. *See generally* DEVELOPING LABOR LAW, *supra* note 61 at 1155–1209.

70. *See generally* DEVELOPING LABOR LAW, *id.* at 761–855.

71. *Supra* note 68.

72. Houde Engineering Corp., 1 NLRB (old) 35 (1934). *See* Ch. 2 *supra* at notes 62–95. *See generally* Russell A. Smith, *The Evolution of the "Duty to Bargain" Concept in American Labor Law*, 39 MICH. L. REV. 1065 (1941).

73. 1 LEGISLATIVE HISTORY OF THE NLRA, 1935 (1949) (hereinafter 1 LEGIS. HIST.) at 1419.

74. Consolidated Edison Co. v. NLRB, 305 U.S. 197 (1938). *See* Ch. 5 *supra* at notes 12–16.

75. *See* Ch. 5 *supra* at notes 12–16.

76. NLRB v. Highland Park Mfg. Co., 110 F.2d 632 (4ᵗʰ Cir. 1940).

77. *Id.* at 637.

78. *See infra* at notes 104–109.

79. *See generally,* DEVELOPING LABOR LAW, *supra* note 61 at 918–32.

80. *See* note 66 *supra*.

81. *Cf.* Ch. 1 *supra* at notes 142–43.

82. The Hoover Co., 90 NLRB 1614 (1950). *See* Ch. 5 *supra* at notes 31–38.

83. Roger Blanpain, INTERNATIONAL ENCLYCOPAEDIA OF LABOUR LAW AND INDUSTRIAL RELATIONS, *Belgium* monograph 114–17 (1977) (hereinafter INTERNATIONAL ENCLYCOPAEDIA).

84. Thomas Kennedy, EUROPEAN LABOR RELATIONS 119 (1980).

85. See DEVELOPING LABOR LAW, *supra* note 61 at 415–17.

86. Matthew W. Finkin, *The Road Not Taken: Some Thoughts on Nonmajority Employee Representation,* 69 CHI.-KENT L. REV. 195, 212 (1993).

87. 117 INTERNATIONAL ENCLYCOPAEDIA, *supra* note 83 at 117.

88. *See* Ch. 3 *supra* at note 73–74, 77–78.

89. *See* Alan Hyde, *After Smyrna: Rights and Powers of Unions That Represent Less than a Majority,* 45 RUTGERS L. REV. 637 (1993) (hereinafter Hyde).

90. *See generally* DEVELOPING LABOR LAW, *supra* note 61 at 1857–1960.

91. Communication Workers v. Beck, 487 U.S. 735 (1988). *See* Ch. 6 *supra* at notes 7 & 62–63.

92. Steele v. Louisville & Nashville RR, 323 U.S. 192, 198 (1944), which established the DFR doctrine under the Railway Labor Act. *See* Ford Motor Co. v. Huffman, 345 U.S. 892 (1955), where the Court applied the same doctrine to the NLRA. *See also* Hyde, *supra* note 89 at 651 n. 42.

93. Beginning with the Sherman Antitrust Act of 1890, 15 U.S.C. §§1–7.

94. Securities Act of 1933, 15 U.S.C. §77; Securities Act of 1934, 15 U.S.C. §78a *et seq.*

95. Adolf A. Berle and Gardiner C. Means, THE MODERN CORPORATION AND PRIVATE PROPERTY 11 (rev. ed. 1967).

96. *Id.* at 12.

97. The first known mention of trade unionism appeared in a pamphlet of 1669. Sidney and Beatrice Webb, THE HISTORY OF TRADE UNIONISM 21 (rev. ed. Longmans, Green 1920, reprint Sentry Press 1973). For a description of early American trade unions, *see* Foster Rhea Dulles, LABOR IN AMERICA 20–34 (3rd ed. 1966).

98. *Id.* at 26.

99. *Id.* at 40.

100. *See* Derek C. Bok, *Reflections on the Distinctive Character of American Labor Laws,* 84 Harv. L. Rev. 1394 (1971). Professor Bok attributes the underlying difference primarily to American patterns of behavior, particularly "the absence of 'class consciousness' or 'solidarity' among working people in this country," *id.* at 1401, for worker organizations here "grew up in a society which stressed the ideals of classlessness, individual initiative, and opportunity." *Id.* at 1403. In contrast, the rise of the working class in Europe coincided with and was closely related to the rejection of political alienation, which produced an ideological component not characteristic of the American labor movement. "Because American unions had to appeal to employees on material rather than ideological grounds, they pressed harder for higher wages and protective work rules and became, in Selig Perlman's phrase, 'the most hard hitting unionism in any country.' As a result, collective bargaining was particularly burdensome to employers and provoked greater resistance here than abroad." *Id.* at 1411, *citing* Selig Perlman, A THEORY OF THE LABOR MOVEMENT 169 (1928).

101. *See* Ch. 1 at notes 5–13, 27–36.

102. *See* note 94 *supra.*

103. Ch. 90, §7(a), 48 Stat. 195 (1933). *See* Ch. 1 *supra* for detailed discussion of this provision.

104. 1 LEGIS. HIST. at 22.

105. *Id.* at 24.

106. *Id.* at 1318.

107. Congress later addressed the matter of labor racketeering and internal union democracy in the Taft-Hartley Act of 1947, 29 U.S.C. §186, and the Landrum-Griffin Act of 1959, 29 U.S.C. §§401–531. As of this writing, Congress is still in the process of exploring and crafting legislative responses to the corporate, brokerage, and investment scandals and fiascos of 2001 and 2002. Union democracy, which is regulated by the Landrum-Griffin Act (Labor-Management Reporting and Disclosure Act), notwithstanding its obvious importance, is not the subject of this book, which focuses only on workplace democracy pursuant to the NLRA.

108. 1 Legis. Hist. at 1319.

109. *Id.* 1411.

110. NLRB v. City Disposal Systems, Inc., 465 U.S. 822 (1984). *See* Ch. 5 *supra* at notes 29–30.

111. *Id.* at 835. Emphasis added.

112. Paul Osterman, *et al,* Working in America: A Blueprint for the New Labor Market 152 (2001) (hereinafter Osterman).

113. *Id.* at 152.

114. *Id.* at 169–80.

115. *See* text *supra* following note 63 and Ch. 11 *supra* at note 3.

116. 29 U.S.C. §301. *See* Developing Labor Law, *supra* note 61 at 1298–1303.

117. United Steelworkers of Am. v. American Mfg. Co., 363 U.S. 564 (1960); United Steelworkers of Am. v. Warrior & Gulf Navigation Co., 363 U.S. 574 (1960); United Steelworkers of Am. v. Enterprise Wheel & Car Corp., 363 U.S. 593 (1960). *See* Charles J. Morris, *Twenty Years of Trilogy: A Celebration,* in Proceedings of the 33rd Annual Meeting, National Academy of Arbitrators 331 (1981); Martin H. Malin, *Foreword: Labor Arbitration Thirty Years after the Steelworkers Trilogy,* 66 Chi.-Kent L. Rev. 551 (1990).

118. *See* Theodore J. St. Antoine, *The Law of Arbitration,* in Labor Arbitration under Fire (James. L. Stern & Joyce M. Najita eds. 1997); Calvin William Sharp, *Judicial Review of Labor Arbitration Awards: A View from the Bench,* in Proceedings of the 52nd Annual Meeting, National Academy of Arbitrators 126 (1999).

119. *Cf.* Ch. 11 *supra* at notes 11–28.

120. An extensive bibliography documents the subject of labor arbitration and the body of recorded arbitral jurisprudence that has accumulated over more than half a century. See, *e.g.,* the published volumes of the Proceedings of the National Academy of Arbitrators, of which the 55th volume is Arbitration 2002, Workplace Arbitration: A Process in Evolution, Proceedings of the 55th Annual Meeting, National Academy of Arbitrators (2003). *See also* Alan Miles Ruben ed., Elkouri & Elkouri, How Arbitration Works (6th ed. 2003); Charles J. Coleman & Theodora T. Haynes, Labor Arbitration: An Annotated Bibliography (1994).

121. "X-inefficiency refers to a situation in which a firm's total costs are not minimized because the actual output from given inputs is less than the maximum feasible level." (Footnote in original.) Toke Aidt and Zafiris Tzannatos, The World Bank, Unions and Collective Bargaining: The Economic Effects in a Global Environment 26 (2002) (referencing the following sources: Faith, R. L. & J.D. Reid, *An Agency Theory of Unionism,* 8 J. of Economic Behavior & Org. 39–60 (1987); Freeman, R. B. & J. L. Medoff, *The Two Faces of Unionism,* 57 Pub. Interest 69–93 (1979); Freeman, R. B. & J. L. Medoff, What Do Unions Do? (1984)).

122. Fact Finding Report, Commission on the Future of Worker-Management Relations, U.S. Dep't of Labor & U.S. Dep't of Commerce, 41 (1994) (The *Dunlop Commission*).

123. Osterman, *supra* note 112.

124. §2(5), 29 U.S.C. §155(5). *See* note 43 in Ch. 7 *supra.*

125. §8(a)(2), 29 U.S.C. §158(a)(2).

126. A vast literature documenting these trends has developed. *See, e.g.,* Saul A. Rubinstein, Learning from Saturn: Possibilities for Corporate Governance and Employee Relations (2001) (hereinafter Rubinstein); Eileen Applebaum et al, Manufacturing Advantage: Why High-Performance Work Systems Pay Off (2000) (hereinafter Appelbaum); The Changing Nature of Work (Frank Ackerman et al. eds., 1998); Eileen Appelbaum & Rosemary Batt, The New American Workplace (1994) (hereinafter Appelbaum & Batt); Workplace Industrial Relations and the Global Challenge (Jacques Bélanger et al., 1994); Thomas A. Kochan & Paul Osterman, The Mutual Gains Enterprise: Forging a Winning Partnership Among Labor, Management, and Government (1994).

127. As Applebaum & Batt reported in 1994, "Joint labor-management programs have been established at approximately half of all unionized establishments [and] many of the best-known examples of high-performance production systems are occurring in unionized plants—such as Corning, Saturn, Xerox, Levi Strauss, NUMMI, and AT&T." *Id.* at 152. *And see* the series of annual conferences and accompanying publications entitled Unions & Management

Working Together: Improve Productivity, Quality and Cost Effectiveness with Effective Labor-Management Relations sponsored by the Manufacturing Institute, a division of the Institute for International Research, website http://www.irr-ny.com. *See also* note 133 *infra.*

128. Richard B. Freeman & Joel Rogers, What Workers Want 4–5 (1999). *See* Ch. 11 *supra* at note 38.

129. §9(a), 29 U.S.C. §159(a).

130. *See* NLRB v. Wooster Div. of Borg-Warner Corp., 356 U.S. 342 (1958), and Ch. 11 *supra* at notes 43–69.

131. *See* §§8(a)(2) & 9(a) and Electromation, Inc., 309 NLRB 990, *enforced,* 35 F.3d 1148 (7ᵗʰ Cir. 1994).

132. Testimony of Eileen Appelbaum before the Commission on the Future of Worker-Management Relations, U.S. Dept. of Labor, U.S. Dept. of Commerce (Dunlop Commission), transcript Jan. 19, 1994, at 9.

133. *See* note 127 *supra. See also* the analyses of high-performance work systems in the unionized steel industry in Appelbaum, *supra* note 126 ("A study by Black and Lynch (1999) of a nationally representative sample of establishments found that unionized plants that adopt various high performance practices have labor productivity that is 9 percentage points higher than nonunionized plants with similar characteristics." *Id.* at 136–37, *citing* S. Black & L. Lynch., *How to Compete: The Impact of Workplace Practices and Information Technology on Productivity* (1999) (unpublished manuscript, Tufts University). *And see* Rubinstein, *supra* note 126 regarding the Saturn experience at General Motors.

134. Robert D. Putnam, Bowling Alone (2000).

135. *Id.* at 19

136. *Id.* at 81.

137. Cynthia L. Estlund, *Working Together: The Workplace, Civil Society, and the Law,* 89 Geo. L.J. 1, 3 (2000). Professor Estlund elaborates on the thesis described herein at notes 138–43 *infra* in her recent book, Working Together: Workplace Bonds Strengthen a Diverse Democracy.

138. *Id.* at 4.

139. *Id.* at 5.

140. *Id.* at 6.

141. *Id.* at 70.

142. *Id.*

143. *Id.* at 77. Although Professor Estlund bases her thesis on the prevailing view of the law, not on arguments for democratization of the workplace she acknowledges that such arguments are "powerful and appealing," but they are distinct from the claims she advances. *Id.* at 73.

144. *See* note 88 *supra.*

145. *See generally* John Kenneth Galbraith, American Capitalism: The Concept of Countervailing Power (1952, 1956).

146. Kevin Phillips, Wealth and Democracy: A Political History of the American Rich 129 (2002). *See especially* charts 3.9a, 3.9b, & 3.11 at 128–31. *See also* Lawrence Mischel, et al, The State of Working America 2002/2003 (2002)

147. *See supra* at notes 2–40.

148. Dicker, *supra* note 25.

Appendix to Chapter 2

1. Kenneth Casebeer, *Drafting Wagner's Act: Leon Keyserling and the Precommittee Drafts of the Labor Disputes Act and the National Labor Relations Act,* 11 Indus. Rel. L. J. 73, 102 (1989) (hereinafter Casebeer *Keyserling Drafts*).

2. *Id.* This draft follows the section format of the Railway Labor Act, 45 U.S.C. §§151–88.

3. *Id.* at 102–103.

4. *Id.* at 103. Boldface emphasis added.

5. *Id.* at 104–105. Boldface emphasis added.

298 | Notes to Pages 232–239

6. *Id.* at 105.

7. *Id.* at 75–77, 80.

8. *Id.* at 109–110.

9. *Id.* at 111.

10. *Id.* at 111.

11. At this point the authors abandoned their initial emulation of Railway Labor Act section-numbering style.

12. Casebeer *Keyserling Drafts, supra* note 1 at 112. Boldface emphasis added.

13. *Id.* Boldface emphasis added.

14. *Id.* Boldface emphasis added.

15. *Id.* at 112–13. Boldface emphasis added.

16. *Id.* at 113.

17. *Id.* Boldface emphasis added.

18. *Id.* at 114.

19. *Id.* Boldface emphasis added.

20. *Id.* Boldface emphasis added.

21. *Id.* Boldface emphasis added.

22. *Id.* at 115.

23. *Id.*

24. *Id.* at 115.

25. *Id.* Boldface emphasis added.

26. *Id.* Boldface emphasis added.

27. *Id.* at 116.

28. *Id.*

29. *Id.*

30. *Id.* at 117.

31. *Id.* Boldface emphasis added.

32. *Id.* Boldface emphasis added.

33. *Id.* at 118.

34. *Id.* at 119–20.

35. 1 Legislative History of the NLRA, 1935 (1949) (hereinafter 1 Legis. Hist.) at 1.

36. Boldface emphasis added.

37. 1 Legis. Hist. at 11. Boldface emphasis added.

38. *Id.* at 1070.

39. Casebeer *Keyserling Drafts, supra* note 1 at 93–94; Irving Bernstein, The New Deal Collective Bargaining Policy 72 (1950).

40. Irving Bernstein, *id.* at 74, *citing* N. Y. Herald Trib., May 24, 26, 1934; N. Y. Times, May 26, 1934.

41. Legis Hist. at 1085. Boldface emphasis added.

42. *Id.* at 1094.

43. *Id.* at 1095. Boldface emphasis added.

Appendix to Chapter 3

1. Kenneth Casebeer, *Drafting Wagner's Act: Leon Keyserling and the Precommittee Drafts of the Labor Disputes Act and the National Labor Relations Act,* 11 Indus. Rel. L. J. 73, 120 (1989) (hereinafter Casebeer *Kyserling Drafts*).

2. As designated in Casebeer's reproduction.

3. *Id.* at 121. Boldface emphasis added. The only relevant difference between this provision and the language in the Walsh bill is the substitution of the word "full" for "complete" so as to read "full freedom of association." Additional prefatory language also precedes this provision.

4. *Id.* at 123. Boldface emphasis added.

5. *Id.* Boldface emphasis added.

6. *Id.* at 123–24. Boldface emphasis added. This language is basically the same as that contained in the 1934 Walsh bill, 1 Legislative History of the NLRA, 1935 (1949) (hereinafter 1 Legis. Hist.), at 1087, which was similar in substantive content to Senator Wagner's original bill (S. 2926), *id.* at 4.

7. Casebeer *Kyserling Drafts, supra* note 1 at 124. Boldface emphasis added.
8. *Id.* Boldface emphasis added.
9. *Id.* at 123–24.
10. 1 LEGIS. HIST. at 1295.
11. *Id.* Boldface emphasis added.
12. *Id.* at 1299. Boldface emphasis added.
13. *Id.* Boldface emphasis added.
14. *Id.* at 1299–1300. Boldface emphasis added.
15. *Id.* at 1300. Boldface emphasis added.
16. *Id.*
17. *Id.*
18. Casebeer *Keyserling Drafts, supra* note 1 at 130–31.
19. The proposed changes in this draft are reproduced by Casebeer in the Appendix to his article, *id.*, although under the misleading heading, *"NLRA Draft 2—February 15, 1935—New Preamble, Amendments in Committee Annotated by L. Keyserling in Margin."* The document is clearly a *third draft*, not the second draft (the second draft was S. 1958 as introduced on February 21, 1935), nor are all of the changes "amendments in Committee"—some were and some were not. In his description of the draft earlier in his text, *id.* at 86, Professor Casebeer does explain that the draft "represents the National Labor Relations Act as introduced February 15, 1935, together with amendments of the Committee on Education and Labor annotated by Keyserling as to their source or sponsor." That clarification, however, is partially inaccurate, for only some of the inserted proposals were ultimately adopted by the committee. The photocopy in my files (Ch. 3 *supra* at note 36) shows that it is a revision superimposed on an officially printed version of S. 1958 that was introduced on Feb. 21, 1935 (which is the calendar day, although it also bears the session date of Feb. 15, 1935). All of the changes on the document appear either in handwriting or as typed copy on inserted flaps—the latter being how the two versions of §8(5) noted herein appear, but with the handwritten identification "Biddle." (There are also other handwritten marginal designations elsewhere in the document showing the sources or sponsors of the changes, except, presumably, when Keyserling was himself the source or sponsor.) Comparisons of the proposed changes inserted into the document with the written proposals attributed to various sources by the Senate Committee in its March 11, 1935, *Comparison of S. 2926 and S. 1958*, 1 LEGIS. HIST. at 1319–71, and also the changes that were incorporated into the bill as reported by the committee on May 2, 1935, show that this was a preliminary and tentative committee mark-up of the original bill, in other words, a *working draft* composed during committee consideration during the period from Feb. 21 to March 11, 1935. Most but not all of those changes were incorporated into the bill as reported, which demonstrates the preliminary nature of the draft's mark-up status, and—more important—that every change or proposed change included in this draft occurred within the Senate committee and thus received the consideration of that committee.
20. *Id.* at 130. Boldface emphasis added.
21. Professor Casebeer inadvertently failed to include this change. Casebeer *Keyserling Drafts, supra* note 1 at 131, Appendix. However, the change clearly appears in handwriting (presumably Keyserling's, *id.* at 130) in the photocopy in my possession (*see* note 19 *supra*). Boldface emphasis and boldface italics added. The boldface italics point up the identity of the phrase compared with the same phrase appearing in the second version of §8(5) submitted by Francis Biddle. *See infra* at note 24.
22. *Id.* at 131.
23. Boldface emphasis added. This version of the proposed §8(5) first publicly appeared as Francis Biddle's proposed amendment in the Senate Committee's memorandum of March 11, 1935, comparing S. 1958 with the last version of S. 2926. 1 LEGIS. HIST. at 1319, 1331.
24. Boldface and italicized emphasis added. This is the version of the proposed §8(5) that was rejected.
25. 2 LEGISLATIVE HISTORY OF THE NLRA, 1935 (1949) (hereinafter 2 LEGIS. HIST.) at 2285.
26. A nonsubstantive change appeared in the conference committee report (hence in the final version of the Act) relative to the pertinent declaration-of-policy paragraph in §1. *See Final Draft infra* at notes 31–35.
27. 2 LEGIS. HIST. at 2414–15.

28. *Id.* at 3227. The House version contained a number of differences from the Senate version, primarily procedural and administrative differences; however, the substantive provisions here relevant were not changed.

29. This was not a change from the Third NLRA Draft, which was a preliminary mark-up draft (*see* note 19 *supra*); however, it was a change from the bill as introduced (*Second NLRA Draft*).

30. 2 LEGIS. HIST. at 2290. Boldface emphasis added.

31. *Id.* at 3270.

32. *Id.* 3260 & 3267.

33. *Id.* at 3252 & 3258.

34. *Id.* at 3268.

35. *Id.* at 3270. Boldface emphasis added.

Index

Note: Case names are italicized.

A. Roth and Co., 254n28
A.M.F. Bowling Co., 290n46
Abbott Laboratories v. Gardner, 286n29
Abood v. Detroit Board of Education, 115,
  127–28
Ackerman, Frank, 296n126
Acme Industrial Co., NLRB v., 291n72
Adair v. United States, 269n17
Adams, Roy J., 142, 281n92
Administrative Procedure Act (APA), 177–
  79, 182–83
Agar Packing & Provision Corp., 159, 161
Age Discrimination in Employment Act,
  294n62
Aidt, Toke and Zafiris Tzannatos,
  296n121
Allied Chem. & Alkali Wkrs. Local 1 v.
  Pittsburgh Plate Glass Co., 291n62
Allis-Chalmers Mfg. Co., NLRB v.,
  273n127
Almendarez-Torres v. United States,
  268n99
Amalgamated Clothing Workers Union,
  262n4
Amalgamated Meat Cutters, Local No.
  189 v. Jewel Tea Co., 291n66
American Federation of Labor (AFL), 33,
  50, 82, 142–43
American Federation of Labor v. NLRB,
  176
American Hosp. Ass'n v. NLRB, 288n63
American Locomotive Co., 285n107
American Red Cross Blood Services, John-
  son Region, 269n106

American Steel Foundries v. Tri-City Cen-
  tral Trades Council, 112, 120,
  245n53
Americans with Disabilities Act, 294n62
Anderson, Clifford H., 208
Antitrust laws, 219–20
  Clayton Act, 123, 269n17
  Sherman Act, 123
Applebaum, Eileen, 296n126, 297n132
  and Rosemary Batt, 226n126
Arizona Portland Cement Co., 290n37
Arrow Elec. Co., Inc. v. NLRB, 282n19
Arthurs, Harry W., 277n11
  and D. D. Carter and H. J. Glasbeek,
  289n7
Asakura v. City of Seattle, 146
Associated Provincial Picture Houses, Ltd.
  v. Wednesbury Corp., 179
Associations (intimate and expressive),
  113, 270n29
Atleson, James B., 263n26, 264n51
Auto Workers Local 259 (Fanelli Ford
  Sales), 291n74
Autodie Int'l, Inc., NLRB v., 289n10
Automobile Labor Board, 38
Automobile settlement, 38–51

Babcock & Wilcox Co., NLRB v., 275n27
Bacharach, Samuel B., 245n66
Baker v. IATSE, 287n32
Bakery Drivers v. Wagshal, 272n109
Balanyi v. Local 1031, IBEW, 287n32
Bankruptcy Act, 248n50
Bartnicki v. Vopper, 270n42
Bassiouni, M. Cherif, 279n52
Bastarche, Michael, 125